Muirhead Library of Philosophy

VALUATION

MUIRHEAD

Muirhead Library of Philosophy

METAPHYSICS
In 17 Volumes

I	Time and Free Will	*Bergson*
II	Reason and Analysis	*Blanshard*
III	Appearance and Reality	*Bradley*
IV	In Defence of Free Will	*Campbell*
V	Person and Object	*Chisholm*
VI	Non-Linguistic Philosophy	*Ewing*
VII	The Foundations of Metaphysics in Science	*Harris*
VIII	The Concept of Meaning	*Hill*
IX	Philosophy and Illusion	*Lazerowitz*
X	The Relevance of Whitehead	*Leclerc*
XI	Dialogues on Metaphysics	*Malebranche*
XII	The Philosophy of Whitehead	*Mays*
XIII	Studies in the Metaphysics of Bradley	*Saxena*
XIV	The Intelligible World	*Urban*
XV	Language and Reality	*Urban*
XVI	Valuation	*Urban*
XVII	Philosophy of Space and Time	*Whiteman*

VALUATION

Its Nature and Laws

WILBUR MARSHALL URBAN

LONDON AND NEW YORK

First published 1909 by
Swan Sonnenschein & Co., Lim.

Published 2013 by Routledge
2 Park Square, Milton Park, Abingdon, Oxfordshire OX14 4RN
711 Third Avenue, New York, NY 10017

First issued in paperback 2014

Routledge is an imprint of the Taylor and Francis Group, an informa business

All rights reserved. No part of this book may be reprinted or reproduced or utilized in any form or by any electronic, mechanical, or other means, now known or hereafter invented, including photocopying and recording, or in any information storage or retrieval system, without permission in writing from the publishers.

The publishers have made every effort to contact authors/copyright holders of the works reprinted in the *Muirhead Library of Philosophy*. This has not been possible in every case, however, and we would welcome correspondence from those individuals/companies we have been unable to trace.

These reprints are taken from original copies of each book. In many cases the condition of these originals is not perfect. The publisher has gone to great lengths to ensure the quality of these reprints, but wishes to point out that certain characteristics of the original copies will, of necessity, be apparent in reprints thereof.

British Library Cataloguing in Publication Data
A CIP catalogue record for this book
is available from the British Library

Valuation
ISBN 978-0-415-29604-5 (hbk)
ISBN 978-1-138-88423-6 (pbk)
Metaphysics: 17 Volumes
ISBN 978-0-415-29532-1
Muirhead Library of Philosophy: 95 Volumes
ISBN 978-0-415-27897-3

VALUATION
ITS NATURE AND LAWS

BEING

AN INTRODUCTION TO
THE GENERAL THEORY OF VALUE

BY

WILBUR MARSHALL URBAN, Ph. D.

FORMERLY CHANCELLOR GREEN FELLOW IN MENTAL SCIENCE, AND READER IN
PHILOSOPHY, PRINCETON UNIVERSITY; PROFESSOR OF PHILOSOPHY,
TRINITY COLLEGE, HARTFORD, CONN.

LONDON
SWAN SONNENSCHEIN & CO., LIM.
NEW YORK: THE MACMILLAN CO.
1909

TO
JAMES MARK BALDWIN
AS A MARK OF
APPRECIATION AND RESPECT

PREFACE

THE "point of view," the unexpressed assumptions in the half-light of which any book, even the most "scientific," is written, and which sometimes find their way into the preface, are often more informing and more interesting than the book itself. This should be eminently true in the case of a book on Values, for here, if anywhere, the writer might, perhaps, be permitted to wear his heart on his sleeve. It is not my purpose, however, to add this glimmer of possible human interest to an otherwise dull book. In so far as the statement of such presuppositions may have any significance for the main developments of the book, they are presented with due objectivity and detachment in the Introduction, and carried—with equal care, it is to be hoped—to some of their more obvious conclusions in the final chapter. It is unnecessary to anticipate them here. But with regard to the more general background—the relation of such a book to the characteristic assumptions of the time—the situation is different. Here a prefatory word may be a word in season; it may not only illuminate some of the dark places, but may even give the key to an appreciation if not to a complete understanding of the entire discussion.

Until recently there was little question as to what should be the suppressed major premise of any serious inquiry, whatever its subject-matter might be. To science and the scientific method belonged the whole "choir of heaven" as well as the "furniture of earth." To leave this assumption unquestioned was felt to be the only correct attitude, and where its acceptance was not whole-souled, half-hearted imitation took its place.

For some time, it is true, this assumption has not been without its disquieting effects upon life and art, upon morals and religion. The sophistication and even pruriency of thought and feeling to which some of the expressions of the scientific spirit have given rise, have led to a reaction against intellectualism which if not widespread is at least profound. But it was not until the triumphant march of science led to the soul and its inmost values that this reaction took definite form. The realisation of the capacity for large ineptitudes no less than for small futilities, which an uncriticised application of scientific method may display, has led to a questioning of its most fundamental assumptions. Vague distrust has developed into outspoken *alogistic* and even *misologistic* tendencies, until the counter-assumption, that values lie beyond the ken of knowledge and science, bids fair to rival its opponent in honour. In our theory as well as in our practice we have reached a point of equivocation, not to say contradiction, at which we must either take refuge in a new doctrine of "two-fold truth" or else, if there is any practical meaning in the principle of the dialectic, await with patience a middle ground of unification.

In the meantime, this dilemma of the Time-Spirit demands a new and rigid alignment of principles, and any book which enters the "fighting-zone" owes it to itself to be clear on this point. The present work places itself frankly on the side of knowledge rather than of edification, in the full belief that the latter presupposes the former. For better or for worse, we are caught in the grip of an immitigable will to know, a will to know which claims for its province "the human soul and its limits, the entire range of its hitherto acquired experiences, the entire history of the soul and its still unexhausted possibilities." Short of this we cannot stop except by the loss of the energy of this will which means the decadence of values as well. Nor does it shun the bringing together of the concepts of value and science. If science when it has followed this track has sometimes shown qualities meriting the term "dismal," it does not follow that when it has penetrated more deeply it may not be "gay." We may well believe that the period of a crude and external dominance of the human spirit by an inhuman conception of science is approaching its zenith, if indeed it has not already begun to decline; but it would be a mistake to infer that with such decline will go that deeper and more intimate control of the individual and social will alike which is made possible through the interpretation of their meanings in terms of reflective thought. Because certain limited conceptions, as well as unlimited claims, of science are being modified, it does not follow that the power of science, in the older and better use of that term, will be lessened. Rather may we confidently look for its increase. For faith and feeling also make unlimited claims which only the discipline of the scientific spirit enables us properly to appraise. There will always be new ventures in faith and science alike, and new ventures must always be followed by new evaluations. But such evaluations are not to be secured by reference to a closed system, either of truths or of values, but only by that orderly progression from actualities to possibilities and certainties which is the method of science. In the interest of true evaluations, the present time is committed to the full development of all that is implied in the concept of science rightly understood.

In comparison with this task—in its larger aspects by no means that of the merely technical philosopher, the aim of the following pages is much more modest. Limited as they are to certain "first works" which must in the nature of the case be largely technical, the writer must be content merely to hope that they may affect, at least indirectly, the larger issues.

The first six chapters, beginning with "definition and analysis," and culminating in the chapter on the general laws of valuation, seek to lay the foundations for an understanding of the different types of value judgments, their implications and their limits. In the development of this portion, chapters

IV. and V. are in a sense an interruption, since they are wholly psychological; and, while they treat of matters necessary to the complete understanding of the more general topics that follow, might have been handled in separate sections as required. On the whole, it seemed better to bring them together in one systematic treatment. Chapters VII. to XIII. inclusive apply these results to a genetic and synthetic investigation of the consciousness of value from its lowest to its highest levels. Without laying claim to comprehensiveness or completeness, it may be said, I think, that there is no significant form of worth experience which is not adequately enough treated to show its relation to the general system of values. Finally, in chapter XIV. an attempt is made to show the bearing of these results on what I have ventured to call the *axiological* problem of evaluation. The views which I have felt justified in presenting in the limited space of a single chapter represent but in outline certain philosophical conclusions to which the study of the phenomenology of valuation has led. The work was originally planned to be merely such a phenomenological study, and as such it must be judged, but the unity which the entire work gained by the addition of this chapter seemed to compensate for any inadequacies which the chapter might appear to have when viewed by itself. In this connection I wish to express my regret that Münsterberg's *Philosophie der Werthe* appeared too late for the utilisation, except in the last chapter, of any of the valuable suggestions which I have got from its study. While my general position has remained unmodified, I could not have remained uninfluenced, in many details at least, by his brilliant and persuasive presentation of a view which is essentially opposed to my own.

In acknowledging my indebtedness to recent writers for many of the ideas contained in these pages, I have first of all to express my specific obligations to the oral as well as written teachings of Professor Baldwin. My deeper sense of obligation

Preface

he has most kindly allowed me to express in the form of dedication. Of my indebtedness to Meinong and Ehrenfels, as well as to others of that school, my references to their works give visible proof. These do not, however, adequately suggest the valuable help that I have received, not only from their researches in this special field, but from all their writings. To the French psychologists, Ribot and Paulhan, whose studies in "feeling" have yet to be properly valued, I am also greatly indebted. In conclusion, I have to express my gratitude to Professor J. H. Muirhead, the editor of the *Library of Philosophy*, for his very kind interest in the work, as well as for many valuable suggestions and criticisms. My colleagues Professor G. A. Kleene and Professor Arthur Adams have also rendered me great assistance, the former with expert suggestions on points in economics, the latter in connection with the reading of the proof.

Chapters II., III., and part of IV. have already appeared as articles in the *Psychological Review*. They have in each case been considerably modified to suit their present purpose. The general Introduction is an expansion and modification of a paper printed in the *Philosophical Review* under the same title.

TRINITY COLLEGE, HARTFORD, CONN.
December, 1908.

CONTENTS

CHAPTER I

INTRODUCTION

PAGE

The Function of a General Theory of Value: its Nature and Sources . 1
The Psychological Problem and Method—The Presuppositional Method of Psychological Analysis: a form of the Genetic Method . . . 9
The Axiological Problem and Method—Facts and Norms—Genesis and Validity 16
The Relation of the Psychological and Axiological Points of View . . 18

CHAPTER II

DEFINITION AND ANALYSIS OF THE CONSCIOUSNESS OF VALUE

The Judgment of Value—Worth Predicates as Affective-Volitional Meanings—Equivocations in Judgments of Value leading to Analysis of Presuppositions 21
Values as Meanings of an Object for a Subject—The Subject of the Value Judgment—The Subject in Different Attitudes—Classification of Attitudes: Simple Appreciation, Personal and Over-Personal or Impersonal—The Object of the Value Judgment—Objects of Condition, Personal and Over-Individual Value—The Relation of Subject and Object . 26
Psychological Analysis of Worth Experience—Worth as Feeling with certain Cognitive Presuppositions—The Worth-Fundamental is Feeling, not Desire—The Presupposition of Reality not exclusively Existential Judgment: Criticism of Theory of Existential Judgment underlying this View—The Presupposition of Reality: Presumption, Judgment and Assumption of Existence of Objects—Analysis of these Cognitive Attitudes . 35
The Genesis and Relations of these Presuppositions—Genetic Levels of Valuation 49
Résumé of Definition and Analysis 53

CHAPTER III

MODES OF THE CONSCIOUSNESS OF VALUE—PRIMARY AND ACQUIRED

Appreciative Description of Feelings of Value: its Nature and Method . 55
The Fundamental Appreciative Distinctions in Feeling—Descriptions of Reality-Meanings of Feelings of Value, not of Simple Feeling

abstracted from Cognitive Presuppositions—The Three-Dimensional Theory of Feeling: Interpretation—Correlation of Appreciative Meanings with Cognitive Presuppositions 59
Meanings Acquired by Development from the Fundamental Modes—Value-Movement—Acquired Meanings of Simple Appreciation—The Impellent Mode: Feelings of Obligation—The Semblant Mode: Æsthetic Feeling 67
Acquired Meanings of Characterisation and Participation: Personal and Over-Individual Values 71
The Quantitative Meanings of Worth Feeling—Analysis of the Concept of Degree—Degree of Worth (Depth and Breadth) and Degree of Intensity: Independently Variable—Intensity-less Appreciation: Illustrations—Theories of this Relation—Suggestion of a Genetic Theory to be developed later 72
The Bearing of this Analysis on Further Problems 78

CHAPTER IV

THE PSYCHOLOGICAL BASIS OF A THEORY OF VALUATION

The Nature of Feeling and Will and their Relations—Dualistic Theories of Feeling and Will: Criticism—Monistic and Genetic Theory—Interpretation of the Monistic Theory: its Relation to the Definition and Analysis of the Consciousness of Value 81
Further Analysis of Feeling: Structural and Functional—Feeling as a Kind of Sensitivity—The Appreciative Distinctions in Feeling as "Forms of Combination" of the Elements 96
Correlation of Structural and Functional Analysis—Changes in Functional Meaning and Changes in Sensitivity: Passion and Emotion, Sentiment and Mood, and Affective Sign—Theory of their Genetic Relations . 103
Corollaries from the Preceding Theory—Their Significance for the Theory of Valuation 108

CHAPTER V

THE CONTINUITY OF AFFECTIVE-VOLITIONAL MEANING

The Acquirement of Recognitive and Generic Meanings on the Part of Feelings: The Problem 11
Affective Memory—Types of Affective Memory—The Criterion of Recognitive Meaning as applied to Feelings—Theory of Affective Memory . 113
The Generic Meanings of Feeling: Affective Generalisation—The Phenomena of Affective Continuity: Substitution, Subsumption, Transition 120
Psychological Theory of Generic Meanings of Feeling—Imageless Apprehension and Intensity-less Appreciation—The Process of Affective Generalisation 124
The Rôle of Affective Generals in Processes of Valuation—Worth Continuities: Illustrations 133

Contents

CHAPTER VI

THE LAWS OF VALUATION

The Laws of Valuation: Their Nature and Range of Application—
Economic and Extra-Economic Values—Classification and Interpretation   142
The Law of the Threshold: General Meaning—Economic Thresholds,
Upper and Lower: The Existence-Minimum and Final Utility—Modification of the Threshold through Acquired Meanings: Complementary
Values—General Function of Threshold in Processes of Valuation—The
Independent Variability of Hedonic and Worth Thresholds   .   . 146
The Law of Diminishing Utility: Its Historical Significance and Relation
to a General Theory of Value   , ... 156
The Psychological Basis of the Law: Dulling of Sensitivity with Repetition
and Satiety—Critical Examination of these Laws—Their Application
limited to Sense-Feelings and to the Hedonic Redundancies of Feelings
of Value—Restatement of the General Law of Limiting or Diminishing
Value   158
Extent of the Application of this Law: Its Application to all Instrumental
Utility Values, but not necessarily to Intrinsic Ideal Values—The Law
of Marginal Utility and its Explanation—Certain Limitations of this Law   167
The Law of Complementary Values—As Modifying the Law of Limiting
Value; In Economic Valuation; In Extra-Economic Valuation,
Ethical and Æsthetic—General Characterisation of the Law: Its
Psychological Basis—Interpretation   173
The Application of these Laws to Ideal Objects of Intrinsic Value—The
Limits of this Application   181
General Conclusions: The Problem of the Limits of Acquirement of Value—
Inferences from this Study of the Laws of Valuation—Their Bearing
upon Further Studies   185

CHAPTER VII

VALUES OF SIMPLE APPRECIATION

Values of Simple Appreciation: their Origin and Nature—Objects of "Condition" Worth, Primary and Derived   190
Value Movements in General: Definition and Classification—Their Relation
to the Laws of Valuation   194
Value Movements of Simple Appreciation: Ethical and Æsthetic Values
thus Acquired—Modification of Economic Values of Acquisition and
Consumption   205
The Ethical or Impellent Mode of Simple Appreciation: As the Result of
Inward Value Movement—Pre-Ethical and Quasi-Ethical Impulsions
and Obligations: their Sub-Personal and Sub-Social Character—Illustrations of Instinctive, Quasi-Ethical Obligations—Modification of Economic Valuation by these Acquired Obligations   207
Æsthetic or Semblant Mode of Simple Appreciation: as Special Form of
the Value Movement toward Activity—Pre-Æsthetic and Quasi-
Æsthetic Forms of Activity: Their Individual and Sub-Social Character
Conditions of Movement to Activity in its Pre-Æsthetic Form—The
Special Differentia of the Æsthetic   216
Modification of Economic Valuation by Acquired Æsthetic Values   .   . 229

CHAPTER VIII

PERSONAL AND OVER-INDIVIDUAL VALUES—THEIR ORIGIN AND NATURE

Personal and Over-Individual Values: their Origin and Nature—Their "Common Meaning" Presupposes Sympathetic Participation . . 232
Sympathetic Participation (*Einfühlung*): its Relation to Simple Appreciation and Feeling 234
The Psychology of Sympathetic Projection: Its Nature and Conditions—The Inducing Conditions of Affective Projection 236
Levels of Sympathetic Participation—The Presuppositions of Sympathetic Feelings: (*a*) Organic Sympathy, with Vague Presumption of Existence; (*b*) Rise of Assumption-Feelings and Emergence of Distinctions in Presuppositions—Sembling; (*c*) Judgment-Feelings: Conceptual Reconstruction of the Inner Life in Terms of Dispositions 244
Sympathetic Participation (*Einfühlung*) as a Process of Valuation—The Nature of the Feelings of Value Involved: the Projected Feelings "Real" Feelings—Value Movements in Participation and Characterisation 249
The Distinction between Personal and Impersonal Participation—Intensive and Extensive Projection: Resulting in Differences of Presuppositions of Feelings 253

CHAPTER IX

PERSONAL WORTHS: VALUES OF CHARACTERISATION

Definition: The Personal Attitude in Valuation—The Presuppositions of this Attitude—The Ideal of the Personality—How assumed in all Judgments of Personal Worth 260
The Character of the Ideal Person as determined by the Processes in which it is Constructed—Idealisation involved in Sympathetic Participation—Division of the Personality—Extrusion of the Negative Elements—Further Stages in Idealisation: Æsthetic Individuation of the Person; Acquirement of Complementary Value 263
The Laws of Valuation as applied to Personal Worth—The Problem in the Light of our General Study—Special Examination of Feelings of Personal Worth 270
The Activities of Idealisation and Characterisation—Not Subject to the Law of Diminishing Value: Feelings of Personal Worth not Subject to Dulling of Sensitivity and Satiety 272
The Effect of Idealisation on our Actual Feelings and Judgments—The Semblant Mode in Characterisation—Dispositions Created which affect Actual Judgment 275
Absolute Personal Values: They exist as Practical Absolutes . . 277

CHAPTER X

PERSONAL WORTHS—*Continued*

Analysis and Interpretation of the Concrete Judgments of Personal Worth: Imputation and Obligation—Definition of the Subject, Object, and Terms of Estimation Presupposed in such Judgments 282

Contents xvii

Difference between the Personal or Ethical and the Impersonal or Moral Standpoints 288
The Relative Estimation of Personal Worth—The Thresholds and Norms of Personal Obligation and Imputation : Their Origin in the Processes of Sympathetic Participation 291
The Normal Threshold : The Norm of Characterisation—The Upper and Lower Limits of Personal Worth : The Characterisation-Minimum—How Presupposed in all Judgments of Personal Worth 293
Laws Governing Feelings of Personal Worth: as Illustrated in Imputation of Merit and Demerit and in Personal Obligation 298
The Axiological Question of the Validity of the Implicit Assumptions or Presuppositions of these Judgments 309

CHAPTER XI

IMPERSONAL OVER-INDIVIDUAL VALUES

Definition : Over-Individual Values of Participation and Utilisation—The Impersonal Attitude in Valuation—The Morally Qualified Act and the Morally Qualified Judgment—Relativity of the Distinction between the Personal and Impersonal Attitude 311
The Presuppositions of the Impersonal Attitude : Over-Individual Demands —Over-Individual Demands as Collective Desire and Feeling—Their Origin and Nature—Social Synergies : Demand and Supply—The Relation of Subjective to Objective Participation Value . . . 317
Subjective Participation Value—The Individual's Feelings of Participation Value as Determined by Social Sympathy—Extensive Sympathetic Participation—The Laws of Social Sympathy 320
The Objective Participation Value of Dispositions as Deduced from the Laws of Social Sympathy—The Law of Marginal Participation Value . 328
Corollaries from the Law of Marginal Participation Value—The Laws of Social Synergy—Social Value Movements—Social Differentiation and Segregation—The Norms and Limits of Participation Value . . 331
The Limits of Acquirement of Social Over-Individual Value—The Question of Absolute Social Values 342

CHAPTER XII

IMPERSONAL OVER-INDIVIDUAL VALUES—*Continued*

Analysis and Interpretation of Concrete Moral Judgments—The Moral Value of an Act as determined by its Participation Value—Estimation of Moral Value in Terms of Egoism and Altruism—The Significance of these Terms 350
The Thresholds and Norms of Moral Judgment—The Norm of Participation : The " Correct " : The Normal Expectation of Social Participation—The Lower Threshold : The Participation-Minimum—How Developed in Social Participation and Presupposed in all Judgments of Moral Value . 356
Laws Governing Objective Participation Value as reflected in Imputation of Praise and Blame and in Moral Obligation—Moral Obligation Relative, not Absolute 358

CHAPTER XIII

SYNTHETIC PREFERENCE

The Relative Value of Different Classes of Worth Objects—The Levels of Valuation 366
Rationalistic and Monistic Theories of Valuation—Criticism—Intuitionism and Scepticism 368
Analysis of the Facts of Synthetic Preference as exhibited in Judgments of Obligation and Imputation of Value—Conflicts between the Ideals and Obligations of the Different Levels of Condition, Personal and Impersonal Over-Individual Values—The Resolutions of these Conflicts in Actual Experience: In so far as Uniform and Unequivocal, Reflections of the General Laws of Valuation—Break-down of these Laws at the Limits . 371
Conclusions from the Analysis of Synthetic Preference—Restatement of the Criticism of Monistic Theories—The Doctrine of Supreme Moments or Practical Absolutes—The Supreme Moments of Intrinsic Appreciation Transcend all Distinctions of Appreciative Description—The Bearing of these Conclusions on Larger Philosophical Problems . . . 378

CHAPTER XIV—*Conclusion*

VALUATION AND EVALUATION

Restatement of the Axiological Point of View—Reflective Evaluation—Normative and Factual Objectivity 384
Analysis of Axiological Distinctions of Reality and Truth employed in Reflective Evaluation—The Meanings of Existence: Outer and Inner—The Meanings of Truth: Outer and Inner 386
The Relation of Normative to Factual and Truth Objectivity—Their Meanings only Partially Identical: The Objectivity of Values not wholly Reducible to Existence and Truth—Proof of this Conclusion in the Value Judgments of Religion 390
The Sufficient Reason or Sanction of Valuation—The Ground of Value—The Rationalistic Criterion; The Pragmatic Criterion; Criticism—Formulation of the Sufficient Sanction of Valuation in the Light of the Ultimate Meaning of the Presupposition of Reality and of its Fulfilment 395
Axiological Necessity and Sufficiency—The Well-Founded Value—Axiological Possibility and Compossibility—Formulation of a Criterion of the Well-Founded Value 405
Application of this Criterion to Specific Practical Problems—Again the Monistic Ideals 414
Philosophical Conclusions—Truth, Value, and Reality: Their Ultimate Relations 422

INDEX 429

VALUATION
ITS NATURE AND LAWS

CHAPTER I

INTRODUCTION

I. THE FUNCTION OF A GENERAL THEORY OF VALUE

THERE has seldom been a time in the history of thought when the problem of " value " has so occupied the centre of attention as at present. Fundamental changes in the actual values of mankind, giving rise to what has been well called " our anxious morality," with its characteristic talk of creating and conserving values, have brought with them what may, without exaggeration, be described as a gradual shifting of the philosophical centre of gravity from the problem of knowledge to the problem of values. The problem of knowledge has itself become, in some quarters wholly, in others partially, a problem of value.

The historical causes of this, until recently silent, change of attitude are, in a general way, clear enough. The change from intellectualism to voluntarism, the rigorous discipline of the human soul through the almost universal application of the concepts of evolution and the struggle for existence, with their ideas of selective and survival values—these are explanations which immediately suggest themselves; and yet they are but general and superficial characterisations of a still more fundamental crisis of the social will, a crisis which has its roots deep in the necessities of things, and which we are as yet scarcely able to understand.

Whatever the causes, the effects are everywhere in evidence. This gradual change in actual values has found a mouthpiece, if somewhat rhetorical and rhapsodical, in Nietzsche's cry of " transvaluation of all values." But this cry has been echoed by other hearts and minds, and that which began as a species of poetry has passed into sober prose. Of chief importance is the transition from the accumulation of knowledge to its evaluation. To say nothing of the growing attempt to evaluate the results of physical science in the interests of a more comprehensive natural philosophy—a movement which may or may not have some connection with Nietzsche's arraignment of science in its present form, we may find sufficient evidences of this change of heart in the social and moral sciences, where the problem of value lies closer to the surface. "While formerly," we are told, "it was almost wholly the external structure of the social life, and the economic values which it produces, that received attention, now it is the meaning of this life for the human soul, its spiritual origin and spiritual effects, which finds expression."[1] In short it is the problem of evaluation.

Corresponding to this change in practical attitude, has appeared the more theoretical consciousness of, as it were, a new side of reality. We have been scarcely aware, so we are told, that our entire life, on its conscious side, is one continuous series of feelings of value and evaluations, of explicit judgments and implicit assumptions of value; and that it is only by reason of the very fact, *that they are valued*, that the mechanically determined elements of reality in any sense have meaning for us. Far from being a mere fact among other facts, that which we mean by our evaluation of objects is something independent of this world, and so little merely a part of it that it is rather the whole world seen from a special point of view. Over against a world of facts is set a world of values.

But if this growing consciousness of the problem of value has indeed reached a point where we are conscious of a world of values, where the terms ethical, æsthetic, and even "truth" values, are in every mouth, and where the thought of a special "theory of value" is no longer novel, with it has also come the realisation that philosophy, and the philosophical disciplines which are traditionally concerned with values, are, in their present form, not quite in a position to take possession of the new world. It is true that for some time metaphysics has seemed to many to be but a theory of value; but the traditional problems

---

[1] This quotation is taken from the "Prospekt" of *Die Gesellschaft* (Verlag der Literarischen Anstalt, Ruten & Loenig, in Frankfurt A. M.), a collection of social-psychological monographs in which the various institutions of society are studied from the point of view of their values for the individual. Some of the titles are Religion, Speech, Custom, Commerce, The State, Politics, War, The Strike, etc.

Introduction 3

as well as the traditional methods of that discipline are still such as to make the question of values subordinate to the question of "being." Nor are the special sciences which deal with facts of value able, as such, to cope with the changes, in both form and content of discussion, which this new setting of the problem has brought about. An harmonious division of labour between economics, ethics, and æsthetics has produced results which, for various and sufficient reasons, do not meet the need. It is rather precisely because of this division of labour, unwisely conceived, that the results are unsatisfactory. More and more the conviction gains ground that a general theory of value, which shall comprehend in a systematic and scientific way all types of human values, is an absolute necessity.

II. The Sources of Such a Theory

It has been said that the most fruitful metaphysical thought of the present is to be found in the special sciences. While perhaps not quite true, such a statement has this element of truth, that it is within the special sciences that the most significant questions of philosophy first make their appearance. Similarly, the necessity of solving certain special questions of value within the sciences of economics, ethics, and æsthetics, has developed concepts the significance of which extends far beyond these limits, and which therefore afford the material for more general and systematic reflections.

Of first importance is the " theory of value " which economics has developed for its special purposes. Narrow as this theory is (for it is not so long ago that an economist, F. von Wieser, although of the opinion that he had fulfilled his intention of "treating exhaustively the entire sphere of worth phenomena without an exception," did not once in his investigations go beyond the region of economic goods), nevertheless, the very limitation of its activities to a narrow range of problems has led to an intensive analysis of certain facts and laws of valuation which should have long since furnished an example to ethics, and which must now furnish both the stimulus and the discipline for any one who seeks to comprehend the larger field. But this limitation of interest has obscured wider relations, knowledge of which would have been fruitful for the special work of the economist himself, and, in some cases, has led to fallacies of both observation and inference, which a more philosophical treatment of facts would have corrected. These limitations are, however, being overcome. The necessity of translating economic into sociological conceptions, of correlating economic with larger social values, has brought about a notable change. Indeed, much of the movement in the direction of a more general theory comes from economics itself. Gradually the opposition to theory in this sphere is giving way, and at the same time the feeling increases that economic values are but a special class of human worths, and that they can be understood only in their relations, especially in their relation to ethical values.[1]

Ethics, likewise, has its contributions to make to a general theory of value. Chief among these are its appreciative analyses and descriptions of qualitatively different attitudes and dispositions, and its elaboration of a doctrine of the norms of obligation and virtue in which the appreciative distinctions of the race have been fixed. To this must be added the development of hypotheses as to the nature of the ultimate good, which, while they have not led to any final solution, have nevertheless served to develop and organise the normative point of view. But it is precisely because of this pre-occupation with ultimate norms and abstractions that ethics is in no position to meet the advances of economics. For ethics, as it is commonly understood, still remains too much in the traditions of the Greeks, and, instead of seeking a theory of value founded upon an adequate psychology, contents itself with a theory of abstract goods, consisting in an external and often arbitrary classification and evaluation of objects of desire without a sufficiently vital sense of the great problems involved in the processes and laws of desire themselves.

Especially harmful, moreover, has been the Kantian distinction between the " empirical " and the " intelligible " will, and the narrowing effect of the concept of abstract imperatives. Although no longer held in its original form, it still exercises influence through the unfortunate antithesis of facts and values, of genesis and validity. For where such distinctions are made ultimate, where the laws of the empirical will are conceived to be irrelevant, or even hostile, to the will that values, there a science of values is impossible.

Where, on the other hand, ethics has broken loose from these bonds, the new-found freedom has given rise to such a multitude of irreconcilable principles that it is immediately apparent that

---

[1] Compare in this connection Hadley's article on " Economic Science " and the present writer's article on " Worth " in the *Dictionary of Philosophy and Psychology*.

the certainty of method, which makes possible internal unity of principles and harmonious external relations with other sciences, is still lacking. It has even been seriously doubted whether ethics can maintain its place as a special science—whether it is not doomed to break up, on the one hand, into a part of psychology, the task of which shall be to analyse the individual feelings, judgments, and acts of will, the content of which has the moral predicate, and, on the other hand, into a part of sociology, which shall portray the forms and content of the common life which stand in relations to the ethical obligation of the individual. Its double character will, it is thought, ultimately prove its undoing.[1]

Doubtful though such predictions may rightly be held to be—for the boundaries of sciences are determined by other motives than those of mere logic, and there are practical reasons which will plead strongly for the integrity of ethics as a separate discipline, still there can be no doubt that the inconsequent character of the science, in its present state, unfits it for leadership in the attempt to conceive valuation in its more general aspects. Like economics it has, to be sure, recently been looking beyond its narrowly conceived province, and seeking points of contact with its neighbours—the breaking up of its solidarity is, in one sense, but an outward sign of an inward grace; but this is in itself not sufficient to make of ethics the science of values *par excellence.*

Nor is such a science to be developed by a merely external fusion of elements from both of the preceding sciences, with perhaps the addition of a few judicious reflections upon æsthetic and religious values. To meet the obvious necessities of the situation there is required, rather, a systematic treatment of human values in their mutual relations, together with the psychology of feeling and will upon which such a theory must rest. What is needed is a point of view and method which shall go beyond the special motives of economics and ethics, and thus find common ground in a conception and purpose which unite them both. Thus, while economics has been thought to be a descriptive and explanatory science, and has contented itself with description of the empirical laws of valuation for the purposes of control, it has really been shot through with assumptions of a normative character, and has been fruitful in disclosing actual standards of value which ethics has often failed to estimate at their proper

[1] Simmel, *Einleitung in die Moralwissenschaft,* Berlin, 1893, Vol. I, Preface.

worth. On the other hand, ethics, although claiming to be a normative science, has found it necessary to investigate the phenomenology of feeling and will, without, however, as I shall seek to show later, succeeding in making these investigations sufficiently fruitful for its more ultimate purposes. The desideratum, therefore, seems to be to find a method which shall unite in some more fruitful way the descriptive and the normative points of view, a method which shall know how to interpret the norms of the so-called "intelligible" will in terms of the laws of the "empirical" will.

Is such a Science Possible?

The preceding statement of the problem of a general theory of value shows it to consist in two main problems, closely connected, the descriptive or psychological and the normative or axiological. And such a conception of the problem seems necessitated by the facts with which we are concerned. For the function of valuation has two aspects. On the one hand, we *feel* the values of objects; on the other hand, we evaluate these objects and ultimately the experiences of value themselves. The first aspect is a *process*, the conditions and laws of which are to be determined; the second is a *function*, the meaning and norms of which are to be developed. To a preliminary characterisation of these two problems we might now proceed immediately, were it not for the dogma of the antithesis of the "intelligible and empirical" will which, in its various forms, has stood in the way of a science of values, and must therefore receive brief consideration.

This dogma, appearing under various names, now as the antithesis of genesis and validity, again as the antithesis of facts and values, has become especially familiar, not to say insidious, in its latter-day formulation, Appreciation versus Description.

It is not difficult to understand the motives of the antithesis in its present form. The gradual usurpation of the whole field of description by certain specialised scientific methods brought with it inevitable disappointment. The psycho-physical and biological methods, approaching as they did the problem from without, and finding irrelevant all aspects of experience except such as could be connected with the conceptions of these sciences, soon showed their inadequacy as means of describing experiences of value. The simplest solution of the difficulty seemed, therefore, to be in looking upon values as merely appreciable and not communicable in terms of any objective description. Value is always the *meaning* of an attitude of a subject, and is therefore not describable in terms of mental elements. An attitude can be merely appreciated.

It would seem that the antithesis is falsely conceived, and that it arises primarily from the fact that we have to do here with a false way of setting the problem. Instead of going directly to facts, the point of view here disclosed starts with a wholly arbitrary and narrow conception of description. Having assumed this, and finding a mass of experience which escapes its categories, the logic of the situation leads to the conclusion that there is appreciation without description. Let us first consider the abstract merits of the antithesis, and then we may turn to a critical examination of the concept of scientific, and therefore psychological, description which underlies it. From this we may be able to determine the function of psychology in a general theory of value.

As a preliminary distinction the antithesis does well enough. For a moment, perhaps, one's appreciation seems to be one's own "incommunicable dream," but the need of participating with others in the social concourse presses upon us the necessity of objectifying our experience, of searching for presentations with which the experience may be connected. Through them the attitude becomes objectified to consciousness and communicated to others, and behold appreciation has itself increased. The very condition of continuous and progressive appreciation is some sort of description.

It is no less true that there can be no description, even the most scientific, without an appreciative element. Here again the ideal of a scientific description without the element of appreciation is merely an ideal limit, set for certain purposes, but a limit not realised in actual experience. It would not be difficult to show that, when in any science we make abstractions, the direction and extent of these abstractions are determined by an act of appreciation. All abstraction is in the last analysis purposive. Whether the product of our abstraction is in any sense the concrete thing with which we started, or has any useful relation to it, is finally to be decided by an act of appreciation.

So much for the antithesis in its general form. The twofold assumption that there may be appreciation without some form of description, or description without an ultimate moment of appreciation, proves untenable in both aspects. It is true that there may be a blind sort of feeling of significance before the rise of any cognitive acts objectifying the experience, but that feeling, with all its brute immediacy, has scarcely reached the level of explicit appreciation or feeling of value. It is also true that the total meaning of an appreciation is never exhausted in any description. There is always an element which just escapes. But some of the meaning is conserved; otherwise it is not description. We may, it is true, describe—satisfactorily for certain limited purposes—and at the same time ignore certain aspects of the total appreciation, but never all, otherwise it is no description.

From these general conclusions more specific inferences may be drawn of immediate and practical importance for the discussions that follow. In the first place, there are varying types of description of any phenomenon, types determined by the purposes of the description, and therefore by the degree of appreciation retained in the descriptive terms. The antithesis between appreciation and description is accordingly reducible to a distinction between two types of description, appreciative and scientific, and we may probably infer that there is at least an *appreciative* description of experiences of value.

In another connection[1] I have sought to show that there is such appreciative description—and communication—of individual experiences of value, and to develop its characteristics and principles. A brief summary of the conclusions will be sufficient for the present purpose. Such description has as its object the communication and objectification of the intrinsic meaning of individual experience in the interest of facilitation, either conservation or increase, of appreciation. This communication and description are accomplished through connection of individual experiences with ideal psychical objects, already shared and over-individual, projected affective-volitional meanings embodied in ideal persons and states. Through identification or contrast with these the individual experience is communicated, both in its quality and degree. Such communication and description is essentially norm construction. For the ideal object, thus projected and shared, contains the *funded* meaning of past experiences, and constitutes not only the presupposition, the medium, of all communication of present experience, but also the norm of its control.

---

[1] "Appreciation and Description and the Psychology of Values," *Philosophical Review*, November, 1905.

When we ask what it is that this appreciative description seeks to communicate, and what it is, according to the view criticised, that cannot be communicated and described, we find it to be certain references of the attitude beyond the present experience, meanings acquired in individual and social processes. These are always references of the present state to something presupposed. They may be described in general terms as *transgredient* and *immanental*. The transgredient reference, as expressed, for example, in such appreciative categories as obligation and desert, is a present feeling, but includes in it a reference beyond the present state. The immanental reference—as, for instance, the worth suggestions of æsthetic states—is a present state, referring, not beyond the present state, but to something more deeply implicit, something presupposed in it. These references, communicated, as we have seen, by connection, either through identification or contrast, with projected ideals or norms, really point to the psychical processes in which these norms were constructed and in which their meaning was acquired. Whether these processes can be described, whether the genesis of these attitudes and meanings can be reconstructed, is the problem of the psychology of worth experience, and this includes the question of the relation of appreciative to scientific description.

III. The Psychological Problem and Method

The first task of a general theory of value is psychological analysis. Strictly speaking there is no problem, scientific or unscientific, which does not have its psychological side. Not only the questions, but also the objects in connection with which these questions arise, belong in the first place to the psychical life. It is further apparent that the fact of value itself cannot be described otherwise than by reference to determinations which are taken from the psychical life and which therefore belong to psychology. The most convincing proof of this is the fact that it has never occurred to economics, which is in the main free from abstract questions of methodology, to attempt to define the nature of value without reference to psychology. Reflections of this nature would seem to lead to the inference that it is in psychology and its analyses that we must, in the first place, look for those general categories of description which shall form the basis of a general theory of value, and for the general laws of psychical process which shall enable us to correlate the different types of valuation. Such, indeed, is a plain inference from the facts, but here again certain *a priori* theories of the nature and function of psychology call a temporary halt.

Upon the general question, as it relates to psychology as a whole, there are a multitude of counsels at the present time. There are those who see in psychology and its descriptions chiefly a propædeutic to the interpretation and appreciation of actual psychical reality, the categories of which are teleological. It is the fundamental *Geisteswissenschaft*. It is upon the basis of such a conception of psychological purpose and method alone that we may ascribe to psychology the rôle of the science of abstract mental laws which shall make possible the interpretation of the concrete mental reality with which the sciences of ethics, æsthetics, etc., are concerned. In direct opposition to this view, both historically and logically, is the view which denies the possibility of description except through connection of the psychical with physical objects, and which therefore, in view of the artificial transformation of the psychical which results, also denies its function as interpreter of the psychical objects of ethics and æsthetics. Finally, there are those who, while perhaps not sure as to the precise logical basis for the recognition of two distinct types of method within the same science, are yet forced by a broad view of the facts to recognise two distinct purposes in the reconstructions of psychology, the one having as its end the construction of abstract concepts which shall be instrumental in the interpretation of actual historical psychical reality as a process of acquirement of meaning, the other the control of the psychical through its connection with mechanical process.

Upon any conception of the function of psychology other than the second, the facts of worth experience are, *as such*, the material of psychology. That view is obviously but a special application of the general antithesis between appreciation and description, and must in the last analysis share its fate, but a brief consideration of this special expression of the dogma will clear the way for our positive conceptions of the function of psychology in a general theory of value.

Briefly it runs as follows. All description and explanation have as their motive the communication and ultimately the control of experience. Such communication and control of the subjective and individual are possible only through linkage with objects which have common meaning and which, therefore, are, through

Introduction

abstraction, as far removed as possible from individual appreciations. The only objects which fulfil these conditions are the physical objects, the abstractions of physical science which have lost all intrinsic meaning and have become wholly instrumental. The ideal of psychology is therefore connection of the psychical with physical objects, and only in such connection do we have description and explanation which merits the name of scientific.

The consequences of this are obvious. For if the only description which merits the name scientific is connection with physical objects, then in the reconstruction of our immediate appreciations abstraction must be made from all appreciative moments in the psychical, and the immediate experience must be broken up into non-appreciative elements, preferably sensations, which may be connected with the non-appreciative elements of the physical construction. What this means for the psychology of those aspects of the psychical which form the basis of worth experience is evident. Feeling and will, the basis of this experience, *intend*, in both the transgredient and immanental references of their states, psychical objects as well as physical, and can communicate these intents, these acquired meanings, only through connection with such ideal objects. These objects are, however, always projected will and feeling, and scientific description, if it is of the nature assumed, can make no use of these psychical objects, and therefore no use of the abstract conceptions of feeling and will in its reconstructions. Such continuity as it may establish is not psychical, but must be wholly in terms of physiological dispositions. If this view of psychological description is justified, Münsterberg has drawn the only conclusion possible, viz., that there is no psychology of the worth experience possible, and therefore no relation between appreciative and scientific description.

Clearly the whole question revolves about the more ultimate problem of the purpose of psychological description. The question is not whether physical objects are the only media for any description—we have seen that they are not, but rather whether they are the most useful for the purposes of psychology. That there are other objects than the physical through which communication and description are possible, we have seen. If our initial assumption, that appreciation without description and description without appreciation are but abstractions and ideal limits, that all concrete thought activities contain both moments in different degrees, is valid, then there can be scientific constructions making use of terms in which the process of abstraction from appreciative connotation shows different degrees of completeness, according as the purposes of the reconstruction require. It follows that the absolute contrast between appreciative and scientific description disappears, and we have left merely the practical problem of the degree to which appreciative differences shall be retained in our constructions. This is wholly a question of the purpose of the description.

Historically, and in present practice in so far as it is fruitful, the motive of psychology is primarily one of interpretation. The region of possible control of mind through its connections with the body, although we cannot limit it *a priori*, is small indeed in comparison with the regions of possible interpretation through psychical conceptions. Even in the region where the motive is primarily one of direct control, the conclusion is rapidly gaining ground that control is possible only through appreciative interpretation of the mental life. Especially noteworthy is the change of view in the field of mental pathology, where the necessities of practice are leading to a reaffirmation of the fundamental conceptions of emotion and conation, as against the purely neurological conceptions.[1] Even if this were not so, it is impossible to ignore the larger region where the function of psychology is wholly interpretative. And here the motive determines the method. For concepts, in order to be instrumental for interpretation, must conserve, and contain, at least implicitly, the acquired meaning which they seek to describe. The explanation must be in functional terms, and functional terms are in the last analysis refinements of appreciative description.[2] The question whether there is any relation between

---

[1] Compare in this connection the psychological conceptions of Janet, i.e. of *emotion* and *conation*, with the neurological of Wernike and Ziehen. Also the introductory paragraphs of James's Presidential Address, *The Energies of Men*.

[2] Moreover, with the growing recognition of the close relation of economic objects and values to other psychical objects and their values, already referred to, comes the recognition of the fact that the psychology of values is concerned with the *interpretation* of individual and social worth processes and only indirectly with their *control*. With this recognition of the interpretative function comes the necessity of the use of terms which may be instrumental in interpretation, terms with appreciative connotation. As soon as the economic philosopher seeks to use his constructions as a means of interpretation of concrete reality, to connect economic with ethical and æsthetic worths, he must restore the appreciative aspects. Interesting illustrations of this appear in the works of Veblen—*A Theory of the Leisure Class* (Macmillan) and *A Theory of Business Enterprise* (Scribner), one of the most significant aspects of whose method consists in making technical essentially appreciative terms, and more marked still in Simmel's *Philosophie des Geldes*. It is an interesting fact that while official psychology in some of its tendencies seeks to exclude all appreciative descriptions, the economic sciences are becoming more psychological by restoring them.

appreciative and scientific description is then the better known problem whether psychology should be a "functional" or a "content" psychology. For the latter a psychology of value is impossible; for the former it is possible, and what is more, a present fact.

When, therefore, we narrow this general problem of psychological method to the more specific question of the psychology of worth experience, it is possible to draw certain inferences as to method which find substantiation in the actual procedure of psychology. In the first place, values are facts, to be described as any other mental facts. The sharp antithesis of facts and values might temporarily delay the appeal to psychology, but the simple and inevitable necessity of the situation—that every assertion of a worth involves likewise the assertion of its conformity with actual or possible experiences of feeling and will—makes the appeal to psychology ultimately unavoidable. But the recognition of this abstract proposition does not help us until we have a clearer conception of psychical fact. Whether psychological analysis can serve as an instrument of interpretation and appreciation of values depends upon what we conceive its function to be. Here the principle maintained throughout this discussion must be final. If experience is conceived to be cognisable as a fact only when it is viewed as a passive state loosed from all relations with the object which it cognises and appreciates, then the experience of value cannot be cognised in this sense. If, on the other hand, psychology is a science which, although it makes use of abstractions, still deals with reality, then a value can be cognised as a fact, as well as appreciated. To cognise it as a fact, related in certain uniform ways to facts of the same order, requires that it shall be subsumed under general concepts; but in order that these concepts shall really define it, they must have meanings common to all appreciation. Psychological description must then start with appreciative description. To describe thus appreciatively a valuation, its meaning as an attitude must be communicated; but this meaning can be communicated only by connecting it with the ideal objects toward which the attitude is taken, and by characterising the predominant moment in the attitude, whether feeling or will, and the cognitive presuppositions which determine it. Consequently, when we attempt to describe and classify, and to derive genetically the various attitudes in valuation, we must retain in our abstractions such concepts as *feeling* and *will*, functional terms which have still enough of appreciative connotation in them to be instrumental in the interpretation of appreciations.

Here then finally we see the relation of appreciative to scientific psychological description. Appreciative description communicates the meanings of feelings acquired through connection with psychical objects toward which the feeling is directed. These objects are, as such, not the material of psychology alone any more than are the physical objects. As objects they belong to the normative sciences. But while they are not the material of psychology alone — inasmuch as they are projections beyond the individual, nevertheless the processes by which they have been projected and objectified and the processes by which the individual, when once they have become psychical objects, participates in their meanings—in other words, the presuppositions, conative and cognitive, which determine his feeling attitudes toward them—are distinctly the material of psychological study.

THE PRESUPPOSITIONAL METHOD—A FORM OF GENETIC METHOD

The method of psychological worth analysis we may then characterise as the Presuppositional Method. It begins with analysis of presuppositions. The key to the position is to be found in the fact that worth experience is always an attitude. An attitude is an immediate experience which contains in it a reference—in our terms, either transgredient or immanental—to presupposed psychical process. Its determinants are the actual cognitive acts of the present experience—for all worth experience presupposes some form of cognition of reality—and the conative dispositions, the assumptions and postulates, which form the platform of the present experience. The varying worth attitudes must be defined in terms of their presuppositions, actual and dispositional. But further, if any worth attitude, when viewed thus psychologically, is an immediate feeling *plus* the acquired meaning or reference, then this reference, which is for immediate appreciation the sign of worth continuity, must find a psychological interpretation in a continuity which is psychical, and not in one established indirectly through connection with physiological dispositions. With this our method becomes genetic.

The genetic method in psychology, broadly viewed, is capable of different formulations. Thus Baldwin, Paulhan, and Stout, although making the idea of development fundamental, make use of somewhat different principles. Accommodation and Habit, Systematisation and Arrest of Conative Tendencies — such are the differing functional conceptions with which they work. But the conception which underlies them all is, I think it may be safely said, that the progressive differentiation and correlation of the content of consciousness, by which new meanings are acquired and appreciatively distinguished, must be referred for explanation to functional readjustments of consciousness as an organic whole. Different levels of meaning are thus distinguished and transitions from one level to another accounted for. One of the most important consequences of this genetic, functional method is that what appears from one point of view as habit or disposition, may in a new adjustment find a place in the content as a meaning; so that the functional meaning of disposition, viewed as habit, is conserved on the new platform of accommodation in the new arrangement of content. This unification of functional habit and content under the genetic categories finds its most notable expression, on the cognitive side of experience, in the doctrine of the general concept it is able to contribute. Whereas from the purely analytical point of view the general concept finds no satisfactory psychological equivalent, from the genetic its functional meaning receives due recognition. " Selective thinking may then be viewed as the systematic or progressive and continuous determination of the stream of thought in the individual's mind."[1]

When now this genetic method is applied to the worth aspect of consciousness, a similar problem presents itself—how valuation may be conceived as a continuous, progressive, and systematic determination of the stream of conation and feeling in the individual's mind. Here again, psychical continuity is the important point, and the special form in which it here appears stands in close connection with the problem of the derivation of the different attitudes of appreciation as genetic modes of one continuous process of acquirement of meaning—of showing how the acquired meaning of one attitude, having become dispositional, functions as an assumption or presupposition of new feelings and modes of valuation. This involves the concept of psychical development or *value-movement*, the conditions and laws

[1] Baldwin in the *Dictionary of Philosophy and Psychology*, Vol. II, article on "Selective Thinking."

of which must be explained in terms of still more general laws of feeling and will.

The presuppositional method as thus described, lies midway, so to speak, between the teleological analysis and explanation of the normative sciences—which assume an end or ends as the instruments of analysis of the stages of meaning and the ordering of the psychical objects, and the causal method which abstracts from all meaning, and may thus break up the whole concrete attitude, including the functional presuppositions, into as many parts as it finds convenient in the working out of the relation of mind and body. The presuppositional method assumes no specific end for psychical process. It contents itself with carrying over from the sphere of appreciation the merely functional concept of "acquirement of meaning." But assuming conative continuity in which meaning is acquired, it takes the differences in meaning distinguished by appreciative description, which would be ignored in the purely causal analysis, and asks what functional adaptation is presupposed by this difference. And since all adaptation which is psychical consists of conative and cognitive acts, its problem is to analyse out the conative and cognitive presuppositions of worth-feelings.

IV. The Axiological Problem and Method—Facts and Norms—Genesis and Validity

The second task of a theory of value is the reflective evaluation of objects of value. We not only *feel* the value of objects, but we evaluate these objects and ultimately the feelings of value themselves. Clearly another point of view than the psychological is here involved, a point of view which requires, not only to be clearly defined, but also to be properly related to the psychological. If our problem were that of the determination of the validity of objects and processes of knowledge, it would be best described as logical or epistemological, but the term epistemology is too narrow to include the problem of the evaluation of values, and we may therefore make use of a special term to define the problem as it here presents itself. On the analogy of the term epistemology we have constructed the term axiology, and may hereafter speak of the relation of the axiological to the psychological point of view.

The chief problem for axiology, as for epistomology, is bound up with the distinction between subjective and objective, a distinction made use of in connection with judgments of value as well as judgments of knowledge. We recognise values as in some way independent of individual acknowledgment, for between the subject and the object there are relations of feeling and will, felt as demands and obligations, just as inviolable as those of the sense impressions imposed upon us from without. Between the subjectively desired and the objectively desirable in ethics, between subjective utility and sacrifice and objective value and price in economic reckoning, between the subjectively effective and the objectively beautiful in art, in all these cases there is a difference for feeling so patent that in naïve and unreflective experience the feelings with such objectivity of reference are spoken of as predicates of the objects themselves.

For reflection, however, there is a difference between the meaning of this distinction in the sphere of values and that which it has in the sphere of truth, and it is at this point that the specific character of the axiological problem appears. In the theory of knowledge the dispute still rages, and is especially fierce at the present time, as to whether there is an objectivity which transcends all subjective process, whether qualities inhere in the thing apart from experience. For the theory of value the problem is simplified. All values are in one sense subjective. All are founded on some process. But we recognise that our concept of subjectivity must make room for a kind of objectivity, that the feelings or desires developed in one process may exercise a control over feelings and desires determined by other processes, and that this control gives them a form of objectivity.

When we seek a name for this form of objectivity, we find one at hand in the concept of the norm and of normative judgments. The practical significance of an objective value is that it forms the norm for subjective feelings of value, that it determines subjective feeling in some way. An examination of the character of this determination indicates its uniqueness. The norm is the product of appreciative description and construction of subjective feeling; but when it is thus objectified and projected, it becomes a demand, the acknowledgment of which is the condition, or presupposition, of further appreciations, or subjective feelings. The acknowledgment of the normal exchange value, the price of an object, is the condition of its further utilisation by the individual, the acknowledgment of permanently desirable dispositions is the condition of the realisation of certain subjective ethical values, the acknowledgment of objective beauty is the

c

condition of permanent æsthetic satisfactions. Still more apparent is the relation in the case of the extreme objectifications of religion. Ideals of a supernatural character are the product, phenomenologically speaking, of individual and racial appreciative constructions; but the assumption, or postulation, of their existence is the presupposition of certain subjective feelings of value, such as reverence and inner peace. In general the norm is an assumption or postulate of existence representing the permanent aspects of desire, underlying changeable feelings and judgments. Its function is the control of appreciation.

The norm is thus seen to have the double character of subjectivity and objectivity. The normative judgment represents at the same time a subjective appreciation and an objective description. Its subjective reference is seen in the fact that it is only through these projected ideal objects, assumed to exist independently of the subject, that the subject's individual feelings can be communicated. Norm construction is, as we have seen, a product of appreciative communication and description. As such the norm has a psychological genesis and character; it is an assumption, a postulate, determined by certain dispositions. Its objective character is apparent, on the other hand, in that, having passed beyond the subjective control of the moment and become, through its character as a presupposition of belief, the condition of further subjective appreciations, it in turn exercises control over these feelings.

From this double character of normative objectivity certain characteristics of axiology and axiological method may be inferred. The axiological problem is the reflective evaluation of values, and this evidently consists in determining the validity of distinctions between subjective and objective already developed in worth experience. Now, the distinction being what it has been shown to be, it is clear that the question of the validity of any such distinction is bound up wholly with the question *whether the objectivity postulated fulfils its function as the necessary presupposition of the continuity of valuation, in its two aspects of acquirement and conservation of value.* Other questions may indeed be raised—as for instance whether the reality which an object of value thus has is equivalent to existence apart from subjective process, but they are not axiological. It is also evident that such a criterion must remain wholly abstract and general until the phenomenology of valuation, its processes, its objects and laws, has been developed. To the application of the criterion we shall return in the concluding chapter, contenting ourselves for the present merely with its formulation.

When, however, the problem of axiology is stated in this way, it is immediately apparent that a certain definite relation to psychology is involved. For immediate experience this normative objectivity appears in an immediate appreciation of value which has as its cognitive presuppositions certain assumptions or postulates, but for reflection these very assumptions show themselves to be the product of a selective, genetic differentiation of our desires—through arrest, effort, and consequent readaptations and reconstructions, in which some of our desires have developed into permanent and objective demands. Out of the general level of immediate appreciation has emerged a development which has its conclusion in a new kind of objectivity or reality. It is clear, then, since all values, whether subjective or objective, are founded on some process, that the ultimate question as to their validity is whether they are well-founded or not. It is also clear that whether they are *well-founded* or not depends upon their conformity to certain ultimate laws. Every assertion of a value implies at the same time an assertion of its conformity to the laws of feeling and will.

To this inference from the preceding study of the nature of the normative judgment, the dualism between appreciation and description is likely again to reply with a doctrine of absolute values, and to insist that the evaluation of objects of value is wholly independent of their genesis, the norms of their evaluation being in no sense related to, or determined by, psychological laws. It is unnecessary to recall our previous discussion in order to point out that the axiom " no description without appreciation " has as its converse " no appreciation without description," a proposition which we have also accepted as justified. If it is true that there is no description and communication without its stimulus and control in appreciation, it is also true that there is no appreciation except through the media and the control of objective descriptions. But what is reflective evaluation but the highest form of appreciation, and how can that reflective evaluation proceed in its task of distinguishing between subjectively and objectively determined values without a study of the genesis of these differentiations ? The situation may be stated in still another way. Whatever may be the abstract formulæ for the normative sciences of the norms of validity, they cannot be anything else than the development in other terms, and for other purposes, of what, from another point of view, we call psychological laws. We may well believe that psychological description is not the whole of a theory of value, but it certainly is not irrelevant to the normative problem. It is at least necessary that the assumptions and postulates embodied in these norms shall be psychologically possible, that " they shall be in harmony with the general laws of the conscious life and only special and detailed developments of what lies in these laws." [1]

[1] Quoted from Höffding's discussion of the relation of logical laws to psychology, *The Problems of Philosophy*, p. 76, translation, Macmillan, 1905.

CHAPTER II

DEFINITION AND ANALYSIS OF THE CONSCIOUSNESS OF VALUE

I. WORTH PREDICATES AS FUNDED AFFECTIVE-VOLITIONAL MEANINGS—ANALYSIS

1. *The Judgment of Value.*

A CURSORY examination of the more general terms of worth description, good and bad, useful and useless, beautiful and ugly, noble and ignoble, etc., or indeed the terms worth and worthless, valuable and valueless themselves, and the manner in which they are applied, makes us immediately aware of the fact that, for the unreflective worth consciousness, they are at first tertiary qualities, as much a part of the object as the so-called primary and secondary qualities are parts of the physical object of cognition. This is especially noticeable in the case of the ethical and æsthetic predicates, but it is no less true of the unreflective use of the terms utility and value, as for instance when we say that iron has utility or value even when the conditions of its applicability are lacking. The intrinsic worth judgment is psychologically the more fundamental, whatever may be inferred upon closer inspection and reflection.

But while as qualities of objects, as terms employed in appreciative description, they have a certain kind of objectivity, they are nevertheless felt to differ from the other qualities in that they are subjectively conditioned in a way that the so-called primary and secondary qualities are not.

The judgment of value has accordingly been described as a mere assertion of the meaning of the object for the subject, or as an appreciation. When I say that the object is good or beautiful or noble, I assert a direct relation of the object to my feeling and will, a harmony between the object and my subjective dispositions which is relatively independent of my judgment of existence of the object or judgment of the truth of the idea I have of the object. Existence is perceived; truth is thought; value is felt. But while the worth predicates are in the first place felt and not cognised, while they are at the third remove from pure objectivity, nevertheless, there is presupposed in every appreciation, in every judgment of value, a reference to reality and truth. This reference comes to the surface as soon as I ask such questions as these: is the object *really* good or useful? is it *truly* noble or beautiful? The feeling of value includes the feeling of reality. Appreciative meanings presuppose reality meanings.

2. *Equivocations in the Value Judgment, leading to Axiological Distinctions in Existence and Reality Meanings.*

Accordingly, when we attempt a further analysis of these predicates we find certain references to reality, always implicit in the judgment, which demand to be made explicit. Prior to such reflective analysis they give rise to equivocations in their meaning, equivocations so confusing that more than one thinker has counselled entire scepticism in the matter, not without a show of reason, it must be admitted. But that this initial scepticism is merely a salutary warning becomes apparent as we follow these equivocations to their sources, for it is precisely in this process, this study of the grammar of the worth consciousness, that we find both the nature of these predicates and the basis of their classification. The character of the confusion may be seen at a glance by observing the distinctions which worth analysis has developed, in all the concrete worth sciences, economics, ethics, æsthetics, for the removal of the equivocations. Worths are said to be subjective or objective, real or ideal, actual or imputed, intrinsic or instrumental.

The first distinction, between subjective and objective worths or values, gives the key to the situation. The same objects, let us say diamonds, may have little worth or indeed be distasteful to me personally, although in another attitude I may ascribe great value to them and, indeed, think of them as intrinsically valuable. My friend's action may be sanctioned by me in immediate appreciation, although from an objective, moral point of view I must needs condemn it. Such contradictions can only be resolved by a distinction between subjective and objective values. Closely connected with this equivocation is that which arises when the distinction between intrinsic and instrumental values is ignored. An object which is worthless, or indeed the object of negative worth judgments of harmful or bad, may acquire the worth predicate when it becomes instrumental to some object of immediate or intrinsic value. Similarly, within the sphere of instrumental values or utilities of economics, we find an equivocation which can be removed only by the use of the distinction between subjective and objective. On the one hand, if any thing is of worth because it is utilisable, it is always so for a subject and with reference to concrete conditions. But on the other hand, we are led to ascribe value to an object, for instance when we say that iron has value, irrespective of its relation to an individual subject and to concrete conditions: by a process of abstraction we give the object value in itself. For these differences in meaning the economists have used the terms subjective and objective value; or the latter is sometimes called objective exchange value.

From these illustrations we see that the attitude expressed by a worth judgment, whether the worth be described as subjective or objective, is an attitude of a subject, but the difference in attitude is determined by the inclusion or exclusion of certain presuppositions, the nature of which is to be determined. The other distinctions, between real and ideal, actual and imputed values, show the same desire to remove the equivocations inherent in worth predicates.

Sometimes we attribute worth to an object when we mean that it deserves to be valued, irrespective of its actual valuation by any person or group of persons. Such value is said to be ideal. Again, there are objects of valuation, the existence or non-existence, or the possibility or probability of realising which is not inquired into, but which are abstractly valued and said to be ideal values in contrast to the real value of objects where the judgments of existence or possibility are true or grounded judgments. In both cases the real and the ideal values are equally functions of the relation of the object to the subject. The difference lies in the attitude of the subject, in the different presuppositions of the feeling in the two cases. Confusion of meaning arises only when these presuppositions are not made explicit.

The distinction between actual and imputed values, like the other distinctions considered, is one which is not found in the immediate worth experience itself, but which develops when the presuppositions of the worth judgment are made explicit through reflective analysis. The total worth predicated of an object is often seen to have more than one determinant and, under certain circumstances, the element in the total value corresponding to one subjective determinant will be described as actual, while the other element will be described as imputed. Thus the elements of a total complex, food for instance, will each be said to have its actual value arising from its capacity to satisfy separate desires, or to satisfy desire when consumed separately. On the other hand, such worth as an element may get from its combination with the other elements is said to be an imputed value. In a similar way, when an act of a person has value as manifesting a disposition instrumental to the fulfilment of social ends, this is described as its actual value, while an additional value attributed to it as a part, or manifestation of the total personality, is described as an imputed value over and above the actual value of the act. It is obvious from these illustrations that the different moments in the total worth of the object have different subjective determinants, and that these go back to the different objects or aspects of the object upon which judgment is directed, in other words, to the cognitive presuppositions.

3. *Interpretation of these Equivocations—As due to Different Presuppositions.*

The meanings thus differentiated may be described as the *reality-meanings* of the worth predicates. As distinguished from the purely appreciative meanings previously considered, they represent modifications in worth predication determined by differences in cognitive attitude toward the object. The necessity of such distinctions arises from the fact that the appreciative meanings are not wholly independent of the reference to reality involved. As simple acts of appreciation, the presuppositions of existence may not be explicit; indeed the most primitive judgments of worth are assertorial—without any conditional element whatever. But as soon as the question of *evaluation* of the worth predicates themselves is considered, as soon as the axiological problem of the differentiation of subjectively conditioned values from objectively conditioned, is raised, then the presuppositions of reality must be made explicit. By making them explicit is understood the acknowledgment of the

Definition of the Consciousness of Value 25

presupposition of reality, present in all judgments of value, in all appreciations, in specific judgments of existence. In what *way* are the values real? In what *way* are the objects of value existents or realities?

From this study of the various meanings of the worth predicates, it becomes clear that the worth judgments express not attributes of objects apart from the subject, even when the value is described as actual and objective, but rather functions of the relation of subject to object. When we speak of an object as having absolute or objective value, it is only by a process of temporary abstraction from the subject in some specific attitude, not from the subject itself. The other differences of meaning in the worth predicates reflect the same fact. Thus when I attribute value to an object, meaning that it is actually valued, my attitude is determined by certain presuppositions of judgment, which are the product of participation in the worth judgments of others. When, however, my judgment means that the object is ideally of worth, *deserves* to be valued, that judgment expresses a modification of attitude brought about either by exclusion of certain presuppositions of judgment, as when I pass my judgment in opposition to temporary judgments about me, or by inclusion of other presuppositions, as when, for instance, I appeal from a narrower actual worth judgment to a possible more universal judgment. The situation is the same in the case of the distinction between actual and imputed values. The actual value is always the meaning of the object for a subject in some attitude—never an attribute of the object itself. The imputed value added to the actual value arises from attitudes of the subject, negligible or irrelevant from the standpoint from which the actual value is determined.

From all this it is apparent that whatever meaning we may ultimately give to the objectivity of worth predicates, whatever validity may be assigned to the presupposition of reality implicit in all judgments of value, we may unhesitatingly assert that these predicates are meanings pre-determined by antecedent psychical processes. While at first sight they appear to be tertiary qualities of the object, on closer inspection they are seen to be acquired meanings of the object for the subject, as, in fact are some of the so-called primary and secondary. As thus predetermined they may be described as *funded* meanings, in that they represent the accumulated meaning of these processes. Furthermore, we may now see that the equivocations in the value judgment which have been analysed arise, just as do certain contradictions in cognitive predication, through abstraction of the predicates, as qualities of the objects, from the processes of acquirement of meaning in which the meaning was funded.

But this analysis enables us to add something more to our definition and characterisation of worth predicates. We have defined them as funded meanings, pre-determined by antecedent psychical process. It is possible to limit still further the concept by defining them as *affective-volitional* meanings, thus distinguishing them relatively from the attributes employed in cognitive predication. Relations to judgments of truth and existence are presupposed in all appreciations and judgments of value, but as we have seen, in the first place only *implicitly*. As assertorial judgments, they assert a relation of the object to feeling and will —either an immediate actual experience or a possible experience of feeling or will—that is, belief in the power of the object to call such experiences into being.

II. Further Analysis of the Value Judgment as Expressing Affective-Volitional Meaning of the Object for the Subject

1. *Axiological Distinctions as Clues to Analysis.*

Two important consequences follow from this conception that worth or value is the funded meaning of the object for the subject in different attitudes, or as predetermined by different dispositions and interests. In the first place, while the distinctions we have been discussing are developed from the axiological standpoint of the determination of the relative validity of worth judgments, we have in the analysis underlying these distinctions at the same time a clue to the psychological analysis and classification of the different attitudes involved. In all these differences of meaning the sources of the difference were found in the nature of the cognitive presuppositions. All valuation, as attitude of the subject, is primarily an act of immediate appreciation; but this primitive attitude may be modified to give various meanings by the inclusion of various types of judgments, existential, instrumental, judgments referring the object to the self or others, judgments of possibility or probability of acquisition and possession, etc. While for the axiological point of view the truth of these presuppositions is significant, for psychological

Definition of the Consciousness of Value

analysis their importance lies in the changes in worth experience, which follow upon changes in these presuppositions. In the second place, as a result of this conception of worth as the affective-volitional meaning of the object for the subject in different attitudes, the way is now open for an analysis of the worth subject and for a classification of the fundamental worth attitudes.

2. The "Subject" of the Value Judgment—The Subject in Different Attitudes—Classification of Attitudes.

The equivocations in the meaning of the worth predicates already considered, indicate certain fundamental differences for the subject of the experience. The distinctions between subjective and objective worth, between actual and ideal, are reducible to differences in the judging subject. These differences have led to the conception of different subjects for different types of worth judgments. Thus Kreibig[1] distinguishes between a primary and secondary worth subject, the primary being the individual as such, the secondary being the group or race consciousness. So also Meinong,[2] in treating of the difference between ethical and moral judgments, distinguishes the more personal "ethical" from the impersonal, "moral" subject. The former is the concrete ego in his relation to the alter; the latter is neither the ego nor the alter but an abstraction, a third person, the "impartial spectator" who sits in judgment upon both. These distinctions, appearing as they have in the effort to do justice to fundamental differences in worth predication, point in the right direction. But they are nevertheless open to the criticism which attaches to all conceptual constructions employed as instruments of analysis, that they are in danger of being hypostatised into separate realities and conceived as real even when abstracted from the individual subject. For certain purposes of social and ethical philosophy, we may, perhaps, speak of a group consciousness, of a general or over-individual will, without a serious distortion of the facts; but for the empirical analysis of worth judgments, it is nearer the truth to say that the subject in the rôle of the individual, of the group or race, or of the impartial spectator, is the individual in different attitudes. The problem is then to

---

[1] Kreibig, *Psychologische Grundlegung eines Systems der Wert-theorie*, Wien, 1902, p. 5.
[2] Meinong, *Psychologisch-ethische Untersuchungen zur Wert-theorie*, Graz, 1894, pp. 72, 163, 216.

account for the origin, differentiation, and fixation of these relatively permanent attitudes.

The worth judgment of an individual may then express the affective-volitional meaning of an object for the subject, as qualified by the subject's participation in and explicit cognition of the worth attitudes of others, of single persons, of social groups, or perhaps of an over-individual worth consciousness which transcends even group distinctions, giving the impersonal attitude of the "impartial spectator." The difference in attitude is determined by the inclusion or exclusion of judgments as part presuppositions of the meaning. The psychological problem is the tracing of the processes by which this participation in, and cognition of, the attitudes of others is realised, the more specific problem of worth analysis itself being to determine how this modification of the attitude of the subject also modifies the worth predicated of the object.

In a preliminary way we may distinguish three fundamental attitudes of the self or subject of worth judgment: (1) Simple appreciation of the affective-volitional meaning of an object for the self; (2) the personal attitude, in which the worth of the object is determined by explicit reference of the object, whether a physical possession or a psychical disposition, to the self or the alter, and in which characterisation of the self or the alter is presupposed; and (3) the impersonal attitude, in which the subject of the judgment is identified with an impersonal over-individual subject and the value of the object is determined by explicit reference to the over-individual demand.[1] All three are forms of appreciation of worth, but while the first is *simple* appreciation, in that the presuppositions are simple, the personal and impersonal attitudes are complex and derived, having as their presuppositions judgments and assumptions which have had an historical genesis.

3. *The "Object" of the Value Judgment—Classification of Worth Objects.*

As the subject of value experience, one of the moments in the value function, is constantly changing, expanding and contracting through inclusion and exclusion of presuppositions of

[1] This classification corresponds in principle with Baldwin's classification of cognitive meanings in the first volume of his *Thought and Things*, chap. VII, p. 148, where he distinguishes: (1) Simple and private; (2) aggregate and con-aggregate; (3) social and public meanings.

Definition of the Consciousness of Value

judgment, so also the object of valuation undergoes modification. Broadly speaking, the object of worth belongs to the presentational side of consciousness, is the object of immediate apprehension with its implicit presupposition or explicit judgment of existence. It is, therefore, in the first place, the not-self the external object of feeling and will, those aspects of experience which are from the beginning presentational. But there is scarcely any aspect of consciousness which cannot become presentational, cannot be presented to consciousness, and thus become the object of judgment. Even the attitude of valuation itself, which we may describe as "psychical" pre-eminently, is susceptible of representation, translation into ideal terms, and of thus taking its place on the objective side of the value function. The psychology of this representation of the psychical will engages our attention at those points where we shall make use of the principle. Here it is merely important to insist that the general class, worth objects, includes physical and psychical and, among the latter, the attitude of valuation itself.

A more significant distinction among objects of valuation is that between primary and secondary or between simple and *founded* objects. By a founded object in general we understand one built up by processes of ideation and judgment upon primary sensations and perceptions. Such a founded object is, strictly speaking, not the object of perception but of ideation or judgment, and may be said to be pre-determined by these processes. Thus certain ideal objects of presentation and judgment, while themselves neither sensed nor perceived, may be said to be founded on sensation and perception. The processes of sympathetic realisation of the feelings of another, are in the first place perceptual in character, but upon the basis of these processes certain ideal objects, the self and its dispositions, are built up, and these become the objects of imputed values. To them is imputed the funded meaning of the processes of feeling and conation involved in their construction.

These founded objects may be of two kinds, according as they are founded on processes of perceptual or ideational activity. Illustrations of the former are: (*a*) beauty or grace of form in objects of perception; (*b*) founded qualities acquired in the sensational and perceptual activities of consumption of food, or more broadly of various instinctive activities, such as cleanliness, manners. Any harmonious grouping or arrangement of the activities of living creates secondary objects of worth, founded upon the primary.

As illustrations of the secondary worth objects, founded on processes of ideation and judgment, we may take the *person* and his affective or conative dispositions, built up conceptually on the basis of the immediate appreciations of sympathy by a process of inference, which, in turn, become the objects of secondary judgments of merit and demerit, etc. To these may be added a third group of founded worth objects which may be described as over-individual. These are the products of the ideal re-construction of objects of primary worth, as determined by participation in the worth processes of larger social groups or of society at large. To this class belong the ideal moral and cultural goods of society, economic goods as objects of exchange, including the medium of exchange which has over-individual worth exclusively. In distinguishing thus between founded objects as products of perceptual and ideational activities, we cannot of course make the distinction absolute, for in the case of many such objects both activities have been at work in their construction.

A preliminary classification of worth objects would then include the following groups : (1) Objects of *simple appreciation*. These objects may be either physical or psychical and include the founded psychical objects built up in perceptual activity. The worth of these objects may also be described as " condition " worth for the reason that when the feeling of value is made the object of reflection it is referred directly, as feeling of pleasantness or unpleasantness, to a modification of the condition of the organism, and is set in contrast to personal and social values. (2) Objects of personal worth such as qualities and dispositions of the person (the self or the alter) objects founded in the processes of *characterisation* of the person. (3) Objects of over-individual or common worth constructed in processes of social participation, ideal constructions developed in the interest of social *participation*, or of *utilisation* and *exchange* of objects. In general these objects of worth correspond to the fundamental attitudes of the subject of the value experience.

4. *The Relation of Subject and Object—Further Development of the Term " Affective-Volitional Meaning ": its Extension and Intension.*

The analysis of the meanings of worth predicates, and the consequent differentiation and classification of the fundamental types of the subject and object of the judgment of value, bring

Definition of the Consciousness of Value 31

us to a third problem, namely, a more definite characterisation of the term affective-volitional meaning and an analysis and classification of the modes of consciousness corresponding to its various meanings. As long as we were concerned merely with a preliminary differentiation of cognitive meaning from that aspect of meaning described as worth or value, it was sufficient to describe the latter as a meaning pre-determined by processes of feeling and conation, and the judgment of value as an appreciation or acknowledgment of that funded meaning. But when this criterion is examined more closely and the attempt is made to determine more precisely just what aspect of meaning is represented by the different types of worth judgments, appreciation, characterisation, participation and utilisation, just what the determining processes of feeling and conation are in each case, more detailed psychological analysis becomes necessary.

When we seek to make more specific this very general description of the worth relation, we are confronted with two possible views of worth which may be described as a broader and a narrower view.

The narrower view recognises only two types of value judgment, the ethical and economic, thereby limiting the term value to such feeling attitudes as follow upon the *affirmation* of the existence or non-existence of an object for the self or its purposes. This limitation denies, therefore, the character of worth attitude to all immediate feeling of the meaning of the object for the subject, prior to the distinctions which we describe as economic and ethical, and likewise to all forms of higher immediacy of feeling attitude as we have them primarily in the æsthetic consciousness. This view, which has been presented most definitely by Witasek[1] and H. W. Stuart,[2] logically excludes the æsthetic from the sphere of values, in the view of the former because the æsthetic is prejudgmental, i.e., is feeling which has merely presentations as its content, in the view of the latter because he conceives it to be post-judgmental, an appreciative state in which all judgment has lapsed. Either mode of cutting the æsthetic attitude off from its closely related ethical and economic attitudes is, we shall find, open to serious criticism.

The reasoning which underlies the formulation of this criterion

[1] Witasek, *Allgemeine Æsthetik*, Leipzig, 1904.
[2] Stuart, *Valuation as a Logical Process*, in Dewey's *Studies in Logical Theory*, Chicago, 1903.

is well expressed by Stuart in the following paragraph : " Our general criterion for the propriety of terming any mode of consciousness the value of an object must be that it shall perform a logical function, and not simply be referred to in its aspect of psychical fact. The feeling or emotion, or whatever the mode of consciousness in question may be, must play the recognised part, in the agent's survey of the situation, of prompting and supporting a definite practical attitude with reference to the object. If, in short, the experience enters in any way into a conscious purpose of the agent, it may properly be termed a value."

Now, in examining this criterion one recognises immediately that it provides a good definition of a certain type of reflective value judgments which we may call secondary. A very large group of our worth judgments are determined by the conscious inclusion of the feeling or emotion as presented content, and as partial determinant of the judgment. The typical economic judgment takes place only upon the occasion of adding to or taking from our store of objects, and is motived by a reflective inclusion of the worth feeling in our total practical attitude. The ethical judgment, in its typical reflective form, may be shown to be of the same character in that the subject's own mode of experience or way of feeling, presented in terms of a disposition or quality of the self, enters as a determinant in the total situation. But the secondary and derived character of these reflective judgments soon becomes evident. How can the feeling or emotion as presented content " play a recognised part " as a value " in the agent's survey of the situation," unless, as a motive to previous unreflective judgments, i.e., before it was presented as a conscious determinant, it was also a value or at least suggestive of value ? We may say, then, that, while much of valuation is a logical process in this sense, nevertheless valuation in itself has its roots in experiences of simple appreciation, where the emotion, while determinative, is not so consciously, as object of presentation or judgment, and must, therefore, be referred to simply in its aspect of psychical fact.

We must, accordingly, interpret our definition of value as affective-volitional meaning in a broader way—so as to include modes of feeling or desire, as the case may be, which are merely appreciative of the object, which merely apprehend the object with its funded meaning. We cannot confine it to attitudes in which this meaning, abstracted from

Definition of the Consciousness of Value

the object, becomes a motive in the subject's survey of the situation. We shall then be enabled to include both the attitudes of lower immediacy, which are pre-judgmental, and those of higher immediacy, which are post-judgmental, recognising the intermediate rôle of the reflective judgments, existential, instrumental, possessive, etc., and recognising also that the reflective and the unreflective, the intrinsic and the instrumental, are constantly passing over into each other, a phenomenon which we shall later describe as value-movement.

In close relation to this first problem which arises in the attempt to make more specific the general definition of worth as affective-volitional meaning, a second problem arises, namely, the question of the specific manner in which we shall set the worth-moment in relation to its psychological equivalents, feeling and conation. In the use of the double term *affective-volitional* itself in our preliminary demarcation of worth experience, there inheres a certain vagueness which, while excusable when viewed in the light of the purpose of the term, must be subjected to explicit analysis if we are to find equivalents for worth experience which shall form the basis for a scientific reconstruction of the processes of valuation. The significance of this double term lay in the fact that it marked off a species under the generic term, meaning. Not that there could be cognitive meaning without worth references or affective-volitional meaning without cognitive presuppositions. Indeed, we shall see that these terms are not very clear at the limits. Merely to indicate a relative distinction, by means of emphasis on different aspects of meaning, was the purpose of this differentiation.

In the second place, the double term was necessary for the reason that only in such a definition could all the attitudes toward objects, recognised as worth attitudes, be included. For our ordinary usage, at least, makes a clear distinction between feeling and will and recognises, as objects of worth, objects toward which both types of attitude are directed. Prior to more scientific analysis, this double relation must be taken as descriptive of the worth attitude. But here again, when this general definition is subjected to psychological analysis, we find that the distinction between feeling and conation in some of its forms is far from clear, and it is consequently difficult to say under which of these terms the immediate experience which is the bearer of these meanings, is to be subsumed. On the one hand, we find experiences of preference and obligation where

D

feeling, in the form of passive pleasantness and unpleasantness, is scarcely present, or, if present at all, is irrelevant—so irrelevant in fact that some theories of worth experience (e.g., the voluntaristic theories of Brentano and Schwartz) find the *locus* of value in what they describe as "intensity-less acts of preference," denying the worth aspect to feeling and its intensities. On the other hand, we find worth experiences, such as the æsthetic, apparently purely affective, where desire, or conation in all its forms, is at a minimum, and appears to be significant, if significant at all, merely as a disposition or presupposition. While, then, in view of these facts the general term affective-volitional meaning was necessary to define the various meanings of objects included under the term values, it is nevertheless evident that the definition can become serviceable for further psychological analysis and explanation only when it is determined which of these elements, the affective or conative, is primary and which secondary—that is, which is always present actually as conscious experience and which as a merely dispositional determinant.

In the light then of these considerations, it would appear that the course of our further analysis is clearly indicated. We are compelled, on the one hand, to include both the concepts of feeling and conation in our psychological equivalents for the worth moment; otherwise we should not have a true equivalent for the funded meaning of the object described as worth. On the other hand, when we seek to analyse the content of the experience, we find they are present in different degrees and different ways, and the question arises which is the more fundamental. Is then the worth-fundamental feeling or desire?

In the second place, whichever of these two aspects be taken as fundamental, a second question necessarily arises—is worth coextensive with feeling or desire, or is there a further demarcation within the sphere of feeling or desire? In other words, have all feelings or desires, whatever their conditions, however fleeting and however caused, the transgredient and immanental references which characterise the worth attitude of the subject toward the object?

Definition of the Consciousness of Value

III. PSYCHOLOGICAL ANALYSIS OF WORTH EXPERIENCE—WORTH AS FEELING WITH CERTAIN COGNITIVE PRESUPPOSITIONS

1. *The Worth-Fundamental is Feeling, not Desire—Criticism of Ehrenfels.*

Both of these problems have been in the forefront of recent psychological analysis of value.[1] They are questions which are forced upon the attention as soon as we attempt to co-ordinate and reduce to common terms the varying attitudes which have been included within the definition of worth experience. It is true that there is a point of view from which these finer distinctions are irrelevant. One can see that for the limited purposes of economic analysis, which requires but a short excursion into psychology, we might speak of the worth moment, now as feeling, and now as desire. Ehrenfels is also probably right in saying that the general laws of valuation and the forms of mutation of values or value-movement, hold true whether we define worth experience as feeling or desire, and that changes in judgment of value are due to modifications of feeling or desire. Nevertheless, a complete analysis of the worth consciousness, in all its phases, requires the solution of both these problems.

It is in connection with the first problem that the first divergence in definition appears, as typified in the different formulations of Meinong and Ehrenfels. Ehrenfels defines the worth of an object as its desirability and makes actual desire the fundamental, assigning to feeling a merely dispositional rôle; while Meinong, on the other hand, identifies actual worth experience with feeling, desire appearing in his definition only as presupposed disposition. In some sense, we have seen, both terms, feeling and conation, must enter into our psychological definition; the question is which shall be given the rôle of fundamental, *actual* experience, and which that of disposition.

Ehrenfels[2] takes desire as the actual psychological worth-fundamental. Value, we are told, is proportional to the desirability of the object—and he continues, as though it were self-

---

[1] For a detailed historical statement and criticism, see the writer's article "Recent Tendencies in the Psychological Theory of Value," *Psychological Bulletin*, Vol. IV, No. 4, March 15, 1907.
[2] Ehrenfels, *System der Wert-theorie*, Leipzig, 1897, Vol. I, chap. I, especially p. 35.

evident,—'i.e., to the strength of the actual desire which corresponds to it." The first part of the definition is certainly true. The funded meaning of an object is its desirability, its capacity, under certain circumstances, of calling out desire. The second part does not, however, necessarily follow. It does not follow either that judgments of worth are determined by actual desire, or that the worth of the object is proportional to the strength of the actual desire. As to the identification of value or desirability with actual desire, a consideration of certain simple but typical worth experiences indicates, that it is not exclusively an actual, but, ultimately, merely a possible desire or desire-disposition with which worth is to be equated, a modification of his earlier definition which Ehrenfels himself accepts. When I think of an absent friend, I may feel his worth to me without the slightest trace of actual desire for his immediate presence, although the presupposition of that feeling is a disposition so to desire. Or again, my consciousness of the objective value of objects of economic use may be independent of any actual desire, although not of my knowledge of their desirableness under certain circumstances. It is equally true that the degree of worth or desirability of an object cannot be straightway identified with the degree of actual desire. It is undoubtedly proportional to the strength of desire-disposition presupposed, but the strength of a conative tendency or disposition is not always measured by the intensity of actual desire; is often inferred indirectly from its effects on volition, or through the intensity of the emotional disturbance following upon arrest. The assumption that the strength of a desire-disposition is given directly in immediate modifications of consciousness, is one which introspection makes highly improbable, and Ehrenfels, at least, with whose definition we are here concerned, does not admit it.

It is clear, then, that while desire, and conative tendency in general, must find a place in our worth definition, it cannot be taken as the psychological fundamental in the sense that it is the conscious correlate of the funded meaning of the object. This conscious correlate is feeling. Ehrenfels thus brings feeling into his definition. Desire is not determined by mystical qualities of objects but by aspects of our consciousness which can be reduced to psychological terms. "All acts of desire are determined, in regard to their direction as well as their strength, by the relative increase of pleasure which they, according to the affective dispositions of the individual in question, bring with them upon their entrance into, or continuance in consciousness." Feeling is, therefore, after all, primary. The worth of an object is directly proportional to the strength of desire, but this strength of desire is determined by the difference of the place of the object in the hedonic scale.

In this conception of Ehrenfels the whole psychological problem of the nature of feeling and desire and of their relations, is involved. Into that larger question we cannot here enter. It will be sufficient to notice certain fundamental difficulties which have been generally recognised by the critics of the position. The criticism turns upon the concept of the *determination* of desire by feeling, upon the idea of the causal relation involved. It is maintained with justification that for a feeling to be a cause of desire it must be actual, that is a present state of consciousness. But according to Ehrenfels' conception it is not always a present state, but often a state which does not yet exist, which is said to be the cause. It is the existence of an object not yet realised or the non-existence of a present object, which is desired. The hedonic accompaniment of a not-yet existent object, itself therefore not existent, cannot in any causal sense be the determinant of desire. But it may be said that it is the difference of these two states that is the cause. In that case it must be either the unfelt, uncognised difference, an abstraction, which is the cause, or else a new feeling following upon the judgment of the difference between the actual present feeling and an imagined feeling arising from the assumption of the existence or non-existence of the object. In the first case, we have a conceptual abstraction made the cause—which is impossible. In the second case, a feeling difference has become the object of judgment, and a value moment is already present prior to desire. It is clear that in some sense feeling or feeling-disposition is always presupposed by desire, but the relation cannot be described as causal.

Ehrenfels recognises, that upon this causal view of the relation of feeling to desire, the proposition must be modified to read: desire is determined by feeling or feeling-dispositions. But we have already seen that worth cannot, in every case, be identified with actual desire, but only with the capacity of being desired or desirability. Thus Ehrenfels is finally left without any conscious correlate for the worth moment. Both the feeling and conative aspects tend to become dispositional.

2. The Criterion of Worth Feeling—Presupposition of Reality.

For reasons of the nature of those developed in our criticism of Ehrenfels's worth definition, Meinong [1] makes feeling the worth-fundamental. The sense of worth is given in feeling-signs, Werth-gefühle, which are determined in character and degree by the nature of their *presuppositions* (Voraussetzungen).[2] These presuppositions he further conceives, in the case of worth feelings, to be always judgments (or according to his later formulation, judgments and assumptions—Annahmen), and are therefore distinguishable from feelings which have merely sensations or presentations as their presuppositions. Leaving out of account for the moment the question of this limitation of the class, worth feelings, we may accept Meinong's general position. The preferability of feeling as the fundamental element seems to me to be beyond doubt, and for the following reasons. In general our argument would be : There can be no sense of worth without a meaning which may properly be described as *felt* meaning, while there can very well be a sense of worth without that qualification which we describe as desire and volition. More specifically, even in those experiences which we call explicit desire or volition, the essence of the desire can be equally well described in terms of feeling without doing violence to our speech. The essence of desire is the feeling of lack or want. We "*feel* the need" of something. What further qualifies desire is the kinæsthetic sensations which are irrelevant accompaniments from the standpoint of the essential worth moment. But it is by no means in the same sense true that every worth experience involves explicit desire. We may actually feel the worth of objects without the slightest trace of that qualification of our feeling which we describe as actual desire for their presence, although a conative disposition is presupposed and may become explicit under suitable conditions. The same is true of æsthetic and mystical states of repose where actual desire is in abeyance.

What this means for our definition is clear. In actual worth experience desire is not necessarily present although

---

[1] Meinong, *Psychologisch-ethische Untersuchungen*, Part I, chap. I.

[2] In presenting Meinong's position I have translated Voraussetzung "presupposition" rather than pre-condition, as better adapted to convey his meaning, and have retained this broader usage of presupposition throughout, although in the usage of Baldwin it is confined to the higher reflective level, that is, if I understand his position correctly, his presupposition is always a "presupposition of belief."

Definition of the Consciousness of Value

feeling is. The desire is present often merely as a dispositional moment which, however, may become actual under certain definite circumstances. In so far, therefore, as our definition includes the element of desire, we must enlarge it to read—an object has worth in so far as it is either desired or has the capacity of calling out desire, has, in other words, desirability. This definition includes the mystical and æsthetic states of repose already referred to, for no object can become the object of such feelings which has not been desired and may not under some circumstances again be desired. Conation is present dispositionally (how we shall see later) even in these states of repose. But the case is different with feeling. In defining worth as feeling with certain characteristic presuppositions we mean that every actual worth judgment implies actual feeling—even in those cases where the worth attitude is scarcely distinguishable from the cognitive.

Feeling having been taken as the actual conscious correlate of worth predicates, the second problem arises—whether worth feelings are coextensive with feelings in general, or whether some further differentiation within the general class, feeling, is required. It is at this point that the definition of Meinong, that feelings of worth are exclusively "judgment-feelings," becomes important. This view, which may be described as the intellectualistic theory of worth experience, has given rise to so many important developments in ethics and æsthetics that it demands the most careful consideration. Negatively viewed, it denies the character of worth experience to all feelings which have as their presuppositions mere presentations, to all feelings which may be adequately described as the mere feeling-tone of the presentation or as the effect of the entrance of the presentation into consciousness. It differentiates "worth feeling" from mere "pleasure-causation," i.e. pleasure viewed as mere reaction to stimulus.

Before considering in detail the psychological grounds for this view, it will be well to observe the more general fact that, whether worth experience be defined in terms of desire or feeling, it cannot be made co-extensive with either. Desire, in itself, does not constitute the experience of valuation: there are fleeting desires which do not attain to the level of valuation, a fact which leads Krüger in his definition, which is in terms of desire, to make the differentia of worth a certain *constancy* of desire. Again, as Meinong points out, illustrations are plentiful of valuation without actual consciousness of pleasure, while a fleeting pleasure does not necessarily involve valuation. Reflection upon these facts of experience leads to more strictly logical considerations such as those which appeared in our criticism of Ehrenfels's definition. The sense of value cannot be identified with the mere feeling of pleasure, although of course a feeling of pleasure when it is made the object of judgment may become a value, for the feeling of value is conditioned not only by the presence of objects, but also by their absence. The mere absence of the object is not the condition of the feeling, but the cognisance (in Meinong's terms the judgment) of non-existence. The hedonic state which would be the effect of the presence of the absent object is not actual, and can therefore not be, in any causal sense, the condition of the desire and of valuation. Moreover, the cause of the pleasure is often quite distinct from the object of the feeling of value, often physiological and unconscious. The feeling of value can therefore not be viewed as the effect or accompaniment of sensation or presentation of an object, but as conditioned by some presupposition of the existence of the object. In the case of the reflex feeling of the value of life, conditioned by organic sensations, the feeling is objectless but contains a primitive presumption of reality which then maintains itself, as an explicit judgment of value, by attaching itself to objects which form the concrete content of life.

The negative aspect of Meinong's position, the denial of the character of worth experience to mere presentation-feelings, appears justified from this analysis of the facts. A fundamental distinction seems to exist between feeling which is a mere feeling-tone, accompaniment or effect of a sensation or revived image, and feeling-attitude which is characterised by the direction of the feeling toward the object. Feeling-attitudes alone seem to contain the worth-moment. It is undoubtedly true that feeling-tone of presentation, when it reaches a certain degree of intensity, gives rise to a feeling-attitude, to the presentation of the cause as object and the direction of judgment toward it, and thus to feeling of worth. But this feeling or desire, as the case may be, is distinguished from the feeling-tone by the presence of additional presuppositions; whether exclusively judgmental or not is a question to be determined.

A critical consideration of this positive aspect of Meinong's definition requires a closer examination of his use of the term presupposition (Voraussetzung). Under this concept he includes

Definition of the Consciousness of Value

all those conditions of feeling which are psychical in character, as distinguished from other causes of feeling which may be dispositional and physiological. In this sense a presupposition may be any psychical process, presentation, judgments, the various types, categorical, hypothetical, etc., and other types of function, perhaps, such as assumption. In every case where the presupposition of a feeling is spoken of, the feeling is directed toward an object and is conditioned by some psychical act, of presentation, of imagination with its assumption of reality, or of judgment, which is for Meinong a fundamental form of psychical process. The significance of this distinction is to be found in the fact that the characteristic meanings of feelings which distinguish them as feelings of value, are not to be differentiated in terms merely of the objects toward which the feeling is directed, nor yet in terms of the causes of the feeling, but in terms of the cognitive acts or attitudes which relate the object to the subject.

(a) The Presupposition of Reality not exclusively Existential Judgment—Criticism of Meinong.

Is then the presupposition of worth feeling exclusively judgmental, as Meinong maintains? To this question our answer must be negative. But we may admit, to begin with, that many types of worth attitude do have existential judgments as presuppositions, and that all secondary modifications of worth attitude are determined by the inclusion or exclusion of judgments, existential and relational, as part presuppositions of the feeling. But that there is no primary immediate consciousness of value without explicit judgment of existence or non-existence of the object, cannot be maintained. As was pointed out in our discussion of the equivocations in the worth predicates, ideal and imputed values may be attributed to objects when the question whether they exist or may be acquired is not raised, and when, accordingly, the attitude can never reach the point of explicit judgment. The activities of imagination and idealisation abundantly prove that the feelings directed upon their objects are really feelings of worth and are determinative of worth judgments, although they presuppose mere assumptions of the reality of the objects which do not require to be converted into, or explicitly acknowledged in, existential judgments.

Meinong has indeed found himself compelled upon further reflection to modify his definition to the extent that he includes with the judgment-feelings assumption-feelings (Annahme-gefühle). He recognises, that "often one values an object at a time when there is entirely wanting all chance of judgments of existence and non-existence, because it is not yet determined whether the object thought of as in the future will exist or not." Moreover, "it is possible, and it frequently happens, that we value an abstractly presented object without inquiring after its existence."[1] And in a later paper[2] he further qualifies his position by recognising that it is only *some universe of reality* which is necessarily presupposed, in that the presuppositions are not necessarily categorical existential judgments, but may be hypothetical or disjunctive. Now in all these cases where the object is "abstractly presented," assumed to exist, or asserted to exist conditionally, reality is presupposed in some sense; there is some reference to reality. It is also clear that in all these cases the feeling characterised as feeling of value is, by this very reference to reality presupposed, in some way differently qualified from the feeling of pleasantness or unpleasantness. The question at issue is merely as to the proper characterisation of the reality-meaning, whether it rests exclusively upon existential judgment or not.

(b) *Criticism of the Theory of Existential Judgment underlying this View—Existential Judgment merely Acknowledgment of a Presupposition of Reality.*

This question is still more ultimately conditioned by a theory of the existential judgment. To this theoretical problem we shall presently turn, but it will be in the interests of clearness to seek a preliminary characterisation of this presupposition of reality. There can be no question, in the first place, that wherever there is the feeling of value, there is reality feeling. When once an object, the existence of which was what I desired or what conditioned my feeling of value, is explicitly judged non-existent, the object undoubtedly loses its value for me. The essential condition of its being valued is eliminated.

---

[1] Meinong, "*Über Werthalten und Wert,*" *Archiv für Systematische Philosophie*, 1895, pp. 327–46. Also his later work, *Über Annahmen.*
[2] "*Urtheilsgefühle, was Sie sind und was Sie nicht sind,*" *Archiv für die gesammte Psychologie*, Vol. VI, 1905.

Definition of the Consciousness of Value 43

My appreciation of the worth of an object does not, however, necessarily, and in every case, rest upon such explicit judgment of existence, but at most upon a primary undisturbed *presumption* of reality. By this primary presumption of reality, of a reality, moreover, in which the more specific existence meaning has not yet been differentiated, is to be understood the mere act of acceptance, *taking for granted*,[1] prior to the explicit *taking up* of the object into a pre-determined sphere of reality through the existence predicate, and prior to the assumption of existence of an object in the interest of continuity of any trend or activity, whether of the type of cognition or valuation.

As illustrative of this attitude of primitive presumption we may consider first the reality-feeling which attaches to perception and presentation simply because of the " recognitive meaning "[2] which they have. Distinctions between existent and non-existent arise later—more especially in the case of presentations in the fancy or imagination mode. They are presumed to be real until the entrance of illusion-disturbing moments which require the presumption to pass over into explicit judgment and conviction either of existence or non-existence. The fairy world of the child is a world neither of pure presentation nor of existential judgment but of presumption. The same may be said of many ideals of the more developed mind, as for instance, the religious, about which questions of existence and non-existence are not seriously asked. In all these cases some psychically pre-determined *demand*, whether arising from a more objective cognitive factor of recognition or a more subjective factor of conative disposition or interest, creates a presumption of reality.

Such presumption must be carefully distinguished from both

---

[1] The use of the term *presumption* to characterise this relation to reality is, I think, fully justified both linguistically and psychologically. Our ordinary speech, it is true, frequently fails to distinguish between presumption and assumption, and has, moreover, read into the word presumption a certain ethical connotation which partially unfits it for the present use. On the other hand, the original meaning of the Latin *praesumptio* is much nearer to the use that we have in mind—it had more the meaning of *taking for granted* prior to explicit judgment and was quite different from the conscious assumption of reality as we have it in hypothesis. The modern English dictionaries give as one of the renderings, *taking for granted*, the meaning here emphasised. The use of the term in formal logic, as in fallacies of presumption, while at first apparently against our usage, on closer inspection seems to favour it. A presumption is a material fallacy, an unconscious pre-logical taking for granted. Finally, the value of the introduction of this term for our immediate purpose is to be found in the possibility it affords of using the prefixes *præ*, *sub*, and *ad*, with the same root, to designate modifications of cognitive attitude.

[2] Baldwin's distinction referred to above.

judgment and *assumption*. The existential judgment arises, we shall see, only after disturbance in a sphere of reality already presupposed; it is an act which takes place only after some disposition, some tendency to recognition, or to renewal of attitude of feeling or will meets with opposition or arrest. It must be equally clearly distinguished from the later, more developed, attitude of assumption of existence which presupposes dispositions already created by actual judgment. The assumption, except when it is what we describe as an unconscious assumption (and then it is really an approximation to presumption), recognises the possibility of the non-existence of the object, and in some modes of playful assumption (the "semblant modes" of Professor Baldwin) it is, so to speak, on the verge of explicit judgment of non-existence. But in the making of the assumption the act is determined by a subjective factor, a demand arising from already existing dispositions and interests. The assumption is an acknowledgment of this demand.

It is obvious, after this analysis, that the definition of feeling of value under consideration, as feeling with existential judgment as its presupposition, is possible only on the theory that the primitive form of judgment is the mere act of acceptance (acknowledgment) [1] or rejection and involves no relational aspect, no separation of two elements, subject and predicate. The existential judgment is identified with acceptance and the non-existential with rejection. If this view of judgment (Brentano's)[2] can be maintained, it follows necessarily that there can be no feeling of value without a judgment as presupposition, for all attitude is primarily acceptance or rejection, and the feeling of value is an *attitude*, not mere presentation plus feeling. But can mere acceptance or rejection be identified with judgment of existence and non-existence, and at the same time any useful conception of judgment be retained? I think not, and for the following reasons.

The view that they can implies: (*a*) That presentation

---

[1] The use of the terms *acknowledgment* and *rejection* as correlative is most unfortunate, for it prejudices the whole question. Rejection, as any dictionary tells us, is not the opposite of acknowledgment. Acknowledgment has as its opposite disavowal, while the opposite of rejection is acceptance. This linguistic relation corresponds precisely to the psychological. Acknowledgment and disavowal both represent the explicit judgmental acts by which a reality already presupposed is affirmed or denied. Mere acceptance or rejection of an object presupposes nothing more than a presumption of reality or disturbance of that presumption.

[2] For a presentation and discussion of Brentano's theory of judgment see Stout, *Analytical Psychology*, Vol. I, chap. v.

Definition of the Consciousness of Value

and judgment (acceptance or rejection of the existence of the presented) are two different and irreducible elementary aspects of consciousness ; (b) that while the affirmation or negation of A (as function) adds something to its mere presentation (as function), the affirmation or negation of A's existence (as content) adds nothing to the affirmation or negation of A (as content). The first thesis is the key to the position. Is there such a thing as simple apprehension, presentation without acceptance, or does apprehension involve apprehension of existence? At first sight the former of the two possible alternatives seems to be true. From the standpoint of analysis alone, we seem to find cases in which the element of affirmation is at a minimum, or is even entirely lacking, and in which a merely presentational consciousness remains. Leaving out of account the case of doubt or suspended judgment where, although at a minimum, tendencies to judgment still remain, we may turn immediately to the typical case of æsthetic contemplation. Here it is said we have a strictly presentational consciousness, at least when the contemplation is pure, when the æsthetic is unmixed with other factors. This view we shall find it necessary to reject, and for the following reasons. In the first place, æsthetic contemplation is an attitude—not mere presentation ; in it there is, as Ehrenfels says, at least a resting in reality, " ein Haften an der Wirklichkeit," either outer or inner. As such it is more than mere presentation. While for the purposes of the psychologist the idea of a purely presentational consciousness is sometimes a useful abstraction, every actual experience presupposes a minimum of acceptance or rejection. The procedure, therefore, which takes this abstraction, made for purposes of analysis, as a picture of reality, and from it infers, for instance, the unreality of the æsthetic object and experience and its exclusion from the sphere of worth experience, is vitiated by serious fallacy.

But if the merely presentational consciousness be but an abstraction, there still remains the question—to what extent, in actual concrete cases of æsthetic contemplation, all acceptance and rejection may be seen to be excluded and the purely presentational approached. Perhaps the difference is negligible. Most æsthetic attitudes, it is recognised by all, fail to give us this contemplation pure. In the sublime and tragic, for instance, pseudo-æsthetic factors, so called, enter in, in the form of acknowledgments and rejections, judgments of various kinds. Even beauty, in its narrower sense, contains, as partial moments, normative judgments. If we are to find any concrete æsthetic experience of "pure contemplation," it must be in the simplest perceptual forms and form-qualities. These are indeed usually taken as the typical æsthetic objects when the æsthetic is thus defined. But even here it is doubtful whether the element of acceptance and rejection, or of conation, can be excluded. It is true that these forms and form-qualities, when abstracted from the elements in which they inhere, may be viewed as the objects of purely presentational activity. Nevertheless their construction was the product of conative activity which involved spontaneous acceptance and rejection, presumption of reality. Viewed genetically, every æsthetic feeling of form presupposes a disposition created by preceding conative activity.

The distinction between simple apprehension and acceptance is, then, even in æsthetic contemplation, a relative one. What shall be said of the second part of the thesis—that acceptance or rejection of an object, A, is identical with the affirmation or negation of the existence of A, or, in other words, with judgment? Acknowledgment or rejection does undoubtedly presuppose the reality, in some sense, of the presentational content. This is the same as saying that all conation is directed toward objects presumed to be real. It does not follow, however, that explicit existential judgment is involved. We must, I think, look upon the existential judgment as derived from a simpler and more ultimate attitude toward a reality presupposed in all conation, even on the perceptual level. Acceptance and rejection involve presumption of existence but not necessarily judgment.

Such a distinction between presumption and judgment involves of course a theory of the nature of judgment. Into the logical questions here raised we cannot go in detail, but this much at least may be said. The position maintained by Sigwart (among other logicians)—that judgment "must be regarded as establishing a relation, even in its existential form," seems necessary if our conception of it is to retain any useful significance.[1] When the relational aspect is allowed to lapse, judgment becomes practically indistinguishable from conation. It is true that the existential judgment occupies a unique position. It does not establish a relation between its subject and the predicate, "being," "but between an object as idea and an object as intuited." Affirmation of existence or non-existence presupposes,

[1] Sigwart, *Logic* (translation), Vol. I, p. 72.

as mere acceptance or rejection does not, at least the beginning of the differentiation of subject and predicate.[1]

3. *The Presupposition of Reality—Presumption, Judgment, and Assumption of Existence of Objects—Analysis of these Cognitive Attitudes.*

On the theory of judgment here developed, the existential judgment and the pure presentation, in so far as "contemplation" is pure presentation, are secondary attitudes, derived from the primitive *presumption* of reality presupposed in all acceptance or rejection of an object. The difference between the presumption and judgment is that, while in the former we have merely acceptance and rejection, in the latter we have acknowledgment and disavowal, acceptance and rejection *plus* belief or disbelief. Returning then to the question of the necessary presuppositions of the feeling of value, it is clear that there must be the presumption of reality, for without it there can be no attitude toward the object, seeing that attitude involves either acceptance or rejection, or disposition to accept or reject. But it is equally clear that the existential judgment cannot be the sole and necessary presupposition of the feeling, for there can be no such explicit judgment (acknowledgment or disavowal) except as there is already some reality meaning, some presupposition of reality. Again, the hypothetical *pure* presentation, in so far as there is any such mode of consciousness, is equally secondary and derived. It is the result of abstraction from the primitive presumption of reality, the result of arrest of this presumption implicit in all conation. Meinong's use of the expression "abstractly presented" is significant in this connection. To present abstractly means to strip off the reality feeling involved in the first experience. This relation to reality feeling may, however, be partially restored by a further movement of conation in which the presented object is *assumed* to exist, an attitude we find characteristic of certain secondary contemplative æsthetic experiences.

---

[1] The following quotation from Baldwin's *Thought and Things*, Vol. II (chapter II, on "Acknowledgment and Belief," p. 17), puts the situation admirably: "The existence meaning which the judgment always presupposes in the sense given, may, *when explicitly asserted, be called a predicate* but not an *attributive predicate*, not a separate element of presented context or of recognitive meaning, attributed to the subject matter. It is only the explicit assertion of the presupposition of belief in the sphere in which the subject matter is constituted an object of thought."

We are thus led finally to a consideration of the relation of the attitude of assumption to the primitive presumption of reality and to the existential judgment. This question is important for the reason that the special modification of feeling which has assumption as its "presupposition," the feelings of the imagination (Phantasiegefühle) of Meinong's school, has been made much of in recent discussion. For one thing it has been asserted that these feelings are not real and therefore not feelings of value, although under certain circumstances they may stand for, or represent, real feelings. Our own view, which will be developed more fully later, is that they are real feelings in any sense which has significance for psychology and that they have a presupposition of reality, although from the point of view of reflective evaluation of the objects of such feelings (the axiological point of view) the judgments which spring from these feelings may be invalid. But a more adequate characterisation of the attitude of assumption itself is our first problem.

Assumption, as a cognitive attitude, has two meanings. According to its first meaning it is an acceptance, a taking as existent, of an object when there is an underlying sense of the possibility of its being non-existent. In this sense it is a halfway stage between the primitive presumption of reality and the existential judgment. In this sense also it is a secondary movement or act of cognition within a developing sphere of reality, bounded by the primitive presumption of reality and the existential judgment, affirmative or negative. From the point of view of conation, it is an act determined by the momentum of a subjective disposition or interest. In its second meaning it is not pre-judgmental but post-judgmental, that is, a permanent assumption is created by habitual judgment; it presupposes dispositions created by acts of judgment and is derived from the judgment attitude. In this case the assumption approaches closely to the presumption, and for this attitude the two terms are often used interchangeably. It is important to emphasise these two meanings[1] for the feeling attitudes involved are in many respects quite different, and the confusion of the two has led to misinterpretation of worth experience. Thus the feelings which attach to assumptions of the first type may be described as feelings of the imagination; they belong to the mode of

---

[1] Baldwin's recently published theory of "schematic" function recognises both these modes of "assumption," the existential judgment lying, genetically, between them. *Thought and Things*, Vol. I, chap. v.

semblance or "make-believe." But those which attach to assumptions of the second type are more accurately described as feeling-abstracts or affective signs and represent the acquired or funded meanings of past judgment feelings. To this class, we shall see later, belong all those feelings or funded meanings which inhere intrinsically in general concepts. Such terms as truth, virtue, duty, etc., have functioned in particular existential judgments, and it was upon the basis of these judgments that the feelings of value for which these terms stand arose. But when they are thus formed they are abstractly valued without explicit judgments of existence or non-existence. They represent an assumption which has arisen through formation of habit. Explicit judgment is always the terminus of a process of adaptation. From the primitive presumption arises, through arrest, assumption, which in turn passes into judgment and the later assumption.

We are now in a position to summarise our view as to the nature of simple appreciation or primary feelings of value, in so far as it is related to Meinong's criterion. We agree with him to the extent that we include among the feelings of value only such feelings as have reality meanings, that is, have some presupposition of reality. As to the nature of that presupposition of reality we differ. We deny its limitation to existential judgment and include the two attitudes of presumption and assumption. This may be said to be the result of our critical analysis of the meanings of experiences of worth. There remains still the question of the functional and genetic account of these different presuppositions. Before undertaking this we must glance briefly at another criterion of feeling of value recently developed, more especially by Lipps.

IV. THE GENESIS AND RELATIONS OF THESE PRESUPPOSITIONS OF THE FEELING AND JUDGMENT OF VALUE

1. *Criticism of the Theory that All Feelings of Value Presuppose Reference to the Personality.*

It is maintained that all feelings of value are feelings of personality—that the analysis which finds the criterion of feeling of value in the nature of the attitude toward a transcendent object, really overlooks the significant moment, which is the reference of the feeling to the subject, the personality. Feelings of value are feelings of activity of the subject, the acts of judgment, etc., being of only secondary importance. Such a criterion is presented in the formula of Lipps :[1] " Der Wert jeder Lust ist bedingt durch einen Persönlichkeitswert." Now, while it is undoubtedly true that there are types of feelings of value which have as their presupposition explicit reference to the personality—i.e., those feelings described as values of characterisation, including feelings of obligation, desert, etc. It must nevertheless be recognised that these values are secondary and acquired, that they presuppose judgments referring the attitude to the presented self, the self being the product of an ideal construction based upon preceding experiences of value. The only sense in which Lipps's statement may be said to be true is that in primary feelings of value, as distinguished from simple pleasure, there are certain modifications, certain implicit meanings which, when reflected upon, lead to their reference to the self. Such a modification of his view we may accept.

The meanings which appear on the level of simple appreciation prior to reference to the self, Krüger[2] has described as depth and breadth of the feeling in the personality, and he conceives them to constitute a third dimension of feeling, besides its intensity and duration, a dimension which is determined by a relative constancy of disposition. His development of the criterion is both analytical and genetic. Valuation is distinguished from mere desire and simple "pleasure-causation" by a moment of relative constancy of desire. Desire of itself does not constitute valuation, and valuation is never mere desire or a series of desires. He further conceives the relation of this "desire-constant" to the individual desires on the analogy of the relation of concepts to particular sensations and percepts. A valuation always presupposes a relatively constant disposition, and this disposition appears as an actual element in consciousness only in a corresponding judgment. Yet the judgment of value is not the valuation itself. This is given rather in the characteristic modification of the experienced desire and feeling, which he conceives to grow in depth with the development of the "desire-constant."[3] He suggests that it is probable that in the first stages

---

[1] Lipps, *Die ethischen Grundfragen*, Leipzig, 1899, Chap. I.
[2] Krüger, *Der Begriff des absolut Wertvollen als Grundbegriff der Moral philosophie*, Leipzig, 1898, chap. III ("Zur Psychologie des Wertes").
[3] One point, however, he has left undetermined. Is the worth experience given in feeling or desire? In some passages he speaks as though the sense of worth were given in feeling as determined by or as determining desire, in others as though it were given in the experiences of desire themselves. As a matter of fact, he does not seem to have

of conscious life only that was consciously striven after which brought with it relative increase of pleasure, and that the consciousness of value has probably taken its rise in such strivings, but every desire has a tendency to develop a relative constancy and thus to pass into a valuation. It leaves behind in the personality constant dispositions, and with them traces of value. The mechanism of pleasure-causation is thus broken through by the formation of values; and as soon as the function of valuation is formed at a single point, the will ceases to be exclusively determined by the intensity and duration of expected pleasure. Through the fact of valuation the affective-volitional life gets, so to speak, a third dimension; the value of a constant desire is determined by its breadth and depth in the personality.

The interest of this definition of Krüger's is to be found in the fact that it is an attempt to connect the appreciative distinctions which differentiate feelings of value from other feelings, which lead ultimately to the characterisation of the self and to the explicit reference of the object to the self, with the functional, dispositional conditions of the feeling, and it has been presented here at some length because this concept of conative constants or dispositions as the necessary conditions of feelings of value, feelings with depth and breadth, is precisely the concept which we need to connect these appreciative meanings with the reality meanings which the preceding analysis has distinguished. At an earlier stage it was seen that both the concepts of feeling and conation must find a place in the definition of worth expeiience. It is now seen that feelings of value are not completely characterised by reference to their presuppositions of reality, presumption, judgment and assumption, but that we must go more deeply into the conative dispositions which determine these acts of presumption, judgment, and assumption.

2. *Genetic Levels of Valuation.*

How then shall we conceive this relation of the two determinants of feelings of value? If we describe the acts of cognition as the *actual psychical presuppositions* and the conative

faced this question at all, as the following passage indicates: "Where the capacity or function of valuation is to some degree realised, there the individual experiences of feeling and desire are in a peculiar manner heightened and deepened, they have a personal character. They find, so to speak, in the personality a fuller and more individual resonance. We can in such a case speak of a more highly developed 'Gemütsleben'" (p. 50).

tendencies as the *dispositional conditions*, our problem would read : What is the relation of the actual presuppositions to the dispositional conditions as determinants of feelings of value ? The answer to this question must be in genetic terms. We have already seen that there is a certain genetic relation between the attitudes of presumption, assumption, and judgment. Each, in its way, represents a functional attitude toward a psychically pre-determined object, the acceptance of a demand, acquiescence in a claim to control, and each therefore is a type of reality meaning. But these demands or controls vary at different stages of the genetic series. An analysis of the manner in which the dispositional factor functions at the different stages of development should give us a point of view from which to unify the results of our study.

The condition which determines the primitive presumption of reality seems to be that the object shall have recognitive meaning for a conative tendency. At this point the cognitive and conative moments can scarcely be distinguished. As far back as we can go in our analysis, interest and conation seem to determine recognition, and recognition is the condition of the first reality-meaning which characterises feelings of value. In the primitive presumption of reality the dualism between subjective and objective controlling factors has not yet emerged. It is with the first arrest of a conative tendency, through the development of an independent cognitive interest, and through differentiation of the recognitive factor from the conative, that the innocency of primitive presumption is disturbed and a differentiation of subjective and objective demands or controls appears. Here the attitude of assumption emerges, determined largely by the subjective control factor of the conative disposition, often in opposition to objective controls already established—but not necessarily so. Assumption of the existence of an object is the acceptance of a subjective demand, after arrest of primitive presumption, and constitutes a transition stage between presumption and explicit acknowledgment of a control as objective.[1] From the assumption attitude emerges the existential judgment, either positive or negative. It represents not merely the acceptance or rejection of an object, but the explicit acknowledgment or disavowal of a certain control factor. It is important to ob-

---

[1] I am inclined to agree with Professor Baldwin that a pure fancy mode or play of fancy, described by him as the first semblant mode, constitutes a genetic transition between presumption and assumption, but for our purposes it is negligible.

Definition of the Consciousness of Value

serve that this control factor may be either an objective or subjective factor and that the existential judgment may be acknowledgment of either. But in the latter case the subjective has, by that very process, been transferred to the objective side of the equation.

V. Résumé of Preceding Definition and Analysis

The material is now before us for a summary restatement of our original definition of value, as funded affective-volitional meaning, in terms of psychological equivalents. The psychological equivalent of the worth predicate is always a feeling, with certain meanings determined by actual cognitive presuppositions or types of cognitive reaction which actualise pre-existent conative dispositions. The value or funded meaning of the object is its capacity of becoming the object of feeling and desire through actualisation of dispositional tendencies by acts of presumption, judgment, and assumption.

The conative disposition is the fundamental determinant of the feeling of value or appreciative meaning of the object, but the disposition may be *actualised*, represented in function by different cognitive attitudes or acts, of the types enumerated, and according as it is one or the other of these types is the feeling qualified in the manner described.[1] Underlying the feeling of value attached to the idea of my friend is the conative disposition, the interest created by former desires for his presence and satisfaction of those desires, but that feeling may now arise upon mere momentary assumptions of his existence without a trace of desire for his immediate presence. All "disposition-feelings," however actualised, are feelings of value because they represent the funded meaning of affective-volitional process,

[1] In the consideration of the relation of the actual presuppositions to the dispositional conditions there are still certain questions which have considerable bearing upon later discussions. Thus Witasek maintains, that while it is probably true that feelings of worth arise upon the mere presentation of an object related to desire dispositions, nevertheless, since desire presupposes judgment, and these dispositions have been formed by preceding judgments, the worth feeling is ultimately still a "judgment-feeling." Now it may be admitted that judgments enter into the formation of these desire dispositions, but as dispositional they are merely conative tendency, for it is the essence of judgment to be explicit and actual. Again, it is argued (by Saxinger), that the dispositions corresponding to judgment feelings are different from the dispositions correlated with assumption feelings, and he bases his arguments upon differences in the laws governing the two kinds of feeling. Into the consideration of this question we cannot enter here—that will be reserved for later study. We may simply emphasise our own position that worth feeling is a function of conative disposition, whether conation expresses itself explicitly in judgment or assumption.

although they have different reality-meanings. From the standpoint of the extension of the term, the class, feelings of value, includes æsthetic feelings, feelings of the imagination so-called, as well as practical and ethical attitudes.

In general, then, we may conclude that feeling of value is the feeling aspect of conative process, as distinguished from the feeling-tone of simple presentations. And by conative process we understand the total process of development by which affective-volitional meaning is acquired, the total process including actual and dispositional moments. How these dispositions, and with them the feelings which they condition, are modified, both qualitatively and quantitatively, at different stages of this development, by changes in presuppositions, and more especially by the inclusion of secondary judgments of relation, etc., is the problem of the next chapter.

CHAPTER III

MODES OF THE CONSCIOUSNESS OF VALUE— PRIMARY AND ACQUIRE

I. THE APPRECIATIVE DESCRIPTION OF FEELINGS OF VALUE— DESCRIPTION OF MODES OF REALITY FEELING

1. *The Nature of Appreciative Description.*

THE course of the preceding chapter has led to a demarcation of those meanings described as worths or values. Beginning with the preliminary definition of worth as the affective-volitional meaning of the object for the subject, we advanced by successive stages of analysis to the more specific statement that worth experience is always a feeling attitude which presupposes the actualisation of some conative disposition by acts of presumption, judgment, or assumption (implicit and explicit). This definition obviously involves a certain theory of the nature of feeling and of its relation to conation. For one thing, this broader use of the term feeling involves a relative distinction between feeling-attitude and affective tone of sensation, a distinction which has in fact been insisted upon, and it also leads to the view that feeling, as worth feeling, has appreciative distinctions not found in passive affection. To this theory of the nature of feeling, and to the more abstract psychological analysis which it involves, we must turn our attention later. For the present—and indeed as a necessary preliminary to this later study—our problem is the further development of the appreciative distinctions of feeling.

Earlier in our study a distinction was made between the "appreciative" and "reality-" (including existence-) meanings of worth predicates. Starting with the analysis of the latter, we developed the definition of value in terms of its functional presuppositions. But in the course of that very analysis we came upon certain appreciative distinctions in feeling, as, for instance, in the study of the criteria of Lipps and Krüger, such as feelings of the personality, breadth and depth of feeling in the personality, which were taken as descriptive of feelings of value. Logically, this analysis of appreciative descriptions of feeling should, perhaps, have come first in our own study, but the order of presentation chosen has this advantage, that the critical studies of the preceding chapter have, by their results both positive and negative, defined the sphere of worth experience, and have given us the clue to the interpretation of the different qualifications of feeling which are suggestive of worth, that is, which give rise to those meanings of objects which we call worth predicates.

The worth predicates themselves, as tertiary qualities of objects, are, in their manifold modifications, appreciative distinctions arising from differences in the meaning of feelings. They are projections into the object of distinctions within feeling. The supposition immediately presents itself that, since they are funded meanings of feeling processes, they correspond directly to fundamental differences in feeling itself, and that there are as many differences in feeling as there are worth predicates. Reflection, however, makes it clear that appreciative description of objects, while the expression of worth feelings, is not necessarily the appreciative description of those feelings themselves. These predicates are *what* we feel about the object, not *how* we feel. We feel beauty, goodness, nobility, sublimity, obligation, but when we describe how we feel in such cases a transition has been made to the appreciative description of the feeling itself. The feeling has been made the object of presentation and description, and it is quite possible that in such appreciative description of the feeling one of these general worth predicates may stand for different modifications of feeling, or for several at the same time. Thus the predicate good may, when applied to an act, have as its equivalent a feeling described as the tension of obligation, at another the feeling of satisfied repose. In order to describe adequately the feeling I have when I call an object sublime, it may be necessary to use the terms elevation and repose; and, if I wish to add to my description quantitative terms, to speak of the depth of the feeling. It is apparent, then, that what is meant by the appreciative distinctions in primary worth feeling are those descriptions of his feelings which the subject seeks as the equivalents of his worth predicates applied to objects. The ultimate terms in which such feelings

Modes of the Consciousness of Value

of simple appreciation are described should give us the fundamental modifications of worth feeling.

2. *The Relation of Appreciative Description to the "Scientific" Description of Feeling as Content—Theories of Feeling.*

It has been said that there are innumerable nuances of feeling, and in the same breath it has been asserted that all these differences are reducible to differences in intensity and duration of a one-dimensional continuum, pleasantness-unpleasantness, these differences being due to differences in the sensational, perceptual, or ideal content with which the feeling is connected. With the first part of this statement we may agree, but the second requires critical examination. The consciousness of the inadequacy of this conception of the dimensions of feeling has been growing recently, and the demand for new analysis has arisen from two distinct quarters—from the study of the psychology of worth experience, on the one hand, and from non-appreciative psycho-physical analysis as illustrated in Wundt's three-dimensional theory, on the other hand.

In the case of the "worth psychologists," with whom we are in this connection primarily concerned, the logic of this analysis is clear enough. When they turn from the worth predicates of objects to a description of the experiences which determine these predicates, they find the old terminology, intensity and duration of pleasantness-unpleasantness, inadequate for the reconstruction of this experience. In the analysis of Krüger which we have already considered, worth feeling, which is distinguished functionally from pleasure-causation by the fact that it presupposes conative constants, is distinguished appreciatively by a new dimension, depth and breadth in the personality. Simmel,[1] who likewise makes feeling the fundamental element, also finds it necessary to distinguish the aspects of depth and breadth of feeling from intensity. Another class of analysts, who hold a voluntaristic theory, find modifications of worth experience, which cannot be correlated with feeling if feeling be conceived merely as intensity of pleasantness-unpleasantness. Brentano[2] is compelled to assume quasi-logical dimensions of acts of preference, to which pleasantness and unpleasantness are related merely as redundant passive phenomena and more

---

[1] Simmel, *Einleitung in die Moralwissenschaft.*
[2] Brentano, *Psychologie.* Also *Ursprung der sittlichen Erkentniss.*

recently and definitely, Schwartz[1] has found it necessary to distinguish fundamentally between degrees of worth experience, satisfaction (Sättigung des Gefallen) and intensity of feeling, and on the assumption that feeling is passive pleasantness-unpleasantness, to seek a voluntaristic basis for worth experience. Despite the differences in theory of the nature of the worth-fundamental, it is clear that these analyses all have in view the object of doing justice to appreciative distinctions in worth experience, whatever that may be found to be, in terms of psychological equivalents.

3. The Problem and Method of Appreciative Description.

If then we hold to the view already developed, that worth experience is feeling with certain characteristic presuppositions, our task is naturally to seek some conception of feeling which lies between the two views propounded—both of them unworkable for our analysis—the proposition that feeling has innumerable modifications, and the view that it is merely intensity of pleasantness and unpleasantness. Now the key to our procedure is to be found in the fact that " pleasantness-unpleasantness " covers but one class of terms which may be applied to the description of the concrete feeling attitude, that there are other class terms which are equally fundamental for the communication of the qualitative differences in feeling. As a description of the subjective experience corresponding to the worth predicate, the qualitative differences, pleasantness-unpleasantness, are insufficient. Moreover, when this has become clear, it will also appear that in order to express quantitative differences in worth feeling it will be necessary to make use of other conceptions than that of intensity, in its narrower sense, which has been transferred from sensation to the pleasantness and unpleasantness which accompanies sensation.

The problem then is—what are the fundamental nuances of feeling corresponding to the tertiary qualities or worth predicates attributed to objects? The answer to this question would naturally take the form of a classification of the appreciative descriptions of feeling attitudes and indeed a desideratum of the greatest importance in the present situation of the psychology of feeling is precisely such a "natural" classification of the appreciative terms used in the first stages

---

[1] Schwartz, *Psychologie des Willens*, chap. II; also Appendix I.

of introspection. As I have elsewhere[1] pointed out, the psychology of religious, ethical, and æsthetic feeling must build its generalisations almost entirely upon the results of such introspections, gathered, for instance, by the questionnaire method, and its possibility rests ultimately upon the existence of uniformities in such descriptions. Partial contributions to such a classification already exist—notably in the sphere of religious experience—but in default of any adequate view of the whole range of such descriptions, and in view of the impossibility of attempting such a classification here, we may resort to the more usual and more direct method of analysing our experience directly for the primary fundamental meanings of feeling, and then seeking to develop the secondary derived meanings by "genetic progressions" from the fundamental. This special application of the genetic method of analysis will have the advantage of presenting our results in such a form as to connect them immediately with the results of the preceding analysis of functional presuppositions, and the two will act as mutually supplementary and corrective.

II. THE FUNDAMENTAL APPRECIATIVE DISTINCTIONS IN FEELING—QUALITATIVE AND QUANTITATIVE

1. *Qualitative : Directions and References—The Three-dimensional Theory.*

What, then, are the primary, irreducible aspects of feelings which must be distinguished in order to fix their place in a system of meanings? As has been suggested, these aspects must be expressed in terms both of quality and degree. Our first concern is therefore with the qualities of feeling. Every concrete feeling attitude has two primary aspects or meanings, its *direction* and its *reference*. Its direction is either positive or negative. Its reference is either transgredient or immanental. Of the first aspect little need be said. It is that fundamental duality of quality which, when feeling is viewed retrospectively as passive and as abstracted from conation, is described as pleasantness-unpleasantness. As direction or meaning of feeling attitude, however, it presupposes relation of the attitude to conation. What have been described

---

[1] "Appreciation and Description and the Psychology of Values," *Phil. Rev.*, November, 1905.

as the references of feeling specify more completely, on the other hand, this relation to conation ; they are aspects of the feeling which refer to something presupposed, to a disposition already acquired for which the object has a meaning. In the case of the transgredient reference it is the sense of a subjective control leading on to other states. In the case of the immanental, it is a sense of a more objective control leading to continuance or repose in the same state. When it comes to describing these directions and references, their different nuances and suggestions, use is made of metaphorical and analogical terms, the significance of which we must consider.

The simplest analogy here made use of is that of contrast pairs from the different sense regions. Feelings are described as sweet or bitter, bright or dull, soft or hard, etc. They specify for finer discrimination and description the two fundamental directions of feeling, the positive and the negative, pleasant and unpleasant. Of these it is not necessary to speak in detail, for while they help to describe the worth or affective-volitional meaning of objects for the subject, their external and analogical origin makes them only indirectly the means of communication of worth experiences.

A more important group of terms employed in differentiating the worth suggestions of feeling-attitudes are those which may be described as *dynamic*. They describe the dynamic suggestions of the feeling, specify the transgredient reference. This transgredient reference is ordinarily described metaphorically in terms of forms of movement from the external world. Of the large number of such forms made use of in these descriptions a slight study of the literature of such appreciative introspection makes us immediately aware. It is full of terms for different *nuances* of movements of the crescendo or diminuendo type—of soaring, uplifting, of sudden breaking in upon consciousness, of dying away, of height and depth, etc. They can probably all be included under the general terms tension, restlessness, and perhaps contraction, the nature of which dimensions, and the theory connected with their classification, we shall consider presently. From the point of view of content such forms of movement are probably complexes founded on relations of intensity and duration among more ultimate elements. However that may be, the characteristic of these symbolic, dynamic descriptions is that they describe transitional aspects of experience, transitions from one aspect of content to another by which meaning is acquired. By this I mean that in

Modes of the Consciousness of Value

the present feeling there is always a transgredient reference to a past or future attitude. The present experience is always the foreground of a background, past or future, which is still, or already, dimly felt. Of course in such a feeling there is always reference to conation, and it might be objected that we are here dealing with impulse and desire rather than with feeling, if it were not that, as we shall seek to show, feeling cannot be completely abstracted from conation.

A third, and qualitatively opposite, class of terms is used to characterise appreciatively the *nuances* of immanental reference of feeling. They may all be grouped, I think, under the general terms, repose, relaxation, and expansion. Feelings of expansion have an unusual wealth of descriptive terms at their service. Favourite descriptions are in terms of pervasion and possession. The subject of the emotion describes himself as pervaded—as by an ether, a fluid—as swallowed up by the emotion, and in the mystical amorous and religious literature, of which such descriptions are typical, it is with love, with the glory or the will of God, that the subject is filled. These suggestions or meanings of feelings are likewise probably aspects or qualities founded on more elementary content.

This immanental reference of repose, with its cognate expansion of feeling, is a meaning which the feeling gets when the conative tendency or disposition, presupposed, has reached the stage of habit after accommodation. The object of the feeling occupies the whole consciousness, but into the meaning of the object is taken up all the accumulated meaning of the processes of accommodation for which the disposition now stands. The reference of the feeling is not beyond the present state, but to something more deeply involved in it.

In the case of the term expansion (and contraction its correlative transgredient term), it is obvious that such descriptions are metaphorical transferences from the spatial world of perception, but I think it can scarcely be denied that, as appreciative descriptions, they are as fundamental as the other descriptions transferred from the experiences of intensity and duration. It has been objected to the three-dimensional theory of feeling that, if the analogical terms, tension-relaxation, restlessness-quiescence are introduced, there is no reason why the terms contraction-expansion should not also be applied. There is none in fact—the only question is whether they are equally irreducible as terms of appreciative introspection. With an introspection which is not appreciative we have in this connection no concern.

That contraction and expansion are in this sense fundamental aspects of feeling there can I think be no question. And in this connection it is interesting to note the fact that, in a recent study of feeling by experimental methods, without these appreciative distinctions, it was found impossible to distinguish the feeling-tone of simple sensation from a mood or disposition-feeling. "The former attaches, so to speak, *to* the stimulus-complex (taste) while the latter spreads *over* the whole consciousness." It was further found that they have different pneumographic expressions. The former is attended by quickening, the latter by slowing of respiration.[1]

(a) *The Three-dimensional Analysis a Description of Reality-Meanings of Feelings of Value—not of Simple Feeling Abstracted from Cognitive Presuppositions.*

The relation of this analysis to the so-called three-dimensional theory of feeling developed by Wundt may be stated as follows. We accept the analysis; but for us the terms of this theory are descriptive equivalents for appreciative meanings of total feeling attitudes, while for Wundt they are qualities of simple feelings. The difference arises necessarily from the different points of view from which the description of the same experience is approached. The appreciative descriptions try to fixate the meaning of the conative references (transgredient and immanental) implicit in the feeling attitude, i.e., references to preceding and succeeding conation. The analysis of Wundt, on the other hand, seeks to fixate the same experience by terms from which the worth connotation is more completely abstracted, and in which the implicit reference to the self is ignored. Royce, it should however be noted in passing, finds the "interest" in the hypothesis in the "statement it makes possible of the relation of feeling and conduct, not adequately conceived on the one-dimensional theory"—a clear recognition of the fact that he is concerned with appreciative description.

That the three-dimensional theory constitutes a true description of total feeling attitudes is scarcely open to dispute. The slightest appreciative introspection enables us to distinguish

---

[1] G. Störring, "Experimentelle Beiträge zur Lehre von Gefühl," *Archiv für die gesammte Psychologie*, Bd. I., Heft 3.

between the exciting pleasure of hope and the tranquil pleasure of peace, between the painful tension of dread and the equally painful relaxation of despair. The question at issue is not, then, whether these differences are appreciable among total feeling attitudes and thus constitute worth suggestions, but rather whether they are equally characteristic of sensation-feelings. On this question there is no conclusive answer to be given at the present time. Wundt has brought forward experimental evidence in favour of the view that these additional qualities belong also to simple sensation-feelings (the feeling tone of colours and sounds, for instance). As to the value of the evidence, there is, of course, still doubt; some experimenters do not find the modifications of the curves corresponding to the three-dimensional analysis. But even if there were no question in regard to the facts themselves, the meaning of these facts would not be unequivocal. We cannot, for one thing, be sure that while the stimuli are so-called simple sensations, the feeling reactions are simple feelings. They may be — and, indeed, probably are — on the emotional level, the organic and muscular sensations due to the surplus excitation. It is certainly true that the results are most apparent, both in the graphic registration and in introspection, as reference to Wundt's studies will show, in those cases where the reactions are on the emotional level. Besides, as has already been pointed out, although the feeling tone of sensation is itself not worth-suggestive or on the level of worth feeling, nevertheless, when the stimulus has reached a certain intensity or duration, it gives rise to a feeling attitude which is worth-suggestive. Until the experimental evidence is more unequivocal, both introspection and logic would rather lead to the view that these dimensions of feeling which seem to belong to simple feeling-tone of sensation are really qualities of a secondary feeling attitude following upon pleasure-causation. Störring's analysis, already referred to, would seem to indicate the truth of this view.[1]

[1] Recent criticisms of the three-dimensional theory have been entirely justified in saying, on the one hand, that these qualifications of feeling are taken from the side of conative meaning, and on the other that when we look for equivalents in content, we find them only in sensations, kinæsthetic and organic. Both statements are true and at the same time consistent with each other, as will appear in our later studies of feeling. It is only in the appreciatively described total meaning of the attitude that they appear as primary qualities of experience. When we take the abstract point of view of function they break up into relations of affirmation and arrest of tendency. When we take the abstract point of view of content or structure, they break up into complexes or series of sensations. The way of reconciling structural and functional points of view in psychology is to correlate them both with the appreciative description from which both take their origin.

(b) Worth Feelings are on the Emotional Level.

Be this as it may, I think it may, nevertheless, at least be said that these aspects of experience, whether that experience be a hypothetical affective or sensational content, become *worth-suggestive*, acquire the transgredient and immanental references only on the emotional level, only when the feeling is a feeling attitude toward an object. And I think it may further be said that the criterion of such a feeling attitude, or emotion (the term emotion being used in its broadest sense to include passion, sentiment, and mood, as well as emotion proper), is the presence of the cognitive presuppositions already analysed, presumption, judgment, and assumption. What is meant by this, to state the point more fully, is that the differences in feeling-attitude appreciatively distinguishable appear only in total feeling-attitudes, and are not varieties of the mere feeling-tone of sensations. It may be that the content which acquires these meanings is certain simple affective or sensational elements, but it acquires these meanings only on the level of emotion.

The view here developed involves, further, that the criterion of an emotion or feeling-attitude is to be found in the presence of a cognitive act (presumption, judgment, assumption) as the presupposition of the feeling. Can this view be maintained? I think it may not only be reasonably maintained, but is, in fact, inevitable, if we approach the study of emotions as above defined from the standpoint of their meaning. There is, to be sure, another point of view, that of more abstract study of content and emotional expression, from which this scarcely seems to be the proper criterion, as for instance, in the case of the inherited instinctive emotions, of which the instinctive fear of animals is a good illustration. But while this is true—and with this view of the facts our present analysis must, in its proper place, be brought into harmony, it is, nevertheless, also true that, as a meaning, an emotional attitude always presupposes such cognitive acts. Joy and sorrow, the two typical and fundamental emotional attitudes which have these worth suggestions or meanings, become meaningless when conceived apart from these presuppositions. They are usually judgment-feelings, although not always such (as Meinong maintains), for they may follow upon simple presumption or assumption of reality. The joy in the presumed, assumed, or asserted reality of an object is *toto genere* different from the pleasantness

Modes of the Consciousness of Value

of a sensation. And the same is true of those modes of emotional attitude, such as fear, dread, despair, hope, elation, in which the cognitive act is further modified in the direction of possibility or necessity. It is further to be observed that, from the point of view of appreciative analysis, these emotional attitudes are variously specified according as the fundamental positive or negative direction has transgredient reference with its tension or restlessness, or immanental reference with its relaxation and repose. Joy or sorrow, as we have seen, may be of either type. The inevitable conclusion seems to be that these meanings arise only when there is that *totalisation* of attitude, the condition of which is the actualisation of conative dispositions through acts of the type described.[1]

(c) Objectless Feelings not an Exception.

There are, however, certain phenomena which constitute an apparent exception to this law, namely, objectless feelings (emotions, sentiments, and moods), which, although objectless, are clearly worth suggestive and find expression in worth judgments. Practically all the concrete emotional attitudes—joy, sadness, anger, fear—may appear as worth feelings without concrete perceptual or ideal objects. A nameless sadness or fear, an objectless anger, may arise in consciousness with all the worth suggestions of enhanced or thwarted conation, but without any object towards which it is definitely directed. This does not mean that there are no adequate conditions (physiological, and even psychological), but merely that there is no presupposition, no judgmental reference to the existence or non-existence of objects. They appear at first sight to be without such presuppositions. In reality, however, they are to be viewed as in the main analogous to exclamations and some forms of impersonal

---

[1] Wundt (and, it may be added, Höffding also) makes much of the principle of totalisation, of total resultant, in his analysis and theory of feeling. Whatever be the nature of the simple feelings, they all tend to merge in a total resultant, a unitary feeling. This principle of "Einheit der Gefühlslage" is referred to the principle of unity of apperception for its explanation, all feeling being viewed as the subjective aspect of apperception. The truth of this general proposition is beyond question, but there are different grades of apperception and different degrees of totalisation. Undoubtedly when attention is held by a sensation of sound or colour, or by an organic sensation, its feeling-tone tends to dominate consciousness and to fuse with it all other feeling-tones. But it is not until there is explicit reference of the sensation, as object, to a conative disposition through judgment or assumption, that the totalisation of attitude takes place which gives rise to the worth suggestions of feeling. In such a totalisation the feeling-tone of sensations, as such, becomes irrelevant and subordinate to the worth feelings of the attitude as a whole.

F

judgment in the sphere of cognition. As in these cases there is no directly asserted subject of the predicate discoverable, so in objectless emotions and moods there is no directly asserted object of judgment to which the worth predicates implied in the feelings of joy, sorrow, etc., are applied. Reality is implied —the feelings are real and "earnest," but there is no existential judgment about any definite object in reality. There is merely an undifferentiated presumption or assumption of reality as presupposition; but this is sufficient to make them worth feelings.

The psychology of the impersonal judgment scarcely leaves us room to doubt of its nature. There is for such judgment neither subject nor predicate, nor reference of the one to the other. It is, so to speak, the amorphous, protoplasmic germ of later reflective judgments which do involve a separation of subject and predicate. Whatever, in the interests of systematic logic, we may seek to supply as the subject of such judgment in order to bring it within the classifications of a logical system— whether we describe the subject as universal and undetermined, the whole of reality, or as a determined and particular sensation of the moment, the fact remains that psychologically the "*it*" of the impersonal judgment is contentless. Similarly, in the objectless worth feeling the object is no presentation either universal or particular, no sensation either peripheral or organic. Subject and predicate, presentation and feeling, are not discriminated. We have to do here with a protoplasmic worth attitude without judgmental presuppositions but which may, nevertheless, become definite through the inclusion among its presuppositions, which are now merely conative and dispositional, of some explicit act of judgment.

3. *Correlation of Appreciative Meanings with Cognitive Presuppositions.*

Can we, then, correlate the meanings of worth feelings, thus described, with specific types of cognitive presuppositions? The necessary presupposition of worth feeling is, as we have seen, the actualisation of a conative disposition through acts of presumption, assumption, and judgment. Can we connect the specific type of reference of the feeling with a definite type of actual presupposition?

The two directions of worth feeling (positive and negative), as distinguished from mere pleasantness-unpleasantness, contain some presupposition of reality—witness our study of joy and sorrow, love and anger, hope and despair. And as we shall see later, positive and negative worth may vary independently of pleasantness-unpleasantness. But it is with the other qualification of feeling, the reference to conation, that we are chiefly concerned. When we turn to the transgredient reference, with its tension, restlessness, contraction, and to immanental reference with its relaxation, repose, and expansion, we find that they are closely connected with changes in the presupposition of reality.

In general the transgredient reference appears in all those emotional attitudes where an habitual presupposition of reality meets with opposition or arrest, where, for instance, primitive presumption passes into assumption and judgment. In such a case it may be, either the *subjective* control factor—the conative disposition which is felt in the background and which gives rise to the assumption—or the more *objective* factor of control, the recognitive, determining and giving rise to judgment. In either case, however, the transgredient reference is to a disposition in the background, in the process of determining a new accommodation.

The immanental reference to reality, on the other hand, represents the emotional attitude which goes with accommodation realised. It is the feeling which attaches to judgment-habit or to the assumption of the second type arising out of that habit. The fact that habit has its own feeling, its own worth suggestions, is a point which must be emphasised throughout.

III. Meanings Acquired by Development of these Fundamental Modes—Value-Movement

1. *Acquired Meanings of Simple Appreciation.*

With the analysis of these primary aspects or meanings which feelings disclose, we are led to the problem of derived or acquired feeling attitudes.

There are two possible conceptions of the nature of these attitudes and of the process of their derivation. The first of these is the concept of fusion or mixture of feelings, purely analytical in character. On this view the aspects of feeling, the meanings of appreciative description, are hypostatised as elements, and all acquired meanings are conceived as fusions or mixtures of these elements. The second concept, genetic and functional in character, looks upon the derived attitude, the acquired meaning, as a new aspect, the product of a new " totalisation " of consciousness in which the old aspects are taken up into the new, but in which the new meaning is not exhausted by its analysis into the old elements. The new feeling-attitude is a new accommodation, a development, in terms of worth theory, a value-movement.

The former of these views, of very limited applicability at the best in any region of psychological explanation, is wholly inapplicable to the explanation of the meanings of feeling-attitudes. Wundt is, unfortunately, despite his three-dimensional theory, still too much under the influence of this conception, although in applying his fundamental law of psychical causality, the law of resultants, he explicitly asserts that there is an acquired meaning in the resultant complexes or fusions not found in the elements. It is better to abandon the concept of elements entirely in this connection and to make use wholly of the genetic concept of acquirement of meaning through change in presuppositions.

The acquired meanings of feelings may be divided into two groups : (1) the acquired meanings of simple appreciation, and (2) those of characterisation and participation. If we recall these distinctions, previously made, it will be remembered that simple appreciation of an object is an appreciation of its affective-volitional meaning or worth prior to explicit reference of the object to the ego or the alter or to other objects, prior, in other words, to secondary possessive or instrumental judgments. On the level of simple appreciation appear, then, certain qualifications of the general transgredient and immanental references of feeling.

(a) The Impellent Mode-Feelings of Obligation.

The first of these acquired meanings to be considered is the feeling of *oughtness* or *obligation*. The feeling of oughtness that *a thing should be*, that an act should take place, is a specific form of the feeling of value. As such, upon our view, it should be defined in terms of its presuppositions. Appreciatively described, it is an acquired modification of the general feeling of transgredient reference or of tension, and may be best described as the Impellent Mode. Apart from appreciative description it is an experience of mere strain—perhaps, from the point of view of content, a mere strain sensation. Its differentia is to be found in the precise character of the transgredient reference, and therefore in the character of its cognitive presuppositions. Now the feeling of oughtness, in its simplest form, attaches to objects, to things. It is felt that if a thing does not exist it ought to. As thus applied, for instance, by a child who as yet has practically no sense of personal, ethical obligation, it means little more than that the thing is desired. But just that little additional meaning is the important modification. Is it possible to define this additional meaning ?

The point of difference is to be found, I think, in the fact that the presuppositions of the feeling of oughtness are not simple, as in the case of a simple mode of feeling or desire. The feeling of oughtness is, in fact, a transition mode between two existential judgments, in which an existential feeling is qualified by an assumption-feeling. The object does not exist, and we have the corresponding feeling or desire, but so strong is the conative disposition presupposed that it gives rise to an assumption of existence. This assumption is felt to be not merely possible, but necessary, and thus, as Simmel has said, obligation is in one aspect a mode of thought lying midway between possibility and necessity.[1] The source of this assumption is the subject's conative disposition and the feeling of oughtness is the feeling of that subjective control ; but since the subjective control is not explicitly acknowledged in judgment, the oughtness is felt as a tertiary quality of the object.

The transgredient reference of the assumption is therefore to the disposition. To refer again to the figure of the foreground and background of consciousness, the judgment of existence or non-existence of the object is in the foreground, the modification of the feeling which we describe as oughtness having reference to an object in the background which at first is revealed merely in this modification of feeling, but which later, through the activities of ideal construction and judgment, becomes an explicit ideal object, the self or the social will. When this is developed ethical obligation is felt. In a sense the simple feeling of oughtness is objectless until this stage of ideal construction is reached, and corresponds to the impersonal judgment.

[1] Simmel's masterly study of the modes of oughtness, *das Sollen* (*Einleitung in die Moralwissenschaft*, chap. 1) can be merely referred to in passing, fuller treatment being reserved for another connection. The important point is that it is a fundamental mode, at the same time cognitive and affective-volitional.

(b) The Semblant Mode-Æsthetic Feeling.

Corresponding to the feeling mode of oughtness, the primary impellent mode out of which ethical obligation develops, we find a second mode of simple appreciation which represents a special qualification of the immanental reference of feeling, the " semblant " or æsthetic mode.[1] This mode, the æsthetic feeling, is always appreciatively described in terms of repose and expansion, and its worth, in so far as the experience is purely æsthetic, is immanental. Here again we have, not a simple aspect of feeling with simple presuppositions, but an attitude implying transition and accommodation, and therefore characterised by typical changes in cognitive presuppositions.

The characteristics of this mode of feeling, its repose, relaxation, and expansion, have their origin in the fact that the judgments of existence and non-existence, and with them explicit conation, desire, are inhibited, reduced to a minimum, and remain, in fact, merely as a dispositional presupposition, while consciousness is largely absorbed in presentational content. With the laws which govern the ordering of that content, and which condition the arrest of desire and the inducing of repose, we are not at this point concerned; it is sufficient to note the general fact that formal principles of æsthetics owe their significance psychologically to the fact that they are instrumental in producing this effect. But as has already been pointed out, it is not an adequate view of æsthetic feeling to regard it as a purely presentational consciousness. While explicit judgment is reduced to a minimum, its place is taken by assumptions which relate the object to a desire which is now merely dispositional. These assumptions, we have seen, may be of two types, the explicit and the implicit. In the first case we have the primitive semblant mode, in the latter the more developed mode of contemplation.

In general, then, the æsthetic mode of sembling or contemplation is a complex, derived mode of feeling of value in which the presuppositions are presentational content and assumptions. To use again the figure of the foreground and background of consciousness, the foreground is taken up with presentational content, the psychical energies involved in judgment are occupied

---

[1] For the use of the term "*semblant* mode," see Baldwin's *Thought and Things*, Vol. I, especially chap. VI. As to his complete identification of *sembling* with *Einfühlung*, I think there is some doubt, since the latter, in at least some of its aspects, is earnest, and the feeling has presumption and judgment—not merely assumption—as its presupposition.

with the activities of mere apperception of content in its relations, with contemplation, while in the background remains the assumption of existence, with its reference to conative dispositions. While the object is detached from immediate desire, its relation to desire is not absolutely severed.

An illustration will show the situation with greater clearness. The æsthetic appreciation of feminine beauty is a psychosis grafted immediately upon desire and desire-dispositions. The process by which the æsthetic psychosis supervenes upon that of crude desire is one of arrest, social and individual, and of rearrangement of the elements of the object, presented either unconsciously, or consciously as in art, in such a manner as to fill the foreground of consciousness with presentational activity, and to detach the object from immediacy of desire. An implicit assumption of the existence of the object for desire is, however, a necessary presupposition of the æsthetic appreciation. Should the conative disposition become explicit in actual desire, the æsthetic repose would cease and a new adaptation take place.

In both these appreciative modes, it should finally be observed, worth or affective-volitional meaning has been acquired. The deepening of the transgredient or immanental reference, as the case may be, becomes part of the funded meaning of the object, and is imputed to the object. The recognition of this fact is of far-reaching importance, for all the meanings acquired in these modes of appreciation enter as determinants in later judgments of value.

2. *Acquired Meanings of Characterisation and Participation.*

Simple appreciation, with its two primary modifications described, is further differentiated into secondary acquired meanings which we may describe as *personal* values of possession and merit, instrumental or utility values of *utilisation*, and the common values of *participation*. The characteristic of all these modifications of primary feeling of value is to be found in the fact that they arise through the establishment of *relational* judgments between the object and the disposition presupposed. Otherwise expressed, the merely *felt* transgredient or immanental reference of simple appreciation is now referred to its explicit object which is acknowledged in judgment.

An analysis of the personal feelings makes this point clear. The feeling of possession is more than the feeling of the worth of the object, as presumed, judged, or assumed to exist. The object acquires an imputed value through the explicit acknowledgment of the subject for which it exists. Similarly, the feeling of personal obligation or merit arises on the basis of a reference of the valued disposition to the personality. In general we may say that the personal feelings have an additional presupposition of reality which the primary feelings have not. But the more developed modes of these primary feelings, the impellent and the semblant, contain the germ of these personal values. They are transition stages in which a new feeling mode is introduced, through the transgredient or immanental reference arising upon assumptions. In the case of the personal value the assumption becomes an existential judgment of acknowledgment of the self. Of course such a transition requires ideal construction of the self, and this involves an extension of simple appreciation through sympathetic *Einfühlung*, a process to be studied in another connection.

The impersonal feelings of the participation values or utility-values of dispositions and objects involve a further extension of this acquirement of common meaning. In addition to the presupposition of the reality of the desired object, there is an additional presupposition of similar desires and feelings in the minds of others which gives rise ultimately to judgments and assumptions of over-individual demands. How such presuppositions arise is, again, of course, a problem of genetic psychology, more especially of the study of the laws of sympathetic imitation and *Einfühlung*. The main point here is that the appreciative differences in the meaning of the feelings arises through explicit acknowledgment of references which were previously merely implicit.

It should be noted finally that, just as the transgredient and immanental references acquire depth of meaning through the obligation and æsthetic modes, so in these experiences primary feeling is further deepened and broadened.

IV. THE QUANTITATIVE MEANINGS OF WORTH FEELING—DEGREE OF ACQUIRED MEANING AND DEGREE OF INTENSITY—THEIR RELATIONS

1. *Analysis of Concept of Degree of Worth Feeling—" Depth and Breadth."*

Worth predicates have been defined as the funded meanings of objects. These predicates or meanings correspond, we have seen, to certain qualitative aspects of feeling, primary and derived. But they have also a quantitative aspect—of degree. To what aspects of feeling do these differences of degree correspond? It has already been pointed out that many psychologists have found it necessary to distinguish between degree of feeling of value and degree of intensity of sensation-feeling, and some have used such terms as depth and breadth of the feeling in the personality to characterise quantatitively the worth suggestion of the feeling. And when we examine more closely the appreciative distinctions made in the sphere of worth experience it becomes clear that some such distinction is necessary. For, in the first place, it is to be observed that, if we make use of those appreciative descriptions of feeling subsumed under the general terms transgredient and immanental references, we cannot properly apply the quantitative term, intensity. While, for instance, we may speak of the degree, we cannot properly speak of intensity of repose or expansion, and thus seem to be driven to some such terms as depth and breadth. Thus we find Münsterberg[1] accepting the ordinary formula, that intensity of feeling decreases with repetition, and at the same time, in his desire to do justice to the concrete facts of worth experience, insisting that repetition may increase the *depth* of feeling tone. Clearly depth and intensity are here definitely distinguished and admitted to be independently variable. It appears, then, that we must make a distinction between degree, or intensity in the broader Kantian sense, and intensity in the narrower sense of sensational intensity, between degree of feeling of value and intensity of pleasantness-unpleasantness as feeling-tone of sensations. Intensity in this latter sense applies to all sensation-feelings, to "pleasure-causation," as we have described it, and probably to all sensation feelings which enter into a total feeling complex, but not, properly speaking, to feeling-attitudes, not to the worth aspect of feeling.

What, then, is the relation between the degree of acquired meaning or value of a feeling attitude and intensity of pleasantness-unpleasantness? How are they related for appreciative introspection and analysis, and how shall this empirical relation, when determined, be connected with our analysis of the conditions, actual and dispositional, of these two aspects of feeling? This question is of the utmost importance, because in the solution

---

[1] Münsterberg, *Grundzüge der Psychologie*, Leipzig, 1900, p. 39.

of this problem is involved the whole question of the measurement of feelings of value, to which we must presently turn.

2. Degrees of "Worth" and Degrees of Intensity Independently Variable—Illustrations.

We find, then, that not only is worth experience distinguishable from pleasure-causation in the aspects both of quality and degree, but also that degree of value varies independently of hedonic intensity. Two phenomena of our worth experience indicate this relation. (1) Feeling of positive worth may exist side by side with unpleasant experiences and feeling of negative worth with pleasant. (2) Degree of worth feeling may increase with decrease of hedonic intensity, and there are numerous instances where worth feelings are practically intensity-less. These facts have led to the general conception of the irrelevance of the hedonic aspects of a total attitude for worth judgment and to the formulation of Brentano's doctrine of "hedonic redundancies."

We shall examine the facts briefly, and then turn to a consideration of the theories of the relation of the two distinguishable aspects. The first phenomenon is well illustrated in the classical description of Lessing. In a letter to Mendelssohn he writes : " In this we are then agreed, my dear friend, that all passions are either strong likes or dislikes. Also in this, that in every such feeling of like or dislike we are conscious of a greater sense of reality, and that this consciousness cannot be other than pleasant. Consequently, all passions, even the most unpleasant, are *as passions* pleasant." [1] The paradox of calling that which is unpleasant pleasant, and the lack of adequate analysis in this description, should not blind us to its essential truth. While the same feeling cannot at the same time be both pleasant and unpleasant, it is quite possible that we are concerned here with two actual feelings in certain definite relations to each other.

Plausible explanations have been given from the point of view of the identification of worth feeling with a form of simple pleasure. It is said that we have to do here with an illusion of judgment, that what was formerly unpleasant has now become pleasant through change in physiological disposition, and that the unpleasantness instead of being real is merely a memory of former unpleasantness. It seems hardly necessary, however,

[1] Quoted from Hirn, *The Origins of Art*, London, Macmillan, 1900, p. 60.

Modes of the Consciousness of Value

to deny in the interests of theory what is a fairly constant deliverance of appreciation, namely, that feeling of positive worth may be co-existent with actual unpleasantness. Or it might be said that we have a simple case of mixed feeling. A pleasant and unpleasant sensation-feeling may exist side by side in the same state of consciousness, as for instance, the pleasant taste of sugar and the unpleasant sensations of satiety as they are just beginning to appear—why then should not two worth feelings or worth feeling and simple pleasantness or unpleasantness ? To this we may answer that the two cases are not parallel. The inapplicability of the concept of mixture or fusion to feelings of value we have already pointed out, and in this case the figure is especially misleading.

If we look at Lessing's description more closely we find that his paradox really arises from a failure to analyse—to distinguish between two aspects of the total psychosis, the feeling of value and the irrelevant hedonic accompaniments. The situation he describes admits of two interpretations. On the one hand, the passion, of anger let us say, is really a feeling of negative worth, with certain cognitive presuppositions—unpleasant, as Lessing says. It is quite possible, however, that the organic disturbance may be pleasantly toned, especially after long-continued arrest, with its unpleasant strain sensations. We should then have pleasant accompaniments of a feeling of negative worth. On the other hand, it is equally possible that what Lessing calls the pleasantness of the unpleasant passion may really cover a gradual transition from one feeling of value to another, and that what he calls the pleasantness of the psychosis may be a feeling of value of the personal type. The object itself may have negative worth, while the entire experience of having such a passion, or, in fact, the knowledge of the capacity for such reaction, may give rise to a feeling of satisfaction, of personal worth. This might even extend to such passions as have unpleasant hedonic accompaniments. Feelings of value would then be accompanied by unpleasant sensation feelings.

The second group of facts which lead to this differentiation of degree of intensity of pleasantness-unpleasantness from degree of worth or meaning of the feeling, are the so-called intensity-less attitudes or acts of valuation and preference. Here, it is maintained, quasi-logical modifications take the place of intensity. If we begin with the two primary modifications of simple appreciation, the ethical and æsthetic, we find intensity giving place to other modifications. A quiet sense of obligation may reveal a degree of worth of an ideal object which the intensest passion or emotion does not suggest. Similarly in the æsthetic, or semblant mode, a degree of immanental worth may be suggested in the depth and breadth of the feeling when the element of intensity is reduced to a minimum. But still more evident do these facts become when we pass to the secondary, derived feelings, the personal and the impersonal over-individual references. In a case of preference between objects to which these feelings correspond, a relatively intensity-less feeling of personal worth may have an affective-volitional meaning which the intensest passion connected with sense objects has not. And so with the over-individual feelings. If, then, by intensity we mean, not the broader Kantian conception of any modification of degree of inner experience, but that particular degree which applies to sensation and feeling-tone of sensation, there can be no question but that worth feelings, as determined by judgment and assumption, may be practically intensity-less. These acts are, of course, causally connected with sensation tendencies, both peripheral and organic, and every such act has as its accompaniment secondary hedonic resonances of more or less intensity, but the point is that appreciatively we can distinguish the two factors, and are aware that the latter do not determine the worth judgment.

The facts upon which this hypothesis of independent variability of the two factors in a total worth attitude is based are now before us, as well as the subordinate rôle which the hedonic resonance plays in worth judgments. We are, however, as yet wholly without any conception which will enable us to understand this relation functionally.

3. *Theories of this Relation—Suggestion of a Theory to be developed later.*

There are two general theories of this relation, which may be described as the dualistic and the monistic or genetic. The dualistic theory is represented by Brentano and Schwartz. In Brentano's view,[1] as we have seen, any concrete attitude of valuation can be analysed into two aspects, intensity-less acts of preference, acts of love and hate, and the hedonic redundancies

---

[1] Brentano, *Psychologie*, especially p. 197. Also *Ursprung der sittlichen Erkentniss*, especially p. 86.

Modes of the Consciousness of Value 77

which accompany them. To the latter alone, as sensation-feelings, belong, properly speaking, degrees of intensity. In Schwartz's view [1] feeling intensity belongs to the passive side of consciousness, degrees of worth to the active, voluntaristic side. The latter appear in the form of acts of analytic and synthetic preference. The essential point of both conceptions is the dualism between feeling and will, and the reference of worth distinctions to modifications of will.

The facts which have given rise to this theory are, as we have seen, true enough. So also is the conception of hedonic redundancies, in so far as it merely describes the functional relation of these two aspects. But it is far from certain that it is necessary to draw the dualistic conclusion. That would follow only on condition that feeling and will are totally different elements, that the distinction between them as active and passive is ultimate, and secondly, that the only modification of feeling which can be made the equivalent of degrees of worth is hedonic intensity.

Whether these assumptions are necessary must be determined ultimately by a consideration of the whole question of the psychology of feeling and will and their relations, which must be reserved for another chapter. It will be sufficient here to deny the necessity of such assumptions, and in the meantime to suggest a second possible conception, monistic and genetic in character. Feeling, according to our analysis, has other modifications, other meanings than passive pleasantness - unpleasantness, viz., transgredient and immanental references to conative dispositions. These references, which arise only when the disposition is actualised by cognitive acts of presumption, judgment, assumption, are signs of the affective-volitional meaning of the object, its relation to conation. Feeling as passive is therefore not to be separated from will as active. But more than this, these references or aspects may, conceivably—with repeated actualisation of the dispositions—become differentiated, as developed meanings, from the aspect of hedonic intensity, and increase in depth and breadth. If this view should prove tenable, we should have a relation analogous to that between the general concept and the particular presentation. As the meaning of the concept develops with actualisation of the judgment-disposition in successive cognitive acts, the particular presentation becomes less and less significant,

---

[1] Schwartz, *Psychologie des Willens*, chap. II ; also Appendix I.

until we have what is practically imageless apprehension. So also with the development of the meanings of feeling, the hedonic resonance may become less and less significant until relatively intensity-less appreciation of the worth of the object appears. The substantiation of such a conception of affective generalisation involves a more extended excursion into the psychology of feeling. Here we may merely note the fact that such feeling-attitudes exist, i.e., in the case where the presuppositions are assumptions, either of the explicit or implicit type.

V. Conclusion—The Bearing of this Analysis on Further Problems

In concluding this chapter we may with advantage return to a consideration of the preliminary definition of worth and worth predicates from which the entire analysis took its start. This analysis, it will be seen, has given content to that definition. It has also given us the ground-work for further researches into the principles governing the concrete phenomena of valuation of different types, economic, ethical, æsthetic, etc. A more general view, both retrospective and prospective, will serve to give unity to the results thus far attained.

In general, we found worth or value to be the funded affective-volitional meaning of the object for the subject. That funded meaning, as expressed in terms of the predicates, goodness, utility, beauty, obligation, desert, etc., represents the desirability of the object, although not necessarily the fact of actual desire. The funded meaning is acquired through actualisation of conative dispositions by acts of presumption, judgment, and assumption, and this actualisation results in feeling which undergoes certain modifications, with change in presuppositions, and with repetition. This feeling, with its modifications, reflects the funded meaning of the object. Worth predication, in the aspects both of quality and degree, is determined by appreciative modifications of feeling, which in turn are determined by changes in the presuppositions of the feeling.

To these funded meanings, roughly classified as simple appreciation of objects (with its impellent and semblant modes) personal worths of characterisation, and common over-individual values of participation and utilisation, correspond certain classes of objects, primary and derivative, perceptual and ideal. All these derived objects, with their corresponding attitudes, are perceptual and ideal constructions which emerge through certain value movements from simple appreciation. The genesis of these objects, with their corresponding predicates, is one of the chief problems which now present themselves. This differentiation and fixation of objects and predicates of valuation must be traced to fundamental laws of the psychical processes by which affective-volitional meaning is acquired. These laws we may describe as the Laws of Valuation.

But worth predication has a quantitative as well as qualitative side. Worth judgments express preferability of one object over another, as well as degrees of preferability of different amounts of the same object. We are thus led to the problem of the measurement of the worth or funded meaning of objects. At this point several questions arise. Is worth or value, as we have conceived it, an object, a function, to which the concepts of quantity and measurement can be applied ?

In answering this question we must first note the fact that such quantitative judgments do exist. Within the various regions of worth predication numerous empirical uniformities are discoverable connecting quantity of object with degree of worth predicated. Thus in the region of economic " condition " worths, there are certain empirical laws connecting changes in the intrinsic desirability or in the utility (instrumental desirability) of an object with changes in its quantity. In the region of judgments of personal worth the obligation or merit predicated varies in certain definite ways with changes in the amount of the object or in this case disposition displayed. The same is true of those judgments upon dispositions according to their over-individual value for participation. It is clear, then, that empirical relations of a quantitative character may be established between objects and their worth predicates or funded meanings. But such empirical laws would constitute no explanation, nor would they enable us to establish relations of degree between objects of these different types. While we might formulate empirical statements of dependence of degree of value of the object upon changes in the object without formulating any theory of the psychological grounds for this dependence, such measurement must, if it is to lead to any insight into the nature of worth judgments, involve the reduction of these empirical uniformities to more ultimate psychological laws. Thus, to take an illustration from another region of psychology, the significance of the empirical formulation of

Weber's law for perception holds good, irrespective of any theory of its psychological explanation. Or, to take another illustration from a more closely related region of investigation, the law of marginal utility in economics is an empirical law which holds, within limits, irrespective of its interpretation, and is capable of explanation in terms which do not necessitate the hypothesis of continuous change in hedonic intensity. We must therefore distinguish between the merely empirical formulation of more and less and a theory of the psychological determinants of the change in degree of worth or affective-volitional meaning of the object.

The question whether worth, or funded meaning of an object as we have defined it, is susceptible of measurement is reduced, then, to the still more fundamental question whether the psychological determinants of that meaning are objects of measurement. Into the acquired and funded meaning of an object enter various elements presupposing various processes and attitudes. If these can be analysed out, and their contributions to the total worth of the object determined, such measurement is possible. On the view which we have rejected—that degree of value is to be equated with degree of intensity of pleasantness-unpleasantness, or as sometimes formulated, with a function of intensity and duration, the problem is, at least theoretically, simple. The laws of habit, satiety, contrast, etc., for sensation-feelings might be applied directly to feelings of value. But such a procedure is impossible after our analysis. The psychological determinants are for us more complex. Having defined feelings of value as feelings presupposing dispositions actualised by presumption, judgment, and assumption, our problem is the determination of the capacity of the object, as presumed, judged, or assumed to exist, to call out feelings of value. Since the worth of the object is a function of the capacity of the subject for feeling, as determined by these preceding processes of accommodation in judgment and assumption, we must inquire into the effect of these processes upon the dispositions presupposed. The analysis and formulation of these factors constitute the laws of valuation. Such laws are capable of determination, and when determined they enable us to explain the empirical laws of "more and less."

CHAPTER IV

THE PSYCHOLOGICAL BASIS OF A THEORY OF VALUATION

THE preceding studies of worth experience—of "feelings of value," of their meanings and presuppositions—have brought us to a point where new problems present themselves which necessitate new methods of solution. Thus far we have been concerned merely with the analysis of the fundamental modifications of feelings of value and of their presuppositions. Our task is now to make use of the results of this analysis in the determination of the laws of valuation, as a process of acquirement of affective-volitional meaning. Our former problem of analysis and description has now become one of explanation.

The problem of explanation is a genetic problem, in the larger sense of that word. Now the genetic method is, we have seen, but an extension of the presuppositional method. Its task is, in general, to show how valuation may be conceived as a systematic, progressive, and continuous determination of the stream of conation and feeling in the individual's mind, to show how presuppositions become actual in feeling and desire, and how actual feelings and desires, and dispositions when formed, become presuppositions of new feelings and desires, and of further modifications of quality and degree.

When the nature of the task is thus stated, it becomes evident that its successful prosecution involves a further excursion into the psychology of feeling and will. We have as yet no adequate conception of the nature and relations of feeling and will, such as would enable us thus to conceive valuation as a systematic, progressive, and continuous determination of the stream of conation and feeling. We have not yet developed such abstract conceptions of feeling and conation, as would make possible an account of the manner in which actual experiences of feeling and desire create the presuppositions of succeeding valuations. We have no developed concept of affective-volitional determination. To this general problem we must now turn our attention.

For the purposes of this study the general question of the nature of feeling and will and their relations may be reduced to three special problems.

1. In the first place, what is the nature of feeling and of its relation to conation, actual and dispositional, as required by our definition and analysis of worth experience? We distinguished between feeling and desire, and although the distinction appeared to be not very clear at the limits, we found grounds for defining experience of worth as feeling. But we found feeling determined by conative dispositions, and these in turn determined by feeling. How shall we understand this relation? Moreover, in our analysis of the fundamental modifications of worth feeling we used the concept of feeling in a broad sense, which included references to conation in a sense quite different from the definition of feeling as passive affection. Clearly, a psychological theory of feeling and will is involved, which must now be more fully developed.

2. In the second place, the appreciative analysis of the different modifications of worth feeling calls for some further theory of the nature of feeling itself. This demand appears especially in connection with our distinction between degree of intensity of feeling and degree of worth or affective-volitional meaning, but is also involved in our analysis of the transgredient and immanental references and their distinction from pleasantness-unpleasantness. These aspects or meanings of feeling-attitude must be founded upon some actual content or process of consciousness, must have equivalents in terms of content and function.

3. Finally, we have a third problem, which may be described as the problem of the *continuity of worth process*. This is closely connected with the preceding question—how an object may acquire *funded meaning* while the *intensity* of feeling reaction diminishes. The problem presents itself in the following way. The consciousness of value is at any given moment an emotional consciousness. Such emotional states are, however, when viewed as content, discrete and fugitive. While, therefore, worth judgment, viewed in the light of its meaning, is continuous—that is worth experiences of the present are conserved in

succeeding judgments of value—the emotional experiences which find expression in these judgments, seem at first sight discontinuous. Are feeling and emotion thus fugitive and discontinuous, so that their meaning survives merely in the physiological dispositions created? Or is there such a thing as a *felt* continuity, wherein feeling acquires recognitive and generic meanings, which are then taken up into permanent sentiments, and upon the basis of which as presupposition new feelings and volitions are formed? Is there such a thing as an "affective logic" or quasi-logical continuities of affective-volitional meaning? It is in connection with this problem that a satisfactory conception of the nature of feeling as content of experience, and as functional in determining succeeding experiences of feeling and will, is most important. Its solution is possible only after an investigation of the first two problems concerning the nature of feeling and will. To these the present chapter will be devoted, the problem of the nature of this continuity being reserved for a special investigation.

I. The Nature of Feeling and Will and their Relations

1. *The Problem.*

The problem of feeling and will and the nature of their relations is perhaps the most difficult within the entire field of psychological analysis. The reason for this is not far to seek, for nowhere is it more important that the distinction between appreciative and non-appreciative description should be realised and a true theory of their relations formed, and nowhere is there such confusion on these points as in this sphere.[1]

To illustrate my point in detail, the distinction between feeling as passive and will as active is an appreciative distinction. One concrete attitude is relatively more passive than another

---

[1] The consequence has been the widely divergent analyses with which psychologists have been scandalised. The original distinctions within this sphere were made from the appreciative point of view because analysis of feeling and will first began with the worth problem, e.g., Plato and Aristotle and in modern times the English Utilitarians. As the original interest became secondary to that of non-appreciative description, the distinctions developed in appreciative description were applied without reflection to a hypothetical feeling abstracted from its presuppositions. Tradition was all powerful here, for we are naturally conservative in all that concerns the feeling and worth side of experience, and when at last independence of analysis appeared, the question of the retention or elimination of these distinctions seems to have been determined largely by personal inclination rather than by considerations of scientific method.

with reference to its meaning in a series of attitudes, i.e. with reference to what succeeds or precedes; but when we abstract from the meaning of the attitude and apply the distinction to hypothetical content, it involves us, we shall find, if it is made absolute, in contradictions, and is far from representing the facts. The distinctions between feeling, emotion, impulse, desire, wish, and will, are primarily appreciative, made with reference to the meanings of the attitude and, as we shall see later, go back to certain differences in cognitive presuppositions. Similarly, the distinction pleasantness-unpleasantness, and its selection as the dominant in the feeling complex or attitude to the exclusion of other aspects, is one which has been determined largely by appreciative purposes, i.e., it is the abstract aspect which appears emphasised when the subjective attitude is transformed into a state and itself becomes an object. Now when these appreciative distinctions, which are largely concerned with the intent of an attitude rather than with the content of a state, are taken to apply to content from which meaning has been abstracted, interesting difficulties and contradictions arise. When the distinctions between passive and active, feeling and conation, are taken as non-appreciative ultimate distinctions, we have a dualism in affective-volitional meaning which the several different dualistic theories seek to bridge by establishing relations of *causal determinism* between the two aspects. One finds feeling, as a distinct element (passive pleasantness or unpleasantness), the necessary antecedent of all conation; another, giving the primacy to conation, finds in the passive feeling the sign of the satisfaction or arrest of some antecedent active impulse or desire; or, finally, the dualism may be pressed so far (as in the recent work of Schwartz) as to admit the existence of volition without feeling.

The extent to which these fundamental differences colour all worth analysis and theory is obvious. Psychological hedonism, with its incapacity to explain a great part of worth experience, is the result of the first. A theory which is unable to include the æsthetic in the sphere of worths is the result of the second. From the third we get the strained formalism of Kant and Schwartz. In view of these difficulties, no theory of feeling and will and of their relations (and some theory is necessary) is of any value unless it is formed with a clear consciousness of the problem involved in the relation of the appreciative to the scientific description of the psychical.

There are two views which have been formed with this clear consciousness of the methodological presuppositions involved. On the one hand, Meinong tells us, the relation of feeling and will can be determined only from the worth standpoint, while Wundt looks upon the distinctions introduced from the point of view of worth analysis, such as the distinctions between feeling, desire, and will, as "pure logical artifacts, not in the least psychical ultimates distinct from each other." As a consequence, the distinction between feeling and will is for the former ultimate, while for Wundt's monistic theory there is a fundamental identity of feeling elements underlying all these artificial distinctions.

Between two such divergent views, with such different methodological presuppositions, there appears to be no middle ground, and yet to my mind each has a relative validity, and is susceptible of reconciliation with the other. More than this, I am inclined to think that the *Identity* theory, developed from the standpoint of analysis of content, is the only one which will harmonise with the distinctions in affective-volitional meaning, developed from the standpoint of functional intent.

2. *Dualistic Theories of Feeling and Will—Criticism.*

We may begin our study, then, with a brief critical examination of those views which, upon the assumption of an absolute distinction between feeling as passive pleasantness or unpleasantness and conation as active, seek to establish a relation of causal psychical determination between them. If the distinction is one of content viewed apart from its intent or meaning, then it is necessary that experience shall show us, either that passive feeling is the necessary antecedent of all active states which are called conative, or, on the other hand, that all passive states of feeling have as their necessary antecedents arrest or accommodation of conscious impulse or desire, in its very nature, as content, different from feeling.

The first of these dualistic views, in its original form of psychological hedonism, was beautiful in its simplicity. Feeling, as a passive state, is always an effect of content, sensation and idea, and their relations. The aspects, quality and intensity, vary with the changes in sensational and ideal content, and the intensity and quality determine impulse, desire, etc., the active side of consciousness.

A very superficial examination of the facts suffices to show us that, if by feeling we mean simple passive pleasantness or unpleasantness with certain intensities, it is by no means the necessary antecedent of any given impulse or desire. On the one hand we have simple impulses for which there is no such conscious hedonic antecedent. When the impulse to take exercise comes over me at a given time, introspection will show me that it is *necessarily* preceded neither by a conscious feeling of unpleasantness nor by an anticipation of pleasantness, although either *may* be the antecedent. On the other hand there are phenomena of a more developed conation which we have seen described as "intensity-less" acts of preference in which affective disturbance is at a minimum, and which, if feeling be described as passive hedonic intensity, certainly show no such feeling antecedent. Impulses with the note of obligation in them are frequently of this character.

That there are changes in affective-volitional meaning (*Gemüthsbewegungen*, in the broadest sense), described as impulse and desire, which do not presuppose an antecedent passive hedonic consciousness or consciousness of hedonic difference, is clear. If we include in feeling other qualities such as tension-relaxation, restlessness-quiescence, it is merely a verbal quibble to raise any question of antecedent and consequent. We have already attributed to the concrete feeling the essential character of the conative side, a virtual acceptance of the *Identity* theory.

This fact, that there are numerous impulses and desires which follow immediately upon presentation and judgment without appreciable hedonic consciousness intervening, is, moreover, admitted by the upholders of the theory of dependence themselves. Thus Kreibig speaks of dispositional feelings below the threshold as determining impulse and desire, while Ehrenfels speaks of desire as determined by feeling *or feeling-dispositions*. And even when it is actual feeling which is conceived as causally determinative, it is not, as we have seen in our previous analysis of Ehrenfels's worth definition, feeling as a separate antecedent state, but the feeling-difference as determined by the object as existing or not existing and the feeling-disposition of the subject. In the case of the impulse to exercise it would be, not necessarily the unpleasantness of the present state nor the anticipated pleasure, but the difference between the two, which constitutes the necessary presupposition of the impulse or desire.

It is in these admissions, and consequent modifications, that we see the failure of this entire theory of dependence growing out of the separation of feeling from conation. A feeling which does not rise above the threshold is a pure conceptual construction. So also is the feeling-difference when made the presupposition of desire. For a feeling-difference can be an actual psychical determinant in only two ways : either it is an ideal construction, the resultant of reflection upon feelings, and then we have an idea as the presupposition of the desire or else this difference is felt as tension or restlessness, as an expectancy generated by the hypothetical disposition, the active conative moment supposed to be determined by the feeling. Where feeling-difference is conceived to be the presupposition of conation, it is either not distinct from conation or else it is a purely conceptual construction.

The second theory of dependence, which has been developed upon the assumption that feeling and conation are ultimates from the point of view of content, is that all feelings have as their necessary antecedent some phase of conscious conation, and that feeling is the sign of arrest or satisfaction of desire. Here, again—if conation is conceived to be an aspect of consciousness which, as content for non-appreciative description, is distinct from feeling, it is difficult to establish a thorough-going relation of dependence. It is true that affective attitudes on the plane of worth suggestion presuppose the activities of acceptance or rejection, but even here it cannot be said that the relation is one of antecedent and consequent, nor can it be said that the worth feelings are passive pleasantness and unpleasantness. But it is by no means easy to include in such a generalisation all the phenomena of feeling. There are, in the first place, the feelings which accompany simple sensations, the agreeable or disagreeable affective tone of an odour or colour. There are also the sudden emotions of surprise and fear, and finally the instinctive emotions, inherited and appearing at first without any conative experience as their antecedent.

As to the first group of phenomena, those who hold the view that feeling has its rise in arrested conation insist that even these phenomena fall under the general law. So also does the functional theory in general when it is consistent and sharply distinguishes feeling and conation. Thus, in a recent article written from this point of view, unpleasantness is conceived to follow upon arrested conation, while pleasantness appears only when conation is accommodating itself after arrest. States which do not contain conative moments are neutral.

Nevertheless, the difficulties in the way of such an answer are not to be minimised. If we examine the reasons given for this inclusion we find that they are of two kinds—the first being analytical and introspective, the second functional. The first is to the effect that it is impossible to get the feeling-tone of a simple sensation uncomplicated with the aspects of tension-relaxation or restlessness-quiescence, with their suggestion of conative presuppositions. The second or functional argument is to the effect that the law of decrease of affective tone through habit and repetition of stimulus is primarily a law of adaptation of tendency to stimulus, and that, when an odour or tone loses its affective tone through repetition, it does so because the sense-tendency, or need of excitation of the physical organism produced by arrest, has been satisfied. Here again, as in the preceding theory, the relation can be made universal only by going beyond immediate experience and supplementing it with hypothetical conceptual constructions. The aspects of tension-relaxation or restlessness-quiescence, if they appear in the simple feeling-tone of sensation, are analytically separable from the feeling as antecedent content and intrinsically different from feeling; impulse and desire are not *conscious* presuppositions of the feelings. Nor when the intensity of feeling-tone diminishes with repetition does it necessarily mean that actual impulse or desire gradually disappears, but merely that some disposition or tendency diminishes in strength with repetition of the stimulus. The proposition that all feeling presupposes conation holds only when modified to read, "*or* conative disposition and tendency."

The same reflections hold good for the other phenomena of feeling, the sudden emotions of surprise and fear, and the inherited instinctive emotions. When, upon walking through the woods, I am surprised with the odour of flowers, this emotion has as its presupposition no specific experience of impulse or desire. Such surprise is possible with relative passivity of consciousness, although, were there complete passivity, even surprise would be impossible. The situation seems to be that at least some general conative tendency toward objects other than the flower must be arrested in order that surprise shall arise. The surprise is not occasioned by the odour directly, but by the arrest of some other conative interest or tendency. It does not, however, presuppose actual desire. The same may be said of the instinctive emotions. They presuppose dispositional or instinctive conative tendency, not actual conation; they are themselves experiences which may with equal right be described as feeling or arrested impulse. Finally, there is the æsthetic feeling in the case of which, while conation is presupposed dispositionally, certainly no conscious impulse or desire necessarily precedes. Analysis shows the aspects with conative connotation, relaxation and repose, as well as the merely hedonic, but these are aspects of the total attitude, not *different states*, except for retrospective analysis.

The conclusion of these reflections is, then, that a thoroughgoing dependence of feeling, as distinguished from conation, upon conation, can be established only when we modify our proposition to read conation *or* conative disposition or tendency. This is practically the conclusion reached in the examination of the theory which makes conation determined by feeling. But when we have introduced the concept of disposition, that is when we have gone beyond the distinctions of immediate experience, and supplemented them with conceptual constructions, it does not matter greatly whether these dispositions are described as belonging to feeling or desire. As Ehrenfels wisely recognises, for worth theory—which is concerned with the changes in valuation and their laws, as determined by changes in dispositional presuppositions, it does not matter whether these dispositions are described as affective or conative: the laws of valuation will hold on either assumption. The conclusion of real importance, however, is that the distinction between feeling and will is not one of psychical content, but of intent or meaning.

3. *Monistic and Genetic Theory of Feeling and Will.*

The chief outcome of our consideration of these two theories of the relation of feeling to will is that no thoroughgoing relation of dependence can be established either way except by leaving the sphere of psychological fact and supplementing it with the conceptual constructions of dispositions. If, however, in order that we may fill out this relation of dependence, we include among the attributes of feeling restlessness-quiescence, which have the conative connotation in them, it is doubtful whether anything is gained by this complete separation of the two aspects of experience. The "*Identity*" theory denies that this distinction is fundamental, and asserts that it arises only from the difference in point of view from which we look at one primary content of consciousness. My own view is that this theory, rightly understood, affords the most satisfactory basis for a true theory of values, while doing most complete justice to the facts of analysis. We shall now turn our attention to the development of this theory.

In its most general form, it has been well stated by Wundt in the psychological part of his *Principles of Morality*.[1] There we are told that these distinctions are purely conceptual, determined by the point of view from which we observe a series of inner events, the flow of consciousness itself being not concerned with them. "Every act of will presupposes a feeling with a definite and peculiar tone: it is so closely bound up with this feeling that, apart from it, the act of will has no reality at all. On the other hand, all feeling presupposes an act of will; the quality of the feeling indicates the direction in which the will is stimulated by the object with which the feeling is connected."

This view is developed in more detail from the standpoint of psychological analysis of content in the last edition of his *Psychology*. Here the emotion ("*Affekt*" or *Gefühlsverlauf*) is taken as the ultimate of concrete affective-volitional meaning or intent, and this emotion, which, as content, is a complex of feeling elements, may be called emotion, impulse, desire, or will, according to the nature of the movement or complex. "The question is no longer what specific conscious content the will is, but what aspect a feeling must assume to become volition." This specific difference he finds (1) in the character of the "end-feelings" of the emotion and (2) in a certain meaning or intent of the total emotion which can be formulated only in retrospective logical terms. As to the first point, conation or will-process is an emotion which through its movement produces a final feeling which in turn destroys the emotion. It is the *final* feeling of relaxation which distinguishes the conative process from emotion. Again, in the entire *Gefühlsverlauf*, when experienced as conation, there dwells a *Zweck-richtung* which is realised in the end-feeling of relaxation. Primary conative processes, such as impulse, are emotions with this meaning; secondary derived conation, such as desire and will, are emotions in which certain single feelings and presentations, elements in the total emotion, are singled out as the motive for the final feeling of relaxation. So

---

[1] Wundt, *Ethics*, Vol. I, "The Principles of Morality," pp. 6 and 7.

that "desire is not so much the preparatory stage of an actual, as the feeling basis of an arrested conation." The experience which constitutes desire may be viewed as feeling or conation according to the point of view from which it is observed. All these concepts are finally logical abstractions, and not fundamental distinctions of content.[1]

A similar view was, in all its essentials, developed by Brentano,[2] from the point of view of worth analysis, before Wundt's present formulation, in his well-known claim that in a given series of affective-volitional meanings, a vital series of adaptation passing from feeling to will (as, for instance, sadness, longing for an absent good, passing into desire to secure it, courage to undertake to secure it, decision to act), it is impossible at any point to make an absolute distinction between feeling and will. They constitute rather a continuous series of meanings in which these two aspects can be distinguished only relatively and conceptually.

The criticisms passed upon this conception by the upholders of the dualistic views are instructive as showing the contradictions involved in the theories which make these distinctions ultimate differences of content. The upholder of such a dualism must put his finger on the point in the series where feeling ends and conation begins. Ehrenfels finds it immediately after the first stage of the series. Sadness alone is pure passive unpleasantness. All the others have in them the active principle of desire. But both the superficiality and the contradictions in such an analysis become immediately evident. For what is involved? Clearly, to make the distinction at *this* point necessitates the throwing of the emotions of hope and courage from the feeling to the desire side of the distinction, as indeed Ehrenfels does, and the logic of such procedure would be to confine feeling to pleasantness and unpleasantness as passive and unspecified states.

---

[1] *Physiologische Psychologie* (5th edition), Vol. III, chaps. XVI and XVII. *Affekt* is here translated emotion in accordance with the broad use of that term in chapter III, p. 64, and as recommended by the *Dictionary of Philosophy and Psychology*, pp. 316, 317, article on *Emotion*.

[2] The considerations which were influential in this analysis of Brentano were precisely those of which we have already taken cognisance. If feeling be taken as identical with passive pleasantness and unpleasantness, valuation cannot be reduced to determination of conation by feeling, to pleasure-causation. Feeling, it is true, viewed merely as pleasantness and unpleasantness, is present throughout the entire accommodative or vital series, such as that described above, but it becomes less and less significant in the latter stages where the dynamic tension becomes dominant. Hedonic intensities become irrelevant redundancies and we have practically intensity-less conation. The absolute dualism between the worth and hedonic element, as described in chapter III, p. 76, is unnecessary if these distinctions are interpreted genetically.

But when this violence is done, the superficiality of the analysis immediately appears. Can we say that sadness is pure passive unpleasantness? Certainly not. Already in the relatively passive state of sadness we have the preliminary stage of the accommodative reaction, the vital series. This is to be found in the expansiveness of the feeling. The concentration of images in this phase of brooding sadness, the tendency of the feeling to expand, contains already an immanent activity, differing only in degree from succeeding phases of more explicit conation. The fact of the matter appears to be that feeling seems to be *mere* feeling, and passive, only when we separate it retrospectively from the functional whole, the vital series of which it is the first phase. Prospectively, in the first phase of expanding feeling, is already contained a sense of the strength and extent of the conative system arrested, and this feeling passes without a break over into the relatively more active emotions, desire and will, acts which follow as the arrest increases in strength and duration. From the standpoint of the later stages, the initial feeling, viewed as a *cause*, seems relatively passive.

If, on the other hand, we seek, as some do, to find the point of distinction between the more active feelings and decision at the end of the series, the only point of difference that we can find is again an end-feeling of relaxation. The origin of this end-feeling, and of the characteristic sensations which go with it, is to be found in the simple fact that the general disturbance, displayed in the series of emotions preceding the moment of decision, has found a definite motor channel in some specific bodily movement or word-formation. But to separate this final phase, this end-feeling, from the feelings which precede it, is again to give us a mere torso, an unreal abstraction. The entire vital or worth series is one, with a continuity of affective-volitional meaning. Each phase may be interpreted as conation or feeling according to the point of view from which it is observed.

The consideration of these two attempts to mark off the active and passive aspects of experience—to differentiate, in terms of elementary content, the affective and conative phases of a total vital worth series, shows that such an effort must prove unsuccessful. If we abstract from the meaning which the attitude has by virtue of its place in such a series, the distinction between active and passive, and with it that between affection and conation, lapses. We have in these conclusions therefore, without further analysis, the grounds for our negative position with regard to the dualistic theories of feeling and will which find the worth element in feeling conceived as passive pleasantness-unpleasantness or in desire, and for our criticism of any conception of causal determination between them. They afford positive grounds, moreover, for our definition of worth as "affective-volitional meaning," and for the view that the worth experience is a concrete feeling-attitude, in which conation is always present and conative dispositions always presupposed.[1]

4. *Interpretation of the Monistic Theory—its Relation to the Definition and Analysis of the Consciousness of Value.*

Nevertheless, while this duality, this distinction between feeling and will, is not one of elementary content, it is still a duality of meaning which becomes fundamental from the appreciative point of view. Feeling and will are two *meanings* of the same content; but what determines the difference in meaning? How is this differentiation to be understood? Our answer to this question must be in the general terms of the "Identity theory," that is, that the difference can be described only in conceptual, logical, retrospective terms. By this it is meant—to make the general statement more specific—that this duality or distinction is one of recognitive and selective meaning. The passive or active meaning is one which the attitude gets by reason of its place in the vital series, and one which becomes explicit only when the attitude is viewed in relation to preceding or succeeding phases of the series. They are differences of genetic mode.

If we seek to describe retrospectively these two modes, if, in other words, we seek to convey their internal meaning, after the fact, we find that we can do so only in terms of cognition, by description of the cognitive presuppositions of the attitudes. According to Wundt, the special aspect which an emotion must assume to become volition, is an immanental *Zweck-*

---

[1] It is interesting to note that in a recent article, "The Nature of Conation and Mental Activity" (*The British Journal of Psychology*, Vol. II, Part I), Stout, while defining conation "as a complex experience" which, however, contains as one of its elements "a simple and unanalysable element uniquely characteristic of it—an element from which the whole derives its distinctively conative character" (which he describes as felt tendency, and which is not identical either with motor sensations or affection), nevertheless admits that this felt tendency and affection, though distinguishable, do not occur separately, and he proposes to use the term "interest" to express the unity of conative and affective characters in the same process. I cannot see that this view differs essentially from the one developed here. As analysed by Stout, these two aspects are retrospective abstractions.

richtung, and this aspect can be understood only as change in cognitive attitude, not in content. The attempt of Münsterberg to characterise the distinction is also instructive in this connection. " In feeling," he says, " an object, independent of us, is interpreted through conation (*Trieb*). . . . This *Trieb* remains, however, as overtone and as a help in apperception of the object, thought of as independent, which we judge in feeling. If we make the object dependent upon us, so that we perceive it as retained or excluded, then we experience conation and impulse, but not, properly speaking, a feeling."[1] Now, to make the object dependent upon us is to assume its existence or non-existence, as the case may be—that assumption being motived by a subjective disposition presupposed. To think it as independent of us, which, according to Münsterberg's analysis, we do when we feel rather than desire, is again to judge or assume its existence or non-existence, but the motivation of the cognitive act is in this case a control of a more objective origin and character. The significance of this analysis is to be found in the fact that the distinction between feeling and conation is one which, in the last analysis, is reducible to a difference in the immediate functional meaning of elementary content, and that, when this meaning is retrospectively described, such description involves recourse to cognitive presuppositions.

There can be no doubt, however, that this difference in immediate functional meaning, though retrospectively describable only in terms of cognitive attitude, is really *implicitly* present prior to explicit cognitive acts of judgment and assumption, and that below the level of worth experience this duality has its germs in the simplest types of organic accommodation and habit. The " dependence upon " or " independence of " subjective control, which on the higher level is explicitly cognised in acts of judgment and assumption, is implicitly felt in the fundamental attitudes of habit and accommodation after disturbance of habit. If then we view in this more external way such a vital accommodative series as that described by Brentano, we find that what distinguishes the phases which are predominantly affective from those predominantly conative is the degree of inhibition of a presupposed disposition or tendency. Whether we call the phase in question feeling or will depends upon the point in the process of accommodation in which we, so to speak, catch the experience. In Brentano's series the first stages are characterised

[1] *Grundzüge der Psychologie*, p. 366.

by the apprehension of the object as relatively independent of the subject (in this case the apprehension is judgmental)—and in introspection they are interpreted as feeling; in the later stages the object is apprehended as more and more dependent, until in the last phases the belief or judgment that the desire will be accomplished enters and voluntary decision has been reached. Likewise, when Wundt describes the relation in the statement that " feeling may just as well be looked upon as the beginning of a conative process, as on the other hand will may be conceived as a complex feeling-process, and that the emotion is a transition between both," he is distinguishing different phases of one accommodative process.

With this conception of the nature of the duality in meaning of feeling as passive, and desire or volition as active, we are in a position to justify our definition and analysis of worth-experience. Feeling and desire are differences of genetic mode, relative differences of functional meaning, not of content. The worth of an object is therefore its affective-volitional meaning, and is given in feeling-attitudes in which there is always an element, transgredient or immanental, of conation. We describe the worth-fundamental as feeling or concrete emotion, because pure passive affection and pure active conation are limiting terms in the series, and really exist merely as abstractions. But the affective-volitional meaning, or worth, of an object, *its relation to desire and conative disposition as interpreted through feeling*, becomes explicit only on the cognitive level where accommodation is in the form of cognitive acts of presumption, assumption, and judgment. It is the actualisation of the dispositional tendency, either in feeling or desire, through these cognitive acts, which gives to the feeling or desire that meaning described as worth.·

In conclusion it may be pointed out that in this conception of the nature of feeling and will and of their relations we have a psychological basis for the study of the *laws* of valuation. The concrete laws of valuation are not reducible to general laws of feeling, abstracted from conation, nor of desire abstracted from feeling, but rather of affective-volitional process conceived as a whole. If we apply the term *interest*, employed by Stout in the connection already referred to, to designate the conative process in its twofold aspect, we may quite properly speak of these laws of acquirement of affective-volitional meaning as laws of interest.

II. Further Analysis of Feeling—Theory of the Nature and Relation of its Different Aspects

1. *Structural Analysis.*

The theory of the relation of feelings and will already developed has given us a psychological basis for the definition of worth experience as feeling with certain presuppositions. Our second problem, the further analysis of feeling itself, arises from the fact that the appreciative distinctions already made—between the different modes of feeling, between the feeling-tone of sensation and the meanings of feeling-attitudes, which are alone suggestive of worth, between intensity of feeling-tone and depth and breadth of feeling, all demand some further theory of the nature of feeling itself. In our previous analysis of these appreciative descriptions we have already suggested certain elements of such a theory which must now be developed in more detail.

(a) *Feeling as a Kind of Sensitivity.*

We have said that the concrete psychoses which are subsumed under the general terms feeling and will—emotion, passion, sentiment and mood, impulse and desire—are fundamentally different meanings of the same general content. Can we specify more completely the nature of this content? A consideration of the attempts to answer this question may well be preceded by an explicit recognition of the fact that, just as the concepts of feeling and will are abstractions from a concrete whole of meaning which, as such, can be only appreciatively described, so any attempt to reconstruct the appreciative difference of feeling in terms of content, i.e., in terms of non-appreciative description, must involve a process of abstraction which makes one aspect of the total complex do duty for the whole. Simmel has well said of the use of pleasure as synonymous with feeling that: it rises as a concept, as a separate content of consciousness, only after its manifold real characteristics (*Ausgestaltungen*) have determined our actions, and after precisely these differences have had their effect.[1] But when this fact is fully recognised, it still remains true that one abstraction, one equiva-

---

[1] Simmel, *Einleitung in die Moralwissenschaft*, Vol. I, p. 307: "Lust taucht als Begriff, als gesonderter Bewustseinsinhalt erst auf, nachdem ihre realen Ausgestaltungen tausendfach das Zweckhandeln beherrscht und nachdem gerade die Fülle und Verschiedenheit dieser dazu angeregt hat, unter gegenseitiger Verdunklung jenes Verschiedenen dem Gemeinsamen davon eine besondere Beleuchtung zu verleihen."

Psychological Basis of a Theory of Valuation

lent may be more useful for its purposes than another. The chief purpose of a theory of feeling stated in terms of mental elements is, to my mind, and according to the general principles already laid down, its use as an instrument in the interpretation of the functional relation of the general aspect of experience which we describe as feeling to that other aspect which we call cognition; and while from the point of view of our special study there are many questions of analysis which may be left unconsidered, nevertheless, we cannot avoid altogether the formulation of some working conception which will serve this special purpose.

All theories are agreed that feeling is the peculiarly subjective aspect of experience, in contrast to the objective, cognitive, and it has been proposed that the term feeling be applied in a broad sense to the subjective fringe of all cognitive experience. But the question arises immediately just *how subjective*—and we have answers varying all the way between the extremes of those who hold that feeling is entirely unpresentable and is never found on the objective side of the equation, and those who find in it quasi-cognitive functions such as memory and generalisation. Closely connected with this is the question of the degree of independence of feeling of the cognitive aspects of experience, of sensation and image content.

Without going too fully into minor distinctions, we may in general distinguish three main theories of the structural nature of feeling. The first of these is that feeling is not content, but merely the affective tone of content, sensational and representational. But on this view it is necessary to distinguish, as Stout has done, the affective tone of content, sensational and ideal, from the affective tone of process, perceptual and ideational. The fundamental aspect of emotion, sentiment, and mood is, then, the feeling-tone of the *process*, positive or negative, according as it is facilitated or arrested (the feeling-tone of sensations and images, the more objective peripheral, and the more subjective organic, entering as secondary qualifying elements, through surplus excitation). The second theory, Wundt's, is like the preceding in distinguishing feeling completely from sensitivity, but differs in the fact that it conceives feeling to be a special mental element, on the analogy of sensation. These elements have three attributes, pleasantness-unpleasantness, tension-relaxation, and restlessness-quiescence, distinguished in the preceding chapter. Total feelings are then complexes of these hypothetical elements. The third theory, of which

Münsterberg may be taken as representative, holds that these are appreciative descriptions, and that when we turn the feeling-attitude into an object of non-appreciative description, only sensational elements can be discovered. A psychosis called feeling is then but a complex of sensations more difficult of analysis than other more objective complexes.

Leaving specific criticisms of the first two theories to be developed in the course of the discussion, I find certain general considerations which lead to a modified form of the last theory. In the first place the non-sensational aspects of any experience are, in the very nature of the case, only appreciatively describable in functional terms. In the second place the distinction between affectivity and sensitivity cannot, I think, be as completely drawn as is presupposed in the first two conceptions. And, finally, properly combined with the functional genetic conception of feeling and will already developed, it seems adequate to account for all the modifications of feeling-attitude which we have found significant for a theory of feeling and of worth experience.

The breadth of the use of the word feeling in ordinary speech has been frequently commented upon in recent discussions. We *feel* a sensation, an emotion, a mood, or sentiment. We *feel* darkness and distance, the remoteness or nearness of things in memory. We *feel* an impulse, a desire, and we *feel determined* to do a thing. If we start with the last use of the term, we find that, apart from the functional place of the attitude in a vital accommodative series, and the nature of its cognitive presuppositions, there is nothing to distinguish the feeling of desire or will (i.e., of being determined) from the feeling of an emotion or mood, except the character of the sensational content in the two experiences. In the case of the desire or feeling of determination there are certain kinæsthetic or motor sensations which are quite distinct from the organic and systemic sensations which qualify the attitude which we describe as emotion, sentiment, or mood. The difference in the "feel" of the two kinds of attitudes is adequately describable in terms of these sensations and their combinations. In the vital series some distinguishable feeling-attitude has normally preceded (not always, however, as we have seen) the desire or act of will, and its meaning is taken up into the more explicit volition; but the added content which comes with the volitional attitude gives a distinguishing quality to the psychosis. Moreover, in the case of explicit desire or volition the subjective sensational content tends to usurp consciousness, and the perception of the object is a secondary element in the total complex. In the coarser emotions, so called, the sensational elements stand out almost as clearly as in the case of desire. In these, in very truth, the "body" of the emotion is the mass or series of sensations, mostly organic, but also partly motor, since the emotion can never be completely distinguished from the desire. But the "soul" of the emotion, to use a correlative term, its meaning, is found, as in the case of the volition, in its place in the vital series, in its cognitive presuppositions. When, however, we seek to describe this meaning, we can do so only by having recourse to appreciative terms—we describe its positive or negative directions, its dynamic and expansive suggestions, etc.

The preceding attitudes are analysable as psychoses, because their content usurps consciousness even to the partial exclusion of the objects toward which they are directed, and because they represent the result of marked inhibition of conative tendency. When we turn to those "finer" phases of feeling, the sentiments and moods which attach to ideal objects and the "feeling-tone" of sensational and perceptual objects, we find the *object* upon which they are directed, or to which they are attached, more in the ascendent. Those sensational experiences which in the coarser emotions stood out in all their discreteness, now fall into the background, and are recoverable only in case the feeling flares up again through arrest, into a coarser, more fully embodied meaning. What shall we say of the structure of these finer states? I cannot see that we have any other alternative than to say that, as content, the feeling is the *same sensation mass*, but so reduced in intensity as to be for practical purposes inseparable from the objective cognitive content, or so completely fused as to forbid analysis of the separate elements. These finer feelings seem, in contrast to the coarser forms, to lead a disembodied existence, or, better still perhaps, they become embodied in, or fuse with, other presentational material such as the motor or auditory resonance of a word, visual or tonal complexes, in nature, human expression, and art. We speak then of the feeling-tone of the object, or describe the object as suffused with feeling.

Finally, there is a group of experiences, of which we shall have more to say presently, in which the affective state is scarcely distinguishable from the cognitive. The affective aspect, the subjective reference, is so sublimated that it is little more than an accompaniment of the cognitive process. Speaking figuratively, we may perhaps describe them as subtle tones which, in ordinary unimpeded mental process, take the place of explicit fuller embodiment of desire, emotion, and sentiment, and call them "affective signs." The so-called feelings of relation are of this character—the feeling-tones which attach to conjunctions, adverbs, etc., or to the moods of the verb, I shall, I can, I will, I ought, I must. These affective tones are all sublimated forms of explicit emotion and conation, and, with sufficient arrest in the ideational process in which they occur, may flare up into the explicit embodied feeling of which they are the signs, with all its characteristic sensational content. They have consequently been described as vestigial phenomena, survivals of former motor and organic attitudes. It is to be noted too that, while normally they are the affective tones of words, they may, nevertheless, appear prior to and independently of word formation. For the sake of completeness it should be added that the affective tone of abstract and general terms, the affective-volitional meaning acquired in processes of ideal construction, and accompanied by explicit desires and emotions, are of the same general character. But of this more later.

(b) *The Appreciative Distinctions in Feeling as "Forms of Combination" of the Elements.*

To this theory—that feeling, when viewed as content, is a form of sensitivity, serious objections have been raised. Especially these finer forms of affectivity, which seem to be without embodiment in analysable muscular or organic sensations, raise a doubt as to the completeness of our analysis. And, indeed, we may well question its adequacy, as it stands, without any further modification, to account for the different qualifications of feeling as differentiated by appreciative description. Is it not necessary, after all, as for instance in Wundt's theory, to assume special feeling elements to account for these differences?

Both Wundt and Stout have criticised this theory of emotions on the ground of the difficulty of accounting for the qualitative differences in emotion merely as differences in sensation quality of the muscular and organic reflexes, and because of its being viewed as an effect rather than as a cause of the organic resonance. The differences in motor and organic reaction, and therefore in sensation complexes, consistent with the realisation of the same subjective emotional state, necessitate, it is said, our looking elsewhere for the distinctive content of emotional psychoses.[1] In addition, it is held that such a theory wholly ignores in its explanation of the emotions the conative tendencies which they presuppose. "An emotion involves a certain trend or direction of activity which particularises itself in any way it can, according to circumstances."

These criticisms, it may be admitted, are in the main sound, but the modification which the theory requires to make it adequate is one which presents itself almost immediately when one views an emotion in its aspect as content. A closer analysis indicates that what gives such a psychosis its specific *quale* is not the separate sensation qualities, nor yet their fusion in an indistinguishable mass, but rather the structural relations among these elements. In addition to the qualities of the sensations, there are certain temporal and intensity relations among them. Every emotion has, in addition to the object toward which it is directed, the presuppositions which give it its meaning, and its positive and negative direction, its own peculiar organic resonance with its own specific character due to the "form of combination" of the temporal and intensity aspects of the elements.

This concept of a new specific *quale*, or form of combination, giving rise to new qualities which may be appreciatively distinguished, seems to have become a permanent feature of theories of emotional complexes, irrespective of their conception of the nature of the elements in those complexes. Wundt, who holds that these elements are hypothetical feelings, differing *in toto* from sensitivity, reconstructs the different complexes as different forms of *Gefühlsverlauf* among the elements. Witasek, who holds that these "movement-forms" are forms of combination of sensational elements, conceives that the *Gestaltqualität* thus formed becomes the presentable aspect of the total affective complex. It is not necessary to reopen the discussion between the sensation-element and affective-element theories. For the point we are concerned with here, that ques-

---

[1] Moreover, difficulties arise from the genetic point of view. As has been pointed out by Stout, the same emotion—for instance, fear—may arise in connection with very different motor expressions, even in the same animal, showing clearly that the specific *quale* of an emotional psychosis is something which may remain constant notwithstanding considerable variation in the qualities of organic and muscular sensations following upon motor expression.

tion is relatively unimportant. The point of real importance is that such form-qualities exist, and that they are founded on the temporal and intensity relations of the elements.[1]

These form-qualities, moreover, as has been clearly shown by Witasek, may be transposed from the organic sensitivity in which they first inhere to presentational and ideal content. Many of the "finer" sentiments are without embodiment in sensational content, and therefore without this emotional intensity. They consist wholly in the "form of combination" of cognitive content, which, however, still retains the meaning of former fully embodied emotions. Of this fact we shall make further use in our study of the processes of sympathetic *Einfühlung* and the new meanings and values which arise in those processes. Sympathetic projection of a feeling-attitude involves presentation of the psychical, in this case the peculiarly subjective aspect of experience described as feeling. Now, of course, the hedonic intensity and the cognitive presuppositions of the feeling-attitude can be projected only conceptually, as objects of judgment, assumption, etc. But this does not exclude the possibility of the *intuitive presentation* of the *form* of the psychosis, and, therefore, of its specific *quale*. For, if the form of an emotion is the system of temporal and intensity relations among the elements of the complex, this aspect can be abstracted from the elements precisely as any other form of combination (e.g., rhythm), and transposed to other elements. This is precisely what happens, and, when we come to the study of sympathetic projection (*Einfühlung*) in detail, we shall find that the form-qualities of objects, persons, and things constitute the inducing conditions for this intuitive realisation of the emotion, as when the sighing of the wind or the bodily or vocal expression of a person expresses for our intuitive perception the particular emotion in question.

Moreover, on this hypothesis it is possible to understand how the peculiar resonance of an emotion may remain unmodified, notwithstanding great changes in the qualities of the separate sensations and in the absolute intensity of the emotion viewed as a total complex. As on the more objective presentational

---

[1] Wundt—we may merely note in passing—has made some progress in the direction of classifying these various movement-forms: (1) The rapidly rising and slowly falling; (2) the slowly rising and rapidly falling; (3) the intermittent; and (4) the oscillating, and in subsuming the affects appreciatively distinguishable under these rubrics. The most fruitful principle of classification is, I believe, to be found in this direction, but with the actual classification we are here only remotely concerned.

side, the form of combination of the temporal and intensity aspects of sensational elements, as, for instance, a rhythm, may be transposed from one set of elements to another, and, provided the relative intensities and temporal relations are unimpaired, remain entirely clear and distinct with dampening of the intensity of the total complex—so here, even on the assumption that affectivity is a form of sensitivity with a peculiarly subjective meaning, we may see how the specific *quale* of the emotion may still be accounted for.

In conclusion, then, we may say that a complete analysis of any total affective attitude must differentiate four aspects: (1) its positive and negative direction; (2) its presuppositions, dispositional and actual; (3) its sensation content; and (4) the form of combination of that content, or this *quale* transposed to more objective cognitive content, of which it becomes then merely the affective over-tone.

2. Correlation of Structural and Functional Analysis of Feeling.

The outcome of this structural analysis of the different phases of experience which we group under the general term feeling, is the view that the different modifications of feeling are meanings of a certain type of sensitivity. The significance of this conception lies in the fact that, while the essence of feeling is a functional meaning, it is an *embodied* meaning, and we may therefore expect different modifications of that meaning to be correlated with significant *changes in this sensitivity*. These changes in meaning, with their correlated changes in sensitivity, will, moreover, in all probability be connected with changes in functional presuppositions. The working out of these relations would enable us to correlate our structural analysis and classification with the earlier genetic analysis of the accommodative series.

(a) *Changes in Functional Meaning and Changes in Sensitivity-Passion and Emotion-Sentiment and Mood.*

The duality of affection and conation has been interpreted as a differentiation of meaning determined by the place of the psychosis in the accommodative series. Structurally, the emotion is seen to be a shortened form of desire and volition, in which organic largely takes the place of motor sensitivity. In other words, from the standpoint of structural analysis, the nearer a psychosis approaches to explicit desire and volition, the more pronounced becomes that special phase of sensational content which we call strain and effort. It is in these phases that we find inhibition of conative disposition or tendency at a maximum.

But there are other modes of feeling, distinguished by psychological analysis, which represent *various stages* in accommodation, and which show corresponding typical changes in the sensitivity of which they are the meanings. Certain modes of feeling, finer forms of affectivity, such as sentiment and mood, are characterised by the fact that the organic sensations with their hedonic intensity become less and less important while the functional meaning remains unimpaired. There are even certain phases of affective-volitional meaning in which the meaning is without embodiment in analysable organic sensitivity, but in which it appears merely as an overtone of perception or cognitive activity in general. Can we understand these phenomena in terms of our genetic theory?

(b) *Their Genetic Relations.*

In a general way it may be immediately seen that the terms passion and emotion, sentiment and mood, stand for appreciable differences in meaning of affective attitude. One love is best described as a passion, another as a sentiment; one fear as an emotion, another as a mood. It is also apparent that there are genetic relations among them. Emotion may become fixed as a mood, passion may pass over into a sentiment. Sentiment may flare up into passion and mood be stirred into emotion. The significance of these appreciative distinctions is to be found in the fact that they represent different attitudes, different modes of affective-volitional meaning of the object for the subject which, as in the case of Brentano's series, with its distinctions between feeling, desire, and will, go back ultimately to differences in presuppositions. In fact, the transition from passion to sentiment, and its limiting term "affective sign," or from emotion to mood and "affective sign" constitutes a vital series which may be appreciatively segregated for analysis and description in terms of function and structure.

A singularly superficial view of the nature of these dis-

Psychological Basis of a Theory of Valuation 105

tinctions reduces them to differences merely in degree of intensity. This insufficiency of the analysis has been supplemented by Paulhan's study, *Les phénomènes affectifs et le lois de leur apparition*, the general import of which is so thoroughly in harmony with our study that it may be stated in his own terms.

His general theory is that affective states presuppose conative tendencies of varying degrees of strength and systematisation ; that the actual appearance in consciousness of an affective attitude is due to incoördination and arrest of these tendencies, and that in these affective states there are certain aspects of content which disclose the degree of systematisation and arrest presupposed ; that the modifications of attitude, passion, sentiment, emotion, mood, and affective sign may be reduced to differences of degree in which these aspects are present, and therefore to differences in arrest of tendencies presupposed. Those aspects of affective disturbance upon the basis of which a genetic and functional classification is thus possible are : (1) the intensity or vehemence of the disturbance, the force and persistence of the arrested tendency ; (2) the multiplicity of phenomena in the affective state (mass of sensational content) disclosing the complexity of the tendencies presupposed ; (3) the degree of the tendency of the disturbance to absorb consciousness (which we may interpret as indicating the degree of concentration of subsidiary tendencies about the fundamental). All these aspects are interpreted as functions of the two factors systematisation and arrest of conative tendency.

Having established the general fact that all affective attitude involves at least a minimum of arrest, he examines the different attitudes, passion, emotion, sentiment, mood, etc., in the light of the preceding analysis. Passions and emotions disclose these aspects at a maximum and represent the extreme of arrest. On the other hand, sentiments and moods, derived respectively from the passions and the emotions, show these aspects in a less marked degree, and represent, therefore, the beginning of re-adaptation after arrest or the reduction of the moment of arrest. All these aspects are, however, again reproducible in passion and emotion when the conative disposition is again subject to arrest. On the functional side, then, this diminution of intensity, multiplicity, and absorption of consciousness represents the habit which comes with repetition.

In the "affective sign" (a new descriptive term introduced

by Paulhan for affective phenomena not ordinarily observed in superficial introspection), we have a still further reduction of these aspects of the affective experience. It represents a limiting term in the affective or vital series, hard to distinguish from terms in an intellectual series. Paulhan describes the rôle of these affective signs in the following way : " We may describe more clearly perhaps the nature of this class of facts by comparing them with the operations of the cognitive consciousness. We know that cognitive phenomena are often substituted the one for the other. Thus the image replaces the sensation, ideas or words are able to replace images. The substitution takes place so easily that one is not as a rule led to recognise it, and the more ultimate, abstract, and feeble substitutes have consequently been but rarely studied by psychologists. These substitutes are pure abstracts, produced perhaps by the partial excitation, feeble but systematised, of a large number of tendencies. We find in the affective sphere facts of substitution analogous to those which we recognise in the functioning of intelligence. Passion and sentiment are replaced often by other states of consciousness of an affective nature, which become substitutes for them and fill their rôle."[1]

This greater capacity of the affective-sign for substitution or transference from one fundamental to another is functionally its most significant aspect, and, as Paulhan points out, this capacity goes with the fact that it shows intensity, multiplicity of content, and absorption of consciousness, at a minimum. On the side of content it is the relative absence of these aspects which marks the affective sign as the limiting term in the vital series we are considering. But to this negative aspect must be added a positive. This Paulhan recognises in the peculiar tone which the sign, although relatively intensity-less, gives to consciousness. The decrease in these contentual aspects does not, however, mean loss in worth suggestion or affective-volitional meaning. The affective sign has a functional meaning which does not lie in its intensity.

[1] *Les phénomènes affectifs*, etc., Paris, 1901, p. 72. He thus further describes their function in consciousness : " If we recall an affective impression with strength and persistence, we may be able to free ourselves from it partially, as we would not be able in the case of the original affective disturbance, but we feel always within us, not the original impression, but an element which replaces it momentarily and which gives to the state of consciousness a peculiar tone." This *tone* he then goes on to describe as both generic and recognitive in its suggestions. This is a true piece of psychological analysis and introspection, examples of which will be given and discussed in more detail in the following chapter on affective memory and affective generalisation.

Psychological Basis of a Theory of Valuation 107

In this application of the genetic view to the explanation of the relation of the functional meaning of feeling attitudes to their sensitivity, we have not only an important extension of the general principle that the differences in affective-volitional attitudes are reducible to differences of genetic mode in a vital accommodative series, but also the basis for psychological explanation of certain phenomena of valuation. We have found that, on the level of worth experience, accommodation and habit are to be co-ordinated with cognitive acts, feeling and desire being actualisations of conative dispositions through presumption, judgment, and assumption. An obvious inference from this conclusion would be that the differences in meaning of these different modes, passion, sentiment, affective sign, emotion, mood, affective sign, may, in so far as they are significant for worth experience, be conceived in terms of modification of cognitive presuppositions.

This inference is, I think, justified by the facts. Sentiments, moods, and, still more, affective signs, representing, as they do, habituation in varying degrees, are significant in worth experience precisely because they are modes of feeling which go with assumptions of the two types, explicit and implicit. In the preceding chapter we had occasion to point out that, even in the case of those moods apparently physiological in origin, objectless feelings in general, there is really a vague presumption of reality. All forms of affectivity which are worth-suggestive have cognitive presuppositions, and in the case of the modes of feeling which act as substitutes for passion and emotion the presuppositions are assumptions, explicit or implicit. In the first case, as we shall see presently, we are concerned with feelings of the imagination, in the second, with feeling-abstracts. Accordingly, the different modes of the vital series, passion, sentiment, affective sign or emotion, mood, affective sign, represent on the side of presuppositions, and in their aspect of worth suggestion, a gradual, although not always recognised, change in presuppositions. Passion and emotion represent readjustment after arrest, and this readjustment in so far as it is a worth experience implies judgment. But sentiment and mood, and still more the affective sign, stand for the adjustment as it approaches accomplishment. These forms of affectivity represent the affective-volitional meaning of habit, and as such are the psychical correlates of dispositions.

3. Corollaries from the Preceding Theory of Feeling.

In the light of the preceding analysis and theory it is now possible to understand psychologically certain facts of worth experience which the studies of the preceding chapters have brought to light. We have seen that the appreciative distinctions and descriptions of worth experience involve the possibility of differentiation and ultimately independent variability of different aspects of the total feeling-attitude. This appeared most emphatically in our introductory distinction between feeling of worth (with its meanings, references) and pleasantness-unpleasantness, between *degree* of feeling of value and *degree* of intensity of pleasantness-unpleasantness. From the differentiation of these aspects, and from the very fact that they can be presented and described, it was also inferred that the psychical as such, in this case the feeling, must in some way be the object of recognition, presentation, and judgment, and thus approach to the cognitive side of experience. The application of these conceptions constitutes the special problem of the following chapter. Here we shall content ourselves with showing how our theory of feeling makes these conceptions possible.

With respect to the first of these problems—how acquirement of funded meaning may go hand in hand with diminution of hedonic intensity, or how the aspect of hedonic intensity may become redundant in any given worth experience—our concept of feelings as meanings embodied in a certain type of sensitivity is seen to be enlightening. The two directions of feeling attitude, positive and negative, which belong to it by virtue of its relation to conative disposition, become pleasantness-unpleasantness when the attitude is viewed retrospectively, as predominantly passive. When thus viewed, moreover, passive affectivity becomes a form of sensitivity and may properly be said to have degrees of intensity. But since intensity, in its narrower sense, is also, properly speaking, an attribute of sensitivity alone, the meanings of the attitude in its prospective reference, the transgredient and immanental references which it has by virtue of its cognitive presuppositions, have *degree*, but *not intensity*. As an analogy we may take the *meaning* of an idea and its content or imaged substrate. The latter has intensity, but the former intension and extension.

This fact being recognised, we may see the meaning of the

Psychological Basis of a Theory of Valuation

statement previously made that "pleasantness rises as a separate content of consciousness only after the real manifold characteristics have determined our actions," i.e., only when it is selectively differentiated, as passivity, from the other meanings, the transgredient and immanental references. When the other aspects, or meanings, of the total attitude are uppermost, i.e., in the prospective reference of the attitude, the passive hedonic aspect is in abeyance, and for the worth aspect irrelevant and redundant. Thus it comes about, as we have repeatedly seen, that the worth suggestions of the feeling-attitude may be unaffected by the dampening of the absolute intensity of the organic resonance or sensitivity. Intensity is a function of structural modification, of degree of arrest of organic tendency, and, while habit, which comes with adaptation, involves diminution of this intensity, it does not necessarily involve modification of the other meanings of the content. This we have seen in our study of sentiments, moods, and "affective signs."

Thus it comes about also that in any given total attitude (of any duration) there may be variations of hedonic tone, both qualitative and quantitative, which do not in the least affect the worth suggestion or meaning of the total attitude. Sadness is a negative worth attitude and hope a positive, the one is predominantly pleasant and the other predominantly unpleasant; but the sadness as a total attitude may be now pleasantly, now unpleasantly tinged, while hope, though predominantly pleasant, may contain unpleasant moments. Yet this does not, as Stout says, affect in the least degree the strength of the conative aspect of the attitude or, as I should prefer to say, the variations of hedonic tone of the passive aspects of the feeling attitude are irrelevant to the worth suggestion or meaning of the total attitude.

With this conception of the different aspects or meanings of the feeling attitude, differentiated in the process of accommodation, there arises the further question of the possibility of feeling acquiring that objectivity which goes with recognition and presentation. In our structural study we had occasion to note different degrees in which a feeling may be independent of its object. The feeling-tone of the sensation is inseparable from the content to which it attaches, while the emotion, sentiment, or mood, in other words, the "disposition-feeling," spreads over consciousness. The question arises whether this independence, this segregation or detachment of feeling from its object can reach such a point that the feeling itself may acquire recognitive and generic meaning. There are several points in the phenomenology of valuation where such an hypothesis is required, as for instance, in the processes of sympathetic participation in which the feeling as projected object acquires recognitive meaning for the subject, but with these special applications we are not now concerned. Our only interest here is to point out that in this conception of feeling as a meaning, as a form of combination of the elements of subjective sensitivity, itself relatively independent of this sensitivity, we have a basis for this hypothesis.

CHAPTER V

THE CONTINUITY OF AFFECTIVE-VOLITIONAL MEANING

THE ACQUIREMENT OF RECOGNITIVE AND GENERIC AFFECTIVE MEANINGS—AFFECTIVE MEMORY AND GENERALISATION

1. *The Problem.*

A THIRD problem of the psychology of valuation, requiring a special analysis of feeling, is connected with the question of the nature of the continuity of worth experience and judgment. This question, briefly stated in the preceding chapter and reserved for a separate discussion, now becomes answerable in the light of the results of the analysis of that chapter. The question, as there stated, is this : How does the meaning of previous emotional experience, having found expression in a judgment of value, function in new judgments, in new accommodations? Otherwise expressed, How shall we understand psychologically the *funded* meaning which an object acquires through the formation of dispositions?

The view generally held is that feeling is a discontinuous accompaniment of cognitive experience, that it becomes functional merely by the creation of physiological dispositions and tendencies, or by *reflective interpretation* of the past experience in a new situation. One writer states the problem thus : " Now, if it were in a direct way, as immediately felt emotion, that the consciousness of value must be functional if functional at all, then the problem might well be given up ; but it would be a serious blunder to conceive the problem in this strictly psychological way. A logical statement of the problem would raise a different issue— not the question whether emotion, as emotion, can in any sense be functional in experience, but whether the consciousness of value, and emotion in general, may not receive reflective interpretation, and thereby, becoming objective, play a part as a factor in subsequent valuation-processes."[1] Now, it is quite true that from the logical point of view it is "simply a matter of fact" that a present consciousness of value does become a factor in subsequent valuation-process. It is, however, not clear that this dispenses us from the necessity of understanding how this is psychologically possible. It is also clear, on the other hand, that if this continuity is conceived purely physiologically, if the disposition is conceived to be functional without any psychical correlate of conscious meaning, the valuation-process is psychologically discontinuous just as truly as in the logical statement of the situation.

Neither of these views is an adequate account of the continuity of valuation. Immediately felt emotion does indeed become functional through reflective interpretation, i.e., by becoming the object of new judgments and assumptions, but there are also *felt* continuities in which the acquired meaning of past feelings determines directly the meaning of the present feeling. For the explanation of such continuities we must assume an emotional "logic," in which feeling is directly determinative through its acquirement of recognitive and generic meanings. In a preceding chapter, where the difference between hedonic intensity and "depth and breadth" of funded meaning was appreciatively determined, it was suggested that a theory of "affective generalisation," of development of generic feeling-attitudes, afforded a basis for the understanding of these facts. To the consideration of this theory we must now turn.

Certain phenomena already examined afford the starting-point for this theory. Our combined structural and functional analysis of feeling has disclosed certain forms of feeling, sentiments, moods, and, more particularly, "affective signs," which differ in certain definite ways from passional and emotional reactions to specific situations. Their lack of sensational intensity, their character as residual feelings, gives them a representative function, and enables them to play a functional rôle in worth determination, irrespective of their intensity, a rôle analogous to that of the general concept in cognition. As we may speak of a relatively imageless apprehension of cognitive meaning, so we may speak of a relatively intensity-less appreciation of affective-volitional meaning or value.

Now the fact itself—of the existence of such residual feelings,

---

[1] H. W. Stuart, *Valuation as a Logical Process*, in Dewey's *Studies in Logical Theory*, p. 336.

such relatively intensity-less phases of feeling (which take the place of explicit and more concrete emotions and passions)—is, I think, beyond doubt. From various quarters the facts themselves are being recognised. The only question is as to the usefulness of this conception of memory and generalisation, or of recognitive and generic meanings, as a formula under which to group the facts. Of its usefulness as an hypothesis for explaining the unities and continuities of valuation the present writer is persuaded, despite recent criticisms of the conception. Nevertheless, it is important to recognise that it is merely an hypothesis of an analogical character, and that it is valuable only in so far as it enables us to get a deeper insight into the facts of valuation; and that, further, there is no objection to the substitution of another conception if it fulfils this function better. This position I have already maintained in a critical study of Ribot's theory.[1] The reason for the retention of the concept of an "affective logic" is to be found in the fact that the phases of affectivity under discussion do seem to have a representative rôle analogous to that of generals and abstracts in the sphere of cognition, that they do determine actual feeling and worth judgments, as opposed to the view that they are totally different from real feelings and do not affect them. This is the significant point, and a point to which we shall devote a fuller discussion later.

With this view of the nature of the hypothesis in mind, we have the following problems before us: (1) What are the phenomena of worth determination, of affective-volitional process, which give rise to this hypothesis? (2) What is the psychological criterion in terms of content and function, of recognitive and generic meaning in the sphere of cognition? What are the similarities between these and the phases of affectivity under discussion which give rise to this analogical hypothesis? In other words, What is the criterion of affective memory and generalisation? (3) What is the origin of these phases and their function in the unities and continuities of valuation?

II. THE ACQUIREMENT OF RECOGNITIVE MEANING BY FEELING
THE PROBLEM OF "AFFECTIVE MEMORY"

The problem of "affective memory" has recently received considerable attention.[2] In my own earlier studies in this

---
[1] Review of Ribot's *La logique des sentiments*, Psych. Bulletin, Vol. II, No. 9.
[2] The fullest and most recent study of Affective Memory is found in Paulhan's *La fonction de la mémoire et le souvenir affectif*, Paris, 1904.

subject.[1] it was pointed out that a distinction must be made between the *fact* of recognition of feeling as past and our explanation of the phenomenon, and that, moreover, the acceptance of the facts has been hindered by certain prejudices of theory, both as to the nature of feeling and of memory. If we identify feeling with one of its aspects, pleasantness-unpleasantness, and then ask whether an hedonic tone may be *recalled*, there is indeed none but a negative answer to that question. There is no restoration of a past hedonic tone, except in conceptual terms, for every experience of pleasantness-unpleasantness is an actual present feeling. If, however, we put the question as it should be put—does a present feeling ever acquire recognitive meanings ?— the answer is in the affirmative. And, when we further ask: How does it acquire this meaning, and what aspects are recognised ? there is some hope of answering the question. To this question, in so far as it concerns our psychological theory of valuation, we must give some attention, but we may at the outset disclaim any intention of exhaustive treatment and refer for details to the studies already cited.

1. *Types of Affective Memory.*

The facts of affective memory have been collected in considerable number. The restatement of them here would require more space than can be devoted to the subject. Our concern is primarily with the interpretation of the phenomena and the determination of their place in our genetic and functional theory of acquirement of affective-volitional meaning.

We may recall, however, that there are two forms which have been generally distinguished: (1) what may be called voluntary revival, or, more carefully expressed, perhaps, voluntary *re-instatement* of a feeling attitude with recognitive meaning, and (2) involuntary spontaneous recurrence of an attitude, without its accompanying object, but with recognitive meaning.

Of the first type of re-instatement there are numerous illustrations in the literature referred to, and, in fact, in everyday experience. I shall note only one, which is considered by Pillon to be distinct disproof of the view that the so-called revived emotions are really new ones. It is a passage in the *Nouvelle Héloïse* (Part IV, Letter 17) where Saint-Preux de-

---

[1] "The Problem of a Logic of the Emotions and Affective Memory," *Psychological Review*, Vol. VIII, Nos. 3 and 4.

The Continuity of Affective-Volitional Meaning 115

scribes himself as reviving in the presence of the old scenes of love the same emotions, but as falling into rage and despair upon recognising their futility. Pillon considers this evidence that there is a recognised difference between the revived emotion and the new in the mind of Rousseau.

If we examine this illustration of the first type more closely, it appears that we have to do with what has recently been described as "feelings of the imagination." Feelings of imagination are those which follow upon the representation of image content, where the content is not presumed or judged, but merely assumed to exist. Such a feeling may be evoked, either by recalling images of the past with assumption of existence in the past, or by calling them up with assumption of present or future existence. In the first case the feelings have recognitive meaning, and we speak of affective memory; in the latter case we have imagined feelings in the more limited sense of the word. In both cases the "feeling of the imagination" differs from the actual present feeling in its coefficient of reality and in certain aspects of structure.

Some feelings of the imagination (i.e., assumption-feelings) have, then, recognitive meaning, and it is important to note that these feelings with recognitive meaning may be reinstated, either by recalling images of the past with assumption of existence, or by a form of auto-suggestion, motor or verbal, in which the subject induces sentiments or moods by assuming a motor attitude, or by use of verbal symbols having emotional overtones from past experiences of feeling. Toward this reinstated feeling a new feeling-attitude, positive or negative, may be taken, as in the case of Saint-Preux already described. This feeling is the actual present feeling, and presupposes the passage of assumption into explicit judgment of existence or non-existence.

The second type of reinstatement is quite different. In this case the feeling-attitude may recur with recognitive meaning, even without any recognised presentational content or any *explicit* assumption as presupposition. The feeling itself is first recognised, and only later emerge the presentations to which it refers. It is at first of the nature of an objectless feeling, but has, nevertheless, recognitive meaning. A classical illustration of this type is the experience of M. Littré, given by Ribot, where the feeling connected with the death of his sister, which took place in his youth, comes over him unexpectedly in his old age, after the memory of the death had for years ceased to be accompanied by feeling.[1] In such cases the recognition of the feeling seems to be independent of the recognition of presentational content, and is reinstated indirectly through association.

The two types thus distinguished have been called respectively *false* and *true* affective memory, and, as Paulhan recognises, there seems to be a real distinction involved, although not one so ultimate as these terms would indicate. The distinction lies in the fact that, while both are feelings of the imagination with certain definite marks which distinguish them from real present feelings, the evocation of the one is dependent upon revival of image content, while the other, the so-called true memory of feelings, is itself the condition of revival of memory images. To the functional basis of this distinction we shall return, but we must first determine the criterion which distinguishes the feeling of the imagination (in both forms) with its recognitive meaning, from the " present " actual feeling.

2. *The Criterion of Recognitive Meaning.*

The criterion of recognitive meaning (of any experience, whether cognitive or affective) is a certain mark of *pastness* inherent in a present experience or content. This mark of pastness is reducible to certain equivalents in terms both of function and content. On the side of *function* the difference between an experience with, and one without, recognitive meaning seems to be primarily one of *control*, of reality coefficient. In the case of the content which has the mark of the present without any reference to the past, the content is an object cognised as immediately given. Where, on the other hand, it has the mark of pastness, the content is felt not to

---

[1] Reference may also be made to a case cited by Mauxion in an article, "La vraie mémoire affective," *Revue philosophique*, February, 1901, and I may also quote a case from my own experience described in the article already referred to :—

"A few years ago, while living abroad, there came into my consciousness, entirely without associational conditions that were recognisable, a peculiar emotional tone which I recognised as having been experienced before with peculiar intensity. I located it finally as the emotional overtone of a peculiarly desolate bit of anthracite coal region. So strong and marked was it that it developed into particular emotions of great vividness, and sufficient to lead immediately to a bit of descriptive writing. The point of psychological interest is that with the closest search no ideal content could be found which would account for its revival. It is probably explained by the fact that a somewhat similar feeling had that day been generated by wholly different content—the squalor of a certain quarter in a foreign city, and that there had been direct emotional recall through emotion."

The Continuity of Affective-Volitional Meaning

be immediately given, but as so connected with the immediately given that the immediacy can be restored.

This difference is reducible, in its functional aspects, to difference in cognitive acts. All content with the mark of presentness is presumed or judged to exist. The presumption of existence characterises, we have seen, all acceptance of content which is objectively determined, while judgment is but the explicit acknowledgment of that determination. The content with the mark of pastness, on the other hand, is felt to be connected with immediate content the existence of which is assumed. It is this connection with assumed reality which gives it its recognitive meaning.

To this functional difference between the content with past and present meaning there corresponds a difference in structure. Analysis discloses the fact that memory images differ from immediate perception in that they are schematic, and lack the peculiar "sensational intensity" which characterises immediate perception. The schematic character lies in the fact that there has been a "wearing away" of certain elements in the total complex, those elements being retained which through complication and other forms of association are connected with previous experiences. The reduction in intensity is probably to be correlated with the reduction of tendency to motor expression in the case of memory images. However we explain these structural differences between immediate perception and memory image, they are closely connected with the functional criterion of recognitive meaning. The content with these characteristics is distinguished from immediate perception, is inhibited by perception, is thrown back and localised in the past.

3. *The Criterion of Recognitive Meaning as Applied to Feelings.*

From these reflections we should naturally be led to infer that, among the classes of feelings distinguished by our analysis, feelings with presumptions and judgments as presuppositions do not have recognitive meaning, and that assumption feelings alone have the qualification of pastness. And this inference is justified by the facts. For, in the first place, the two types of feelings which have the mark of pastness, where a present feeling seems to be a re-instatement of a past experience (the so-called false and true affective memory), are either "feelings of the imagination," with assumptions as presuppositions, or objectless feelings which, although at first without objects and explicit presuppositions, develop into feelings of the imagination. And what gives them their recognitive meaning, it is easy to see, is the belief that they are reducible to or convertible into, actual immediate feelings, *if* the content which is their object should again acquire the coefficient of reality which goes with perception and its presumption of existence, or *if* the content should again become the object of existential judgment. On the other hand, it is equally easy to see why feelings with presumptions and judgments as presuppositions have no mark of pastness. Each act of apprehension or judgment is itself a new accommodation and involves a new, unique feeling.

Both these types of feeling have, then, this qualification of pastness or recognitive meaning, because of their reference to an actual feeling which it is believed would be reinstated with the reinstatement of perception or judgment. But this conversion is not always possible, and, when attempted, it is frequently followed by a change in feeling—the new feeling being neutral, or, indeed, often opposite in character.[1] New conditions of the present, or changes in the disposition of the subject, often inhibit the judgment-feeling toward which the assumption-feeling points. In the case of Saint-Preux the feelings of the imagination with recognitive meaning refuse to take on the actuality of a present feeling, and are felt to be futile. When one returns to the scenes of his childhood, feeling has often become neutral or opposite in character. The feelings connected with a shipwreck or a death, as long as they are merely remembered or imagined, retain all the aspects of the early experience, except that which gives it its mark of presentness; but the present actual affective attitude toward the past event may become neutral, or at least blunted. This appears notably in the case of the experience of M. Littré, where, although the

[1] It is interesting to note that Angell (*Psychology*, p. 266) admits the existence of affective memory in the practical sense that we feel that we *could*, if necessary, recall events with their former feelings, although, he goes on to say, "if we actually attempt to recall the event we find that sometimes the recollection itself is affectively colourless, sometimes it has the affective character of the original event and sometimes an opposite character." It is this fact that we feel that we *could* recall that is significant. In order that we may have this reference to a real feeling of the past at all, there must be an "affective sign" representing it. Whether that affective sign or feeling of the imagination with recognitive meaning, can be converted into a real feeling or not, whether, owing to change in feeling-dispositions, the present actual feeling differs from the past feeling, is beside the mark. Angell's analysis is here inadequate for the reason that he fails to distinguish between the revived feeling and the present actual feeling, the latter being, of course, a new feeling without the mark of pastness.

The Continuity of Affective-Volitional Meaning

actual feeling attitude toward the past event, the death of his sister, had long since become neutral, nevertheless the feeling of the past, through some chance association, returned in its former character and meaning.

What, then, is this mark of the actual present feeling which distinguishes it from the feeling of the past? Those who have analysed these feelings of the imagination with the mark of pastness agree that the " revived " feeling, whether imaginatively revived or spontaneously recurring, differs from an " actual " present feeling in certain respects analogous to those differences discoverable in the sphere of cognitive images. Like the revived image, the imagined feeling or emotion is schematic. But schematic in this sphere means the absence of the full, rich organic sensations in which the " present " feeling is embodied. With this reduction in sensitivity comes a corresponding reduction in intensity. The revived feeling lacks that " sensational intensity " which actual feeling has. It has its own intensity, which, as has been pointed out by Paulhan and the present writer, and more recently by Saxinger, is unaffected by repetition, and in that respect stands out in marked contrast with the present actual feeling. This so-called intensity of the feeling of the imagination is better described, however, as the *meaning* of the feeling, to distinguish it from the sensational intensity of the actual feeling.

The feelings of imagination, following upon assumptions, have undergone certain modifications which distinguish them from " actual," present feelings. It remains now merely to determine what aspect of the total feeling-complex remains in the feeling of the imagination and acquires recognitive meaning. Upon the theory of feeling developed it is not difficult to answer this question. We have already seen that, while feeling is the embodied meaning of a certain type of sensitivity, that meaning, as a form of combination of the content, is relatively independent of the specific elements of the content and of their intensity. It is this " form-quality," I think we may safely say, that is recognised, and it has recognitive meaning because *it feels as though it could*, were the necessary conditions given, be converted into that fully embodied meaning, with all the reality feeling of immediate perception with its primary presumption of reality or of explicit existential judgment.

This view, much more fully developed in the paper already referred to, receives confirmation in the introspective accounts of "revived" feelings. Notwithstanding the fact that the actual feeling attitude toward a past experience may have changed, the subject may still recall in imagination the precise nuance of emotion, the thrill, the expansiveness, etc., of the feeling from which the mark of present reality has vanished, provided, of course, he is of the affective-memory type.[1] It is a view, moreover, which, if valid, will enable us to understand how feeling may become objective, may be projected, in processes of imaginative *Einfühlung*, into another person, *recognised* and read back into the self.

III. THE ACQUIREMENT OF GENERIC MEANINGS ON THE PART OF FEELING—AFFECTIVE GENERALISATION

With this understanding of the nature of the acquirement of recognitive meaning on the part of feeling-attitudes, we may turn to the consideration of the further hypothesis developed in the effort to account for the continuity of affective-volitional meaning—namely, that certain phases of feeling acquire a generic meaning, relating them to the judgment of value in a manner analogous to the relation of the general concept to the judgment.

The common characteristic of the theories of affective-continuity criticised is, it will be remembered, that there is no *felt* continuity—that habit has no felt meaning. Feeling of worth being identified with hedonic intensity, as feeling-attitude approaches habit actual worth feeling decreases. In the case of the genetic modes of feeling-attitude analysed, passion, emotion, sentiment, mood, and affective sign, we have, with approach to habit, a progressive diminution of intensity, and with it a decrease of actual worth feeling. In opposition to this view we have maintained that these higher genetic modes of feeling-attitude are related to passion and emotion as the general concept is related to the particular percept. As the general concept represents the acquired mean-

---

[1] A passage from Taine's *De l'intelligence*, quoted by Paulhan with reference to the revival of emotions, shows the aspects of feeling recognised on revival. "La seule chose qui en moi se reproduise intacte et entière, c'est la nuance précise d'émotion, âpre, tendre, étrange, douce ou triste, qui jadis a suivi ou accompagné la sensation extérieure et corporelle; je puis renouveler ainsi mes peines et mes plaisirs les plus compliqués et les plus délicats, avec une exactitude extrême et à de très grandes distances; à cet égard le chuchotement incomplet et défaillant a presque le même effet que la voix."

ing of a judgment disposition, so these generic forms of affectivity represent the acquired or funded affective-volitional meaning of particular emotional reactions, and have a functional rôle in worth determination, independent of their intensity, analogous to the rôle of the general concept in cognitive judgment.

1. *The Phenomena of Affective Continuity : Substitution, Subsumption, Transition.*

This analogy between the function of the general concept and the so-called generalised emotion appears more specifically in three types of felt continuity—affective substitutions, affective subsumptions, and affective transitions. Just as an image with generic meaning may, because of its reference to past situations and judgments, take the place of varied image content in our judgments and reactions, so certain affective signs may take the place of specific emotional reactions. As the subsumption of a particular image under a general concept gives to the particular the cognitive predicates of the general, so the colouring of a specific emotion by a sentiment or mood gives to the former the worth connotation of the latter. Finally, as a particular image with generic meaning affords the basis of transition from particular to particular, so the generic meanings of affective states make possible affective transitions analogous to logical judgment, giving rise to an "affective logic."

The phenomena of affective substitution have already been described under the head of "affective signs."[1] There it was seen that relatively contentless and intensity-less phases of affectivity could, as schematic meanings, take the place of particular passions and emotions. On closer analysis it further appeared that these substitutes might be of two kinds, either a feeling following upon explicit assumption of an object (where the assumption is a substitute for judgment) or the emotional connotation of a general term, the feeling in this case following upon *implicit* assumption, but connected either with judgmental habit or with a mere verbal image.

The second group of phenomena, affective subsumptions, has been presented in detail in two papers in the *Psychological Review*.[2] A brief restatement of the chief points of this discus-

---

[1] Cf. pp. 105 ff.
[2] "The Problem of a Logic of the Emotions and Affective Memory," *Psychological Review*, Vol. VIII, Nos. 3 and 4.

sion will suffice. Two forms of this emotional unity or affective subsumption were distinguished: (1) ethical sanction, and (2) æsthetic appreciation. The characteristic of both of these phenomena is that certain particular emotional reactions are subsumed directly under sentiments, moods, or affective signs without the mediation of intellectual relational judgments, thus giving rise to wholly emotional unities. To these may be added certain mystical religious states which represent the extreme of emotional unity, with a minimum of presentational content and judgment.

Ethical sanction of the emotional type is characterised by the fact that some generic dominant emotional attitude having acquired the transgredient reference of obligation, already described, is "felt" to include more particular desires and emotions, and to sanction them. Illustrations of this inclusion appear in such expressions as "holy" anger, "reverent" fear or mirth. In such cases the immediate emotional reaction, the anger or mirth, is coloured by a presupposed sentiment or mood. As will be shown in detail later, an actual judgment-feeling is determined by a generic feeling-attitude, which accompanies an ever-present implicit assumption. Of interest in this connection is also the gradual assimilation of marital under the maternal sentiment, described by Ribot, for it frequently has the character of ethical sanction. These phenomena have generally been described as mixtures of feeling, resulting from the presence in the same unity of consciousness of different images, but such a conception ignores, as we have already seen, the difference in the functional character and presuppositions of the two feelings. The justification of calling them inclusions, rather than mixtures of feeling, is to be found in the fact that the generic aspect of the total attitude gives its meaning to the other aspect—sanctions it, in that it determines its place in a system of worths. The generic feeling is, moreover, often without explicit image content.

The experiences in which this affective subsumption is seen in its most complete form are certain cases of æsthetic appreciation and creation. An *intuitive* "unity in variety" has always been recognised as a characteristic of the æsthetic mode, but recently it has become apparent that such unity may be almost exclusively emotional. The unity for appreciation may be created and retained by inducing certain assumptions, with their corresponding generic sentiments and moods, and by the arrangement of details of imagery in such a manner that the feelings and emotions connected with this imagery may be easily assimilated to the primary sentiment or mood. They do not disturb the assumption, are not, in other words, "illusion-disturbing." As extreme cases of this we may cite certain impressionistic or symbolic styles where the general mood or *Stimmung* is almost palpable, and can be easily segregated from the emotional or feeling tones of the elements—whether words, visual images, tones, or what not.[1] Not only may the generic feelings be distinguished from the feeling-tones of the elements, but, like the sentiments of places, they may often be recalled, and recognised without revival of the particulars.

On the other hand, such generic emotions, sentiments, or moods, may be germinal to æsthetic creation, and the process of creation becomes, in such cases, a subordination or subsumption of particular images under the general mood, according to their emotional values. On the side of active creative expansion of sentiment and mood over particulars we have the interesting account by Poe of the construction of the *Raven*. He tells us that his starting-point was the purpose to express the mood of melancholy. For this mood he found the characteristic refrain, *Nevermore*. His art then consisted in finding particular images, such as the Raven, the locality of the poem, etc., which had emotional tones that could be subsumed under

---

[1] A striking illustration of this is that exquisite mood poem of Tennyson's *The Lotos-Eaters*. All his technique of imagery and rhythm is expended, not only to arouse the grey mood of forgetfulness and indifference, but to carry it on and on, intensified and solidified, until it becomes the mood through which the very gods see the world. That world includes many things which do not fit this mood, yet, like gods,

> They smile in secret, looking over wasted lands,
> Blight and famine, plague and earthquake, roaring deeps and fiery sands,
> Clanging fights, and flaming towns, and sinking ships and praying hands.

And, although these rapid pictures suggest incipient emotional responses of another sort than the dominant mood, they succeed each other so rapidly that it is all

> Like a tale of little meaning, though the words are strong.

The general mood may become so strong that it will spread over all particular emotional tendencies, provided the technique of expression is such as not to allow these particular motor tendencies to get above a certain strength. In this case the technique consists in the rapid piling up of the pictures, thus preventing the particular emotional suggestions from getting in their full motor value. Experiments with people in the reading of this poem have led me to the conclusion that if the mood of the poem is fully appreciated before this passage comes, it may be subsumed under the dominant mood. Otherwise the contrast is too great and the unity of the poem seems to be broken.

The technique of the *Lotos-Eaters*, when closely examined, shows that this subsumption is furthered by the imagery and sounds employed in the poem. The former is always in vague general terms, keeping out the particularised images which with their intenser emotions would overcome the languor of the general mood. The resonances are further damped by the careful use of vowel sounds: "Here are cool mosses deep"—"the ivies creep"—"the long leaved flowers weep."

this mood. And he did not scruple, he tells us, deliberately to tone down or exclude all imagery, the emotional intensity of which was too great for the mood.[1]

The third group of phenomena, described as affective *transitions*, comprises certain continuities in which transition is made from one affective attitude to another through the medium of an affective, rather than ideal or conceptual mean term. In such cases the same phase of affectivity, i.e., the affective sign, which we have seen in the rôle of substitute for particular emotion, or as giving colour, through a kind of subsumption, to particular emotions, becomes a mean term, connecting in one continuity of meaning, particular emotions otherwise different in character. The most characteristic forms of such emotional signs are the residual feelings or abstracts that inhere in general terms and their corresponding words, such as love, duty, God, etc. These may function as transitional mean terms when there is no concrete object of judgment toward which the feeling represented by these words is directed. The objects of such feelings are not definite presentations, but as in the case of objectless feelings, already considered, vague universals—not the object of explicit judgment, but of assumption. But while the emotional suggestion of words is the typical form of transition, it is possible that even the word embodiment may be lacking, and that the vague mood or affective sign may determine worth attitude without embodying itself in any presentation that analysis can discover to be relevant. Full illustrations of such transitions are given in the later paragraphs of this chapter.

2. *The Psychological Theory of Generic Meanings— Structural and Functional Analysis*

The facts which give rise to this hypothesis of the existence of the phenomena variously described as affective generals, abstracts, or affective signs, and of a corresponding " affective logic," are now before us. These facts are, in general, in favour of the view that there are phases of affectivity in some way *different* from the usual emotional reaction to a particular definite situation, therefore (in our terminology), from the particular feeling. They indicate also that these phases acquire reçognitive

---

[1] Poe, *The Philosophy of Composition;* also Paulhan, *L'Invention,* p. 81 ; also Ribot, *L'Imagination créatrice,* where Poe is classed as of the *diffluente* type of imagination, in which the unity is the emotional abstract.

and generic meanings, which enable them to function as substitutes for particular feeling reactions. What, now, is the ground for describing these phenomena as affective generals or abstracts? To answer this question it is necessary to develop a criterion of abstraction and generalisation, and to show that these phenomena fall under such descriptive terms.

(a) *The Nature of Generic Meanings of Ideas: Imageless Apprehension.*

Upon this problem, as it applies to the cognitive side of experience, we are not without some definite conceptions. We may, therefore, take our departure from the psychology of general *ideas* in which the problems are fairly clear, and in which some conclusive results have been obtained. With these before us, we may then turn with some hope of success to the similar problem in the sphere of feeling. The most important analytical problem in the psychology of general concepts may be stated in the following way. The general concept stands for a meaning which has been acquired in the process of judgment; its functional correlate is, therefore, habit or judgmental disposition. But this meaning is always the meaning of some psychical content. What content can introspection discover corresponding to this meaning? If this content be looked for in terms of images, the answer is given—there is no content, or it is inadequate and irrelevant. The final question then is, in the words of Stout,[1] how is "imageless apprehension" possible?

Considering the phases of this problem in detail, we find that for the most abstract concepts there is *no* image equivalent. Words such as liberty, truth, force, may pass through our minds, be intrinsically apprehended, and leave a trail of meaning, without calling up specific images, and even when there are images, these are often wholly irrelevant to the meaning. Moreover, in the case of the most abstract terms, there may be judgments and subsumptions, which approximate to the habitual and automatic, in which the subject finds no image content corresponding to the term. Thus, to sum up the results of Ribot's investigation of general ideas,[2] he finds no characteristic content distinguishing the formation of general ideas, and for the more abstract notions, no analysable content whatever. The conclusion is that the

---
[1] Stout, *Analytical Psychology*, Vol. I, chap. IV.
[2] Ribot, *The Evolution of General Ideas*, chap. IV.

concept can be formulated only in functional terms and must be relegated to the unconscious, which, on his principles, means physiological disposition.

It is true that the criticism of Royce upon these conclusions of Ribot—that the latter's investigations were concerned merely with the most abstract notions, and that the poverty of his results is due rather to the extreme simplicity and automatic character of the judgments and reactions which the experimenter used than to the absence of a psychical correlate, is well founded. It is true, as he maintains, that when judgment takes place with effort, after inhibition, in the attempt to assimilate some novel particular, conscious experience of the process is present. Nevertheless, even here, in the instrumental use of the concept, the particular images called up are not adequate equivalents for this consciousness of meaning, they are often irrelevant—and besides, there still remains the intrinsic meaning of the term, already described, which is present, when there is no inhibition, and which, nevertheless, has no image equivalent. The problem still remains to find some correlate for this consciousness—the question still is: How is imageless apprehension possible?

The approach to the solution of this problem has been but gradual. As long as psychology failed to go beyond the separate presentations and their external associations for principles of description and explanation, it could by no possibility find any terms of description for this additional meaning. Judgments appear to be mere associations after disjunction, and the general concept has no reality except as physiological disposition. The nearest approach along the old lines was when the equivalent of this " meaning " was found in a sort of composite photograph of particulars, a blurred reproduction which is susceptible of recall by a large number of presentations, and which, in the process of recall, receives special emphasis upon that aspect with which the new particular assimilates. But the irrelevance of these images in some cases, and their total absence in others, mark the limits of this conception. The attempt of James to bring this " meaning " within the ken of psychology by use of the metaphor of the psychic " fringe " or overtone to describe our sense of the halo of relations about an image, has been of great historical importance, but it was not until there appeared a much wider extension of the concept of content beyond the limits of an atomistic psychology, that justice could be done to this suggestion. The condition of this extension was the recognition of the fact that between content and function there is no fixed gulf, that what is function on one level becomes conserved as content on a higher level—the recognition, in short, of the genetic point of view. Now, functionally, we have seen, the general concept is a judgment-disposition, an acquired meaning developed in the processes of judgment, and, judgment being a developed form of conation, the positive significance of the general concept is its instrumental use as a means of conative unity and continuity.

The meaning or intent of a general notion is therefore *not the object of presentation at all.* It is the object of judgment. By becoming the object of judgment, however, it also becomes a content of a higher order. This meaning, become content, is therefore, as we have already seen, relatively independent of particular presentations; indeed, the particular presentations may be wholly irrelevant, and the meaning may inhere in mere words which, although they may, in their origin, have been accompanied by associated images, are now wholly independent of them.

Distinction between the Instrumental and Intrinsic Meaning of the General Notion.

It is, however, quite possible to over-emphasise the instrumental character of the general notion. This has been a noticeable characteristic of recent discussions. As a matter of fact, psychological analysis must distinguish two types of meaning of the general notion, genetically related to each other, an *intrinsic* as well as an instrumental. Under the influence of subjective interests and dispositions, an aspect, which has already recognitive meaning, is separated, abstracted from the object, and in the interest of conative continuity is assumed to exist, is given a quasi-existence. This assumption of the first explicit type (arising in the semblant mode, and having schematic meaning, to use Baldwin's terms) passes into judgment when the assumed existence is acknowledged in a judgment relating the quasi-real with the reals of immediate perception. But there is also a function of the general notion in which its meaning is intrinsic, as in the cases of imageless apprehension already discussed, in which words such as truth, liberty, may leave a trail of meaning in our minds without the presence of images. The point of difference lies in the fact that the third stage of the accommodative process has appeared. The judgment disposition created by repeated judgments of an instrumental character has given rise to the implicit assumption of the second type. When the general concept contains this implicit assumption of existence, as in the case of the belief in abstract truth as a reality, intrinsic meaning is hypostatised into a reality. The fulfilment of such an assumption lies wholly in the continuity of the intrinsic meaning, and not in its instrumental reference to a particular situation. This meaning, for which an "objective" is assumed to exist—at least until the implicit assumption is disturbed by new existential or truth judgments, is that which characterises contemplation. This is the origin of all belief in the reality of general concepts. We are not concerned here with the metaphysical validity of such a belief, but merely with the psychological origin of this second intrinsic meaning of the general concept, for we shall find a similar distinction in the meanings of affective generals.[1]

(b) *The Nature of Generic Meanings of Feelings. Intensity-less Appreciation.*

The answer to the question—how is imageless apprehension possible?—has led to a development of a positive functional criterion of generalisation which supplements the negative criterion of relatively imageless apprehension. The problem of the psychical correlate of the meaning of the *affective* general or abstract presents itself in a somewhat similar way. Here the negative criterion is intensity-less appreciation, and the corresponding question is, how is this intensity-less appreciation possible, or if we use emotion in its limited sense of concrete affective disturbance—how is emotionless appreciation possible?

In the first place, it is important to emphasise the fact that this lack of intensity is the characteristic attributed by those who have made a study of the phenomena to the phases of affectivity

---

[1] Thus, as Stout says of the conceptual "now," the word "now" may stand for the moment of the specious present with its sensation content, for the now of an historical epoch, of a year or a day with their varied ideal content. These are instrumental functions involving judgment, and the relative constancy of the meaning of the conceptual "now" is not a function of the sameness of its content, but of the constancy of the judgmental processes of which it is the objective meaning. The word "now" has a meaning (as in the case of the other words studied) even when none of this varied content is present, when it is founded merely upon the auditory or motor sensations which make up the word. This is its intrinsic meaning, and here we have merely the vague assumption of an objective for it, of an existence in which it inheres.

The Continuity of Affective-Volitional Meaning 129

variously described as affective sign, affective abstract or general. When subjected to structural analysis, these feelings are seen to differ from particular feelings in the fact that they lack the intensity and multiplicity of organic sensations which characterise the particular emotion. In the second place, these phases of affectivity have a funded meaning which is independent of increase or diminution of intensity. In fact, the one *criterion* of these forms, however they be designated (as recognised by Paulhan, Elsenhans, and Saxinger), is that they are not subject to the law of diminution of intensity with repetition. In these descriptions, it is true, no clear distinction is made between intensity and degree of meaning, but a careful scrutiny shows that it is degree of funded meaning which they find unmodified by repetition. On our view, which identifies intensity with intensity of organic sensitivity, the term intensity-less appreciation means that the degree of intensity of the sensitivity in which the feeling is embodied is irrelevant for the worth suggestion of the feeling. The question then is, how can the meaning of emotional reactions remain after the particular organic sensitivity, with its intensity, and the particular percepts which called out the emotion have disappeared?

Let us first examine these generic phases of affectivity more closely. The existence of words, with cognitive meaning independent of particular images, was the starting-point of the analysis of the psychology of the general concept. Words with *emotional connotation*, when there is no specific image or emotional content, may properly be the starting-point for our study of the affective abstract. With the emotional connotation of words in its most patent aspects we are tolerably familiar. Burke tells us that he found it "hard to persuade several that their passions (a general term for feeling) are affected by words for which they have no ideas," but that was at a time when a purely intellectualistic psychology as well as art made impossible a true perception of the facts. Certain forms of modern art, as well as a more subtle and sophisticated analysis of our own experience, make us now thoroughly cognisant of the general fact. Ribot has taken as the most primitive type of emotional logic (that is mental movement which has as its mean term the emotional rather than the cognitive connotation of a term), what he describes as the logic of persuasion or appeal.[1] It is "most primitive" because it diverges least from the conceptual

---
[1] *La logique des sentiments*, Paris, Felix Alcan, 1905.

logic; yet the transitions, while giving rise to the illusion of cognitive mean terms, are for the most part emotional. But still more marked is the purely emotional connotation of words in their intrinsic appreciation, where they pass through the mind, leaving a trail of appreciation without raising ideas or definite emotional responses. Such use of words for their purely emotional connotation, as in symbolist poetry, Ribot has taken as a type of affective logic almost pure, and it is these intrinsic emotional appreciations of words, their overtones, so to speak, which Elsenhans takes as the basis for his conception of generalised emotions.

Words, then, may have an emotional connotation for which there is no adequate emotional content-equivalent and no adequate presentational presuppositions. But there are other generic phases of emotionalism which do not have even this embodiment in words. Sentiments are almost wholly connected with words, but moods and affective signs may lack even this embodiment. Of chief importance in this connection are the so-called sentiments or moods of places. Here a certain feeling attitude, with definite recognitive meaning, includes in it the funded meaning of past emotional reactions, which, it is felt, could be individually revived with the revival of the particular presentations. This is also characteristic of the mood we carry away from the reading of a poem, as illustrated in the *Lotos-Eaters* already referred to.[1]

From these illustrations it appears that, as in the case of imageless apprehension of cognitive meaning, so here in intensity-less appreciation of affective-volitional meaning, there are two types, the instrumental and the intrinsic. And this fact underlies, I think, the distinction frequently made between affective generals and affective abstracts. In the case where the feeling with generic meaning functions as a substitute or representative (either as recognitive of former particular emotion or as anticipatory of concrete feeling situations), it may be

---

[1] Lotze has well described this situation in *Microcosmus*, Eng. trans., Vol. I, p. 635: "When we have listened to a poem recited, to a melody sung, and forget the words and tones while yet all that was in them lives on in an abiding mood of our soul; when we first send our glance over the scattered details of a landscape and then, after the definite outlines have long since disappeared from our memory, still preserve an indelible total impression," we make "combination and fusion of myriads of details into the whole of a supersensible intuition, which we but reluctantly again analyse into its constituent parts in order to communicate it to others." In almost the same strain have the writers who argue for affective generalisation and revival described the moods of places, etc., but the value of this description lies in the fact that it comes from one who had no sense of its significance for the psychology of feeling.

The Continuity of Affective-Volitional Meaning

spoken of as abstract or instrumental. On the other hand, in the case of sentiments of places, or sentiments attached to words, the meaning is generic but intrinsic.

In all these phenomena what we have described as "intensity-less appreciation" is the negative characteristic, and may be said to be the negative condition of their generic character and function. In the several cases we have considered—the emotional connotation of a word, representing repeated particular judgment feelings of the past, the "affective sign" as mean term of affective transitions, the generic and schematic sentiment of places—all owe their generic and representative capacity to the fact that, because of some specific difference in functional presupposition, they do not pass over into the full emotional resonance which characterises the particular emotional reaction to a definite situation. They are in the meaning of our terms intensity-less appreciations. To account for this difference in functional presuppositions is to account for these phenomena.

3. The Process of Affective Generalisation—Acquirement of Generic Feeling.

With this analysis of the facts before us, it is now possible to understand the process by which a concrete feeling-attitude acquires generic meaning. Evidently the process has two aspects, one describable in terms of change of function, and the other in terms of modification of structure. On the one hand, how does the meaning become independent of specific image content and cognitive reaction? On the other hand, how does the funded meaning become independent of sensitivity and its intensity? The first aspect is evidently closely connected with the second.

The process of acquirement of generic meaning, or of affective generalisation, may be described as *abstraction from the individual presuppositions of the feeling,* and the substitution of an assumption of existence for specific judgment. Feelings with generic meanings are all assumption feelings, and their intensity-less character may be ascribed to the different attitude toward reality involved.

In understanding this proposition it is first important to note that the acquirement of recognitive meaning is the beginning of acquirement of generic meaning. The recognitive meaning, functionally viewed, consists in the fact that the feeling of the present stands for an actual feeling of the past into which, it is believed, it is convertible. It has a representative capacity. But this same feeling, thus loosed from its immediacy by change of presuppositions from judgment to assumption, has also acquired an anticipatory character, a reference to future actual judgment feelings into which it can be converted. It is here that its generic character is found. Such a feeling anticipates or represents—not one definite actual emotional reaction with its unique and individual presupposition—but a general situation which may be specialised in various particular emotions according to conditions. The derived forms of affectivity, sentiment, mood, and still more, affective sign, have this recognitive and generic meaning in varying degrees. In general, then, the rise of generic meaning is conditioned by abstraction of feeling from its individual presuppositions and the substitution of assumptions.

But this generic meaning we have found to be of two types, instrumental and intrinsic, and one of these, the intrinsic, is closely connected with habit. Every assumption-feeling has, as such, a generic character, in that it is anticipatory of specific judgment-feelings which it qualifies when they become actualised. But, as we have already seen, there are two types of assumption, the explicit and the implicit. The first is an accommodation in the form of imaginative projection as determined by subjective interest. The second is habit following upon repetition of judgment. The explicit assumption is always anticipatory of judgment to come, and is therefore instrumental. The implicit assumption and its feeling is the psychical correlate of judgment-disposition, and its meaning is intrinsic. That which these two types have in common is the important thing, and this is the fact that both are representatives, affective signs, for actual situations in which existence is presumed or explicitly acknowledged in judgment. Their representative function is made possible through their schematic, intensity-less character already described. Both may therefore properly be characterised as *abstractions*, in that their generic meaning is acquired through abstraction from individual presuppositions and by the reduction of those aspects of feeling-attitude which make them specific emotions or passions.

The difference between the two types lies solely in their origin and function. There are two ways in which a feeling is evoked by assumption: (*a*) imagination of the existence of an object or class of objects, in which process the feeling becomes generic and schematic; or (*b*) by repeated judgments passing over into judgment habit and *implicit* assumption, when, embodied in general terms, in mere words, it is an affective sign for particular judgment-feelings.

Specific passions and emotions presuppose explicit judgment. Sentiments, moods, and affective signs may be realised on the mere assumption of the object, the object being often the merest and vaguest universal. Thus it is that these abstracts inhere in mere words. The words God, love, liberty, have a real emotional connotation, leave a trail of affective meaning, because they stand for an object which is implicitly assumed to exist, an assumption generated by previous judgment reactions. Let, however, this assumption pass into judgment, let the explicit judgment, I am free or not free, this is or is not my duty, God exists or does not exist, arise through some arrest of my habitual attitude, and again passion and emotion appear with an intensity which is determined by the desire presupposed and the degree of arrest. We may quite properly speak of the emotional connotation of such words as the funded meaning of previous emotional reactions and the affective abstracts which constitute the psychical correlates of this meaning as the survivals of former judgment-feelings. These residual feelings may, from the point of view of function, be described as affective abstracts precisely because, while every particular emotional attitude presupposes the apprehension and acknowledgment of the existence of a particular object, the affective abstract, the "sign" of these emotional attitudes may be experienced with all its worth suggestion independently of the presupposition of the actual feeling.

IV. GENERAL THEORY OF THE RÔLE OF AFFECTIVE GENERALS IN PROCESSES OF VALUATION—ILLUSTRATIONS

1. *Criticism of the view that they do not determine particular feelings, are not Feelings of Value.*

A view in many respects similar to the preceding is the theory of *Phantasiegefühle*, feelings of the imagination, developed by Meinong and Saxinger, and already referred to in an earlier paragraph. This view demands a special examination here for the reason that, while many of the facts of analysis are true, and while their explanation as assumption-feelings—to which I owe many suggestions for the theory here developed—is sound enough, nevertheless the conception of their rôle in the processes of worth determination is open to serious criticism.

In so far as introspective analysis is concerned, Saxinger practically recognises the existence of such phases of affective-experience as we have described under the terms affective abstract and affective sign, but he gives them another explanation. Elsenhans's generalisation and Ribot's abstraction of feeling have reference, he tells us, to the same emotional phenomenon in different contexts. The generalised feelings are feelings of imagination following upon assumption, the abstract feelings are feelings of imagination attaching directly to "substrate-ideas." For these imagined feelings he finds it necessary to assume the *existence of dispositions entirely distinct from those presupposed by actual feelings*, and accounts for the direct attachment of imagined feelings by assuming that their dispositions may be actualised by substrate-ideas or general concepts, as well as by assumptions. Feelings of the imagination differ from actual feelings in that their intensity is not modified by repetition and in that the corresponding desires of the imagination do not cease with fulfilment. The essential characteristic of this view is to be found in the denial to these feelings of the character of real feelings, and therefore of feelings of value, for the reason that they are not actual, but imagined feelings (*Scheingefühle*); and in the denial, in the second place, that these feelings influence, or are influenced by, real feelings. This last point is the main issue.

Saxinger's grounds for this view[1] are both theoretical and experiental. The theoretical may be dismissed in a few words, for they rest upon certain doubtful assumptions, and in general upon a conception of feeling which we have found untenable. In the first place, it is assumed that feeling is wholly subjective, wholly different from sensitivity, and therefore incapable of undergoing processes analogous to generalisation and abstraction, incapable of acquiring recognitive and selective meaning, a view which our entire analysis has led us to reject.

---

[1] R. Saxinger, Beiträge zur Lehre von der emotionalen Phantasie; *Zeitschrift fur Psychologie und Physiologie der Sinnesorgane*, Vol. XI, No. 3. Also, "Über die Natur der Phantasiegefühle und Phantasiebegehrungen," in *Untersuchungen zur Gegenstandstheorie und Psychologie*, Leipzig, 1904.

The Continuity of Affective-Volitional Meaning 135

In the second place, and closely connected with this, is the assumption that intensity and degree of meaning of feeling are identical, and that therefore the criterion of the real feeling is diminution of intensity with repetition. Any phenomena which do not follow this law must accordingly be, *not* real feelings, but some sort of quasi-feelings which he describes as feelings of the imagination. This criterion of real feelings we must also question, in view of our previous analysis of feeling.

The facts of experience, on the other hand, upon which he bases his conclusions, require closer examination. He finds, as we do, these phases of affectivity similar to other feelings in all respects, except that they do not have that sensational intensity which characterises the so-called actual feelings, and that, in their case, repetition does not affect their meaning. These facts he accounts for in terms of their difference in presuppositions. They are all assumption feelings, having dispositions different from those which give rise to actual feelings. He believes, moreover, that an examination of the facts discloses an independence of real and imagined feelings which makes necessary this hypothesis of different and independent dispositions.

As to the question of fact, we may admit that much that Saxinger has brought forward gives a certain plausibility to this view, but only, I think, when the facts are mis-interpreted. Thus we may admit, for instance, the truth of his statement that, while with time the feeling of sadness following upon the death of some loved one may lose its sting, that is, may decrease in intensity, it is quite possible that the joy in *imagining* the existence of the departed loved one may, within limits, be unaffected by this dulling of the *real* feelings. We may also admit the truth of his illustration where the father gets a certain joy in imagining his son successful, while his feelings, determined by the certain knowledge that his son is a failure, remain unaffected by the feelings of imagination following upon the assumption. A relative independence of these two phases of experience, and the possibility of their existing together, cannot be denied. But it would be a doubtful inference to conclude that they are ultimately independent. Such independence is at the most only temporary. I am inclined to think that in both cases the capacity for such feelings of imagination steadily decreases with the recognition of the inevitableness of the actual fact. In so far as my own introspection goes, with the repetition of judgments of non-existence and their negative worth feelings, the capacity, as well as the desire, for visualisation and assumption of existence of the objects which give rise to the feelings of imagination, weaken, and the former feelings remain only as a mood or affective sign which a word or name suggests. This does not, however, exclude the possibility of involuntary recrudescence of the imagined feeling under certain favourable conditions of general mood or association. The facts of unmediated revival of emotions, examined in the study of affective memory, are too unequivocal to admit of such denial.

Saxinger recognises, indeed, such cases of apparent influence, both of assumption feelings upon judgment feelings and judgment feelings upon assumption feelings, but thinks that such influence is only apparent, and must be explained in another way. The question arises in his discussion especially in connection with the view of Witasek, that the feelings of the imagination in æsthetic experience are influenced by the actual sentiment or mood in which the subject is at the time of the æsthetic experience. It is a well-known fact that some moods and sentiments are completely antagonistic to these feelings and emotions of art. Thus, if we are in a mood of depression, we cannot realise, even imaginatively, the joyous feelings expressed by a work of art. In certain moods tragic emotions are unreal and even absurd. Saxinger finds an explanation for these facts in the theory that we have here not the influence of one feeling upon another, but the influence of intellectual processes of judgment. Certain judgments, with their accompanying feelings, make impossible the activities of assumption, and therefore the feelings of imagination. But precisely in this abstraction of the feelings from their intellectual presuppositions we have the weakness of the argument. Throughout our study of feeling and desire we have insisted that an essential characteristic of the feeling or desire, as the case may be, is its cognitive presupposition. Feelings, as we have shown, do not determine feelings causally, nor do feelings determine desire. All determination of affective-volitional meaning is through change in cognitive presuppositions. When, therefore, the presuppositions of one feeling make impossible or otherwise influence the presuppositions of another, we have influence of feeling upon feeling in the only sense that such an expression has meaning.

Finally, in discussing this influence of one type of feeling on the other, Saxinger has not considered at all the case of those phenomena, the affective signs of words, which he describes as feelings of imagination attaching directly to "substrate-ideas," and which, on our theory, are assumption-feelings of the second type, where the assumption is implicit, following upon presupposed judgmental habit. An examination of these phenomena would have shown him that they constantly influence his so-called real feelings and desires. Their influence is seen in two significant situations: (a) where they act as impelling sentiments or affective signs, negating, inhibiting particular desires and emotions; and (b) in those cases of subsumption of the ethical type where, giving their meaning directly to a particular reaction of desire or feeling, without any mediating associations, they increase its energy or affective-volitional meaning.

Throughout his entire discussion of these phenomena Saxinger has entirely failed to recognise the genetic relation of assumptions of both types, explicit and implicit, to judgment, a relation which the analysis of our first chapter made clear, and which has been persistently emphasised in the discussions that follow. Because of their genetic relations to particular judgment feelings, these assumption feelings are representative, both in a recognitive and anticipatory capacity, of actual feelings, and determine them in ways already described, and to be shown in more detail presently.[1]

2. *The Rôle of Affective Generals in Worth Determination.*

How, then, shall we characterise the rôle of these phases of affective experience in the continuity of affective-volitional meaning? If the results of this criticism of Saxinger are valid, if these phases do determine actual feelings, that is, immediate

---

[1] In this connection a paragraph from James's recent presidential address, *The Energies of Men*, is suggestive. "As certain objects awaken love, anger, or cupidity, so certain ideas naturally awaken the energies of loyalty, courage, endurance, or devotion. When these ideas are effective in an individual's life, their effect is often very great indeed. They may transfigure it, unlocking innumerable powers which, but for the idea would never have come into play. 'Fatherland,' 'The Union,' 'Holy Church,' the 'Monroe Doctrine,' 'Truth,' 'Science,' 'Liberty,' Garibaldi's phrase 'Rome or Death,' etc., are so many examples of energy-releasing abstract ideas. The *social* nature of all such phrases is an essential factor of their dynamic power. They are forces of detent in situations in which no other force produces equivalent effects, and each is a force of detent only in a specific group of men."

reactions to concrete situations, if the distinction between real feelings and feelings of the imagination is not ultimate, but the result of a neglect of their genetic relations, and if, finally, the inference as to the existence of distinct dispositions is not necessary, there is nothing in the way of our conception of an "affective logic." On the other hand, our structural analysis of these phases (and our functional analysis of their origin) has shown the validity of their description as generic forms of affectivity, and affords a basis for the concept of affective logic. We may now seek to develop in more detail the quasi-logical relation of these phases to the so-called actual feelings.

Our main proposition is that these affective generals and affective signs are the bearers of a funded meaning which is independent of their intensity, and that they represent particular feelings—in relations of substitution, subsumption, and mediation—in the continuity of valuation. It is this representative function which should be emphasised. Saxinger recognises, indeed, the representative character of feeling, but does not see that this involves a *real* function in the processes of valuation. "Assumption-feelings," he tells us, "take the place of feelings of value. The objects are measured according to their *subjective* worth when their existence or non-existence is assumed." Meinong is more alive to this real function of the assumption feelings of the two types in the processes of valuation. He makes a distinction between *Werthen* and *Werthalten*, and recognises a subjective *Werthen* in the case of assumption feelings and a more objective *Werthalten* in the case of judgment feelings.[1] He even goes so far as to give a certain advantage to these representative feelings in the process of valuation, in that they are often present when the conditions of judgment are impossible. The importance of these quasi-feelings, as he calls them, for the continuity of affective-volitional meaning is beyond dispute.

We may accordingly describe the function of affective generals and affective signs in the following general terms. The assumption-feeling, whether a feeling following upon an actual explicit assumption of the existence or non-existence of an object, or attached directly to a word or general idea, with its assumption of a corresponding objective, or connected with an habitual judgment which has passed over into an implicit assumption of existence, as in the case of belief, is

[1] Meinong, *Ueber Annahmen*, Leipzig, 1902, chapter VIII, §§ 53, 54, 55.

representative of our actual capacity for a particular worth feeling in a particular situation. If the assumption is explicit it tells us, in imagination, how we should feel in the actual situation. Attached directly to a word or general concept, it stands for a series of judgment-feelings in the past. Attached to an habitual judgment or belief of the present it is the representative of a judgment-disposition.

3. *Illustrations of the Rôle of Affective Generals in Worth Continuities.*

This general statement may be made more explicit by applying it to certain concrete cases of affective substitution, subsumption, and transition, with which our studies began. We may note especially the cases of ethical and æsthetic subsumptions where a generic phase of emotion, sentiment, mood, or affective sign gradually takes the place of particular explicit emotion, and assimilates new emotional attitudes to it, thus affording the basis for transitions of feeling.

In the case of ethical sanction we have a union of assumption and judgment. All affective abstracts are as such, as "intensity-less appreciation," assumption-feelings, while judgment-feelings are particular passions and emotions, and therefore show the aspects of intensity and multiplicity of content. Now in an ethical situation which is emotional an existential judgment is always presupposed and we have always a particular passion or emotion. But we are familiar with changes of ethical attitude where a new attitude becomes merged into an old, or where the old remains as a qualifying or sanctioning undertone of the new. Such cases we found in the phenomena of holy anger, or of a sexual love becoming predominantly maternal in its nature. Examination of these subsumptions (which we found are not mixed feelings), shows the situation to be of the following type. A new object, or new aspect of an old object, becomes the object of an existential judgment, and therefore of a new emotion, while the old judgment does not immediately vanish, but is represented by an assumption which has an affective abstract as its correlate. In the case of holy anger the existential judgment about God is in abeyance; is for the time represented by an assumption. The feeling corresponding to it is an abstract, generic religious feeling, while the concrete object is judged and reacted to emotionally. Now the importance of the analysis lies in the fact that, while the resultant attitude seems to be a fusion, as a matter of fact it is a real subsumption, for it is on the basis of the capacity of retaining the assumption that the union is possible. Should the attendant circumstances of the anger be such as to suppress the underlying religious assumption, the religious tone would fall out. In the other case, the presence of the feelings of the wife and the mother in the same attitude toward the husband, the existential judgments which call out the particular emotions are directed upon aspects of the object which appeal to the maternal instinct, but the disposition formed by the marital relation persists as an undertone in a feeling which has a vague assumption as its presupposition.

One more illustration, one frequently used as an extreme example of mixture of apparently opposing feelings, but which is really a limiting case of subsumption, will show the situation clearly. Rousseau's *Confessions*, which remains a classic of appreciative introspection, describes how the repeated assumption that Madame Martens was his mother passed over into a situation where mere imagination became almost belief, and the correlated filial feelings followed. But when the relation altered and became a liaison, at first the new feelings were coloured by the sanctities of the old attitude, which had now passed back into an assumption. Such a colouring did not, he tells us, and indeed could not, last. The assumption, with its accompanying feeling, was forced out, and in the process he suffered the pangs of remorse. In this extreme case, which indeed seems perhaps pathological, we have nevertheless a type of the emotional logic or fallacy, as the case may be, which is characteristic of all ethical sanction or re-adaptation. When, for instance, a man wakes to find his beliefs, which are largely emotional, changed, it means simply that the old belief has for a long time been merely an assumption which now at last a new judgment has finally suppressed.

Æsthetic subsumption is of a different type. Here the immediate object of the feeling attitude is merely *presented*, not judged, although there are cases where judgments enter in as partial presuppositions. In the cases of the *Lotos-Eaters* and the *Raven*, already described, the actual objects of the particular feelings are all objects of presentation, not of judgment. It would, however, as we have shown, be superficial analysis to deny the presence of conation and desire, at least dispositionally.

The Continuity of Affective-Volitional Meaning 141

In these cases the disposition is represented by an assumption, in the one case of the existence of the desired rest, and in the other of irrevocable fate. The mood in each case is the affective correlate of the underlying assumptions. Now genetically these assumptions are the products of previous actual desires and existential judgments—only thus could the objects of the assumptions have the interest to hold the æsthetic attention, but the possibility of holding all the various particular emotions in the unity of the mood is conditioned by the fact that the mood modifies the feelings connected with the specific imagery, arrests their tendency to pass over into specific actual feelings, i.e., to acquire an intensity which would disturb the æsthetic illusion.

CHAPTER VI

THE LAWS OF VALUATION

I. Laws of Valuation—Their Nature and Range of Application

ALL worth analysis and theory has as its ultimate aim the discovery of laws according to which objects, goods, or worths are valued relatively to each other, are set in equivalence or in a scale of affective-volitional meaning. The processes which underlie any system of worth objects are acts of preference, and since these acts of preference, these judgments, express the funded meaning of the objects, in order to discover the laws of preference it is necessary to examine the psychological laws inherent in the processes through which this funded meaning is acquired. If the funded meaning of an object is its desirability, and if this desirability is determined by actual feeling as qualified by the worth disposition presupposed and by the type of cognitive presupposition which connects the object with the disposition, then the psychological laws of valuation are the laws governing the change in actual feeling as determined by changes in its presuppositions actual and dispositional.

There already exist certain formulations of such laws, developed for the specific purposes of economics. Upon the assumption that worth feeling is identical with pleasure-causation, and consequently upon the further assumption that all worth objects can be analysed into sensational elements and the worth of the objects be reduced to a sum of these sensation-feelings, these laws have been extended uncritically to all types of valuation. But if the relation of the object to its worth feeling is not causal—and this was certainly the conclusion of our earlier studies, and if, further, some of these objects are, strictly speaking, not sensations or presentations at all, but meanings of these elements, then these laws do not necessarily hold for all types of worth process. Nevertheless, since these formulations *have* been made, although upon an inadequate analysis of worth experience, and therefore have a definite place in worth theory, a critical examination of their foundations and the extent of their application constitutes our first problem.

1. *The Laws of Valuation applicable to Extra-Economic Values.*

These psychological laws have been sought primarily by the science of economics for the purpose of measuring the preferability of one object over another within a *restricted field of goods*. The method of investigation is to study the laws of preferability growing out of the laws governing the consumption of separate goods by an individual—i.e., the laws of subjective value—on the assumption, made, apparently, by most writers in economics, that these values are unmodified by the individual's participation in the economic activities of a group. The laws of objective value may then be developed from the laws of subjective value. In general it may be said that this means of simplifying the problem has justified itself in the results attained, and in investigating the larger problem of valuation in general we shall first study the laws governing the worth feeling of the individual apart from those complications introduced by participation in the worth feelings of others, leaving this aspect of the problem to be treated separately in another place.

The investigation of the laws of valuation has been described as a larger problem than that contemplated by the economic doctrine of consumption. The meaning of this will appear when we reflect that, while valuation is feeling-attitude toward objects in general, physical and psychical, economic valuation is concerned only with those feeling attitudes towards objects, appreciation of which is conditioned by consumption. Consumption is but a special case of appreciation. Although other modes of appreciation, such as the ethical and æsthetic, may enter in to modify the worths of consumption, and thus to change the total worth or funded meaning of the object, they are nevertheless, strictly speaking, no longer worths of consumption. The general term, appreciation, includes, therefore, besides the worth feelings which arise in the process of consumption of physical goods, other feelings which have as their objects psychical qualities of a higher order, growing out of the physical objects by processes of perceptual and ideal construction. Such are the æsthetic worths imputed to a feast as the result of arrangement of the objects of consumption in an harmonious manner. Such also are the values which we describe as cleanliness and thrift, objects of appreciation which emerge in processes of consumption, and which, although qualities inhering in these processes, may nevertheless be abstracted from them and become the objects of appreciation. The laws of valuation must take into account the laws governing the change in worth feelings corresponding to these different types of objects.

But valuation, and therefore its laws, must include a wider range of feelings than these. Out of the elementary processes of consumption and appreciation are developed other ideal objects and constructs (not objects of sensation and presentation at all, but merely of judgment and assumption), which may both modify the primary worths of appreciation and also come to be independently valued. The worth of an object of consumption, as it is being enjoyed, may be modified by instrumental judgments as to its utility for other purposes, or by judgments regarding its exchange value as determined by reference to its demand by other subjects. Likewise the simple "condition" worths of appreciation, cleanliness and thrift or other qualities of this nature, may become the objects of a new type of feelings when they are acknowledged as attributes of the self; they become psychical objects of personal worth. Our feeling of the worth of these psychical objects may be further modified in a significant manner by subsidiary judgments regarding the existence of these objects in social groups or in society at large, in some cases heightened by judgment of their absence.

All these facts lead us to recognise the extent of the phenomena which the laws of valuation must include in their generalisations, the variety of objects of worth feelings, and the variety of processes and attitudes which these feelings presuppose. Our problem, from the standpoint of a general theory of value, is to examine the psychological laws of feeling and its modifications, developed for the purposes of economics, and to determine the extent of their application to other types and objects of valuation.

2. *Laws of Valuation as Laws of Affective-Volitional Meaning— Classification and Interpretation.*

These psychological laws may in general be described as laws of relativity of worth feeling. They are formulæ describing the modifications in worth feeling following upon modifications of the dispositional presuppositions of the feeling. The first, the law of the Threshold, states the fact that the power of an object, or rather of a given quantity of an object, to call out worth feeling and judgment, is a function of a disposition created by previous feelings. The second, the law of Diminishing Value, is a statement of the fact that the change in the capacity of an object for valuation is a function of the effect of previous worth feelings. Quantity of actual feeling, whether in the form of repeated reactions or of intensity of a single reaction, diminishes the capacity of the disposition for further actualisation in the form of explicit feeling and judgment. The third law, that of Complementary Values, is a formula for the description of the modification of the capacity of an object for calling out worth feeling, as determined by the combination of the primary object with other objects. Under certain conditions the working of the law of Diminishing Value is thus modified and the value of the object increased.

The interrelation of these laws is apparent. The threshold of worth judgment is determined by both the second and third laws. The second law, working alone, has the effect of raising the threshold, but this effect is modified by the factor introduced by the third law. It is, accordingly, the effect of these laws in determining the value, or affective-volitional meaning, of different types of objects that constitutes the ultimate object of their study. They are further interrelated in that they constitute the laws, formulate the conditions, of psychical *progression* or *value movement*. Movements to new objects, or changes in attitude toward old objects, of desire and feeling are to be interpreted in terms of these laws.

Finally, it is to be observed that these laws are descriptive formulæ for the effect of actualisation of a disposition, in actual feeling, upon the strength of the disposition presupposed, and therefore upon its capacity for further actualisation. When this is recognised, the importance of our preceding analysis of the presuppositions of worth feeling, the types of acts through

L

which feelings are actualised, becomes apparent. The actual effect of these different presuppositions, presumptions, judgments, assumptions, upon the feeling, and its corresponding disposition, is a problem for specific analysis. It is only in the case of dispositions corresponding to the feeling-tone of sensation that the relation can be conceived as one of direct causal stimulation. In the case of feelings of value the relation is of another type, and the underlying dispositions must be clearly distinguished.

II. THE LAW OF THE THRESHOLD—ITS GENERAL MEANING

With these general considerations in mind, we may turn to a study of the first principle of relativity of worth feeling, that which we have described as the principle of the *Threshold*.

In general this principle is an expression of the fact that the power of an object to call out a feeling of worth, or a feeling of worth difference, depends not upon the object alone, but upon the feeling or conative dispositions of the subject as well. If this principle is put into quantitative form, the question relates to the least quantity of the object which will produce a modification in the feeling of worth. The importance of this principle is obvious. All worth theory is concerned with the determination of the principles of relative preferability of objects, that is their relative importance or affective-volitional meaning. In order that such degrees of preferability may be established, it is necessary that fixed starting-points for such estimation should be found at the limits of relative worth, i.e. where relative worth passes over into worthlessness on the one hand, or into absolute unlimited worth on the other. These upper and lower limits of relative worth we may, on the analogy of the laws of intensity, call the upper and lower thresholds.

This concept of limits has been defined with accuracy for the limited sphere of consumption and utilisation. The upper and lower limits of valuation in this sphere have been described respectively as the "existence-minimum" and the "final utility."

But that this concept of limits is susceptible of extension, of a much wider range of application in worth analysis and theory, a very superficial reflection makes evident. The objects of worth judgment, we have seen, may be physical objects of consumption, or qualities of these objects for appreciation; they may be psychical objects, such as acts of persons, or affective-volitional dispositions expressed by those acts. If we take the second group of objects, acts and dispositions presupposed by these acts, and consider the ethical judgments called out by them, we find that the same act, or the amount of disposition disclosed by that act, may have worth or be worthless according to the disposition presupposed in the subject of the judgment. Thus, as an object of personal worth it may rise above the threshold of value, when it has not reached the minimum required to call out the social moral judgment. So, also, a given act may call out a judgment of disapproval, personal or social, when it is not sufficient to rise above the threshold of legal judgment. There are thus, so to speak, qualitatively different thresholds marking off the different spheres of meaning in which the judgments are made. To these correspond different modifications of feeling, the actualisation of which requires different types of objects or different amounts of the same object. This fact finds illustration even in the case of objects of strictly economic valuation. A physical object of mere *condition* worth, the value of which consists solely in its capacity of satisfying some desire of the senses, may, with increase or decrease in amount, call out feelings and judgments of possession or of instrumental value which modify the worth feeling, not only in the direction of degree, but also by introducing new aspects of quality.

From these facts several important consequences follow. In the first place, by discovering the upper and lower limits of a given type of valuation—the boundaries within which differences of worth are determined wholly by differences in quantity of the object, we are enabled to mark off the different levels of valuation. The qualitative thresholds mark the limits of these regions. Thus we shall distinguish thresholds of condition worth of appreciation, thresholds of personal worth of characterisation, and thresholds of social worth of participation and utilisation. In the second place, in determining these limits and their mutual relations, we have a basis for the analysis, not only of the laws of preference within a given sphere of meaning, but also of the laws of value-movement from one sphere of meaning to another, and therefore the laws of preference of one type of objects over another.

The different levels of valuation and the different objects

of value are the products of perceptual and ideal constructions in the process of acquirement of meaning. While the thresholds represent conceptual limits within which the valuation of a given type of objects moves, they nevertheless correspond to actual appreciatively recognisable differences in feeling-attitude, determined by difference in presuppositions. A genetic study of these presuppositions, and therefore of the expectations or *demands* to which they give rise, will enable us to fix the limits of these demands.

With this understanding of the larger significance of the concept of the threshold in worth theory, we may now return to a detailed study of the psychology of the economic threshold of condition worths.

2. *Economic Thresholds—The Existence-Minimum and Final Utility.*

The limits within which the relative valuation of an object of condition worth moves may be described as the "existence-minimum," and the point of "final utility."

The minimum of existence is that conceptual point at which absolute value passes over into relative value. Until the minimum of a given good which is necessary to existence is reached, there can be no estimation of relative value, for any quantum of the good has absolute value and is capable of calling out indefinite sacrifice. The good has no substitute, and it is only among goods with "capacity of substitution" that relative worth or degrees of preferability can be established. The upper threshold of relative value in consumption is, then, the first increment of satisfaction which rises above the indispensable *minimum*. The psychological meaning of this concept of the upper threshold is to be found in the fact that until this point is reached the entire personality is involved, that is, about the fundamental want or desire, whether it be for food or warmth, or any other object, the entire system of conative tendencies is concentrated, through arrest of the fundamental desire, and is directed toward the one object. When the minimum of existence is reached, and the tension or arrest of the fundamental tendency is relaxed, the estimation of worth becomes *relative*, that is, each successive increment of the good is estimated with reference to the importance of the isolated particular wants and desires. It need scarcely be said that for many goods there is no such upper threshold or minimum of existence. They find substitutes or otherwise cease to be desired long before this point is reached, but their place or relative importance in a system of values is determined by their relations to certain fundamental goods without capacity of substitution, relations which become apparent as soon as our habitual valuations are disturbed and we are forced to ultimate preferences.

The *lower* threshold, or the point of *final utility*, is again that conceptual point at which the minimum of worth tends to pass over into worthlessness. It is the smallest quantity of the good which has the capacity of satisfying the least important of the subsidiary wants or purposes of the subject. Psychologically expressed, it corresponds to the most remote of the subsidiary conative tendencies connected with the fundamental to which the good ministers. Now, whether any such point of final utility actually exists in any concrete experience or not, it is, like the minimum of existence, at least an ideal limit useful in describing actual processes of valuation.[1]

In the case before us—which is concerned with the instrumental values of economics, and therefore with worth feelings which have as their presuppositions, in addition to judgments of existence and non-existence, subsidiary utility judgments, it is clear that these points represent limits of relative instrumental valuation. Thus the lower threshold, the quantum of minimal worth, represents that point at which the judgment of its existence or non-existence has the least importance, that is where, with this judgment, goes an instrumental judgment referring it to the least significant purpose. Any quantity below that is worthless, or is valued, if at all, in some other attitude, i.e., intrinsically. Thus to the rich man the small coin, a penny, may be instrumentally worthless, while as a part of an individualised whole, his wealth, it may have an intrinsic worth.

---

[1] The use of the term Final Utility in this way requires some explanation and perhaps apology. As introduced by Jevons, and employed by economists generally, it describes the intensity of desire satisfied by the last increment of a commodity purchased or consumed, i.e., *last in any given process of acquisition or consumption*, and may fall far short of the hypothetical last increment before worthlessness is reached. It is therefore only relatively final and is identical with the concept of Marginal Increment or Marginal Utility which is now gradually displacing it. Since, however, Final Utility in this sense is held to be determined by the law of Diminishing Utility, according to which the value of any stimulus is the degree of satisfaction obtained by its last repetition, and therefore varies with the amount or rate with which the stimulus is furnished, final utility as marginal *tends* to become identical with final in the sense of minimal value. The very fact that the somewhat inept use of the term as identical with Marginal Utility is passing into disuse, may perhaps serve as an excuse for the special application made of it in this connection.

The point of minimal or final utility is, then, the psychological point where all relative instrumental judgments fall away or at least are not called out. The minimum of existence, on the other hand, the point where relative valuation passes over into absolute, is psychologically the point of arrest or suppression of all instrumental judgments, where value becomes intrinsic. We have at this point the extreme of arrest, and, as a consequence, concentration of all subsidiary tendencies or dispositions about the fundamental. The feeling, in this case passion, has all the acquired meaning of the other dispositions, but it is implicit and immediate, all relative judgments being suppressed.[1]

There are two points, therefore, at which relative and instrumental value passes over into intrinsic: (*a*) the upper threshold where the value becomes *practically* absolute; and (*b*) the lower threshold, where minimal worth passes into worthlessness *unless* the minimum in some way acquires intrinsic worth. The first of these situations we may easily understand. The transgredient reference of the feeling to presupposed conative dispositions has become an impellent mode of quasi-obligation. Desire and feeling are unconditional, undetermined by any specific particular end. Here, we shall find later, arise certain quasi-obligatory feelings even in the sphere of economic values. The other situation—where the object which is worthless or below the lower threshold of instrumental value, acquires intrinsic worth, requires more detailed analysis.

[1] This concept of upper and lower limits of relative valuation has been developed for the purpose of making possible descriptive formulæ for concrete worth attitudes. To what extent do these conceptual points correspond to concrete situations? What are these situations in terms of our analysis? Have they actual correlates or are they purely conceptual? It is obvious that, although possible, concrete psychological dispositions represented by the conceptual points are rarely actual moments in experience. We approach them, but they always tend to remain ideal limits. In what sense then do they enter as actual determinants into experience? Do they at all? They do, it would appear, and in this way. Although the actual feeling correlated with these thresholds is scarcely realisable, for the limiting judgments which constitute their presuppositions are largely hypothetical, nevertheless such judgments are frequently represented by assumptions, and the feelings following upon these assumptions complete the worth series. Of this concept of the substitution of assumption feelings, as affective signs in the continuity of real valuation, we shall make important applications later. Here it is necessary merely to note the phenomenon, and to observe that while these substituted feelings lack the intensities which they would have in real situations where the presuppositions are existential judgments, they have nevertheless the worth suggestion, in this case the transgredient reference, which gives them a functional place in actual valuation.

3. Modification of the Lower Threshold through Acquired Meanings —Complementary Values.

The acquirement of intrinsic worth on the part of an object or quantity of an object, in itself below the threshold of value, must be viewed as a modification of feeling brought about by inclusion of a new presupposition. It is already apparent that an object, the mere existence of which does not call out worth feeling, may rise above the threshold when it is related through instrumental judgment to other worth objects and their feelings. It is also true—and this is the phenomenon with which we are here concerned, that a worthless object may acquire intrinsic value through relation to an individuated whole which is assumed to exist, and which has intrinsic value. Such acquired values may be described at *complementary*, and to the more detailed study of such values we shall devote a later section. Here we may content ourselves with a study of the manner in which they modify the threshold. In the case cited, the simple intrinsic appreciation of the penny, when it has no instrumental worth for the subject, is a worth feeling with presuppositions different in certain important points from the threshold of instrumental worth, namely, in the subsidiary presuppositions. In the place of the instrumental judgments and their feelings, which the object in itself does not call out, there enters as a substitute an assumption-feeling, having as its presupposition an envisaging, and momentary assumption of existence, of wealth as an individualised whole, of which the minute object, though instrumentally worthless, is a part. That which raises the minute object above the threshold of value in such a case is not the intensity of the immediate feeling, but the subsumption of the judgment-feeling under the assumption-feeling described.

A like phenomenon is observable in other regions of valuation than the economic. Thus in the ethical sphere we frequently find that the theft of a pin, or some other minute commission or omission, although utterly insignificant instrumentally, may call out feelings of intrinsic worth or *un*-worth. Here, again, it is not the mere existence or non-existence of the act which calls out the worth feeling, but the subsumption of the act under the general concept imputes to the act all the worth suggestion of the affective abstract which the assumption of the existence of the object, corresponding to the concept, involves.

Similarly, in the sphere of the æsthetic, we shall find that an element, worthless in itself, may, as part of an *intuitively* individuated whole, acquire the value of the whole. The feeling may be said to expand to include the element, in itself worthless. With the characteristics of intuitive individuation and with the nature of complementary æsthetic values we are not here concerned. It will be sufficient to note that even in the region of economic objects of condition worths this law is at work. In certain quasi-æsthetic combinations of utilities—as in a festal meal or the style of a suit of raiment—a detail, valueless in itself, as a single utility, may acquire an extraordinary value.

From the illustrations before us the general principle is apparent, that an object below the threshold of value may become the object of intrinsic valuation when there is imputed to it the worth which comes with the assumption of the existence or non-existence of an individuated whole of which it is a part. The ordinary explanation of this fact is in terms of association, the rise above the threshold being conceived as due to a summation of minute dispositional feelings below the threshold, aroused through the stimulation of dispositions associated with the affective disposition corresponding to the primary object. This concept of mere summation, which is inevitable, when worth feeling is defined as pleasure, is, however, untenable.[1] The modification of worth feeling which follows upon the intrinsic ethical or æsthetic valuation of the object, is not a summation of hypothetical feeling elements, but a new total feeling following upon an apprehension of a new-founded object either conceptual, or, as in the case of the æsthetic, intuitively given, which is the object of assumption. We are concerned here with a phenomenon of subsumption of feeling, not summation, with a change in cognitive presuppositions, not change in stimulation. The worth threshold, in contrast to the simple hedonic, must be viewed as cognitive in character.

4. *The Independent Variability of Hedonic and Worth Thresholds.*

The threshold of value, whether of simple appreciation with its intrinsic reference or of utility with its instrumental refer-

---

[1] Höffler, *Psychologie*, Vienna, 1897, p. 448.

The Laws of Valuation

ence, has, it will be seen, a cognitive character, which distinguishes it from the merely hedonic threshold. The confusion of these two conceptions, a procedure fairly common in worth analysis and theory, has led to serious fallacies which can be avoided only by insistence upon this point. The independent variability of worth feeling and of pleasantness and unpleasantness, already pointed out in a preceding chapter,[1] is further confirmed by our study of the worth threshold. For it is possible that, as Krüger pointed out, an object may call out a fleeting pleasantness or unpleasantness or momentary impulse without crossing the threshold, and it is, on the other hand, equally possible for an object to rise above the worth threshold without an appreciable affective disturbance.

As an illustration of the first possibility we may consider the case, an entirely possible one certainly, where a trivial musical phrase in its aspect of mere auditory stimulation (or, still better, a momentary organic sensation) may call out a fleeting pleasantness or unpleasantness which does not reach the point of worth judgment. We are conscious of the hedonic change, but there has not been that totalisation of affective attitude through cognitive reference to the object which constitutes the presupposition of worth feeling. The second possibility, the rise of an object above the worth threshold without accompanying pleasure causation, is illustrated by the many cases where a disposition to worth judgment has been formed on the basis of immediate pleasure-causation, and where the judgment of the existence of the object then calls out worth feeling even when the object fails, although sensed or presented, to give pleasure. Thus when the point of satiety has been reached, it frequently happens that actual enjoyment of the object (of taste, for instance), or imaginative presentation of its enjoyment, is no longer accompanied by pleasure, but the judgment that the object still exists, or that it does not exist, may call out feelings of value.

This principle of the independent variability of the simple hedonic and worth thresholds is further substantiated when we turn from the stimulus-threshold to the threshold of difference. There may be appreciable differences in the hedonic intensity without changes in worth feeling, and changes in the worth attitude without appreciable changes in hedonic intensity. For the first of these possibilities a simple illustration will suffice.

[1] Chapter III.

In the apprehension of an object, more especially a work of art, we may distinguish between the emotional attitude toward the object as a whole, and the particular affective tones of the elements, as attention passes from one phase to another. Thus there may be appreciable changes in feeling-tone which are sufficient to lead to movement from one aspect to another in readaptation of attention, but not sufficient to lead to that readaptation of judgmental attitude which is presupposed in value movement—or in change of worth attitude toward the object as a whole. Similarly, repeated acts of apprehension may lead to appreciable changes in feeling-tone, due to fatigue of the nervous dispositions connected with sense stimulation, without necessarily leading to a change in worth attitude, that is to the change in cognitive presuppositions presupposed in such change of attitude. The worth feeling toward the object, founded on these elements of presentation, presupposes another disposition. These phenomena, we shall find, are of considerable importance when we come to consider the second law of valuation.

A similar situation exists in the case of economic feelings of value, that is where the feeling follows upon instrumental judgments. Let us take the concrete case of an individual in the enjoyment of any object which causes pleasure. Within the total attitude, which may vary in time length, there may be appreciable differences in pleasure, as, for instance, in the consumption of a food, without cognisable change in valuation until there has entered a change of attitude, that is a change in the judgment presuppositions of the feeling, through the judgmental reference of the object to other purposes, to purposes of the future, etc. Here again cognisable differences in worth feeling do not coincide with the least perceptible hedonic changes.

The second possibility—variation in the worth attitude without variation in intensity of pleasure—may also be illustrated from the sphere of feelings of economic value. From the point of view of pleasure it is a matter of indifference whether, besides the quantity of the object being enjoyed, other objects of the same nature exist or do not exist, but for the worth feeling it is of considerable moment. The inclusion within the presuppositions of the feeling attitude of such accompanying judgments may bring about a cognisable difference in the feeling of value, while the feelings of simple pleasure remain the same.

In these phenomena of difference in variability of the threshold of difference for pleasure-causation and the threshold of difference for feelings of value, we have a situation analogous to that which has been pointed out in the sphere of sensation and perception. It has been argued that there also a distinction must be made between the threshold of difference for sensation and for perception. Within limits a stimulus may be varied without producing an appreciable difference in the object cognised. There is a difference for sensation, but not for perception. This means that the perception of difference involves the acquirement upon the part of the sensations of a meaning which expresses itself in readaptation, in modification of attitude in the form of judgment. Between these changes in meaning, or attitude, are changes for sensation which are not significant for cognition.[1] In a somewhat similar way it may be said that worth feeling and feeling of worth difference belong to the cognitive level, i.e., are emotion, sentiment, and mood, and not the hypothetical element of pleasure. There may, therefore, conceivably be change in the hedonic redundancies without any change in the value reaction. This means, simply, that variations may be superficial in the sense that they do not involve any totalisation of consciousness in a unitary affective attitude. They do not penetrate into or involve the personality.

The formulation of this distinction—between the hedonic and worth thresholds, involves important consequences for our theory. For, the fact having been established that the rise of an object above the threshold of worth or worth difference involves cognition of affective-volitional meaning, transgredient and immanental reference, and therefore judgment or assumption as presuppositions, it will now be necessary, in examining the psychological laws operating to modify these thresholds, to study each type of worth feeling for itself, and to refuse to extend uncritically the laws modifying pleasure-causation, and therefore the hedonic threshold, to worth feeling and the perception of worth differences in general.

[1] Stumpf, *Tonpsychologie*, Vol. I, p. 33. Also Stout, *Analytical Psychology*, Vol. I, p. 48, and *Manual of Psychology*, p. 120.

III. THE LAW OF DIMINISHING (OR LIMITING) VALUE: CRITICAL STUDY OF ITS PSYCHOLOGICAL BASIS—INTERPRETATION

1. *Its Historical Significance.*

The preceding study of the concept of the threshold of value, and its relation to the hedonic threshold, has made it clear that for an object to call out a feeling, or a feeling of difference, of worth or value, a change in its cognitive presuppositions is necessary. Whether in a given psychological situation a given object or quantity of an object will rise above the threshold of worth feeling, or feeling of worth difference, depends upon the attitude or disposition (conative and judgmental) created by previous valuations. The problem immediately arises as to the existence of definite laws governing this relativity, whether any factors can be discovered which modify in a uniform way the dispositional presuppositions of worth feeling, and thus the worth feelings themselves.

The theory of value developed for the purposes of economics has formulated a law of relativity for utility in consumption, basing its formulation upon the psychological laws governing the modification of "sensation-feelings" and their corresponding dispositions. The factors of frequency of stimulation, quantity of stimulation, and limitation of capacity for stimulation, in producing the effects of habit, or dulling of sensitivity and of satiety, afford the psychological basis for the general law of Diminishing Value and for the more specific law of Marginal Utility connected with it. On the assumption that all feeling of value is identical with pleasure, it would follow that this law of relativity would apply to all types of worth feeling.

But on this point there is difference of opinion. Thus, on the one hand, we find Ehrenfels contending for an extension of the principle of *Grenz-nutzen* to a more general principle of *Grenz-frommen*, while Kreibig maintains that this principle is a special formulation of the general law of relativity, applicable only to the limited sphere of the instrumental values of economic goods. It is clear that the answer to this question depends upon the more fundamental problem—whether these psychological factors which affect the dispositions underlying feelings of pleasure act in precisely the same manner upon the conative and judgmental presuppositions of worth feelings, whether habit and satiety which correspond to the factors of repetition and quantity have the same functional meaning for worth feelings as for pleasure-causation. These questions can be answered only in the light of a psychological analysis of these factors.

As a preliminary to this analysis we must examine more fully the formulation of this principle of relativity, and bring to light the psychological assumptions upon which the law rests. The first formulations go back to Bentham and Bernoulli.[1] The problem of Bentham was the relation of wealth to happiness, and it arose in connection with the question of the relation of the distribution of goods to his "greatest-happiness" principle. As a result of his analysis, he develops, in the *Panomial Fragments*, the following principle which he dignifies with the name of an axiom: "The effect of wealth in the production of happiness goes on diminishing as the quantity by which the wealth of one man exceeds that of another goes on increasing ; in other words, the quantity of happiness produced by a particle of wealth (each particle being of the same magnitude) will be less and less at each particle ; the second will produce less than the first, the third less than the second, and so on." The common element in his various formulations of the principle may be expressed in the following way. The minimum of existence being assumed as given, when this quantity of the good increases in any constant relation, happiness, the primary worth, increases, other things being equal, within certain limits, but not in the same proportion ; rather is the rate of increase of happiness in relation to wealth a constantly lessening one, although Bentham does not formulate any law governing the rate of decrease. Bernoulli's famous law also assumes the minimum of existence, and he finds, as does Bentham, the increase of happiness, in proportion to the increase of wealth, a constantly lessening quantity. Bernoulli goes beyond Bentham, however, in attempting to formulate the law quantitatively. Happiness is conceived to grow in arithmetical proportion as the quantity of wealth increases geometrically. Finally Gossen, under whose name the law of Diminishing Value has largely entered into Political Economy, formulates the law in the following words, thus leading up to the concept of marginal or final utility: "With

---

[1] For a general sketch of the history of these formulations see Kraus, *Zur Theorie des Wertes*, Halle, 1901, chap. IV ("Grundlagen der modernen Werttheorie"), especially pp. 58-69.

the increase of the quantity of the object the worth of each additional increment must suffer decrease until finally zero is reached"; or, again, "The first increment of an object of value has the highest worth, the second less worth, until finally worthlessness is reached."[1]

These formulations of the law of Diminishing Value all agree in the general conception that the satisfaction of desire or pleasure, when it is increased quantitatively, finally results in the loss of capacity for that desire (and with it feeling)—and, therefore, in movement of desire to new objects, and the formation of new dispositions. For this reason, in view of the functional aspect of the law, as a cause of new adaptations, we shall describe it henceforth as the law of *Limiting Value*.

2. *Psychological Basis of the Law—The more General Laws of (a) Dulling of Sensitivity with Repetition, and (b) Satiety—Critical Study.*

When we seek for the psychological basis of the law, we find that all these formulations of Bentham, Bernoulli, and Gossen alike, assume the identity of worth feeling with pleasure, and therefore the dependent variability of the two. All that was necessary, therefore, to establish psychologically this general principle of relativity was an appeal to the laws governing the physiological conditions of sensitivity to pleasantness and unpleasantness. Bentham definitely based his formulation of the principle upon the more fundamental psycho-physical laws of dulling of sensitivity through repetition and habit, satiety, and limitation of capacity of appropriation; and Fechner likewise, in subsuming the law of Bernoulli under his more general law of sensitivity, does so on the assumption of the universal applicability of these laws.

But this assumption immediately arouses suspicion of its soundness, and cannot be admitted without careful scrutiny. If, as our studies of the threshold indicated, pleasure-causation and worth feeling may vary independently, i.e., the intension and extension (depth and breadth in the personality) may vary independently of the intensity and multiplicity of the hedonic redundancies, and if there may be, to that extent, intensity-less acts of appreciation, the presuppositions of which are conative

[1] Gossen, *Entwickelung der Gesetze des Menschlichen Verkehrs und der daraus fliessenden Regeln für Menschliches Handeln*, 1853, p. 31.

and judgmental, and not sense stimuli, it would follow that these psycho-physical laws governing sensation-feelings, and the general principle of relativity built upon them, should not be uncritically extended to judgment and assumption feelings— that is to worth feelings, without a special analysis in each case. In fact, Fechner himself, even on the assumption that pleasure and feeling of value are identical, warns us against any overhasty generalisation of the principles governing the pleasure values of simple sensation to cover more complex feelings. In the *Vorschule der Aesthetik* (p. 76) he says: "A really mathematical, merely psycho-physical measure of the intensity of pleasantness and unpleasantness could be found only in connection with a knowledge of the universal ultimate cause of pleasantness and unpleasantness; until then it can be nothing more than an estimate of more or less."

Much more, then, if the relative independence of pleasure-causation and worth feeling be established, is a separate examination of the application of these laws to the latter class of feelings necessitated. As Brentano truly says: "For all psychical phenomena which have their grounds in psychical occurrences within the organism (not in external stimuli), or are called forth by other psychical phenomena, a measure of intensity fails." It is entirely conceivable, for instance, that in total attitudes of appreciation, or valuation, two components of the total feeling may be distinguished, the worth feeling which has psychical presuppositions, conative tendency and judgment, and the hedonic redundancies with their sensational conditions both organic and peripheral. To the latter aspect the laws of dulling of sensitivity and satiety might apply, while for the former, already found to be independently variable, the factors of repetition and quantity might have another significance. It is at least conceivable that increase in depth and breadth of feeling tone might go on side by side with the reduction of the intensity and multiplicity of the hedonic redundancies.

(a) *The Law of Dulling of Sensitivity. Critical Analysis—Its Application Limited to Sensation Feelings and the Redundancies of Feelings of Value.*

The two principles of dulling of sensitivity and satiety are often confused, and treated as identical because of their having the same practical effect upon the estimation of the utility of objects of consumption corresponding to isolated organic wants or tendencies. Thus in estimating the utility of a given increment of sugar, it is a matter of indifference whether the lowered utility imputed to it is the result of diminution of desire, through lowering of nervous sensitivity by repetition of stimulation, or whether it is the consequence of the peculiar organic sensations of satiety produced by the quantity of the stimulus. The practical consequences for the estimation of utility are the same. But when we come to examine the psychology of the two phenomena, differences appear of such a nature as to make separate studies of the two cases necessary.

It was, we have seen, to the effect of repetition of satisfaction of desire in producing habit and dulling of sensitivity (and to its corollary, limitation of capacity of appropriation) that Bentham chiefly appealed to substantiate his general principle of Limiting Value. Repetition of stimulation so modifies the physiological or dispositional conditions of the feeling as to change the relative intensity of the feeling in the direction indicated by the law. It is clear that the degree of worth feeling which follows upon the judgment or assumption of the existence or non-existence of any object will be determined by the disposition created by previous acts of consumption or appreciation, but it does not follow that repetition will have the same effect upon all these dispositions. As the presuppositions of the different feelings vary, so on the side of the object, the factor of frequency or quantity may vary in meaning. We must therefore consider the influence of the factor of repetition upon the different types of feeling separately.

The effect of repetition upon one type of worth feeling, the case where the feeling of value is conditioned by preceding sensation-feelings, is simple and evident. An object which has the capacity to satisfy a sense-tendency becomes an object of worth when it is judged or assumed to exist or not exist. The sensation feelings which arise in the process of consumption are not worth feelings, but the worth feelings are determined solely by the dispositions created by the processes of consumption. The repetition of stimulation, the dulling of sensitivity, lowers the capacity of judgment or assumption of existence to call out our worth feeling, for the reason that, in this case, the modifications of sensation-feelings are the sole determinants of the worth feelings. Thus sugar is an object of worth because it satisfies a sense-tendency, and the stimulation of the sense-organ gives pleasure. But the fatigue of nervous substance through successive stimulations reduces the sensitivity. There is, to be sure, a limited degree to which fusion of sensations, and the simultaneous moderate stimulation of different sense-tendencies, may produce a greater degree of pleasure for a longer time. But this qualitative sublimation of the gross quantitative factor is possible only within very narrow limits. Ultimately sensitivity is dulled, and the judgment or assumption of the existence of the stimulating object fails to call out worth feelings, unless the judgment is modified by secondary instrumental judgments. Conative activity is arrested, and we have value movement toward another object.

When, however, we turn from immediate pleasure-causation to the study of worth feelings, that is feelings where the relation of the object to the disposition is not one of immediate stimulation, but is mediated by presumption, judgment, and assumption, it is not so certain that the principle of habit or dulling of sensitivity can be applied directly as a description of changes in worth feeling. We must rather examine in detail the effect of repetition on each type of feeling.

Let us first consider certain feelings of simple appreciation, following upon presumption or existential judgment. Personal fame, as expressed in the applause of others, is normally the object of worth feeling. This feeling is not the result of the stimulation in the applause, but of a judgment of existence of an ideal object which the applause expresses. Repetition of this applause and of the accompanying judgment is ordinarily followed by emotional indifference. That which was first recognised with intensity of emotion is finally recognised without emotional disturbance. Or again, we may take the case of a man (e.g., a miner) whose occupation brings him face to face with constant danger. The judgment of the existence of the danger is at first accompanied by more or less intense emotional disturbance, but with repetition of the judgment his sense of danger becomes dulled. It would appear, then, that repetition of judgment feelings involves dulling of sensitivity, and therefore diminution of worth feeling.

The first part of this inference is certainly true, and the latter seems to be a necessary corollary from the first. But before admitting its necessity we must observe more closely what actually takes place in such cases. The phenomena are more complex than appears at first sight. Can we logically infer that, because of this dulling of sensitivity, the conative dispositions corresponding to these two objects, fame and danger, have been equally diminished, and that the objects have lost their worth, positive or negative? I think not. For, in the first place, the sensitivity which is dulled is the emotional disturbance, and this owes its first intensity to contrast, to the disturbance of some presumption or judgment habit which preceded, and to the effort involved in the readaptation incident to realisation in a new judgment of the existence of the formerly non-existent object. With the growth of conviction the emotional disturbance disappears and the intensity of sensitivity diminishes. But it does not follow that the meaning of the feeling, its transgredient or immanental reference, its depth and breadth in the personality, has diminished. As a matter of fact, experience shows us an entirely different situation. When once the conviction of the existence of the fame or the danger, as the case may be, has been formed, the feeling as sentiment, mood, or affective sign is always present as an undertone in the emotional experience of the person, colouring all his worth judgments. It constitutes a presupposition of all succeeding experience.

The psychological explanation of this fact is to be found in the substitution of assumption, implicit or explicit, for judgment. In another connection[1] it was shown that existential judgment is of the relational type, that is, it appears only after arrest, is association after disjunction. In all other cases reality is assumed. In all existential judgment, adaptation, and therefore emotional disturbance, is involved, with its corresponding intensity. As with repetition the judgment passes over into assumption, the intensity decreases, the energy involved in emotional disturbance is used up, and dulling of sensitivity follows. But this sensitivity is only one aspect of the feeling-attitude. When judgment has given place to assumption, with its feeling of the imagination, its generic sentiment or affective sign, the sensitivity has indeed diminished in intensity—the feeling becomes practically intensity-less—but the *meaning* of the feeling, its depth and breadth in the personality, may remain unimpaired, or may even increase. In the illustrations considered, the funded meaning of the idea of fame or of danger remains in the form of such affective correlates. These correlates may be

[1] Chapter II, p. 42 ff.

reinstated, either by the *explicit* assumption with its feeling of the imagination, or by the implicit assumption embodied in a general concept, the feeling-tone of words. When the feeling is of the first type, the subject often continues to realise in imagination the *felt* meaning of objects and ideas when actual sense experience or specific adaptive judgment is without affective reaction. In phenomena of the second type the mere affective abstracts themselves, which have the funded meaning of past experience (e.g. of fame and danger), and still more—as shown in the illustrations of the preceding chapter,[1] those which have a social origin and meaning, continue as *felt* presuppositions of further emotional experience.

The question arises, finally, as to the effect of repetition upon the assumption feelings of the two types described, the feelings of imagination and the affective abstracts or signs which take the place of particular emotional reactions. Repetition does not, I think, reduce the worth suggestion of these affective experiences. They are modified only when judgment makes the assumption untenable.

The fact that these phases of affectivity are *in some way different* from sensation feelings and particular emotions or judgment-feelings, has not escaped the observation of students of these phenomena. This difference is ordinarily described as consisting in the fact that the feelings of the imagination (Saxinger) or the affective abstracts and signs (Paulhan) are *not* subject to the law which governs particular, "real" feelings, i.e., the law of diminution of intensity with repetition,[2] and has been explained by the theory that the actualisation of these feelings, whether by explicit imagination or by the verbal correlate of habitual judgment, does not involve, as in the case of other feelings, the expenditure of energy, and therefore the diminution of the capacity of the affective dispositions for actualisation. Now the fact of this difference we may admit, but not its explanation. Repetition affects the intensity of all sensitivity, even of the hedonic accompaniments of worth feeling, but the meaning of the feeling is relatively independent of its intensity. Dulling of sensitivity for emotional disturbance cannot be correlated with decrease in worth or affective-volitional meaning.

[1] Chap. v, p. 137, note.
[2] Chap. v, p. 128.

(b) *The Law of Satiety does not apply to Feelings of Value.*

The second psychological principle to which the law of Diminishing Value is referred for its foundation is the principle of satiety. In determining whether these formulations are applicable to all acts of appreciation, we found it necessary to treat separately the two principles of habit and satiety, although from the standpoint of their practical effect upon the determination of the utility of objects they could be treated as identical.

What is to be understood by satiety seems perfectly clear in the case of the consumption of a simple good which corresponds to an isolated sense tendency. As described in the most general terms, it is a law connecting intensity of sensation with quality of feeling. With increase in the intensity of the sensation there is a relatively slower increase in intensity of pleasure until a critical point is reached where the pleasure begins to fall off. Finally, a second critical point in the curve is reached where the positive coefficient of pleasure passes over into a negative coefficient of unpleasantness or pain. The second point is described as satiety or *Übersättigung*. Now this conception of an entire change in quality of the affective tone of the sensation quality, while a description quite sufficient for the uses of the economist in his account of the effect of quantity upon utility, is, from the standpoint of psychological analysis, a fiction, an undue simplification of the phenomenon. As a matter of fact, the situation is not so simple. What we have here is, not pure pleasure until a certain point is reached and then a sudden change to unpleasantness, but rather a mixed phenomenon. The pleasure arising from the stimulation of any organic tendency is made up of the affective tone of the sensation itself plus the affective tone of organic sensations associated with it. With over-stimulation the latter gradually become unpleasant, but at first not sufficiently so to modify the dominantly pleasurable tone of the total psychosis. That which constitutes the moment called satiety is really the predominance of the unpleasantly toned organic content. Such a thing, then, as transformation of pleasure into its negative does not exist. What has been so described is really a driving out of the pleasure feeling attached to the content, as at first experienced, by a more intense unpleasant feeling arising from competing foreign contents.

Now while, as it has been said, this interpretation of the phenomenon does not in any way affect the consequences drawn from the principle of satiety for the utility of goods in consumption, it does modify considerably our conception of the bearing of the principle of satiety upon acts of appreciation in general. In the first place, it is not even clear that we can say that satiety is the normal consequence of satisfaction of desire itself, that is, that it lies in the very nature of desire. It is even abstractly conceivable that, if the successive increments of a good could be appropriated in such a way as not to create organic disturbances and thus introduce new content, the principle of dulling of sensitivity would hold for isolated tendencies, while the principle of satiety would not.

Much more important do these considerations become when we turn to the appreciation of so-called ideal goods. When we recognise that the phenomena of satiety are not inherent in the appreciative activity itself, but are accompanying phenomena, sensational redundancies secondary to appreciation, then new light is thrown upon certain complicated facts of appreciation. In the first place, we may notice that the appreciative consciousness itself makes a clear distinction between the rôle which these accompanying experiences, described as satiety, play in the two cases of consumption and ideal appreciation. We may express this by saying that when the phenomenon of satiety enters into the process of consumption, the subject transfers its meaning to the object of desire; he has enough of the object itself. But when in the pursuit of ideal goods or in acts of appreciation, the unpleasant organic sensations appear as accompaniments of over-stimulation and fatigue, he recognises their secondary character, and does not transfer them to the object; they do not affect the value of the object. This we express in our judgments that the thirst for knowledge, beauty, or goodness is insatiable. Psychologically this means that the sense of value as affective-volitional meaning persists as an undertone in consciousness. The transgredient or immanental reference of the feeling goes beyond the organic unpleasantness of the moment. Desire remains present dispositionally in the form of sentiment, mood, or affective sign. A mere imagination, assumption, of the existence of the object suffices to call up these representative worth suggestions, when the actual processes of perception and judgment involved in the realisation of the objects would be accompanied by the unpleasant conditions which we have described by the term satiety. The worth moment does not lie, then, in the hedonic accompaniments, but in the transgredient and immanental reference to dispositions presupposed, which may persist with change in hedonic redundancies. It is true that these accompaniments, this satiety, may become the object of a negative worth judgment, and that this negative worth may then compete with the positive worth of the object, but in this case we have a new situation. The state of satiety has been presented as an object of worth feeling, and is itself no longer worth feeling, or an aspect of it.

It appears, then, that when the feeling of satiety, the peculiar mass of unpleasant organic sensations that goes by that name, arises in connection with judgment feelings, this does not mean that the worth or judgment-feeling has passed over from a positive to a negative quality, but rather that the physiological processes involved in the presentation and judgment of the object, and in the accompanying emotional experience, have been exhausted and that the pleasurable accompaniments have passed over into unpleasant. It is not the disposition, the capacity for worth feeling itself, which is exhausted, but other dispositions involved in the presentation and judgment of the object. In such cases the valuation may persist in the form of an assumption feeling, during the experience described as satiety.

(c) *Conclusion—The Limited Application of the Laws of Dulling of Sensitivity and Satiety.*

In considering the bearing of these two factors of habit and satiety on worth feeling in general, some such analysis as the preceding is all-important if we would avoid confusion. Thus Gossen, who takes appreciation of a work of art as illustrating the general law of Limiting Value, fails to distinguish the several factors involved in such appreciation. He tells us that " a work of art will bring to the artist who beholds it the highest enjoyment in that moment when he has observed it long enough to grasp all its elements. This enjoyment will sink steadily with continued study, and, after a longer or shorter time, according to the nature of the object and the observer,

The Laws of Valuation

the latter will become tired; satiety will appear, even when he seeks to enjoy works of the same kind. If, after a longer or shorter time, according to the object and the observer, a desire for the repetition of the pleasure arises, he will then, on account of his previous knowledge of the work of art, reach the highest point of enjoyment in a shorter time. But this point will be reached the less easily and the less frequently the more often and the more frequently the repetition has taken place."[1] But in this description Gossen fails to distinguish two different types of feeling involved in this appreciation. Had he observed more closely, he would have found that, while this is a true account of what takes place in the purely sensuous pleasure in the formal factors, nevertheless the sentiment felt toward the content, the object expressed by the work of art, might quite easily have remained unaffected by repetition. The feeling in this latter case is an assumption-feeling and presupposes dispositions quite different from those the stimulation of which affords the pleasure of the formal element. Actualisation of these dispositions has by no means the same consequences as stimulation of dispositions involved in pleasure causation.

IV. Extent of the Application of the Law of Limiting Value to Ideal Objects—The General Problem

The preceding study of the two principles of habit and satiety, upon which the general law of Limiting Value is based, has shown them to hold only for sensation-feelings and for intensities of emotional disturbance involved in judgment-feelings. The latter, the feeling intensities which diminish with repetition of judgment, may, indeed, be sensation-feelings also, resonances of the organism following upon the psychical activity of judgment. To the worth feelings themselves, the affective volitional meaning acquired in processes of judgment and assumption, the laws of dulling of sensitivity and satiety do not necessarily apply, for they are not sensation-feelings. We should avoid, however, at least at this stage of the discussion, the inference that the law of Limiting Value is not universally applicable, as claimed by its founders. Because the psychological analysis upon which, as a theory, it was based, is faulty, it does not follow that it fails as a description of fact. It is entirely conceivable that it represents the fate of all processes of valuation

[1] Gossen, *Entwickelung der Gesetze*, etc., p. 5.

whatsoever, but that the principle rests upon the limitation of other capacities than those of sense stimulation.

There are two types of valuation in which the object as sensed or presented is not the immediate cause of feeling, but in which the feeling-disposition is mediated through intellectual processes of judgment or assumption. They are worth feelings which rise upon processes of ideal reconstruction of the object through judgment. These reconstructions may be either the work of instrumental judgments, in which case the corresponding values are instrumental values, or processes of æsthetic reconstruction which individualise the object as an harmonious whole, and make it of intrinsic value. We must now examine these worth feelings and their modifications to determine to what extent this law of valuation holds.

The objects of such types of valuation, and their funded meanings, are "founded" objects in the sense of our introductory analysis. The various types of such objects already enumerated, the psychical objects of appreciation, such as beauty and grace of form in perceptual objects—founded qualities which emerge in the activities of consumption and in instinctive activity generally, such as cleanliness, manners, etc., the qualities and dispositions of persons, viewed either in their intrinsic worth as worths of the person, or, instrumentally, as the basis of social participation, and finally objects of utilisation, of exchange—more especially the medium of exchange—all these, although they inhere, so to speak, in objects of immediate sensation and presentation, are themselves not the objects of such processes, but rather of judgment and assumption. As such, their funded meaning is not determined by simple feeling, but by feelings which have as their presuppositions the processes of judgment and assumption of which they are the objects. It is of course possible, and it frequently occurs, that these worths or meanings are attributed to the sensations and presentations themselves, and then we speak of them as complementary values of the latter, but for psychological analysis they must be kept quite distinct.

Let us now, with these considerations in mind, turn first to the problem of the application of the law of Limiting Value to the objects of utilisation and exchange, the type of the extension of simple appreciation which takes place through the interpolation of instrumental judgments.

1. *Application of the Law to all Instrumental Values.*
(a) *The Law of Marginal Utility and its Explanation.*

Economic worth theory took its rise from the obvious application of the principle of Limiting Value to objects corresponding to isolated sense tendencies. Its extension to valuation in general was made possible, as we have seen, historically, by the unanalysed substitution of wealth in general, or money, for the particular homogeneous good corresponding to an isolated sense-tendency. In the concept wealth, and still more in that of money, we have the most abstract possible symbol for objective value and thus indirectly for subjective worth. If therefore the principle of relativity developed for isolated processes of consumption holds for the valuation of successive increments of wealth in general, it would seem that the inference as to the universality of its application was justified, and with it the hedonistic assumptions of its founders.

Now, as a matter of fact, we shall see that the merely empirical law of modification of worth feeling, developed by Bentham and his successors, does hold within limits for the valuation of successive increments of wealth; but it does not follow that the psychological explanation of this empirical law is the same in both cases. Since the value feelings accompanying successive increments of wealth are judgment-feelings while in consumption the feelings are sensation-feelings, the presuppositions being different, the law of their modification may be different. As illustrative of our position, we may refer to another region of psychology. If the principle of relativity called Weber's Law, developed first for the perception of differences of intensity, is found, as Wundt maintains, to hold also for the perception of relative differences in pitch, it does not follow that the explanation is the same. Intensity and pitch are two different things, in fact independently variable. The subsumption of this law of relative pitch under the law of relative intensity, because the empirical law is the same, would be unjustified. Likewise, without further analysis, we cannot infer that, because the empirical law of the modification of judgment-feelings in instrumental valuation is the same as that in immediate pleasure-causation, the two phenomena are identical.

The feelings of value corresponding to the concept wealth are, with certain significant exceptions which we shall consider later, judgment feelings. Whatever be the concrete object symbolising wealth, the essence of the conception lies in the fact that, through the interpolation of certain judgments as to its reapplicability for different purposes, whether through extension of simple use or through exchange, the object is removed from the immediacy of simple pleasure-causation, of stimulation or consumption. The presupposition of such a feeling of value is then the fundamental conative tendency as modified by subsidiary judgments as to reapplicability of the object. An object's value in use, notwithstanding the extension of its applicability through exchange, always retains at least a faint reference to the fundamental desires to which it first afforded satisfaction, but the more, as in a "money-economy," it becomes abstracted from this primary reference and fills the rôle of mere symbol of exchange, the more its purely instrumental character becomes emphasised. Now the consequence of this is that successive increments of any good, which, after a certain point in the immediate or direct satisfaction of desire is reached, can then produce a modification of feeling only through exchange for other objects, are not direct stimuli, but can modify feeling only through the indirect process of calling out judgments.

What is the effect, then, of successive increments of wealth, making necessary repeated judgments of reapplicability of the good, upon the economic threshold or threshold of value feeling? Obviously such increase raises the threshold of value. Each new judgment of application diminishes the capacity of the good for application, i.e. with each added increment of the good, especially of the abstract symbol money, the more significant and important fundamental condition worths of the subject become satisfied, the possibilities of reapplication, always for any individual a limited universe, become progressively exhausted and the relation between the object and the immediate appreciation becomes more and more mediated and remote. In other words, in order that a significant instrumental relation may be established between the new increment and a condition or personal worth, the increment must be appreciably greater.

It is clear, then, that the economist is justified in extending the conception of Diminishing Utility or Limiting Value to include all those values mediated by successive judgments of reapplication, as well as to those conditioned by repetition of immediate stimulation. Moreover, the law of Marginal or Final Utility,

The Laws of Valuation

deduced from this more general principle, according to which the value of a sum of goods depends, not upon the "total" utility, but upon the marginal or "final" degree of utility of the last addition, is universally applicable to all objects, the value of which consists in their capacity for reapplication. It is not so clear, however, that this fact is to be explained by reference to the laws limiting our capacity for mere stimulation. It is rather probable that more complex processes of imaginative and ideal construction of ends are involved.

(b) Certain Limitations to the Law of Marginal Utility.

Certain significant limitations of this law will bring the situation into clearer relief. It has been recently pointed out by Simmel[1] that what we may call the curve of value, or funded meaning, of money, for any individual cannot be viewed as a plotting of progressive, gradual changes, but must rather be looked upon as representing a series of discrete stages. Thus, if the individual has a given income, he lives normally in a universe of certain relatively fixed possibilities from which many of the most significant condition and personal worths, such, for instance, as æsthetic satisfactions and social position, in so far as they are dependent upon money, are excluded. Gradual additions to his income are valued by him according to the law developed above, for, within that relatively fixed system, the reapplications become progressively less and less important. But if the increment be of sufficient amount to change the universe of possibilities, the level of valuation is changed. New worths of condition and person come within the individual's horizon, new possibilities of application appear, and the curve begins again on a new level. As Simmel remarks, quantity, when it is grasped as a unified whole, may be transmuted, sublimated, into quality. Of course upon this new level the law again begins to work, modifying the threshold in the manner described above.

A second modification of this law appears closely connected with the one previously described. In the former case, the characteristic feature is to be found in the fact that if a certain sum of money, say a million dollars, is received, its subjective worth is not to be calculated according to the law of marginal utility. It is at first a direct appeal, without mediating instrumental judgments, to the worths of the personality (social

[1] Simmel, *Philosophie des Geldes*, pp. 250–76.

esteem, independence, etc.). The threshold is qualitative, not quantitative. In a similar manner, such a sum of money acquires this qualitative character when it is viewed as an ideal. In the case of the miser, for instance, who sets before himself a certain sum viewed as a unity, as an ideal, the value of the successive increments of money does not follow the law of marginal utility. As he nears his goal the smallest increment may have almost an absolute value, and even in the earliest stages of the process of acquisition, the value of any increment is not to be calculated according to this law. The significant feature of this situation is to be found precisely in the suppression of instrumental judgments and the substitution for them of an assumption of the possible application of the wealth as a whole. To the minute increment is imputed the assumption feeling that goes with the individuated whole, or we may say that the most insignificant moment in the series borrows worth from the end feeling of the series. As we have seen in our study of the threshold, intrinsic valuation of a minute object as part of an individuated whole lowers the threshold of worth for that object. Whereas, then, in the *instrumental* valuation of wealth each successive amount calls forth worth feeling only through the mediation of a series of instrumental judgments—and value decreases with the remoteness of the object from the fundamental desire, in the *intrinsic* valuation of wealth, on the other hand, as an individuated whole, the valuation which follows upon this individuation, is subject neither to the dulling of sensitivity which follows upon repetition of sensation feelings nor to the limitation of judgment capacity which inheres in instrumental valuation.

A consideration of these phenomena enables us then to understand the limited application of the law of marginal utility to the founded ideal objects of economic utility and exchange, without subsuming it under the laws of dulling of sensitivity and satiety, which apply only to pleasure. And—what is still more important—it enables us to dispense with the psychological fiction of the continuous variability of intensity of pleasure with changes in increments of wealth, an assumption which underlies much of economic worth theory. As a matter of fact, however, it must be recognised that some economists have employed this law as a purely empirical principle without accepting the theoretical fiction of infinitesimal changes in worth feeling.[1]

[1] Oskar Kraus, *Zur Theorie des Wertes*, p. 64.

V. THE LAW OF COMPLEMENTARY VALUES; AS MODIFYING THE LAW OF LIMITING VALUE—ITS BASIS IN PSYCHOLOGICAL LAWS

The law of Limiting Value applies, as we have seen, to objects of immediate satisfaction and to objects of more remote instrumental value. In the first case, it is the applicability for immediate sense stimulation, in the second, the reapplicability of the object, which is determinative. In the first case, the working of the laws of habit and satiety raises the threshold of worth and of worth difference until ultimately a point is reached where conation ceases. The object has no longer immediate condition worth and continues to be valued only when secondary instrumental judgments are included as part-presuppositions of the feeling. In the latter case, the object which, as the stimulus of immediate sensation feelings, would not rise above the threshold, nevertheless, through the mediation of instrumental judgments, calls out new feelings of value. This readaptation after arrest is essentially a process of conceptual reconstruction, in that for the concrete objects abstract exchange equivalents are substituted. But while a certain continuity and extension of valuation is attained by these abstract reconstructions, while by the inclusion of instrumental judgments the working of the laws of habit and satiety is modified, it is nevertheless true, as we have seen, that the law of Limiting Value in its special form of Marginal Utility holds for these judgment-feelings also. The factors of repetition and quantity work in an analogous way here, although their effect cannot be properly subsumed under the laws of habit (dulling of sensitivity) and satiety. It is a phenomenon of limitation of judgment capacity, rather than of capacity of stimulation.

There is, however, a second type of reconstruction of objects of desire whereby continuity of valuation is secured, and through which a new development takes place. This reconstruction is intuitive instead of conceptual, and a new form of intrinsic valuation is developed. The construction is intuitive, in that it individuates a group of objects into a whole of meaning, an harmonious group of elements, and out of this process of individuation emerge new psychical founded objects which are intrinsically valued. We have now to consider the nature of these processes of individuation, and to study the laws governing the intrinsic valuation of these psychical objects, more especially the extent of the applicability of the law of Limiting Value.

1. *Description of the Laws of Complementary Values—*
   (a) *In Economic Valuation.*

The general characteristic of this type of reconstruction is to be found in the fact that the elements of a total group of objects, or the part-processes of a total conative process of consumption or acquisition, are so related to each other as to be *complementary*. In other words, when related to each other as elements in an individuated whole, the value of the whole, the degree of satisfaction of the conative tendency presupposed, exceeds the value of the sum of the elements taken separately. The values acquired in such processes are described as Complementary Values, and the objects toward which these feelings are directed are ideal objects. The complementary values thus acquired may, indeed, be imputed to the elements taken separately, but they are not the values of the elements, but of the object founded upon the harmonious arrangement of the elements. We must first consider this doctrine as formulated for economics, and then determine the extent of its application to other types of values.

As a consequence of the law of Marginal Utility, the psychological basis of which we have been considering, the economist without difficulty draws the inference that the value of a supply of goods is determined, not by addition of the utilities actually got from the different parts, that is by the sum of the very different utilities of the different portions, but by the utility of its least important part multiplied by the total number of each equally large part. To this general law an exception is, however, universally recognised, namely, where a sum of goods constitutes a unity and, as such, displays a certain utility effect which is not equal to the sum of the utilities of the separate parts. As a consequence, it further follows that any given part of the whole has imputed to it a utility over and above that which it would have as an isolated good, subject merely to the law of Marginal Utility. A stock illustration is that of the hunter and his powder, ball, and flint. Each of these alone is useless. All of them, taken together with the labour involved in employing them, equal the value, or, in the more accurate terms of the economist, the *discounted* value, of the game.

The Laws of Valuation 175

Because each alone is useless, and is of utility only in combination, the value of each is equal to the value of the whole.

(b) Extra-Economic Valuation—Æsthetic and Ethical.

In this illustration we have a unity, an individuated whole, the *instrumental* value of which arises from the grouping of the elements, the parts of the whole being interrelated by instrumental judgments. But the same general principle is evident in cases where the instrumental judgments recede into the background and intrinsic valuation takes their place. We have already considered cases in which wealth viewed as a whole acquires a complementary value of an intrinsic character, a value which not only exceeds quantitatively the sum of the instrumental values of the parts, but changes qualitatively as well, where quantity is sublimated into quality. In the two cases referred to—where the reception of a round sum of money leads to its intrinsic valuation as a whole (rather than to an instrumental valuation of the parts, according to the law of Marginal Utility, as when the amount is *gradually* acquired), or where the miser values his wealth as a whole without reference to the instrumental value of the parts—in these cases the instrumental judgments have sunk into the background and are represented merely by a vague assumption of instrumental value, the total amount being valued intrinsically without explicit reference to the instrumental value of the parts.

But we find still other cases where the general principle of complementary values applies to individuated wholes, where the element of utility, and of instrumental judgments, is entirely lacking, where both the whole and the parts are objects of intrinsic appreciation. These are perceptual and ideal unities which have an æsthetic or ethical character. Two illustrations will suffice to indicate the character of these constructions. As examples of such *perceptual* wholes we may take a face in which all the features taken together are charming, or a landscape in which the river, the hills, the valleys, are all said to be beautiful. None of them would be beautiful without the others; each has all the beauty of the whole. Of such *ideal* constructs the individuality of a person is typical. The person is an ideal construct, a complex of traits or dispositions all of which, when thus combined to make the unique whole, create that founded object, the *person*. The intrinsic worth of the person is something over and above the separate values of the parts, and to the separate trait or disposition is imputed all the complementary value of the whole.

(c) General Characterisation of the Law.

The phenomena described by the principle of Complementary Values are now before us. From the illustrations given it is seen to be a process by which the range of valuation is *extended*, both in the sphere of physical objects of sensation and perception and in the region of ideal objects of imagination and judgment, a process by which the working of the law of Limiting Value, which holds both for sensation and judgment feelings, is modified. It is this aspect of the situation which has received special attention from Professor Patten[1] in his theory of consumption. The older doctrine of consumption, he tells us, does not take into account all the elements of pleasure and utility. Besides the gross quantity of the goods, and the relation of this quantity to the capacity of the elementary wants, there are in all groups of goods capacities for rearrangement which are outside the category of quantity, that is are qualitative, æsthetic. A group of goods, harmoniously arranged, is capable of giving indefinitely greater pleasure than the mere sum of the separate pleasures of each of the components of the group. The complementary values are then imputed to the components. This principle is conceived as coming in to modify the working of the laws of habit and satiety. These laws, as we have seen, apply to all sensation feelings, and consequently the law of Limiting Value applies to all worth judgments determined by such feeling-dispositions. But since there is in these objects of sensation feeling a certain capacity for harmonious combination which extends their capacity for continued stimulation, these laws are to a degree modified. " Since these æsthetic goods may be said to be goods without the point of satiety which is found in simple economic goods," and " since simple æsthetic goods may be said to be the result of the blending of distinct pleasures into one group and the æsthetic pleasures seem to be the largest harmonious grouping of pleasures that society can produce," it would follow, Professor Patten thinks, that " progress, in the sense of increase of value for the individual and society, must lie in the direction of harmonious consumption." Despite the unfortunate terminology, which identifies worth with pleasure causation and speaks of summation

---

[1] S. N. Patten, *The Consumption of Wealth*, Philadelphia, 1889.

of pleasures, we may accept this as a true account of the extension of the activities of simple appreciation through the rearrangement, reconstruction of the objects of desire and feeling. But Professor Patten has added to this conception another of equal importance for our study. In his pamphlet *Economic Causes of Moral Progress*,[1] he attempts to show that at least many of our æsthetic and ethical ideals, relatively permanent and progressive sources of satisfaction, are but qualitative expressions, names for these complementary goods, the value of which is imputed to the economic goods. Thus comfort, cleanliness, thrift—he might have added taste and manners—are qualitative terms for the process of harmonising goods or objects of sensuous feelings, and of ejection of inharmonious elements. Even the home and its attendant virtues, the state with its justice, are groups of such values, partly economical, partly ethical. If we extend the conception of consumption to include all the activities involved in acquisition and utilisation of goods, we may accept this account of the origin of the primitive ethical and æsthetic objects. The importance of such a conception lies in the fact that, if these qualitatively different worths may thus be related to the elementary economic values as complementary, we have a means of co-ordinating these two groups of values.

But it must be noted, in the second place, that these qualitative expressions for harmonious consumption and activity, these æsthetic and ethical ideals, are new objects of worth feeling, ideal objects, founded it is true on perceptual activities, but nevertheless now no longer the objects of sensation and perception, but of judgment. As such ideal objects of judgment, they themselves now become objects of new worth feelings and are capable of ideal reconstruction into new individual unities or wholes. Thus the worths of the personality, the ideals of goodness, nobility, obligation, inner peace, freedom, perfection, etc., are qualitative terms for complementary values arising from the harmonious co-ordination of these fundamental dispositions. They are objects of desire and worth feeling founded, not in perceptual, but in ideational activity and construction. To what extent these ideal objects may become relatively permanent and progressive sources of satisfaction is a problem to which we must later turn our attention.

[1] S. N. Patten, *Economic Causes of Moral Progress*, Annals of the American Academy of Political and Social Science, Vol. III, Sep. 1892.

3. *Psychological Interpretation of the Law of Complementary Values.*

The extension which has thus been given to the economic concept of Complementary Values—to include all acquired affective-volitional meanings which arise in the process of perceptual and ideal reconstruction of individualised wholes out of the simple elements which constitute the primary objects of desire and feeling—opens up a vista of innumerable objects of secondary acquired value, and raises the question of the limits of such ideal construction and acquirement of meaning. When this process of perceptual and ideal construction is viewed in this larger way, as a form of conative continuity, it is seen that these constructions are all in the service of continuity of valuation and constitute readaptations of conative tendency after arrest. The facts of this conative continuity or acquirement of worth are adequately enough described by this formula of Complementary Values, but the attempt to answer the question of the limits of the process requires that the principle be properly interpreted.

(*a*) *The Objects of Complementary Value: Forms of Combination, Perceptual and Ideal—Founded Objects.*

The interpretation ordinarily given—that the complementary acquired value is in some sense a sum of the quantities of pleasure of the elements, although that product is recognised as being something more than the *mere* sum of the elements—fails to take account of the really significant feature of the process. That feature is to be found in the fact that *the acquired value has as its object, not the elements, but a new object founded on the rearrangement of the elements.* Even in the simple case of the combination of food-stuffs and the order of their consumption, the object of the acquired worth is a qualification, a meaning which, though it may be conceptually abstracted from the process, can be intuitively realised only in the consumption of the elements themselves. When we consider the further complication of these food elements with the objects of other senses— the lights, flowers, and music of the banquet, the refinements of the process of serving and eating, the psychical character of the object of the acquired worth becomes more evident, for we have in the terms "taste" and "manners" the means of separating the form of the process from the material elements. The psychical objects, cleanliness and thrift, though equally forms of combination developed in the processes of consumption, can be still more easily and completely abstracted from the process, as objects of judgment and assumption, and may be referred in judgments of possession to the self, the subject of the process.

This conception of the psychical object as a form quality emerging in conative process may, moreover, be extended to other fundamental instinctive activities, connected with acquisition, the hunt, war, labour, etc., to sex and parenthood, and finally to perceptual and ideational activities involved in knowledge and art. The range of possible psychical objects, the construction of which adds complementary value to the objects of immediate sensation and perception upon which they are founded, is consequently very large. We may, moreover, again recall the fact that personality, when intrinsically valued, is a "character," a form of combination of certain elements. In this case the elements are certain qualities or dispositions which emerge in the process of ideal construction involved in sympathetic *Einfühlung*. Of this special application of the principle we shall make considerable use later.

(b) *Psychological Laws of Complementary Values.*

These psychical objects may, therefore, be founded on perceptual and ideational activities alike; they are the products of individuating activities, both perceptual and ideational. Is it possible to refer this general law of Complementary Value to more ultimate psychological principles, as in the case of the other two laws, of the Threshold and of Limiting Value?

In approaching this question, it is well to observe the fact that we are here concerned with the formulation of general psychological laws of acquirement of meaning through individuation of psychical objects—with general laws, therefore, which have specific application in different spheres of concrete valuation. In the second place, we must distinguish between the general laws of acquirement of meaning, of which the law of Complementary Values is an expression for worth theory, and the particular laws of combination of elements by which the meaning is acquired.

The Law of Complementary Values has accordingly two aspects. From the point of view of conative activity there is progress, to a new (psychical) object. From the point of view of content there is a combination of elements in which an individuated whole emerges with a meaning not found in the elements taken separately. Wundt has described these two aspects as the law of *Heterogeneity of Ends*, and the law of *Creative Resultants*, or more simply, *Resultants*.[1]

The principle of *Resultants* is, then, a law of combination of elements and acquirement of meaning through that combination and reconstruction. Every resultant is an individuated whole, either perceptual or ideal. The complementary value is the affective-volitional meaning acquired in that construction. What are the psychological factors or laws involved?

Wundt formulates but one such law, that of increase through contrast. Here he has in mind the increase of effect for feeling and will which the contrasting elements exercise upon each other. But while the principle of contrast, when viewed in all its aspects, may be said to comprehend all the principles of intuitive construction, nevertheless for our purpose it is necessary to formulate more specific laws for such ordering of content.

We may distinguish, then, three specific laws of intuitive combination of elements into total resultants: (1) the law of *contrast* in its narrower sense; (2) the law of the *total series* (the principle formulated by Fechner for æsthetics as the *Folgegesetz*); and (3) the law of *end feelings* (which Fechner formulated in its æsthetic application as the *Versöhnungsgesetz*). The meaning of these laws may be stated very briefly, for their fuller development will be required at various points where they are applied.

The principle of simple contrast merely states that an object of desire and feeling when contrasted with its opposite, or when its existence is contrasted with its non-existence, gets an imputed value which, by itself, it has not either intrinsically or instrumentally. The law of the " total series " is a formulation of the

[1] Wundt, *Physiologische Psychologie*, Fifth Edition, Leipzig, 1903, Vol. III, chap. XXII; also Kreibig, *Psychologische Grundlegung eines Systems der Werttheorie*, Wien, 1902, pp. 59–63, for a similar study. Wundt describes them as laws of psychical causality in distinction from physical causality, pointing out that, whereas in physical causality there is a quantitative equivalence between antecedent and consequent, in psychical process the resultant always shows an increase or acquirement of meaning. Calling this acquirement of affective-volitional meaning "increase of energy," he finds in this contrast—between equivalence of energy in the physical sphere and increase of psychical energy—the fundamental difference between physical and the psychical causality. While making use of his descriptive formulæ we need not, and shall not, for reasons developed in the introductory chapter and elsewhere in our discussion, conceive them in terms of causality.

The Laws of Valuation

fact that the ordering of objects of desire and feelings in a graded series, or with certain relations of contrast and repetition, as for instance in rhythm, gives rise to an imputed value of the whole which is not a sum of the value of the separate elements. The law of "end feelings" recognises the fact that the worth of a series of elements is determined by the final moment of the series and its relation to the preceding moments. In all these specific forms of arrangement of elements *form-qualities* are created which constitute the real objects of the imputed value.

VI. Extent of Application of the Law of Limiting Value to Ideal Objects of Intrinsic Value

We are now in a position to return to the problem with which this discussion of the founded ideal objects of valuation took its rise—namely the extent of the application of the law of Limiting Value to the intrinsic valuation of such objects. The importance of the question is far-reaching. In the succeeding chapters we shall have occasion to consider the more specific problem of the laws governing the actual concrete judgments of the worth of ideal objects of æsthetics and ethics. Here we are concerned merely with the general theoretical question, whether the nature of these objects, and of their corresponding worth feelings, is such as to make this general law applicable. Upon this question, as we have seen, there is a significant difference of opinion. Kreibig and Meinong deny its application, while Ehrenfels affirms it. The problem is in the first place obviously a question of fact. Are there any objects of desire and feeling which have the power of calling forth continuous intrinsic valuation? It is, in the second place, however, a question of psychological analysis of what is involved in the act of valuation. Thus an analysis which recognises, with Brentano, intensity-less acts of valuation would be in a position to infer the existence of such objects, for the laws of dulling of sensitivity and satiety apply only to hedonic intensities. In general, any theory which makes the fundamental distinction between pleasure-causation and worth feelings, between sensation-feelings and feeling actualised by judgments and assumptions, would leave the question open.

If then we start with the immediately given facts of experience, with our appreciation of those perceptual and ideal objects which emerge in our instinctive conative activities and in our ideal constructions, we are at first sight disposed to admit the working of the law of Limiting Value in this sphere as well. The complementary values which emerge in harmonious consumption modify, it is true, the effects of habit and satiety, and extend the limits of valuation, but ultimately these limits are reached. The acquirement upon the part of a group of complementary objects of sense stimulation, of meanings such as sensuous beauty, taste in eating, etc., removes the object from the immediate gross satisfaction of desire, and postpones the dulling of sensitivity and satiety ; but since these meanings are founded on some stimulations and are conditioned by them, they are ultimately subject to the law inherent in all feelings of sense. Sensuous beauty palls, refinement of living becomes wearisome, and we seek refreshment in crude contrasts of ugliness and coarseness. There is a return value-movement from the acquired to the fundamental.

The same nemesis seems to follow the so-called ideal feelings, the valuation of those ideal objects the worth of which is determined by emotion and sentiment, the ideal objects of knowledge, art, and morals. With the loss of novelty, with each successive act of appreciation, there is diminution of enthusiasm, loss of the emotional uplift which constitutes the peculiar glory of the first realisations. James has described this process in his usual picturesque and impressive way in his chapter on emotions, and it is a phenomenon everywhere present in our appreciation of persons and objects. Friendship begins with full and resonant emotions, love with an ecstatic devotion, to become with use habits with scarcely perceptible affective intensity. Perhaps the most striking illustration of all is the effect of repetition upon sympathetic participation (*Einfühlung*). With each act of participation, the judgment of the existence of the ideal object, the disposition in the *alter*, acquires more certainty, the character is more fully realised, but the realisation has become habit, the emotional resonances are deadened. It would seem, then, that those ideal objects the value of which lies, not in their being sensed, but in their being judged or assumed to exist or not exist, also lose their capacity for calling out intense emotions. If, then, we should equate the worth or funded meaning of these objects with this capacity, there would be no question that the intrinsic valuation of such objects is subject to the law of Limiting Value.[1]

---

[1] And, doubtless, in some moods of retrospection the mind turns from the unded meaning of the object to the emotional accompaniments of the earlier appreciations.

The Laws of Valuation

Apparently, then, we may conclude that the repeated experience of these ideal emotions and sentiments is accompanied by the same dulling of sensitivity for intensity of affective disturbance which comes with repetition and habit in the case of repeated sensation-feelings, and, in those experiences where the intensity of the emotion is unusual, by the phenomena of satiety. We might be led, therefore, to conclude further that the intrinsic valuation of ideal objects is subject to the law of Limiting Value.

On the other hand, with equal truth it may be said that these experiences do *not* modify our feeling of the worth of the objects, do *not* determine our worth judgments, as habit and satiety have been seen to modify our judgments in the case of objects of sensation-feeling. The worth of the object seems to be determined by other modifications of consciousness than this feeling intensity, and to persist throughout these changes in hedonic accompaniments, as relatively permanent and progressive sources of satisfaction. This analysis of the facts of our experience would therefore indicate that in such processes we have a " mixture of phenomena " in which the worth of the object and its capacity for calling out feeling intensities are independently variable. In other words, as we have previously insisted, habit has its own worth feelings, its own affective-volitional meaning.

This apparent antinomy has been clearly expressed in a passage in Münsterberg's discussion of the relation of worth experience to psychology. To a remark of Windelband, that " all interest and appreciation, all valuation on the part of men, have reference to individual and particular appearances," Münsterberg answers : " If by value we mean the psychological feeling-process which is called forth in objective causal happening, such sense of value appertains to repeated no less than to single reactions. Of course there are acts the attraction of which lies in their novelty and singularity, but all that is good and noble gains depth of feeling-tone through repetition just as displeasure with the low and coarse grows through repetition."[1] With the truth of Münsterberg's observation we may, on the basis of our

---

The lover looks back with regret upon his ecstasy, the religious devoté cries out in the words of the hymn : " Where is the blessedness I knew when first I saw the Lord !" And not rarely the artist and enjoyer of works of art alike long for the emotional accompaniment of their earlier appreciations, and, at times, put more value upon them than upon their realised ideals and their attained insights. Nevertheless we rightly look upon these backward movements as temporary phenomena, in what is still a continuous valuation of the ideal object. The lover still loves and believes and appreciates. The ideal objects remain relatively permanent and progressive sources of satisfaction.

[1] Münsterberg, *Grundzüge der Psychologie*, pp. 39 and 40.

own analysis, readily agree. That the increase of depth of feeling-tone, with repetition, is an empirical law of some types of worth feeling no one could deny, unless under the influence of the prejudice that the laws of habit and satiety, which apply to sensation feelings, apply to all feelings. But the recognition of this empirical law necessitates logically, if we are to explain it, a distinction between the attributes, depth of feeling-tone and intensity. Clearly depth of feeling-tone, which is here equated with degree of worth, cannot be equated with degree of intensity of affective disturbance. Depth of feeling must be taken as a description of a modification of a special aspect of feeling, other than the affective tone of sensations and presentations, for the intensity of such hedonic tone is also subject to dulling of sensitivity with repetition.

The question, in so far as it is one of psychology merely, seems to depend for its solution upon the answer to two preliminary questions—namely : what is the nature of these ideal objects, and what is the nature of the psychical acts of which they are the objects ? For the modifications of feeling are, as we have seen, determined by the character of the presuppositions of the feeling.

As to the nature of the objects of this intrinsic valuation, it has already been shown that they are ideal and " founded," and that, while the ideal or conceptual objects of utility-judgments are subject to the limitations inherent in this type of construction, there is, on the other hand, in the case of the individuating type of construction which creates these objects of intrinsic worth, no limit—at least none that can be determined a priori—to the acquirement of meaning. The laws of this individuating construction, already analysed, indicate this fact clearly.

When we turn to the feeling side of this process of intrinsic valuation of ideal objects, and examine the presuppositions of these feelings, we find that the cognitive acts presupposed are judgments and assumptions (explicit and implicit); such ideal objects are not objects of sensation and presentation at all. Now the detailed analysis of feelings conditioned by such acts, has shown us that the laws of dulling of sensitivity and satiety, upon which the principle of Limiting Value is based, do not apply to these feelings, but only to the hedonic redundancies of the acts. Otherwise expressed, the affective abstract, or " affective sign " (an assumption-feeling representing judgmental habit) is not subject to these laws, but rather increases in *depth* of feeling-tone with repetition. The assumption-feeling may, as we have seen, attach itself directly to judgment or to a word which represents a general concept, and, as thus representing the acquired meaning of earlier worth judgments, it constitutes the assured presuppositions of the new judgment-feelings. Each successive judgment of value embodies the assumption-feeling or "habit-meaning" of preceding judgments, and thus makes possible the increase of "depth of feeling-tone," of sentiment.

This increase of depth of feeling does not, however, exclude the phenomena of dulling of sensitivity and satiety as applying to the "hedonic redundancies" of these successive appreciative acts. The causes of these redundancies, accompanying acts of intrinsic appreciation of ideal objects are, as Brentano has suggested, too complex to admit of the formulation of specific laws of their modification. In principle, however, the laws of dulling of sensitivity and satiety are applicable to these, as to all sensation-feelings. When we say, therefore, that the acquirement of intrinsic value on the part of these ideal objects, the permanence of these ideal sentiments, is unaffected by these laws, we mean to say merely that the modification of the intensity of the accompanying sensation-feelings becomes irrelevant for worth judgment. We have already, in a number of connections, seen the independent variability of these two aspects of a total feeling attitude, more particularly in the case of the effect of repeated appreciations of a work of art, already analysed, and in the distinction here made we have the solution of the apparent antinomy in intrinsic valuation.

VII. GENERAL CONCLUSIONS—INFERENCES FROM THIS STUDY OF THE LAWS OF VALUATION FOR DIFFERENT TYPES OF OBJECTS—THE PROBLEM OF THE LIMITS OF ACQUIREMENT OF VALUE

The preceding study of the law of Limiting Value, and of its application to feelings directed toward different types of objects, has been purely psychological in character, in that it was concerned with the application of the laws of dulling of sensitivity and of satiety to feelings with different presuppositions. It can easily be seen that in this principle we have the means of defining different worth objects in terms of their capacity for continuous valuation, and thus for determining the relative preferability, not only of objects of the same kind but of different groups or kinds. Such use of these studies we shall make in the succeeding chapters, which treat of the different worth objects distinguished in the first chapter (objects of condition worth, personal worth, and impersonal or over-individual worth); but before turning to these subjects, and by way of concluding this discussion, we have still to consider a problem of very general theoretical bearings, the problem, namely, whether the principle of *Limitation of Capacity* (capacity of appropriation, as developed for consumption originally) can be applied to valuation in all its aspects.

It was to this general principle, it will be remembered, that the economic theory of value looked for its foundation : to it all other laws were referred. That theory, we saw, is based partly upon analysis of a very limited sphere of experience, and partly upon unwarranted assumptions of an a priori character. Because the dispositions underlying " pleasure-causation " are limited in capacity, it is assumed that all worth dispositions, feelings of value being identified with pleasure - causation, are subject to the same limitation. Now that an empirical study of a larger range of worth feelings, and their psychical conditions, has shown the capacity of some ideal objects for continuous valuation to extend far, perhaps indefinitely, beyond the limits conceived by the theory we have been critically examining, we may turn our attention to this a priori assumption.

The assumption is, of course, that for every ideal worth object which appreciation may distinguish, and for the worth feeling directed toward it, there is a corresponding physiological disposition; that this disposition is part of a system, the total energy of which is a constant and limited amount; that within this system there may be redistribution, but never actual increase of energy; and that the increase of the energy of any disposition is therefore strictly limited by the mutual relations of the elements of the system. This conception is then simply carried over into the psychical sphere and from it are deduced limits for psychical energy and the acquirement of meaning.

Such an assumption clearly underlies Ehrenfels's position when he says [1] that " the ethical dispositions, just as little as any others, however insignificant, possess the power of extending themselves beyond their given limits, that in their tendency so to do they are held fast in their former relations by the same

[1] *System der Werththeorie*, Vol. II, p. 217 note.

The Laws of Valuation

tendency inherent in all other dispositions to maintain their former force." And the same assumption is present when he maintains (in criticism of Krüger's formulation of the supreme virtue, the highest value, as the desire for the increase of the capacity of valuation itself) that, "the claim that every subject of valuation must possess the disposition to value the valuing activity itself is capable neither of a priori nor of empirical proof."[1] Obviously it is assumed that every ideal object constructed has, as its correlate, a definite physiological disposition, and that its place in a system of values is but a reflex of the place of the disposition in a system of energies.

More specifically, the question is raised whether it is possible for us rationally to wish or strive for increase of our worth dispositions in any direction. Can a man, for instance, on the basis of an experience of the sentiment of benevolence, rationally desire an increase in this sentiment, a greater disposition toward benevolence? Ehrenfels's first answer is unqualifiedly negative, but in reply to Höffler's criticism of the same[2] (and this is all that is necessary for our purpose), he concludes that it *would* be rational for a man, let us say in a state of exaltation of benevolent emotion leading to great sacrifice, to desire intrinsically, as a permanent possession, the *same* capacity for benevolent feeling as he experiences on this occasion, that is, more than he ordinarily possesses—and this for the reason that his desire is not for something which transcends the known measure of the capacity of the disposition involved. But to desire an increase in the disposition itself would be irrational, for it would involve the ignoring of the set back which other dispositions would receive through increase over the normal measure of the particular disposition in question.

Obviously the problem, as here formulated, is concerned, not with the instrumental value of the disposition for social welfare—that is another question, but merely with the *possibility* or *desirability* of this increase from the point of view of the individual's worth experience. The question of rationality is then one wholly of internal and intrinsic criteria, the consistency of the desire with former experiences. Thus the desire is to be determined by the judgment of the known measure of actual experience. Now, leaving out of account the secondary question

---

[1] *System der Werttheorie*, Vol. II, p. 171.
[2] Ehrenfels, *System der Werttheorie*, Vol. II, pp. 175, 176; also Höffler, *Psychologie*, p. 599.

of the nature of that measure (which would have to be expressed not only in terms of intensity, but also of extension, that is, of its capacity for expression in all the acts of life, whereas Ehrenfels takes into account only the strength or intensity), we may go directly to the root of the problem. The rationality of the desire for increase of disposition must be determined wholly by the question of experience, whether such an ideal is an object with capacity of continuous valuation, whether with repetition or increase of amount, the worth feeling increases accordingly. The criterion being one of intrinsic and internal meaning, the only way in which the possibility and desirability of the increase of a disposition can be known is by *willing* it, by judging or assuming the object to exist and inferring the truth of such judgment or assumption from the worth experiences which result. The criterion is wholly intra-experiential. But for Ehrenfels the real test of the rationality of the desire is not an intra-experiential test, not a criterion formed in the inductive analysis of the different types of worth feelings themselves. It is inferred deductively from a purely hypothetical and abstract conception which is extra-psychological. It rests upon the assumption of specific nervous dispositions and of the limitation of the energies of these dispositions.

This, it seems to me, is an essentially false way of stating the problem. The " rationality " of any valuation is essentially an axiological problem, and as I hope to show in the concluding chapter, the only possible axiological criterion is an internal one, immanent in the process of valuation itself. From this point of view, the only sense in which the question of " rationality " has any meaning is that expressed by the purely practical question—can I continue to desire and will any object, or its increase, without internal contradictions, contradiction in this sphere meaning, of course, not contradiction of judgment with judgment, but of feeling with feeling or of feeling with will? In the concrete case before us, if I do actually desire increase of a given sentiment, and in that experience there is nothing paradoxical, as there is in the case of the desire for indefinite increase of pleasure, but with each judgment of increase of the sentiment there is an increase of worth feeling, then such a desire is rational in the only sense in which that word has meaning in this connection.

The true way of stating Ehrenfels's problem is rather this—does such a desire for indefinite increase of an ideal object,

The Laws of Valuation 189

as, for instance, the disposition to benevolence, founded on experiences of benevolent feeling, turn out to be consistent with the empirical laws of desire and feeling which an adequate analysis of worth experience discloses? If it does, the desire is well founded, is " rational "—for the assumption upon which it is based is well founded. In this sense it is true, as we pointed out in the introduction, that axiological postulates must not contradict psychological laws. But it is wholly irrelevant to ask that they shall not contradict the hypothetical constructions of a science which is possible only by abstracting from the very experiences which we are here called upon to explain. The criterion is, therefore, experiential, and not to be deduced from abstract constructions foreign to the experience in question. It is true, of course, that if a judgment of the limitation of my capacity physiologically enters as a part-presupposition of my worth feelings, such a judgment will act as a limit to my desires; but the situation is then changed, for the judgment has then become an intra-experiential factor.

The following study of concrete judgments of value will show us that these judgments, and the worth feelings of which they are the expressions, presuppose the capacity of continuous valuation on the part of some ideal objects. The significance of this chapter is to be found in the fact that a psychological analysis of the different types of worth feelings, and the formulation of the laws of valuation based upon this analysis, give us the scientific concepts with which to interpret the concrete facts of valuation which our analysis will disclose. The usefulness of these conceptions for our succeeding studies should not be prematurely prejudiced by the introduction of conceptions from a sphere which is essentially irrelevant.

CHAPTER VII

I. VALUES OF SIMPLE APPRECIATION—THEIR ORIGIN AND NATURE

1. Objects of "Condition Worth," Primary and Derived

A PRELIMINARY classification of worth objects distinguished three general groups—condition worths, or worths of simple appreciation, personal worths, and over-individual or impersonal worths. To these corresponded the three fundamental types of activity of valuation, simple appreciation, characterisation, and participation, the latter including utilisation of objects. On each of these levels of valuation the worth of the object is the funded affective-volitional meaning acquired in antecedent psychical processes, and the different qualifications in worth feeling on these levels, distinguishable for appreciation, go back to differences in the processes by which these worths are funded. Condition worths of simple appreciation are determined by feelings of the individual which presuppose merely presumptions, judgments, or assumptions of existence or non-existence of objects immediately or remotely desirable, that is, objects which correspond to conative dispositions. They are called condition worths because the feelings aroused are, when abstracted from the object and viewed retrospectively, referred not to the idea of the self, but to the affective *condition* of the organism. Personal worths are determined by feelings which presuppose processes of sympathetic *Einfühlung* and ideal construction of dispositions on the basis of that experience, while over-individual worths are determined by feelings which have as their presuppositions still wider processes of social participation, and consequent ideal construction.

The three levels thus distinguished represent relatively distinct stages in valuation, and are related to each other in such a manner that the values of the lower level are implicitly presupposed on the next higher level. Personal and social

Values of Simple Appreciation

values, with their qualitatively distinct feelings and differentiated objects, emerge first in the processes of simple appreciation, being built upon and developed out of objects of "condition" worth. This general process, in which the object of explicit judgment and feeling becomes the object of implicit assumption, and gives place to a new object on a higher level, we may describe as a *progression* or *Value Movement*. The general problem that confronts us in our succeeding studies is, accordingly, the description of the processes involved in these progressions, the discovery of their conditions and laws, and the reduction of their empirical uniformities, in so far as possible, to the general laws of conation and feeling described as the laws of Valuation.

While this is the general problem—the genetic background of our picture, the immediate foreground is taken up by the values and objects of condition worth. These objects are the primary worth objects, and their values the primary values. From these, as has been said, the personal and social or over-individual values are derived. But within the region of condition worths themselves, there are certain phenomena and laws of valuation which require study for their own sake. To this problem the present chapter is devoted, and it may be described as the application of the general laws of Valuation to the specific class of condition worths.

Objects of condition worth are of varied character, and may for convenience be divided into physical and psychical. To the physical objects belong primarily the so-called economic goods, desire for which is conditioned by certain primary sense-tendencies, the stimulation or gratification of the same being described as consumption. To these must be added other objects of sense tendency which for various reasons do not enter directly into economic calculations, although they must of necessity indirectly, such as the satisfaction of fundamental sex and gregarious instincts. Psychical objects of condition worth are the qualities of physical objects, which, arising in the processes of consumption, pursuit, acquisition, become the objects of new appreciations, and either add complementary worth to the primary objects, or, when made the objects of judgment, call out new worth feelings.

This distinction between primary and derived objects and values of simple appreciation constitutes the starting-point for the detailed study of values of condition and their laws.

It is desirable, therefore, to develop the distinction more fully. By a primary value (or *Stammwert*, as Ehrenfels calls it) is understood any object which serves to satisfy immediately any *fundamental* instinctive sense-tendency. The mere presumptions or judgment of existence or non-existence of such objects is followed by a feeling of intrinsic value. By fundamental, in this sense, we understand a relatively constant instinctive tendency, with its corresponding passional or emotional psychosis (or instinct feeling), which may, according to the cognitive acts through which it is actualised, be predominantly desire or feeling.[1]

It is not necessary for our purposes that we should determine just what objects and values are primary and what secondary. For some purposes of ethical and social science such a classification is, it is true, necessary—and many attempts have been made in this direction, notably the recent efforts of Ehrenfels and Schwartz, but for the special ends of the present study, it is quite sufficient to recognise that there are certain fundamental conative tendencies, such as hunger, sex, expression of bodily energy, etc., the satisfaction of which gives immediate and unconditional " condition " worth, that for any given individual they are primary and original, and that the simplest object corresponding to these tendencies are therefore *primary* objects of *simple* appreciation.

Much more important is the derivation of the secondary from the primary. These secondary or derived values emerge, it was said, in the processes of pursuit, acquisition, and consumption of the primary objects. As complementary values, they are first imputed, as additional values, to the primary objects; but they may ultimately be abstracted from the primary objects, ideally reconstructed and independently valued, when they become the objects of personal and social values.

In the preceding chapter we have seen in a general way how these complementary values emerge in the processes of valuation. On the side of the object they are the resultants of

---

[1] The term fundamental carries with it no implications as to higher objective worth or underived character. As Schwartz in his criticism of Nietzsche's worth theory rightly points out, there are no conative tendencies or dispositions which by reason of their originality carry with them implications as to their primary, least of all exclusive, worth. At the same time, when we view the history of the individual as well as that of the race, we find that certain instincts and conative tendencies to which the fundamental passions correspond do, in a certain sense, act as poles about which others concentrate. The individual at birth may from a psychological point of view be looked upon as a group of more or less loosely co-ordinated conative tendencies, impulses, and instincts.

Values of Simple Appreciation

perceptual and ideal reconstruction; on the side of conative tendency they involve reädaptations of attitude after arrest. Continuous valuation of any isolated physical good, satisfaction of any single tendency, is followed by dulling of sensitivity and satiety, and the reconstruction of the object, together with modifications of the attitude, constitutes a value movement in which the continuity of valuation is maintained. Our present task is to study these value movements in more detail, to discover whether these transformations of attitude and reconstruction of objects cannot be reduced to general types, and their conditions and laws determined. To this end we shall seek, first, to classify and analyse the general phenomena of value movement, and then to distinguish those which are characteristic of simple appreciation — those by which primary condition worths acquire complementary value—from the more complete developments from one level of valuation to another. From this understanding of value movements and their relation to the general laws of valuation, we shall turn to the study of two special forms of psychical development, in which objects of condition worth acquire ethical and æsthetic values, and shall seek to show how these acquired complementary values modify our simple economic judgments.

Our general problem may be made more definite by connecting it with the results of the preceding chapter. The law of the Threshold, the law of Limiting Value, and the law of Complementary Values are, we found, the fundamental laws of worth-process in general. We have seen how both of these last two laws modify the threshold. The law of Limiting Value modifies the threshold of value judgment in the sense that old objects and habitual quantities of these objects lose their value, and discontinuous value movement to new objects results. The law of Complementary Values, of which the continuous value movements to be described are but special applications, extends both the lower and upper threshold of valuation. How these thresholds are modified by acquired ethical and æsthetic values constitutes the chief problem of our study.

II. VALUE MOVEMENTS IN GENERAL—DEFINITION AND CLASSIFICATION—THEIR RELATION TO THE LAWS OF VALUATION

1. *Definition of Value Movements.*

By the term value movement we understand, then, any reconstruction of the object, or readaptation of attitude, from which there results continuity of valuation. The term, thus technically used, has acquired a permanent place in the recent contributions to worth theory. The term is primarily due to Ehrenfels,[1] who uses it to describe any transference of worth feeling from one object to another. Schwartz[2] makes use of the same conception, although he gives it another name, Motiv-Wandel, thereby describing the fact that, in the pursuit of one object new objects gradually, and often unconsciously, take the place of the old. Both writers then seek to classify and formulate the laws of these value movements, and ultimately to interpret them in terms of the fundamental laws of value. To these types of value movement they give the term *Directions* of movement, indicating thereby that the changes that take place are not lawless, but disclose certain trends, the causes for, and the meaning of which, it is the function of worth analysis and theory to discover. This conception of value movement we may accept—with the one modification, however, that it shall be understood to include also changes in attitude toward the *same* object, as well as changes in the object, by which meaning is acquired.

With this understanding of the use of the term value movement, we may distinguish two general types, already referred to, the *discontinuous* and the *continuous*. We have the former when, through the working of the laws of habit and satiety, there is simply transference of conative tendency from one object to another. The one acquires meaning, the other loses

---

[1] *System der Werththeorie*, Vol. I, p. 135.
[2] *Psychologie des Willens*, etc., p. 203. This passage may well be quoted in its entirety: "This relation [Value Movement] is found regularly under certain conditions, namely, when, originally only one tendency having moved us, unexpectedly a new note of our will, hitherto unsounded, makes itself heard. As yet we know not what it is that sounds softly within us. We still think we are acting only in the direction of the first motive. But the second gains in force, at first merely as a subsidiary tone of the primary, perhaps never to be heard independently. And yet it may suddenly take the place of the first and be heard for itself. When that happens, when we gradually begin to perform the acts done from the old motive under the influence of the new, and thereby either forget the old or supplement the old with the new, then we have what is called *Motiv-wandel* or value movement."

it. On the other hand, we have continuous value movement where there is *gradual* transference of conative tendency to a new object or a new aspect of the same object, where the new worth feeling becomes complementary to the old or the old feeling remains as an undertone in the new.

2. *Classification of Value Movements—Their Directions.*

By the directions of value movement, then, we understand the relatively uniform types of transference of worth feeling to new objects, or to new aspects or funded qualities, of the same objects, whereby new meaning is acquired. As modes of acquirement of worth or affective-volitional meaning, they are, in the first place, distinguishable only appreciatively; but, since such movement presupposes some psychical process whereby the object is modified, and also certain changes in the functional presuppositions of the feeling-attitude toward the object, these appreciative descriptions may be translated into psychological terms. Their appreciative character appears immediately in the terminology employed in their description. They have been classified as upward and downward, as forward and backward movement, as inward movement and as movement toward activity. In each case the immediate feeling or condition worth of the object has acquired some new reference, transgredient or immanental, not previously distinguishable.

We may best study these phenomena by a critical examination of the classifications of these directions, and of the principles which underlie them. Ehrenfels [1] distinguishes four principal types of direction, the upward, the downward, the inward value movements, and what he describes as the movement toward activity. To such a movement he gives the general name *Ziel-folge,* because, while for the subject of the value movement there is no consciousness of end or purpose, nevertheless, in reflection the transitions may be seen to have an internal meaning. We have a *Ziel-folge nach aufwärts,* upward value movement, when an object valued immediately and intrinsically becomes valued mediately because it is instrumental to the attainment of some new object of value. The reverse of this—where an object valued as a means to an end becomes valued for itself, the former object having been lost sight of, he describes as *Ziel-folge nach abwärts.* We have the inward value

[1] *System der Werththeorie,* pp. 132–141.

movement, *Ziel-folge nach innen*, when the worth is transferred from some object of desire or feeling to the disposition which the worth attitude presupposes. Finally, the movement toward activity takes place when the emphasis of valuation is shifted from the object of desire or feeling to the activities involved in the presentation of the object and in reacting upon it.

Illustrations of these four types are everywhere present in our experience. The upward and downward movements are observable in connection with all fundamental instincts and their objects. The satisfaction of hunger, love, need of exercise, of intrinsic worth at first, may come to be valued as instrumental to ideal and conceptual ends, as when food and exercise may be consciously valued as instrumental to bodily and mental health and power, or when experiences of love are sought consciously as means for the development of artistic powers. The downward movement is, on the other hand, seen in cases where money, knowledge, position, etc., sought at first as instruments to other ends, finally become ends in themselves. Illustrations of this tendency may also be seen in both individuals and social groups, where frugality and self-denial, valued first merely as necessary means to ends, acquire an intrinsic value of their own.

The inward value movement, toward the valuation of dispositions intrinsically, often closely connected with the downward movement, is constantly in evidence. Leaving out of consideration the fundamental ethical dispositions which have been historically developed in this way, such as courage, purity, veracity, etc., the fundamental virtues already fixed for social imitation and valuation, we may see the genesis of new dispositions as objects of worth constantly taking place before our eyes. Every marked change in the conditions of life requiring readjustment, involves further specification of disposition through specification of activities, and these dispositions, e.g., in the capitalist and the labourer, the politician and the scholar, become valued for themselves when the immediate ends are lost sight of.

The movement toward activity is also observable in connection with all forms of conative tendency. As we shall see later, it is at the root of all æsthetic attitudes, using the term æsthetic in the broadest sense. Wherever an activity, at first directed toward some concrete object or end, begins to function with relative independence of the end, we have a transference of the emphasis of valuation. The activities of eating, of the hunt, of love-making, of social communication of all sorts, all instinctive at the start, and with definite concrete ends, may become intrinsically valued as mere *forms* of activity. And with this transference of emphasis, comes rearrangement and ordering of the activities as individualised wholes with a meaning of their own.

Schwartz makes a slightly different classification of these phenomena from a somewhat different point of view. It can be shown, however, I think, that it is really with the same uniformities of direction that his analysis is concerned. He distinguishes three fundamental types of value movement, or *Motiv-Wandel*. These are the forward and backward movements and the movement toward activity. By the forward movement is understood the development from mere condition worth to ideal objects and values, either personal or over-individual. Typical illustrations of this movement are the development of passion into ideal love, of merely organic sympathy into conscious benevolence, of curiosity into love of knowledge and truth. In each of these cases physical objects, the worth or funded meaning of which is determined by the modifications of feeling as a condition of the organism, gradually pass over into founded ideal objects whose worth is determined by feelings presupposing the processes of judgment in which the ideal objects were constructed. This is described as the forward movement because it is the normal direction which worth processes take in continuous valuation.

We have the backward movement, on the other hand, when the emphasis of valuation is transferred from the object of immediate appreciation or condition worth, or, indeed, from an ideal object, personal or over-individual, which has developed out of simple appreciation, to the mere hedonic redundancies of the feeling of value. In this phenomenon, the hedonic resonance abstracted from the total attitude, conceived as passive, and presented in conceptual terms as quantity of pleasure, becomes the object of desire and worth feeling. This backward movement is conspicuously present in all forms of conscious hedonism and epicureanism, but is also to be observed in a more subtle form in sentimental enjoyment of emotions of all kinds—sympathetic, religious, moral, etc.

It will be observed that Schwartz does not distinguish a special type of inward value movement toward the valuation of dispositions. The reason for this is clear when we recognise that it is but one aspect of forward value movement. All forward movement is in the direction of the construction of ideal objects and their valuation. Now the disposition is an ideal construct based upon the experience of condition worths, and referred to the self in judgment. It is, therefore, clearly a type of forward movement of ideal reconstruction of experience in the interest of continuity of valuation. The movement toward activity is closely connected with the backward movement, although not to be identified with it.

A comparison of these attempts to classify value movements reveals two facts which, when properly interpreted, will enable us to explain them psychologically, and to show their origin and function in the processes of valuation. In the first place, as has already been suggested, these directions of value movement are appreciative descriptions of certain uniformities in modification of psychical content and function. When they are described as movements, forward and backward, as inward movement and movement toward activity, we have before us a complete system of possible developments of desire or conation from some simple fundamental desire as a point of departure, a system of possible developments through which worth may be acquired.

In the second place, we find that they fall into two general groups: (1) the value movement as transference of worth feeling along the series of means to ends, the upward or downward movement; (2) value movement to some new object, or new aspect of the old object, which gradually emerges in the processes of desire and feeling directed toward the primary object. Such are the inward movement toward the disposition, the movement toward activity, and the backward movement toward the hedonic accompaniments. It is with the second general class that we are here concerned. They are, as we have described them, "continuous" value movements in that they represent continuous acquirement of meaning.

In those value movements where the continuity is reflective, the change in functional presuppositions consists in the interpolation of a relational judgment between desire or feeling and its object. The object is of value because it is instrumental to the attainment of another object of desire. The disposition when viewed as object is of value because it is instrumental to some desirable act, or because it is identified with the subject. Those value movements, on the other hand, which are character-

Values of Simple Appreciation

ised by a gradual change in appreciative attitude, by a change which takes place within an emotional unity and continuity, have changes in presuppositions of another type. They consist for the most part in the gradual substitution of assumptions for the primary judgments, the addition of new judgments and the combination of existential judgments and assumptions in various ways. Both types of value movement arise, as we shall see, as adaptations of conative tendency after arrest and ' distancing ' of the object of immediate desire and feeling; they differ in the extent to which the readaptation involves conceptual reconstruction.

3. *Analysis of Value Movements in Simple Appreciation.*

When we examine more closely this second group of value movements, i.e., where an object acquires new meanings, it is apparent that they are all characterised by the fact that they begin in a *change of attitude* toward the primary object, in which change new feelings, or modifications of feelings, emerge, leading to the imputation of complementary value to the primary object, and ultimately to the construction of new ideal objects. In the first case we have merely an extension of simple appreciation, in the second case an advance to a new level of valuation, as, for instance, of personal worths. The inward value movement and the movement toward activity are first of all value movements of simple appreciation, but they are the germ of later ideal constructions and values.

This gradual change in attitude—with its perceptual and ideal reconstruction of the primary object—involves certain changes in cognitive presuppositions. In general these changes are of the nature of substitution of assumption for judgment, of gradual change of the primary judgment into assumption, explicit or implicit, and emergence of new judgments. The character of these substitutions differs in detail with the specific type of value movement, but the general nature of the process may be described by saying that the primary object of judgment, desire, and feeling, is gradually *distanced*, falls into the background, the feeling of its existence being retained merely as an assumption-feeling, while a new object or new aspect of the old object comes into the foreground as object of presentation and judgment.

To consider in more detail the changes in functional presuppositions involved in the value movements of simple appreciation, we may start with the type of movements described as substitutions. Here it is obvious—for instance, in the case where the marital attitude becomes gradually coloured by the maternal, or reversely, as in the case of Rousseau, described in a preceding chapter,[1]—that we have to do with phenomena of affective subsumption, the nature of which has already been described. As the new aspect of the old object, or the new object, gradually becomes the object of judgment, and, therefore, of new worth feelings, the old judgment-feeling does not disappear, but gradually changes into an assumption-feeling. The old relation, the old attitude, the marital, for instance, remains as a vague presupposition or assumption, and the affective sign which goes with it colours the new feeling. We have in this phenomenon an emotional *continuity*, whereas in the discontinuous value movement, previously described, the transition from one judgmental attitude to another is abrupt.

The inward movement and the movement toward activity on the level of simple appreciation are phenomena of the same general type, of gradual reädaptation. In the first case, the inward movement, the judgment-feeling is gradually modified until it becomes an implicit assumption, and gives place to a new modification of feeling and a new object. The object of primary feeling is one, the existence or non-existence of which is intrinsically desired. Out of this desire springs an act which is instrumentally necessary and instrumentally valued. With the repetition of that act, and the formation of habit or constancy of disposition, the object of immediate desire is *distanced*, the control factor becomes subjective, and new assumptions and judgments emerge. The act itself is assumed to have an intrinsic value, even when abstracted from the object. It acquires an impulsion, a momentum, so to speak, which persists even when the primary object sinks into the background. Such an inward value movement may be either purely individual and sub-social, or partially social in its origin and conditions. It is with its individual aspect that we are first of all concerned.

Now, as has been pointed out, the *completion* of this value movement leads to the presentation of the disposition itself as object of judgment, and to its intrinsic valuation. But between this and the immediate desire for the object or act lies an *intermediate* stage of inward movement, which is the significant

[1] Chap. v, p. 140.

Values of Simple Appreciation 201

phenomenon in this connection. This intermediate attitude is characterised by an intensification of the transgredient reference or tension, through the formation of the dispositional constant. This modification of feeling has, however, as its functional presupposition, merely an assumption of some ultimate object for the transgredient reference of the feeling. Thus the gradual acquirement of the feeling of obligation with reference to any act, a phenomenon which we shall later consider as the most important phase of the inward movement, consists in adding to the worth of the object or act the transgredient reference acquired in the formation of the disposition, this added feeling having as its presupposition the assumption of the existence or non-existence of a more ultimate desirable object to which the reference points. On the level of simple appreciation, of merely *felt* obligation, this object is always indefinite. It is only through ideal construction and explicit judgment, when this transgredient reference is directed explicitly to such objects as the self or the other, the law, the State, or God, that assumption passes over into judgment. The process by which obligatory character is imputed to an object or act may then be viewed as a continuous value-movement in which an old worth feeling is gradually subsumed under a new, the new in this case being the assumption-feeling corresponding to the dispositional constant created. The acquired worth in this case is an increase of the transgredient reference.

The movement toward activity also consists in the gradual distancing of the primary object of desire and worth feeling and the interpolation of a new attitude or object. In its complete form the activity of conation or feeling becomes the presented object of new judgment-feelings, as when for instance the activities of play, the hunt, or love, as in coquetry, become the object of worth themselves, without any conscious reference to their primary objects. But here again, between immediate desire for the object and the stage of explicit valuation of the activity directed toward the object, there is an intermediate phase of importance for simple appreciation. It is the stage where the gradual substitution of the activity leads merely to the imputation of the new worth thus acquired, to the original object of desire. The process here involved is relatively simple. The original object of desire, the judgment of the existence or non-existence of which is followed by worth feelings, is gradually distanced, and for the judgment a mere assumption is substituted.

As the desired object sinks into the background, the *activity* comes into prominence.

Now, the characteristic of this acquired worth, appreciatively described, is its immanental reference. The distancing of the object from immediate desire, which takes place when judgment passes over into assumption, and the coming into the foreground of consciousness of the mere activities of conation and feeling, make possible repose in the object, together with the acquirement of new worth through the independent functioning of the activities originally directed upon the object. When we come to study in more detail the acquirement of æsthetic worth, as the most important aspect of the movement toward activity, we shall find that the acquired immanental reference of the æsthetic attitude is a worth moment which has as its corresponding object those ideal objects which we mean by the words beauty, grace, sublimity, etc. Finally we may see that the movement towards activity, as a felt continuity, must also be viewed as an emotional subsumption. The new feelings which arise in the perceptual and ideal construction of the object in the interests of mere activity, are subsumed under the fundamental emotional attitude, some sentiment or mood, directed toward the primary object.

4. *Interpretation and Explanation of Value Movements: Their Relation to the Laws of Valuation.*

A general review of the changes in functional presuppositions which characterise all these value movements in simple appreciation, discloses the fact that the common element in them all is the distancing of the primary object of desire or feeling, and the interpolation of new feeling attitudes with modified presuppositions. The change of judgment into assumption, the assimilation of new judgments to these assumptions, and through it all a felt continuity, are the significant factors. It is important to emphasise both the fact and the nature of this continuity. These processes are continuous in that, in contrast with the reflective developments or the movements determined by instrumental judgments, all these movements of simple appreciation, the affective substitutions, the inward movement and the movement toward activity, constitute a gradual assimilation of a new meaning to an old object or a new object to an old meaning. In the second place, the character of the continuity is best described as emotional, as an emotional subsumption. The mean term of the transition is emotional; the assumption feeling, representing the judgment habit of former valuations of the primary object, is retained as the background or "affective sign" which gives colour to the new feeling. Such subsumptions we may describe as forms of *emotional logic*.

The justification of this conception of an emotional as distinguished from an intellectual logic has already been attempted in an earlier chapter.[1] In that chapter also the nature and conditions of these affective subsumptions have been treated in their more psychological aspects, and illustrations of the fundamental types of subsumption developed in detail. Here it is important merely to emphasise the fact that the value movements of simple appreciation are of this general type.

But the significance of these emotional continuities really appears only when they are viewed genetically as readaptations (progressions or regressions, as the case may be), following upon the working of those laws of *interest* or of affective-volitional meaning, described as the laws of valuation. The principal law, the law of Limiting Value, which, we have seen, applies to all objects of condition worth, and to all instrumental constructions growing out of valuation of objects of condition worth, may, in its functional aspect, be interpreted as a law of *arrest*, and the value movements as readaptations after arrest. The general law of acquirement of Complementary Value describes in general terms certain forms of readaptation after arrest.[2]

Functionally viewed, the law of Limiting Value formulates the conditions under which arrest and discontinuity of conative process appear. When reduced to their psychological causes, these arrests were seen to be of two general types. In the first place there is the arrest of any isolated conative tendency due to habit and satiety following upon repetition or over-stimulation of the sense tendencies involved. In the second place, however, and equally important, is the modification of feeling, and arrest

[1] Chap. v, pp. 121 ff.
[2] The importance of the moment of arrest in value movement must be emphasised. The criticism made by Hegel upon those theories of the development of mind which proceed in a purely "affirmative manner" may still hold to-day if we translate their intellectualistic terminology into affective-volitional. In speaking of these methods, he says : "Their ruling principle is that the sensible is taken (and with justice) as the prius and the initial basis, but that the latter phases that follow from this starting-point present themselves as emerging in a solely affirmative manner, and the negative aspect of mental activity by which the material is transmuted into mind and destroyed as a sensible is misconceived and overlooked" (*Philosophy of Mind*, William Wallace, The Clarendon Press, sec. 442, p. 61). So also we may say that, while the condition worths are the *prius* of higher levels of valuation, the later phases arise only through arrest of the primary.

of conation when the limit of instrumental judgment is reached, when the reapplicability of the object in question for the satisfaction of primary wants ceases, or when acts, instrumentally valuable in the attainment of objects, become inapplicable, and when attainment is no longer probable, or even possible.

These then are the causes of arrest of conative tendency which lead to value movement. But it is all important to emphasise the fact that these arrests of conative tendency may be complete or only *partial*, for in the difference of the degree of the arrest we have the source of the distinction between different types of value movements. Where the arrest is complete, the value movement is discontinuous, and we have transference of conation and feeling to a new object. Where, on the other hand, the arrest is only partial, we have value movement of the continuous type, the gradual assimilation of a new object to an old, or gradual change in attitude toward the primary object, by which complementary value is acquired. The value of the primary object remains as an assumption, a presupposition of the new feelings.

Finally we may note the teleological character of these value movements. Functionally viewed, they are reädaptations after arrest, whereby continuity of valuation is secured and meaning is acquired. The description of the directions of these movements or types of adaptations, is, we have already seen, appreciative in character, and therefore presupposes the postulate of all appreciative descriptions, enhancement of worth or acquirement of meaning, and is teleological in its nature. But when these value movements are described as teleological, it is obviously not meant that they are determined by an explicit consciousness of end.[1] Such explicit reference to ends appears only upon the higher levels of valuation. Looking back from these higher levels, we may see that the complementary values of objects of condition worth contain the germ of developments to higher levels, but the objects of valuation on these higher levels are not foreseen in simple appreciation. In the value movements of simple appreciation the teleology is wholly immanental.

[1] The use made of Wundt's descriptive formula (Heterogeneity of Ends) in describing these progressions constitutes an explicit denial of such character to the processes. The complementary values which arise in these movements are unforeseen, are not presented in idea, but gradually emerge in the acquisition or enjoyment of objects of primary condition worth. The teleological character appears rather as immanental and is described by the application of Wundt's second principle the Law of Resultants. The results of these value movements, of these perceptual and ideal constructions of the object, have a worth or meaning not in the elements.

III. ETHICAL AND ÆSTHETIC VALUES ACQUIRED IN VALUE MOVEMENTS OF SIMPLE APPRECIATION — THEIR RÔLE AS DETERMINANTS OF THE ECONOMIC VALUES OF ACQUISITION AND CONSUMPTION

1. *Ethical and Æsthetic Values as Modifications of Feelings of Condition Worth.*

There are two fundamental ways in which the simple appreciation of the condition worth of the object may be modified. The worth attitude may acquire the attribute of obligation or of æsthetic repose in the object. These acquired feelings then become the basis of imputation of new worth to the object.

It is of the utmost importance to recognise the relativity of these appreciative differences. The a priori distinctions drawn by Kant do not maintain themselves upon closer analysis. Genetically viewed, the more primitive ethical and æsthetic values arise in the very processes of consumption and acquisition. The obligation to cleanliness and thrift, the æsthetic values of taste and refinement in living, are acquired almost imperceptibly. And from the analytical point of view also, it is impossible to say that obligation is something fundamentally different from desire or that the æsthetic is desireless appreciation. They are merely appreciative distinctions within the total worth process, modifications of attitude by which meaning is acquired. And, when the problem is approached from the side of economic analysis, it is seen that even the economist cannot keep his province distinct, but is forced to see his general laws modified by the intrusion of ethical and æsthetic motives. These facts, which constitute the bane of the various worth sciences when they seek to work alone, are precisely those which contain the greatest promise for worth theory as a whole. An act or an attitude acquires ethical worth or meaning when it becomes obligatory, and for an act to be felt as obligatory, means that it has become the object of a new kind of worth feeling. An object acquires æsthetic worth or meaning when it becomes, as we say, beautiful, the term being used in its larger sense to include all the modifications of the æsthetic. And for an object to be felt as beautiful, means that it has become the object of a new kind of worth feeling. In each case the oughtness or the beauty of act or object is a funded meaning or worth acquired in some process and imputed to the object or act.

When we seek to describe appreciatively these new meanings, we find that in each case the object has acquired a new capacity, a capacity of calling out certain appreciatively different modifications of feeling; and when we seek to define these modifications, it appears that they may best be described as a deepening of certain modifications of feeling which have already been discovered to be the fundamental aspects of worth feeling. Appreciatively the sense of obligation, as we have already seen in a preceding chapter,[1] is but a deepening of the *transgredient reference* of the dynamic tension, one of the fundamental modes of worth feeling. When an act acquires the coefficient of obligation, it acquires a new impulsion which has its ground neither in the instrumental reference of the act to other acts or objects, nor in its immediate hedonic accompaniments, but in some larger system of meanings which is vaguely felt to be presupposed. Appreciatively described, the sense of beauty is a deepening of the *immanental reference* of the feeling. When the object acquires the quality of beauty, it acquires the capacity of holding us, of confining the energy of conation and feeling to an expansion of feeling, to repose in the object. Such are the appreciative differences in these two modifications of the funded meaning of objects. They have also an aspect in common. Both worths are intrinsic, that is, the worth of the object as revealed in the sense of obligation or in the feeling of beauty, is not felt as an instrumental value rising from the capacity of the object to produce these modifications of feeling, or to bring about such effects indirectly through relations with other objects, but the quality of obligation is felt to be in the act or disposition itself, that of beauty to be in the object as immediately intuited.

These two acquired modes of simple appreciation we have already characterised as the *impellent* and *semblant* modes respectively, and a general sketch of the origination of these modes or attitudes has already been given. Our present task is to develop that sketch in more detail and to show that the progress to these two attitudes, or modes of simple appreciation, is but a special form of the "inward" value movement and particularly the movement toward activity already described.

[1] Chap. III, pp. 68-71.

2. The Ethical Mode of Simple Appreciation—Its Modification of the Condition Worth of Objects.

(a) *Analysis of the Impellent Mode of Obligation.*

An attempt to analyse more completely the sense of obligation shows that it is, in one sense, an ultimate mode of appreciation which is not further reducible. Our description of it as a deepening of the transgredient reference as impellent mode, is in reality only a description and not a definition. Strictly speaking, definition is impossible. If we wish to go further in our fixation of this mode of experience, it must be by a method of interpolation of the mode in a series of equally ultimate meanings, and by determination of their psychological equivalents. But in following this procedure we are immediately met by a considerable difference of opinion. Thus Simmel finds obligation to be a fundamental modality of thought (Denk Modus) ; others describe it as a mode of will and still others as a mode of feeling. On closer inspection it will, nevertheless, appear, I think, that there is no necessary irreconcilability in these different views. Worth experience, of which obligation is a mode, is seen always to be feeling with certain cognitive presuppositions, while the distinction between feeling and will has, on closer analysis, shown itself to be a relative difference of intent and not of content.

Simmel finds obligation, *das Sollen*, in one aspect, a mode of thought which lies midway between the judgments of non-existence and existence. Speaking of the various possible attitudes toward objects, he says: " One could arrange them all in a phenomenological series which extends from the mere presentation of an object for our thought, without existence, to complete reality. Das Wollen, das Hoffen, das Können, das Sollen, all these are, so to speak, mediate stages between non-existence and existence, which, for one who has never experienced them, we could as little define as we are able to say what being or thinking really is: there is no definition of obligation."[1] Here then the attitude of obligation is indirectly defined by giving it its place in a continuous vital series, in much the same fashion that the relations of attitudes of feeling and will were defined in Brentano's series. What is it that distinguishes the attitude of obligation from the adjacent terms or modes in the series ?

[1] Simmel, *Einleitung in die Moralwissenschaft*, Berlin, 1892, Vol. I, p. 8.

Evidently it is its different cognitive presuppositions. It will be recalled that we found the difference between feeling and will in difference of intent or meaning of the same content according as the object is recognised as independent of, or dependent upon, the subject. With the recognition of independence of the object we have feeling, with the recognition of dependence we have desire or volition, according to the degree of the dependence. Now worth feeling is feeling with judgments or assumptions as its presuppositions, and the sense of obligation being a mode of worth feeling, we must look for its differentia in these terms. The feelings, " I wish," " I hope," " I can," " I should," " I must," " I will," represent an ascending scale of changes in these presuppositions in which the dependence of the act or object upon the self comes more clearly to consciousness. " I wish " presupposes merely the judgment of non-existence ; "I hope," this judgment as qualified by an assumption of possibility ; " I must " represents this possibility as having passed over into explicit judgment of existence. The feeling " I ought " lies midway between power and constraint.

Obligation, when thus inserted into a series of cognate attitudes, is seen to be, in one aspect, a mode of thought. But this serial method of interpretation also enables us to answer the other question as to whether it is a mode of feeling or will. Common speech allows either description. For just as we *feel* need or hope, or our power to do a thing, so we may equally well be said to feel the obligation or the necessity of an act. The sense of obligation may, therefore, very properly be described as a mode of worth feeling. On the other hand, when seen prospectively, in the light of the succeeding attitude of will, the sense of oughtness seems to be nearer to, in fact a preliminary stage of volition. The validity of both descriptions appears when we apply the results of our preceding study and recognise that the distinction between feeling and will is itself not ultimate, but that will is also feeling with certain characteristic presuppositions. The sense of obligation appears to be a mode of will, and not feeling, only when the term feeling is limited to those hedonic concomitants which go with emotional disturbance. The feeling of obligation is by no means to be identified with emotional disturbance, for the deepest obligation may be represented by affective abstracts and even by affective signs, often the mere emotional connotation of a word.

If this analysis of the sense of obligation is adequate, it is not difficult to show its place in the system of value movements by which condition worths acquire complementary value. Its subsumption under the inward movement has already been suggested in a preceding paragraph, where it was seen to be a movement from the desire for the object itself to an attitude where the desire is qualified by a consciousness of the disposition presupposed. It is an inward movement in which the object, or act directed toward its realisation, acquires all the meaning of this inward reference. The "distancing" of the object, its detachment from immediate satisfaction through arrest, is followed by the deepening of the transgredient reference, which in turn is the sign of the added element of a subjective control having its *locus* in the pre-formed disposition. The mere feeling of the non-existence of the object is supplemented by the assumption of possibility, the feeling "I can," which then passes over into judgments of existence and necessity. The impellent mode which later develops into explicit sense of obligation is, therefore, a transition stage between desire springing out of non-existence and the sense of the "must be" which comes with the judgment of existence.[1]

(*b*) *Pre-Ethical and Quasi-Ethical Impulsions and Obligations: Their Sub-Personal and Sub-Social Character.*

The feeling of obligation in its simplest, pre-ethical form, as impellent mode, is accordingly merely a new modification of worth feeling. This modification is, as has been already pointed out, at first, in its germinal form, objectless. Its apparent object is still the primary object of simple desire, the simple desire and feeling having been insensibly qualified by the deepening of the transgredient reference. Its real object, however, is the disposition presupposed, and ultimately the ideal construct of the self or the social group, to which the feeling is referred when the progression or value movement has reached the stage of explicit acknowledgment and characterisation of the presuppositions of the feeling. For this explicit acknowledgment

[1] This origin of the movement toward obligation as dependent upon arrest is well described by Simmel in Vol. II, p. 387 of the *Einleitung*, "Das Sollen nimmt eine mittlere Stellung zwischen dem Müssen und dem Wollen ein; beim Müssen stellen sich der Handlung, die schlieslich aus einem überwiegenden Grunde doch gewollt wird, sehr starke Wollungen entgegen; bei dem freien Wollen gar keine; bei dem Sollen eine gewisse Anzahl, deren Überwindung das Maass des sittlichen Verdienstes angiebt." He is here describing obligation on the higher levels of personal and social worths.

P

and characterisation in judgment, certain processes of sympathetic imitation and projection, or *Einfühlung*, are necessary. But the object, later to be characterised and acknowledged, is vaguely anticipated in the transgredient reference of the feeling. The objects of the feeling of obligation are therefore always ideal objects, and it is their worth which is reflected in the feeling of obligation.

The feeling of obligation has, accordingly, different degrees of explicitness. It may be merely felt, as in simple appreciation, or it may be explicitly referred to some ideal object. In the first case some object of the new qualification of feeling is vaguely assumed, while in the second case some ideal object, such as the ideal of the self and its dispositions, or the idea of social good or law, is constructed, and to this the feeling is referred.

We may distinguish three levels of development at which this deepened transgredient reference may appear, and they may be described, in Guyau's terms, as the three *psychological equivalents* of obligation.[1] The *first* equivalent is that which we have described as belonging to the level of simple appreciation, the dynamic suggestion, the transgredient reference which an attitude attains in an individual as the result merely of the formation of conative dispositions or constants through repetition and habit. This equivalent we may describe as the instinctive, pre-ethical, obligation on the level of simple appreciation of objects. The *second* equivalent is the tension, deepening of the transgredient reference, which arises through sympathetic projection (Einfühlung). The presumption of the existence of the feeling and feeling-disposition in another, or in social groups, deepens the transgredient reference of the feeling as condition of the subject. This Guyau describes as tension arising from "fusion" of desires and feelings. The *third* equivalent is the further increase of tension or transgredient reference which arises at the stage of reflection when the object of the feeling is explicitly characterised and acknowledged as a *demand*, personal or over-individual, social or ideal, as the case may be. This third equivalent corresponds to the distinctly ethical obligation. The others may be described as the pre-ethical and quasi-ethical, respectively.

The situations in which this deepening of the worth consciousness, described as the sense of obligation, appears most

---

[1] Guyau, *Esquisse d'une Morale, sans obligation et sanction*, Book I, chap. III, especially p. 127.

Values of Simple Appreciation

marked are, as the Kantian analysis rightly discovered, those in which oppositions between personal and over-individual worths, and between personal or over-individual worths and condition worths occur, where in fact preference and sacrifice appear. Such situations presuppose processes of sympathetic projection and the ideal construction of personal and over-individual objects toward which the feeling of obligation is directed. The feeling of obligation in such cases presupposes, therefore, explicit judgments of the existence or non-existence of the objects and explicit references of them to the self or the alter. With these we shall be concerned in later chapters. But while the higher levels of obligation presuppose these processes of social projection and imitation, it must not be thought that the feeling of obligation is, as simple impellent mode, exclusively social in its origin, or that the value movement toward the ethical is conditioned by the presentation of the attitude as a personal or social worth. This is as far from the truth as it would be to say that the æsthetic mode of worth experience is socially conditioned because most of the specific æsthetic activities are social in their origin. The primary sense of obligation is, as Guyau in his splendid analysis shows, both sub-personal and sub-social. Mere instinctive feeling, as a simple condition worth, prior to its presentation either as an attitude of the self or the alter, has in it the potentiality of that situation of contrast and opposition out of which the sense of obligation arises. Guyau has described this primary sense of obligation as strictly correlative to the sense of capacity. Wherever in the face of arrest emerges the sense of "I can," there tends to follow from it imperceptibly the sense of "I ought."

(c) Illustrations of Various Instinctive, Quasi-Ethical Obligations.

Let us, then, first examine some expressions of this sub-personal, sub-social sense of obligation prior to ideal construction and conscious reference of feeling to ideals. There is scarcely any conative tendency which cannot under certain conditions acquire the sense of obligation. We are hardly aware of the constant undertone of obligation which accompanies our simplest, most instinctive acts. One of the most noticeable, and also most instructive, is the sense of obligation which the mere possession of brute physical strength may acquire. We begin to exert our strength for a given end. If opposition appears, we frequently find ourselves impelled to persist long after the object of the original effort loses its interest. The place of worth has been usurped by the attitude. Inward value movement has taken place. All this would be simple enough in those cases where persistence of effort is, under the stimulus of social imitation and contrast, ideally presented as a personal worth, or as an object with over-individual reference, but the point here is that experience shows us this obligation emerging on the level of simple appreciation, sub-personally and sub-socially, prior to the ideal presentation of the attitude.

And if strength obliges, it is also true that other instinctive activities connected with condition worths acquire the sense of obligation. Sex, for instance, has its impulsions of an instinctive sort, prior to that reference of its attitudes and dispositions to the self and society which creates the ethical and moral obligation proper. Of such instinctive obligation Guyau has given a good illustration in the case of a young girl who cast herself out of the window rather than endure the embraces of a husband who did not call out her love. Her state of mind bore all the characteristic marks of the feeling of remorse, although all the acquired obligations, personal and social, were met. She had obeyed the commands of her parents and the demands of society, but the instinctive obligations of sex triumphed in the form not merely of distaste and unhappiness, but of a primary form of remorse of the most fundamental character. So too the derived emotional attitude of shame, which represents the product of a long series of racial inhibitions, carries with it a primary obligation of such a character that, even after reflective consideration, after the construction of personal and social ideals which tend to modify it, it triumphs in an instinctive obligation which cannot be gainsaid.

An instructive characteristic of these obligations, which may perhaps serve to account for their retention after reflection comes in to modify them, is their complementary worth, heightening the worth of the instinctive activity itself. Indeed one of the most remarkable phenomena of the worth consciousness is precisely this tendency to retain obligations and even to create them. In connection with this very instinct of sex, the innumerable little delicacies of obligation with which it hedges itself about, the inhibitions which it, so to speak, sets itself, often of no social significance and sub-personal in so far as they are not consciously referred to the self, are so many ways of instinc-

Values of Simple Appreciation 213

tively acquiring new worth and meaning. Cases, almost abnormal in character, have been pointed out (Zola describes it in the case of one of his characters) of women who, after a life in which they have abandoned these instinctive inhibitions, obligations, and shames of sex, have, when entering upon a real passion, sought to restore them with a zeal no less than pathetic. The sense of unworthiness in the presence of a true love leads to the development of a conscious cult of modesty which the pure woman who had never felt the loss of these values would never think of building up.

The significance of these phenomena which, although they have been described in the case of but two fundamental conative tendencies, are really characteristic of all, for the instinctive creation of individual obligations is everywhere present in our affective-volitional life, lies in the fact that this primary equivalent of obligation, this tendency to inward value movement, whereby the object of immediate desire is set at a distance, and thus acquires the complementary value of the transgredient reference of the disposition presupposed, is a *normal* form of value movement in the acquirement of affective-volitional meaning. It is a special form of that general law of value movements, the principle of Heterogeneity of Ends according to which conative tendency directed toward an object develops new ends and values not foreseen.

(d) Modification of Economic Valuation by these Acquired Obligations.

The close relation which has been shown to exist between simple desire and instinct and the primary equivalent of obligation gives us a point of view from which we may understand the genetic relation between simple condition worths in general and ethical worths, more particularly between economic and ethical values. The economic value of an object is determined by its capacity to satisfy desire, either intrinsically by virtue of its relation to conative dispositions, or instrumentally through its causal relation to other objects which have this intrinsic capacity. The activities of acquisition and consumption which determine the economic worth of an object are themselves unethical, nonmoral, but may obviously acquire ethical values, and become moralised. Certainly they may become moralised through their relation to personal and social ends presented ideally as intrinsically valuable objects with which the economic activities are instrumentally related. But it would also seem that in the mere processes of acquisition and consumption these condition worths may insensibly acquire an ethical meaning. The instinctive obligations which we have described may become thus qualified, independently of any consciousness of more remote ends, personal or social, presupposed in the processes of mere acquisition and consumption. For such quasi-ethical qualifications there are, as we have seen, definite descriptive terms such as thrift, enterprise, cleanliness, etc. They represent dispositions which, at first merely instrumental to the condition worths of acquisition and consumption, may later be intrinsically valued as personal worths, or imputed as intrinsic complementary worths to the primary objects of desire, of acquisition and consumption. It is with the latter phenomenon that we are here concerned, and an analysis of the principles which underlie this imputation will disclose the essential features of the process by which mere condition worths acquire the coëfficient of obligation; and secondly, the way in which this acquired meaning modifies the laws which govern judgments of economic value.

In our study of the Laws of Valuation,[1] it was seen that valuation moves between the two limits, or thresholds, which mark off relative valuation from worthlessness on the one hand, and from absolute worth on the other. The lower threshold is that minimum of the good which has least importance, that is the smallest increment the existence or non-existence of which calls out a modification of worth feeling. The upper threshold, or the "existence-minimum," is that minimum of a good, without capacity of substitution, the possession of which constitutes the necessary presupposition of all further relative valuation, and which, therefore, itself has absolute value. In the sphere of condition worths, with which we are here concerned, the objects corresponding to these thresholds are quantities of a physical object, the desirability of which lies in its capacity to satisfy certain fundamental sense tendencies. It is in the modification of these thresholds that the acquirement of the feeling of obligation is seen to modify the judgments of condition worth.

It is beyond question, I suppose, that the feeling of the worth of an object which constitutes the *minimum of existence*, and which is without capacity of substitution, is quasi-ethically qualified, has the acquired feeling of obligation. Within limits,

---

[1] See chap. VI, pp. 148 ff.

Values of Simple Appreciation 215

which we cannot here consider, self-preservation is the first law of life. It is the most primitive instinctive obligation which arises when the arrest of conative tendency is carried far enough. There may not be a transgredient reference of the feeling to an idea of the self so explicit that the feeling of personal obligations arises, but there is at least a transgredient reference to the whole system of ideal ends which are founded upon the preservation of life.[1] Now, strictly speaking, the feeling of the intrinsic value of the object, the obligatory character of the act directed toward the acquisition of the object, falls off rapidly after the minimum of existence is passed. Larger quantities of the good have only relative instrumental value, for the reason that they satisfy only secondary and acquired tendencies, and have capacity for substitution. But it is precisely at this point that acquired complementary values with their coëfficient of obligation may come in to modify this law and to change the threshold of relative valuation. If, for instance, the acquired complementary value of cleanliness has supervened upon the consumption of the raw material of desire, and if a corresponding disposition is formed with the coëfficient of obligation, the minimum of existence—the quantity of goods which has absolute value, and for which indefinite sacrifice will be made—will be increased. Whatever is an absolutely necessary condition to a certain irreducible minimum of cleanliness will acquire absolute value. And in fact, as we shall see later, when such a disposition is referred to the personality, and acquires personal worth, its obligation may be of such a character as to lead to the risk of life itself. On this level of simple appreciation the acquirement of the coëfficient of obligation is seen to impute additional value to objects of mere condition worth.

The acquirement of the feeling of obligation is, then, followed by imputation of intrinsic worth to the object. This leads us to the consideration of a second phenomenon, namely, the modification of the *lower* threshold of " final utility " through the imputation of the feeling of obligation to the object. This phenomenon may be more definitely described by saying that

---

[1] This statement would seem, at first sight, to be an illustration of what Baldwin aptly calls the *fallacy of the implicit*. The system of ideal ends founded upon the presupposition of self-preservation is, of course, not present as a motive in any sense. The feeling of instinctive obligation toward one's life is, like any impellent mode of feeling, strictly speaking, *objectless*. All that is meant by this statement is that, after arrest of instinctive conation, affirmation acquires an intrinsic meaning of its own which specifies itself later in various ideal ends.

an acquired obligation, the result of an inward value movement, may make intrinsically valuable a quantity of an object which is instrumentally valueless, i.e., below the threshold. The pursuit of the minimum of existence develops an instinctive obligation in the manner described. The effort itself, the economic virtue of enterprise, becomes intrinsically valuable. So also does the most economic disposal of the goods, describable as the economic virtue of thrift. This acquired intrinsic and complementary value is then imputed as an additional value to the purely instrumental values of quantities of the good, which would, according to the law of Marginal Utility, if it were alone determinative, approach to worthlessness. The illustration of the small coin, instrumentally valueless but intrinsically of worth, described in our study of the concept of the threshold, is a case in point. And in general the very real obligation, often largely instinctive and without explicit ends, which impels men to acquire and conserve property after it ceases to have appreciable instrumental value for them, is of this nature.

III. Æsthetic Appreciation as a Special Form of the Movement toward Activity—Its Modification of Condition Worths

The distinctive attribute of the æsthetic mode of experience, in contrast to the ethical, is its immanency. Both attitudes are intrinsic, but while the ethical mode is appreciatively describable as a deepening of the transgredient reference, the æsthetic is seen to be a deepening of the immanental reference. In our analysis of appreciative descriptions in the first chapter, we found it to be characterised by repose in the object and increase of expansive suggestions of the feeling. From the standpoint of the genetic study of value movements we subsumed the movement toward the æsthetic under the general type of movement toward activity. It remains now to correlate these two points of view, to show how the changes in function and content involved in the movement toward activity are the determining conditions of this repose in the object and expansion of feeling: how in fact in one attitude repose and activity may be combined, and how this combination creates complementary worth which is then imputed to the object.

As in the case of our study of the ethical qualification of

condition worths, through the acquirement of the obligation coëfficient, so our study of the æsthetic qualification must begin with an attempt to define the psychological equivalents of the appreciative description. And here, again, we find the same problem presented. Are æsthetic attitudes modes of feeling, of conation, or of cognition? The answers are varied, and, again, I am inclined to think, not necessarily contradictory. Properly viewed, i.e., genetically, the æsthetic attitude will be seen to be a mode definable in all three terms. Let us begin, however, with an examination of certain attempts to find the equivalent of æsthetic appreciation in feeling, as determined by certain order or arrangement of sensational and presentational content.

1. *Analysis of the Æsthetic Mode of Appreciation.*

In each of these attempts the question is asked, Why do we have this specific ordering or rearrangement of content which is characteristic of the æsthetic experience? And in each case the reply is, if we neglect differences in terminology, in order that there may be the greatest amount of pleasure for the greatest length of time without satiety. But while all reckon with this conceptual abstraction of quantity of pleasure, they, nevertheless, introduce appreciative descriptions of this pleasure which immediately bring the æsthetic experience back into the sphere of worths. It is at this point that the formulations differ, but, upon analysis, they show, I think, a common element which we may accept as a true account of the origin of this rearrangement and of its significance for individual experience.

For Marshall [1] the essential element in the æsthetic rearrangement of content consists in the fact that it constructs a " widened field " of pleasurable revival. The characteristic of this field is that it presents a larger number of moderate stimulations of greater equality of intensity instead of a narrow field of greater intensity. The result is twofold: the satiety which would follow from intense local stimulation is deferred, and with it the consequent value movement to a new object; and, secondly, a qualitative difference of breadth is introduced into the pleasure, and the conditions for dwelling upon the object are created.

For Groos,[2] the essential in the æsthetic is the increase of

---

[1] Marshall, *Pleasure, Pain, and Æsthetics*, p. 335.
[2] Groos, *Der æsthetische Genuss*, Giessen, 1902, chap. I.

pleasure through "playful illusion." Here, again, we have an appreciative differentiation of æsthetic pleasures from others, in that both these terms, play and illusion, have a functional meaning. In his earlier psychological works, which were concerned largely with the genesis of playful illusion as a significant function, Groos was inclined to account for the *pleasure* of both the "play" and "illusion" aspects by connecting it with their biological utility,—as a pleasure arising from the mere activity of these instincts themselves. But in his later work,[1] which is concerned more with the analysis of the æsthetic attitude itself, the emphasis is put upon the rearrangement of the field of content. Here the idea is developed that the playful dwelling in "inner imitation" upon the impressions of things, the temporary identification of the self with other things or persons, with its moment of conscious self-illusion, are the functional conditions which make possible the fusions and complications of sensational and associational content out of which complementary pleasures arise. The changes in content which thus take place are twofold. There is, first, a widening of the field of experience, through inclusion, in the intuitive moment of fusion, of the complementary associations; and, secondly, an elimination of all elements which are inharmonious with the total experience, and which, by their intensity or power to divert the attention, would lead to judgments and value movements—in short, all illusion-disturbing moments. Conversely, it may be added, an arrangement of content which brings about this fusion, and eliminates these disturbing moments, creates the æsthetic illusion. Here, again, the essential features are the widening of the field of experience, and the repose in it, made possible through elimination of the elements which would break up the attitude.

Again, it is held that the essential characteristic of the æsthetic experience is that it combines in a unique way the distinct pleasures of activity and repose. A somewhat incomplete conception of this view may be given in the following quotation: "The diffusion of stimulation, the equilibrium of impulses, life-enhancement through repose—this is the æsthetic experience."[2] Taking these elements of the definition in reverse order, the moment of repose is produced by equilibrium of impulses. Here we have conative activity, but if these activities are in

---

[1] Groos, *Der æsthetische Genuss.*
[2] Puffer, *The Psychology of Beauty*, chap. III.

equilibrium, and if no one breaks loose, so to speak, to become a fundamental, either in the form of desire or judgment, we have repose of desire and judgment, and consequently no value movement. But this equilibrium of impulses, in so far as it is conditioned by arrangement of content, is brought about by a diffusion of stimulation, i.e., by a widened field of well-balanced stimulations. To the technical means employed in the creation of this widened field of diffused and balanced stimulation, we shall have occasion to refer later. The important point here is the definition.

With this sketch of the three formulations before us, it is not difficult to define the common element. This is clearly the concept of the widened ground of diffused stimulation, the *balance* of impulses, so that no one shall constitute an illusion-disturbing moment and lead to readjustment in a new value movement, the consequent *repose* of conation in the object and the *expansion* of feeling which goes with it. The ordering, rearrangement of content characteristic of the æsthetic experience is, therefore, in the service of the deepening, or enhancement of that fundamental mode of worth experience which is appreciatively described as the immanental reference, the expansive suggestion of the feeling. But this repose of conation, with its expansion of feeling, is, as the preceding analysis made clear, conditioned by a characteristic change in the content of the experience, by a reconstruction of this content in such a manner that the foreground of consciousness is taken up with secondary and subsidiary activities of sensation and presentation, with a "play" of impressions which inhibits the fundamental conative tendency with which they are associated. What the technique of this reconstruction of the widened field of attention may be, we have yet to consider, but it is apparent that it must be of the general nature of substitution of a multiplicity of subsidiary activities for the fundamental conative tendency.

This view of the characteristic modification of the content of the æsthetic experience is, however, incomplete without a corresponding analysis of the æsthetic as *attitude*. Such change in content presupposes a change in the presuppositions of the feeling-attitude. Thus far we have considered the æsthetic mode only as a mode of feeling. We must now consider it in its genetic relations to other worth attitudes, as a mode of conation and cognition.

(b) *Analysis of the Cognitive Presuppositions of the Æsthetic Mode —Interpolation in the Vital Series.*

The answer to this problem is possible only through the employment of the same method, the attempt to locate the mode in a vital series of attitudes, used in the analysis of the sense of obligation. When thus viewed, the æsthetic is seen to be not desireless appreciation, as it is sometimes held, nor feeling with mere presentations as its presuppositions. The æsthetic attitude is seen to have both conative and cognitive presuppositions. The object which now presents this widened field is in the first place an object of desire and judgment; the impulses which are balanced in the æsthetic field were first of all impulses subsidiary to some fundamental conative tendency directed toward the object. When the movement toward activity takes place—when the object as desired sinks into the background, is distanced, the fundamental desire becomes, it is true, dispositional, but it is this presence as a desire-disposition which gives the depth of immanental reference in the feeling of repose—as we have already seen in the illustration of the appreciation of feminine beauty.[1] The æsthetic as a feeling mode lies, then, midway between the passivity of sensation feeling and explicit desire, the distinction of feeling and desire being only relative.

Nor is the æsthetic pure "presentation-feeling" without reference to reality. Here, again, the method of interpolation shows it to be a mode of thought midway between the judgment of existence and the judgment of non-existence. Before the movement toward the æsthetic, the object as object of desire, actual or possible, was the object of explicit judgments of existence or non-existence. With the distancing of the object, and the transformation of explicit desire into feeling, there is a change in presuppositions. The æsthetic feeling is no longer a judgment-feeling, neither is it merely a "presentation" feeling, but rather an assumption-feeling. In æsthetic feeling the existence of the object is always assumed, unless explicit judgment of non-existence supplants the assumption.

Here is to be found the element of truth in the description of the æsthetic as conscious self-illusion. This internally contradictory term is a somewhat bungling way of describing a

[1] Chap. III., p. 71

Values of Simple Appreciation

real mode of experience, that intermediate stage of adaptation between explicit judgment and explicit judgment. It is an assumption of reality which will suffice for the temporary repose in the object, and for the realisation of all the values which that object may have for conation when desire is explicit and its presuppositions are existential judgments. But the illusion may be said to be conscious, and to be self-illusion, *only* in the sense that the assumption, although possessing the coëfficient of reality which it has by virtue of its actualisation, in its own special way, of a conative disposition, is under the control of the habits of judgment and implicit assumptions created in former experience, so that ordinarily any tendency of the assumption to pass over into explicit judgment is inhibited. It is not a conscious self-illusion in the sense that its control is conditioned by a conscious reference to the self.

2. *The Origin of the Movement toward Activity and the Æsthetic Attitude—Its Individual and Sub-Social Character.*

The preceding analysis of the structural and functional modifications characteristic of the æsthetic attitude and experience justifies its subsumption under the general type of value movement described as movement toward activity. In the first place, to consider the second aspect first, there is the substitution of assumption for judgment and the *distancing* of the object or its detachment, from immediate desire, characteristic of the semblant mode. With it, in the second place, comes the enhancement of worth through the increased activity of the subsidiary tendencies of sensation, presentation, etc., characteristic of the imaginative attitude. With this account of the nature of the æsthetic mode comes the problem of its *genesis* as a mode of simple appreciation. The problem is in reality twofold : (*a*) what are the conditions of the movement toward activity itself ; and (*b*) what is the origin of the specific form of activity, with its quality of detachment, which characterises the æsthetic ?

(*a*) *Conditions of Movement toward Activity in its Pre-Æsthetic Form.*

As the origin of the inward movement toward the attitude of obligation is thought by many to be wholly social, so also there is a similar tendency to account for the genesis of the æsthetic in merely social terms. The study of the beginnings of art gives a certain plausibility to this view in that much of the rearrangement, reconstruction, of expression of emotions and objects of emotion, seems to be directly connected with the motive of securing social consent in emotional expression, and thus of enhancement of sympathetic participation. The element of order introduced into crude emotional expression is accordingly conceived to have a purely social origin. Nevertheless, while social sympathy may enhance æsthetic worth, and while the motive of social consent may determine many forms of art, both the movement toward the æsthetic itself, and the reconstruction of content involved in that movement, must, it seems to me, like the movement to the ethical, be sub-social and individual in their origin. As a value movement in the individual, its functional conditions must be looked for in the general conditions of value movement, arrest of the *fundamental* through distancing of the object of desire, or through satiety and substitution of subsidiary tendencies.

In his valuable work on *The Origins of Art*[1] Hirn has emphasised this aspect of the origin of art. In the first place, he has distinguished in a very satisfactory way between the question of the functional genesis of the æsthetic psychosis itself and the question of the historical origin of particular forms of artistic expression. He has seen clearly that the various activities in which the æsthetic specifies itself (the concrete origins of art through the secondary social motives of conveying information, display, and self-exhibition, erotic and martial stimulation, etc.) do not explain the antecedent emotional psychosis which they presuppose and express. These are rather activities, emotional and volitional, in which an antecedent need of emotional expression specifies itself. The art impulse itself, or, in our terms, the movement toward activity, must be sought in deeper and more general functional causes. These he finds in the tendency to the development of secondary activities when the primary is subject to arrest. From the standpoint of description in terms of pleasure and pain, art serves either as the reliever of the pain which comes from thwarted conative tendencies, or else as a means of enhancing the pleasure of a fundamental already pleasurable, and of postponing the moment of satiety.

[1] Hirn, *The Origins of Art*, Macmillan, 1900, chaps. I, IV, and VI.

Values of Simple Appreciation 223

Space will not permit a detailed study of the facts of individual and social psychology by means of which this view is substantiated —how sorrowful emotions, and even painful sensations, may really be the relief of deep-seated arrest of activity through the substitution of secondary activities, and may thus attain a positive worth ; how in the social expressions of grief, in the wailing feats of certain savages, and in the *vocero* in general, not only is sorrow relieved, but positive joy of a new sort, joy in expression, in activity, is generated ; how in their orgies the Mænads, by noise, roaring and loud cries, by frenetic dance and wild actions, even by tortures, strove to preserve and recover the faded sense of life which ever baffled their exertions. But enough has been said to show that much of the movement toward activity, out of which artistic activity is ultimately born, is due to the painful arrest of conative tendency. The object of the fundamental conative tendency, of desire and sorrow, is distanced, the full realisation of its existence or non-existence is supplanted by a vague assumption which gives but an undertone to the whole experience, while the activity of the subsidiary tendencies usurps the foreground of consciousness.

This is indeed one mode of origin of the movement toward activity, but it does not include that movement toward activity which results in *enhancement* of the worth of an object already desirable, i.e., possessing the capacity of satisfying a fundamental desire. The movement in this case is to be understood also as an adaptation after arrest, but here the arrest of conative tendency appears at another point. We have elsewhere seen that when once a fundamental conative tendency has through repeated arrests concentrated about it subsidiary tendencies, a too immediate or exclusive satisfaction of the fundamental leads to satiety in which the subsidiary tendencies are left unsatisfied. The movement toward activity of the subsidiary tendencies has as its motive in many cases the distancing of the object of desire in the interest of continuity of valuation of the same object in that to its worth is added the complementary value of the secondary activities.

Of this character are the form-qualities added to the economic activities of acquisition and consumption already discussed ; and the artistic reconstruction of objects of use so that æsthetic repose in them is possible seems to be, from this point of view, of the same general character—the distancing of the object as an object of utility, the feelings of instrumental worth being, as we have seen, by their very nature, quickly subject to the law of limiting value. Finally, the distancing of the object of sex, the movement toward mere activity in both coquetry and idealisation, whatever its biological origin may be, appears, as individual value movement, to be of the same character. It may be said, therefore, that the origin of the movement toward activity is, as has already been shown in our general study of value movements, to be found in the arrest of fundamental conative tendency.

(b) *The Special Differentia of the Æsthetic.*

But it may be properly objected that, while this is a true account of the origin of the general type of " movement toward activity," that while it is true that the causes of this movement are sub-social and individual, nevertheless, these movements, as such, are not necessarily movements to the æsthetic attitude. All movements to the æsthetic are movements toward activity, but not all movements toward activity are æsthetic. Granting the inherent necessity of this movement toward activity, why does the movement not stop with crude and primitive motor and emotional expression—which would suffice to occupy the foreground of consciousness, to still the pain of arrest, and to enhance the faded sense of life, why does the movement develop into that ordered activity which characterises the æsthetic? We have accounted for the pre-æsthetic movement toward activity, out of which the æsthetic attitude itself is ultimately born, but we have not as yet shown why this activity becomes æsthetic.

It is clear that in this question we have the crux of the problem, and, indeed, of all attempts to explain the æsthetic. Nor is the answer to the question altogether easy. It is not surprising that many have finally looked for the point of difference between unæsthetic free play of emotional expression and of activity of the imagination, and ordered æsthetic activity, in social rather than individual causes. But, important as the factor of community of activity and social consent may be in fixing the forms of activity, and in many cases perhaps originating them, it is still possible, I think, to show that this introduction of the element of order, this reconstruction of the content of experience, is inherent in the movement toward activity itself as a stage in individual worth experience. If we grant the truth

Values of Simple Appreciation 225

of our initial definition of the æsthetic mode as a modification of the immanental reference of repose; if, further, we grant that this repose in the object of desire, this tendency to prolong the appreciation of the object is fundamental, and can be achieved only by detachment of the object from immediate desire, in the semblant mode, the question is practically answered. It is precisely because this immanental reference, this *repose in the activity* is *impossible* without such ordered, balanced, and harmonious activity, because without the element of order, the illusion-disturbing moments, the desires and judgments spring again into being, and lead to new value movements, that the movement toward activity, to become æsthetic, must include this rearrangement of activity. The element of form, of order, must, therefore, be looked upon genetically as purely instrumental to the acquirement of æsthetic worth, which is ultimately the affective-volitional meaning of content.

3. *Æsthetic Characterisation of Activities and Objects—The Function of the Element of Order in Creating Æsthetic Values.*

The rôle of the element of order in prolonging the appreciation of objects, in enhancing the immanental worth of objects through detachment from immediate desire, can best be shown by reference to artistic activity, more especially to the primitive arts where the direct relation of the art activity to the fundamental desires and instincts out of which it emerges has not yet been severed, where æsthetic activity has not yet become an end in itself, an independent object of value. Reconstruction of content, we have seen, may be both perceptual and ideal, and æsthetic reconstruction may be of both types. Ordering of our motor activities, as in the dance, ordering of our visual or auditory experiences, constitutes perceptual reconstruction, while the æsthetic characterisation of things or persons as, for instance, in literature, would be ideal construction.[1]

Let us begin, then, with the most primitive and simple form of æsthetic characterisation, the perceptual reconstruction of activities of emotional expression. Ethnology shows us

---

[1] Æsthetic reconstruction should be distinguished from other types of construction, perceptual and ideal, illustrations of which we have already considered. Perceptual reconstruction which facilitates conative tendency, ideal construction of objects and dispositions which, through instrumental judgments, extends the range of conation, may also give rise to new economic and ethical worths. But in the case of these types of reconstruction, conation is explicit, the worth moment is transgredient; while in æsthetic construction, conation is dispositional and the worth moment is immanental.

Q

that primitive dances are invariably the reconstructions of the bodily expressions of concrete emotional states arising out of definite concrete instincts. By this it is meant that primitive dances are always erotic, martial, funereal, or religious. Such reconstructions always have two aspects, the dramatic and the rhythmic. They show forth in gesture and pantomime the motor activities in which these instincts are expressed, and add to these a certain order and rhythm. Both these elements of order involve a certain reconstruction of crude emotional expression, and they constitute the fundamental elements in all æsthetic characterisation. The element of rhythm, besides its social function of securing participation or social consent in movement, has the effect of keeping the emotion and its expression, whether it be martial, erotic, or religious, on a high level for a comparatively long period, to the exclusion of the desire for the object. The object is distanced and the fundamental conation becomes dispositional. This rhythm, usually of the form of advance and retreat, of affirmation and arrest of expression, produces an equilibrium of impulses which prevents the fundamental tendency from breaking forth into overt action.

On the other hand, the dramatic elements of the emotional expression are ordered in a cumulative dynamic " movement-form " which becomes fixed as the characteristic order of the dance. It is generally, as in the erotic or war dance, a conventionalised " movement-form " of the gradual rise, and also the decline, of the fundamental emotion. Beginning with movements and gestures, which are at first rather suggestive than fully expressive, it passes on by gradual transitions to more and more overt and furious expression, until sometimes the distinction between art and reality is finally lost. Here, again, besides its function in securing social participation, this dramatic movement-form introduces a principle of serial order into phenomena by means of which there is individual acquirement of worth. Into the æsthetic experience is carried over a conventionalised form of the very activities which constitute the actual instinct from which the æsthetic has arisen as a value movement toward activity.

The significant and strictly formal æsthetic factor, as the above analysis shows, is, of course, the balance of impulses which detaches the object from *immediate* desire. It constitutes a special application in the sphere of æsthetic reconstruction of that general principle of perceptual and ideal reconstruction.

discussed in a previous chapter under the head of the law of complementary values. But in addition to this, there is also the application of the principles of the " total series " and of " end feelings," characteristic of serial phenomena. In the case before us, the dynamic movement-form of the passions in question is individualised into a total series, and the gradation always has reference to culmination in certain final expressions and feelings which give character to the whole.

The rôle of these formal factors is evident; but it is important to note that the detachment of the object is only partial, that in these primitive dances, in which the object of conation is still not very remote from desire, and where the fundamental desire or system of desires is as yet scarcely dispositional, the " content " factor, the dynamic movement-form of emotional expression, has not reached the point of æsthetic reconstruction which it undergoes in more developed artistic activity. It is still partly extra-æsthetic. When, however, in music and drama, as they become historically differentiated from the dance, a still greater distance is put between the object and the fundamental, the principle of equilibrium is introduced into the movement-forms, and the conative element becomes still more dispositional, remaining present, in fact, as for instance in music, only in the form of a dominant mood.[1]

A word is required concerning the perceptual æsthetic reconstruction of *static* objects in which rhythm and dynamic movement-form do not enter, i.e., æsthetic perception as we have it in the fine arts. For æsthetics pure and simple, this is perhaps the most important field of analysis, but since our interest is confined to the problem of the functional relation of the æsthetic to other worth attitudes, and since we may, therefore, expressly disclaim all desire for completeness in analysis, a mere sketch must suffice. Here, again, we have individuation of the object in the interest of repose. The two significant factors are the arrest and repose of the fundamental through equilibrium of subsidiary impulses and the individualisation and segregation or detachment of the content. To consider the first moment in the light of the results of analytical psychology, it is important to realise that here also we are concerned with a reconstruction of activity, but in this case not of the motor activity of emotional expression, but of an inner activity of attention. Here the activity controlled is not emotional expression,

[1] See chap. v, pp. 122-3.

but attention. The movement toward activity in this case is toward what has been described as a " play with impressions," wherein the objects of sensation and perception are so ordered into groups and " form-qualities," that the separate impulses of attention are balanced, attention being distributed over a field so widened that no portion of the presented whole calls forth feeling and desire of such immediacy and intensity as to break the unity of the whole,—to destroy the illusion and the repose and to lead to a new value movement.

The principles of reconstruction of the æsthetic field in the " non-serial " arts are, *mutatis mutandis*, the same as in the serial arts, namely, the principles of contrast, of "total series," and of " end feelings "; but here these principles are applied to the activities of attention in such a manner as to make possible the widened field of attention and the consequent expansion of feeling.

This widened field of attention is well illustrated in pictorial art. Here the formal conditions of equilibrium and repose are to be found in the disposition of spaces and the composition of the colour elements. The values of these elements of order are in this respect merely instrumental to the equilibrium of the attention-activity sought. The colours used and the objects portrayed have, of course, their intrinsic affective meaning, through association, but this refers to presupposed conative tendency. In so far as the disposition of the *formal* elements *as such* is concerned, it is controlled by special forms of the fundamental laws of æsthetic construction already considered. To this end we have the use of colour contrasts and contrasts of masses, the principle of the " series " which in this case consists in the ordering of the lights and shades in a gradually diminishing scale, with the high light in the centre of attention, and, finally, the use of the principle of " end feeling " which in this case consists in such a balance of elements that the attention always returns to a central point of interest equivalent to the *tonic* in *musical* composition.

The important point for our study is, however, not the detailed analysis of this formal element of order, but rather its relation to the worth element in the æsthetic experience. The object of the worth feeling is always primarily the content expressed by the presentations thus ordered, although there may of course be a secondary worth judgment upon the instrumental value of the form as such, its adequacy to represent or express the object, or to secure and retain the æsthetic repose. This

Values of Simple Appreciation 229

content is always the object of possible desire or aversion. That is, if it were *judged* to exist or not exist it would call out *actual* desire or emotion. But in the æsthetic state these judgments are inhibited, and for them are substituted assumptions. From the standpoint of worth theory, then, the formal element of order is significant only as a means of securing repose in the object (or content) which, when unæsthetically experienced is the object of explicit desire and judgment. What are technically described as the "values" of the particular elements in a work of art (a painting, for instance) are, therefore, relative instrumental values, instrumental, that is, to the enhancement of the primary æsthetic worth, the repose or immanental reference.

Consequently, when, by a movement toward activity, an object acquires complementary æsthetic values, it is not to be understood that this acquired value is the resultant of an *addition* of the values of the formal "elements," but that it is an enhancement of the immanental reference of the worth feeling, an expansion of the feeling over the object as a whole. The desire for the object of the assumption is present dispositionally and actually in the form of the affective abstract, sentiment or mood. The adequacy of the formal element is determined by the sentiment or mood, thus enhancing the worth or affective-volitional meaning of the object.

4. *Modification of Condition Worths through Acquirement of Complementary Æsthetic Values.*

With this account of the nature and genesis of the æsthetic attitude as a form of the movement toward activity, we are now in a position to apply our results to the principal problem of our study, that is, to the determination of the manner in which the æsthetic attitude modifies our primary judgments of appreciation, more especially our economic judgments. The manner in which simple condition worths acquire quasi-ethical qualification has already been studied. It remains to indicate how feelings of condition worth become æsthetically qualified, and how this qualification modifies economic worth judgment and its laws.

In order to understand this problem rightly, it is necessary to recall our distinction between the value movement in simple appreciation and the completed value movement to a new ideal object, or end. In the first case the deepening of the transgredient or immanental reference of the feeling, as the case may be, constitutes merely a complementary value added to the primary object or desire. In the completed value movement, on the other hand, the original object of desire is lost sight of, and a new object, to the construction of which the acquired meaning was germinal, takes its place. The object or activity is independently valued. Now the reconstruction of objects and activities which is, properly speaking, *artistic*, and which constitutes the æsthetic in the full sense of the term—such reconstructions as we have described in the preceding paragraphs, are of this conscious type. The complementary value of "repose in activity," beauty in its various modifications, is sought for its own sake, and the reconstruction of the object is instrumental to this ideal end. But prior to this stage of the æsthetic, there is that phase of movement toward the æsthetic, or toward activity, in which the primary object of desire *remains* primary, and the secondary movement toward activity merely modifies the primary value. These may properly be described as quasi-æsthetic values.

These quasi-æsthetic values, like the quasi-ethical, may appear in connection with all activities, perceptual or conceptual. The solution of a mathematical problem, the performance of a surgical operation, may, in this sense, be beautiful, no less than the "style" or "manners" connected with the more fundamental and instinctive activities, such as eating or walking, or what not. All these acquired values may be described as *style*, the style of life. In their simplest form, however, such manners, together with their values, appear in connection with the fundamental instincts and the acquisition and consumption of objects. Between any fundamental desire or instinct and its satisfaction—such as the desire for food, raiment, love, etc.—intervene these quasi-æsthetic activities, the values of which enter into the funded value of the object. Style in the serving and eating of food, in the forms and colours, and in the actual wearing of dress, the graces and coquetries of love, all extend the primary values of the objects immensely, and give them greater capacity for continuous valuation.

It is this extension of the capacity for valuation which is significant. And while any object, no matter what its simple condition worths may be, may acquire such complementary value, it is especially at the *threshold* and *limits* of condition worth that this function of quasi-æsthetic values is most apparent. We have already seen that an object, or quantity of an object, too insignificant either for immediate appreciation or for re-application, in other words, below the threshold of intrinsic or instrumental value, may, as part of an æsthetically individuated whole, acquire the value of the whole.[1] The same phenomenon, viewed in another way, means that these quasi-æsthetic values modify the laws of satiety and dulling of sensitivity for simple condition worths as well as the law of limiting value as it applies to instrumental values. It will not be necessary to show again how this law enters into the unconscious as well as the conscious technique of life, into the fundamental as well as the more developed activities. It is sufficient to emphasise the fact that it modifies in a significant way all our economic judgments.

[1] Chap. VI, pp. 151–2, also p. 175.

CHAPTER VIII

I. PERSONAL AND OVER-INDIVIDUAL VALUES: THEIR ORIGIN AND NATURE

1. *Their "Common Meaning" Presupposes Sympathetic Participation (Einfühlung).*

THE preceding study of "condition" worths, of the simple appreciation of objects, has emphasised the purely individual, sub-personal, and sub-social character of these feelings. These feeling-attitudes may have both quasi-ethical and quasi-æsthetic modifications without acquiring either the personal or over-individual and social reference which is characteristic of the more developed forms of both ethical and æsthetic experience. But it was also maintained that these modifications of simple appreciation, these complementary values, contain the germ of more *complete* value movements to the higher levels of personal and impersonal social valuation, movements which involve the creation or ideal construction of new objects and new modifications of attitude, the development, in other words, of new levels of meaning where the feelings, and their corresponding worth judgments, presuppose new judgments and assumptions. In succeeding chapters we shall study personal and impersonal social values in detail, defining and classifying their objects and seeking to determine the laws of valuation of these objects. For the present, our study is confined to the genetic problem of the origin of these new objects and attitudes, more especially the origin of the distinctive presuppositions of these feeling-attitudes.

That which personal and impersonal or over-individual values have in common, and which distinguishes them from simple condition worths, is the fact that they presuppose certain processes of acquirement of meaning which simple appreciation does not. This fact appeared both in the nature of the objects of such values and in the character of the meaning of the feelings as expressed in the worth predicates attributed to the objects.[1] In the first place, the objects were described as ideal and "founded," i.e., they are ideal constructions founded on certain processes which they presuppose. In the second place, the meanings of these feelings, as expressed in corresponding worth predicates, are secondary acquired meanings which, as was shown in Chapter III, arise through explicit acknowledgment in judgment of meanings and references of the feelings of simple appreciation, and through their characterisation as a personal or social over-individual demand.

When we seek to define more explicitly what this acquired meaning is, we find that the meaning is "common"; the feeling is both individual and over-individual in its reference, and the objects are founded upon certain judgments or *implicit* assumptions that the feeling and desire of the individual are shared by others. In all feelings of personal worth, it is presupposed that the self and its dispositions or qualities is the object of worth feelings on the part of others. In all personal judgments upon others, it is assumed that objects of desire and feeling have a common meaning. In all judgments of impersonal worth, it is assumed that the individual is representing a wider social consciousness, which is making the same judgments and assumptions.

An examination of the worth predicates in these spheres illustrates the situation more fully. To consider personal worths first, worth is imputed to expressions of feeling or acts of will as manifesting certain dispositions of the personality. The terms of this imputation are approval and disapproval, praise and blame, merit and demerit, according as the disposition exists or does not exist, or ultimately according to the amount of disposition. Corresponding to these judgments of imputation are certain demands upon the person, as a person, to possess and express the dispositions in question. These demands, when expressed in explicit worth judgments, constitute judgments of obligation. Such imputation of praise and blame, and of obligation, may be described as ethical imputation. There is also an æsthetic imputation which finds expression in the predicates of beauty, nobility, sublimity of character and actions, closely related to the ethical predicates. All these judgments of imputation presuppose certain assumptions which we may describe as constituting the common "ideal of personality."

[1] Chap. II, p. 28 ; chap. III, pp. 71-2.

The acts and dispositions in question may, however, be judged from another point of view. Value may be imputed to an act, not because it expresses a personality, but because it is instrumental to certain social, over-individual ends, and satisfies certain impersonal demands. The imputation of merit or demerit, or of obligation, may in this case be described as impersonal imputation, and such imputation presupposes certain expectations or assumptions with regard to the participation of the individual in the social life, therefore constituting what may be described as an ideal of social participation.

If now we describe the first class of values as the *characterisation*-value, the second as the *participation*-value of acts and dispositions, we may generalise to the extent of saying that both types of valuation presuppose the construction of ideal objects, the disposition, the person, the social will, and the emergence of new feelings or modifications of feeling which express themselves in these judgments of imputation. The expectations or implicit assumptions which are presupposed in all such imputations of personal or impersonal value, are in a greater or less degree common and shared. The question of immediate interest is, accordingly, the study of the psychical processes of *participation* in which these new meanings emerge. These have been variously described as imitation, sympathetic projection or *Einfühlung*.

2. *Sympathetic Participation—Einfühlung : Its relation to Feeling and Simple Appreciation.*

It is a commonplace of present-day psychology that the self and the alter are ideal constructions, the material of which are the sensations, ideas, emotions, desires of the individual. It is equally a commonplace that this construction is a social process in which imitation and opposition, or contrast, are at work as the functional, genetic causes. Baldwin has in broad outlines sketched the processes of imitation (projection, introjection and ejection) by which the dialectic of self-consciousness takes place. Royce has emphasised the importance of contrast in the process, and Tarde, from the sociological point of view, has shown the equal importance of imitation and opposition in the generation of new content in the individual and society. But, so far as I am aware, there has been no systematic attempt to show in detail the modifications of the con-

Personal and Over-Individual Values

sciousness of value brought about by this dialectic process. This is due to the fact that the process has been studied largely from the point of view of the psychology of cognition, the interest being primarily in the cognitive content and meaning of the constructs, rather than in the conative and affective side of the process. When viewed in this latter aspect, the process is seen to be one of *Einfühlung*, a process of "feeling-in," in which feeling attitudes are sympathetically projected into another, re-read back into the self, thus becoming the objects of cognition, of judgment and assumption, and ultimately of new feelings of value. It is, therefore, in this aspect, a *value movement* in which new values are acquired.

It is as such a value movement, as the continuation of processes of feeling, of simple appreciation, that Einfühlung is to be studied, and, when viewed in this light, it is seen to be a value movement of the "inward" type, where the movement is *complete*. There is, therefore, no hard and fast line between feeling and "feeling-in" (Einfühlung), between appreciation and characterisation. Activities of appreciation lead gradually and necessarily to characterisation. In the specific case of the feeling of obligation, the felt impulsion which arises in the formation of a conative disposition is gradually referred explicitly to the disposition as a phase of the self or the alter. The vague and uncertain transgredient reference is made explicit in the judgmental reference of the disposition to the ideal construct of the self. It becomes conscious obligation. It is, therefore, as a complete value movement, beginning with simple appreciation of the emotional expressions of others and ending with the characterisation of persons, that Einfühlung is to be studied. We shall accordingly use the term to designate the entire process (projection, imitation, and ejection) involved in the activities of characterisation and participation, and shall consider it, moreover, in its aspect of affective-conative process,[1] for it is a

---

[1] This broad use of the term Einfühlung may perhaps be questioned. It is true that the weight of authority is in favour of confining it to the purely æsthetic type of personalisation and personal construction; it was to explain certain æsthetic phenomena that the concept was first introduced (Lipps and Volkelt). On the other hand, the broader use to which the very structure of the term naturally gives rise—to include all forms of projection or ejection of our own feeling into others—has been employed by some writers, notably by Witasek in his article, " *Zur Psychologie der æsthetischen Einfühlung,*" to which more extended reference is made in a later section of this chapter. There æsthetic Einfühlung is considered to be only one form of the process and is distinguished from ethical. That this broader conception is justified by a genetic treatment of the processes will, I think, become apparent as the discussion proceeds. Baldwin's identification of Einfühlung with *Sembling* is, I think, only partially true. As will be seen later, there is a semblant mode at one stage of the total process, but it is not the

term which includes both feeling and conation, the relations of which have been determined in a preceding chapter. With the change in cognitive presuppositions through participation there comes corresponding changes in feeling, in the aspects both of qualitative and quantitative meaning, in both quality and degree. From these laws of participation are later to be developed the laws governing the valuation of personal and over-individual objects.

II. THE PSYCHOLOGY OF EINFÜHLUNG: SYMPATHETIC PROJECTION

1. The Problem—The Nature of the Projected Feeling—How is Einfühlung Possible?

Projection, in the larger sense of the term, is used to describe all externalisation of psychical content. We project the spatial reference of touch and other sensations into the objects without us. We project ideas, concepts, formed in the inner activities of comparison and differentiation, as the real grounds, external to us, of our sensational experience. In like manner we characterise ourselves and others by reading into our immediate experiences of feeling conceptual constructs. of dispositions, relatively constant, to which these feelings are referred.

But it is immediately clear that just as the first type of projection of constructs is conditioned by immediate perceptual experience, as these constructs are ideal objects founded upon perception, so, in the second type, the conceptual constructs of dispositions are founded upon immediate experiences of *feeling*, in this case upon the " internal perception," the appreciation of the feeling-attitudes of others. Immediate sympathetic participation is, therefore, the condition of the conceptual construction of dispositions of the personality as objects of personal worth feelings. To understand the objects of personal worth it is necessary to analyse the processes of sympathetic Einfühlung on which they are founded.

The phenomena in connection with which sympathetic projection has been chiefly studied are those of æsthetic and ethical personalisation. The simplest form is found in the reading into impersonal and often inorganic objects of the organic

whole of the process. For a general discussion of this term, see Baldwin's *Dictionary of Philosophy and Psychology*, on the topics, " Æsthetic Sympathy " and " Einfühlung " in the article on terminology.

Personal and Over-Individual Values 237

sensations, feelings, emotions, and desires that are really in ourselves. Of this type the attribution of feelings of movement, effort, or strain, to static spatial forms, or to successions in time (the upward striving of a pillar or tower in architecture, the movement of a melody in music) are illustrations. Of sympathetic Einfühlung in the case of persons, we have illustrations in the " feeling-into " persons of emotions such as anger and fear on the basis of expression, facial and bodily, as in the case of the æsthetic appreciation of acting, or in the case of more ethical judgments where we take up practical attitudes toward persons on the basis of this appreciation. It is out of these immediate apprehensions and appreciations of an "inner life" beyond the self, whether that inner life be presumed, assumed, or judged to exist, that the ideal constructions arise. Our first problem is, therefore, to determine the nature and conditions of this process of personalization, which, in its cognitive aspect, is apprehension and, in its affective-volitional aspect, appreciation. The psychological problem is : How is Einfühlung possible ? The solution of this problem is the necessary preliminary to the study of the feelings of value which presuppose these processes.

The psychological problem—how is Einfühlung possible ?—has given rise to considerable discussion in recent literature. This discussion has occasioned a wealth of psychological analysis, but one in which the theoretical problems raised cannot be said to have reached a final solution. The chief source of difficulty is found in the fact that the experience felt into the object, whether a thing or a person, is at once an experience of the subject of the sympathetic projection, and a content of the object, i.e., apprehended as content of the object. The feeling seems to be both experience of the subject, with its own individual presuppositions, and content projected outside the subject, apprehended and appreciated as inner life of the object. How an inner life, other than our own, whether real or assumed, can be interpreted in terms of our own experience, through projection of our own inner states ; and what are the changes which the feeling of the subject must undergo, changes both in content and functional presuppositions, in order to be projected and realised as experience of the alter ; constitutes one of the most difficult problems of psychology.

We may best consider this general problem by taking up in detail certain special questions to which it has given rise. In the first place, it is, as we have seen, upon the basis of some immediate appreciation that the conceptual constructions of character and dispositions are founded. It is as intuitively realised that the feeling in another leads to conceptual characterisation. How shall we conceive this *intuitive* realisation of another's feeling? If it is by a process of projection of our own feelings, what are the aspects of the perceived objects, whether things or persons, which furnish the stimulus to this projection, and how is the fusion of the subject's feeling with the object to be understood psychologically?

In the second place, what is the character of the projected feeling? Is it a "real" feeling, with the same elements of content and the same presuppositions which characterise feeling as an immediate experience, or is there a substitution of presentation for feeling, and a gradual change in presuppositions? What, in general terms, are the changes in content and functional presuppositions which condition participation in the successive stages of the process?

Finally we have a third problem growing out of the preceding. What is the rôle of feelings of participation in the processes of valuation? Is the projected feeling itself a feeling of value, or are the only feelings of value those judgment-feelings which emerge when dispositions in the person are judged to exist. This apparently somewhat subtle question has considerable bearing upon our view of Einfühlung as a process of valuation, for it is merely another aspect of the more general question—whether assumption-feelings or feelings of the imagination are feelings of value.[1]

2. *Sympathetic Projection of Feeling—Its Nature and Conditions.*

Our first problem, then, is to seek to understand how the individual intuitively apprehends and appreciates the inner life of an object other than himself. This is said to take place through a process which is described, in one aspect, as "inner imitation," in another, as "projection." The subject is said to *enliven* the object by projecting or feeling into it his own feeling-content, for which process of "feeling-in," or *inner imitation*, some aspect or expression of the object constitutes the stimulus. For the purely psychological analysis of this process, and the structural analysis of the content of consciousness which conditions the process, it is wholly irrelevant whether the enlivened object is an

[1] Chap. v, pp. 137-9.

Personal and Over-Individual Values 239

impersonal thing or a person; whether the assumption or judgment of the existence of an inner life, which emerges in the process, is valid or not. Upon reflection, the object may be known to be impersonal and the assumption to be invalid, but reflection does not affect this form of inner perception any more than it modifies the illusions of external spatial perception. Here we are concerned in the first place merely with the psychological processes involved.

The process of inner imitation or projection is further characterised as a fusion or complication of one type of content with another. The more subjective content, which we describe as feeling or desire, is said to be complicated with more objective content of peripheral origin. The stimuli of sight and sound, spatial forms, movement-forms, gesture, vocal expression, etc., act as cues for experiences of feeling and organic sensations. The latter constitute the inner imitation, as distinguished from muscular imitation, and these contents, being fused with the peripheral content, become objectified—i.e., acquire the objective reference of that content and are apprehended as qualities of the object. We may, therefore, define the feeling in inner imitation as the induced feeling and the perceptual contents as the inducing conditions.

In order to understand how this fusion is possible, we must get the phenomena more definitely before us. And in the first place, it must be observed that the appreciation of the projected feeling as a quality of the object includes two relatively distinct situations, which may be described as a more emotional appreciation and as an intuitive apprehension. In æsthetic Einfühlung, for instance, two distinct situations are possible. In looking at a Gothic tower we may, either merely *see* the pinnacles striving upward, or be ourselves actually emotionally elevated, i.e., we may have the actual organic sensations attendant upon an inner motor tendency. In the latter case there is a personal participation in the upward urge of the pinnacles, while in the former we have a projection of the movement in terms of representation. In like manner we may realise vividly the affective state, with all its worth suggestions, i.e., anger or fear, in another personality without sharing in the actual organic sensations which make up its content; or, again, when the necessary presuppositions are present, we may experience sympathetically the organic sensations likewise. And, it is important to recognise that when we thus vividly " see " or realise the upward urge of the pinnacles, or the fear and anger of our fellows, we do not simply think them in conceptually, but we also in some sense see them. It is, as Witasek insists, an intuitive (*anschauliche*) representation.

When we analyse these two situations, we find that they differ in two important respects, in the nature of the feeling-content projected and in the nature of the presuppositions of the feeling. We shall see that between the stage of immediate emotional participation, organic sympathy, and the more intellectual intuitive apprehension there is a change both in content and cognitive presuppositions. It is with the first point that we are here concerned; the second will be considered later.

In the case of the more emotional participation, full organic sympathy, there is a fusion of the emotion or desire, with all its subjective meaning, with the more objective perceptual or ideal content. This fusion we have no difficulty in understanding when we recall our analysis of feeling as the " meaning " of a special form of sensitivity, motor and organic. This meaning, we have seen, is embodied in certain form-qualities of the sensitivity, and when this subjective sensitivity is fused with the more objective, under certain conditions presently to be developed, the subjective meaning is felt into the object. On the other hand, the understanding of the more intuitive apprehension of the projected feeling requires the application of that other fact, developed in our analysis of feeling, namely, that the form of combination of the elements may be abstracted from the elements and pass over into presentation. In this way that which is peculiarly *psychical*, i.e., feeling and will, may be presented, and, as in the phenomenon before us, the projected feeling may be intuitively apprehended as a quality of the object.[1]

And now appears a further fact of importance to which Groos has called attention,[2] and which we shall have occasion to consider more fully later. Organic sympathy, Einfühlung as well as feeling, is subject to the law of dulling of sensitivity with repetition. Repetition may deaden the organic sympathy, damp down the intensity of the organic resonance until it finally

---

[1] This is developed more fully in chap. IV, p. 103. Of the four distinguishable aspects of a given affective attitude, its positive or negative direction, its presuppositions (judgment or assumption), the form quality of its elements and the intensity of its resonance, *only the form-quality* is the object of intuitive presentation. The other aspects may become the objects of judgment, they may be conceptually represented. The pleasantness or unpleasantness, with its intensity, and the peculiar individual presuppositions may become the objects of judgment but not of immediate presentation. They belong to the unpresentable side of our experience.

[2] *Der ästhetische Genuss*, Giessen, 1902, pp. 186 ff.

disappears, but the intuitive realisation of the feeling or desire projected, and of its meaning, still remains. We no longer *feel* the upward urge of the pinnacles, or the organic resonance of the angry man, but we apprehend them. We have here, in sympathetic participation, a phenomenon similar to that observed in the case of simple feeling—showing the genetic relation between simple appreciation and participation, namely, that while accommodation through repetition dampens the intensity of the hedonic and sensational aspect of the total feeling-attitude, nevertheless, with the repetition there emerges the affective-volitional meaning, the dynamic and expansive suggestions of the feeling attitude. This phenomenon on the level of Einfühlung, corresponds to facts of the vital series where emotion and passion pass over into sentiment, mood, and "affective sign."

Accordingly, a certain change in feeling, as content, conditions the process of projection whereby the projected feeling is apprehended and appreciated as a quality of the object. The two stages of our illustration indicate phases of this modification. The further development of the process by which a subjective feeling becomes object, requires the study of the change in cognitive presuppositions involved in the process of projection. Before considering this aspect of the problem, we must glance at the inducing conditions of affective projection, those aspects of perceptual content which constitute the stimuli for this projection.

The Inducing Conditions of Affective Projection.

The form-qualities of objects, whether the objects be persons or things, whether the form-qualities be static or dynamic, are the inducing grounds of such intuitive affective projection. It is with the inducing conditions in persons that we are chiefly concerned, but these will be best understood in the light of an analysis of the simpler phenomena of Einfühlung as involved in the æsthetic characterisation of things.

The inducing conditions of all affective projection are, in the beginning, perceptual form-qualities determined by relations of quality, intensity, duration, or extension of simple elements. Rise or fall of melody in the tonal scale, increase or decrease of relative intensities, light and shade, loudness or softness of sounds, gradual increase or decrease of rapidity of *tempo* induce affective states with dynamic suggestions which are then projected as tertiary qualities of the object. The emotions or moods induced by the gradual increase of light at sunrise, or decrease at sunset, the rising shriek of the wind are illustrations. To these must be added the dynamic suggestions of qualitative, intensive, and other contrasts, in which one member of the contrasting pair is emphasised through the opposition of the other; they become the inducing grounds, especially in art, for the suggestion of affective-volitional meanings, the affirmation and arrest of conative tendencies. Rhythmic time relations, both in nature and art, may induce various forms of the two fundamental modifications of worth feeling, the dynamic and expansive, as the peaceful murmur of the brook or the angry lash of the waves. Finally, space forms, such as the upward urge of the pinnacle, or the dim distances of perspective, induce emotions or moods of the dynamic transgredient character, while other forms induce expansive feelings of repose.

When the objects of Einfühlung are persons, the inducing conditions are of the same general character,—form-qualities of perception. The flush that mantles the face has a different emotional meaning, according as its rise is sudden or gradual. Muscular expression of the body, of the face, or even of the eyes alone, emphasis in speech, either of stress or pitch, modulation of the voice, etc., all these are in the first place form-qualities, i.e., relatively permanent relations of quality, intensity, or duration, among the sense elements. They are expressive, that is, they have meaning, because with them fuses the movement form of the emotional attitude.

In all these cases the psychical process may be described as a fusion of an inward with the external movement form, emotions being, as we have seen, in their aspect of content, movement forms of the more subjective aspect of sensational content, muscular and organic sensations, genetically residual traces, vestiges of form remaining over from motor attitudes. But it must be observed that while in many cases we find an actual fusion of the muscular and organic sensations with the external forms, this is not a necessary prerequisite of intuitive realisation of the objectified emotion. As we have already observed in Groos's illustration, we may *see* the upward urge of the pinnacle without feeling it in the sense of having the feelings of effort, the reason being that the essential element of the emotional attitude is the movement-form which may, with repetition, be abstracted from the organic and muscular sensations on which it was primarily founded, and transposed to another series or group of sensations. The external phenomena into which the intuited feeling is projected have acquired this affective-volitional meaning.

It is also important to emphasise the fact that, while the inducing conditions are primarily perceptual form-qualities, they are not exclusively so. Especially in the case where the objects are persons, certain unities and continuities of ideational activity become the inducing grounds of sympathetic projection. Trains of ideas, their types of combination or association, acquire definite movement-forms which are expressive of feeling attitude, more especially those differences in attitude which we describe as temperamental.[1] Without doubt, emotions and moods, and the dispositions which underlie them, frequently determine the associational processes, both as to what images shall be called up, and as to the manner in which they shall be ordered. We cannot be far wrong, then, in describing such image continuities as movement-forms of thought, since in them is embodied some form of affective-volitional meaning. And such types of thought become the basis for intuitive projection of feeling attitude, constituting for the observer emotional expression, just as truly as do the perceptual movement-forms. For when through the expression of his thoughts I realise the affective-volitional attitude of a poet, or of my friend, it is not by a process of inference, a man having such thoughts, such a type of mind, must have such and such feelings or feeling dispositions, but *immediately* through sympathetic participation.

[1] Herein lies the great importance of similarity or difference of temperament as conditions of sympathetic projection, an importance which we can, however, merely suggest and not develop. Differences in temperament represent differences in the capacity of individuals for experiencing different types of emotional attitude, and ultimately of emotional expression. They have, indeed, been classified on the basis of degree of immediacy and intensity of sensori- and ideo-motor response, in impulse and emotion, that is, on the basis of the functional relation of systematic affirmation and arrest of conative tendency. It is not difficult to see, therefore, that sympathetic intuitive realisation of another man's attitude is largely dependent upon the temperamental equipment of the intuiting subject. It is equally apparent that worth judgments which have their grounds in this sympathetic participation, and which we may, therefore, describe as emotional and personal imputation, will vary in a significant manner from those more impersonal judgments which are intellectual in character and have their grounds in conceptual judgment and inference. From this difference important consequences will follow for the later studies.

3. *The Presuppositions of Feelings of Participation.*
(a) *In the First Stage of Sympathetic Projection the Presuppositions are Presumptions.*

The second of these general problems raises the question of the nature of the presuppositions of projected feelings. It has been maintained that there is an ultimate difference between feeling as a simple condition of the individual and feeling as projected or felt into another, and that, in order to be projected, feeling must be presented or imagined. The presuppositions of an actual feeling, as a unique experience of the individual are, it is said, sensations, organic tendencies, and judgments, of the individual alone, which cannot be shared. Therefore the projected feeling is not an actual feeling, but a presented one. In the actual situation of sympathetic Einfühlung it is not the projected feeling which is real, but merely the secondary feeling which follows upon judgment about the disposition of the person into whom the feeling is projected. The projected feeling as such is an imagined feeling.

Now that in the course of the total process of participation there appears a stage where the feeling is imagined and presented, and that this is a significant stage in the formation of personal ideals, is undoubtedly true. There arises a distinction between the feeling as immediately felt and as projected, due to a differentiation of presuppositions. But this is not characteristic of the first stage of the process. At this point the feeling has as its presupposition a simple presumption of existence determined by organic imitation. It has already been pointed out that, when genetically viewed, the distinction between feeling and Einfühlung is not absolute. The latter is but a continuation of the processes of simple appreciation, and we find upon closer study that in its simplest form, as mere organic sympathy, it shows no such distinction between the feeling as felt and the feeling as projected. There are good reasons for maintaining that in elemental organic sympathy there is no presentation of the feeling, and no differentiation between the presuppositions of the feeling as a condition of the subject and the feeling as a quality of the object. It is hard, for instance, to believe that the feelings of effort experienced through organic sympathy are in any way distinguishable from the same feelings when they have their origin solely in the individual, and still harder to believe that there is any difference between the feelings of an infant when he weeps in organic sympathy, and when he weeps because of some stimulus which has its origin wholly within his own organism.

In the first stage of sympathetic projection, we may therefore conclude, the presupposition of the feeling is a simple *presumption* of existence of an inner life—not, it should, however, be observed, of an inner life as definitely localised either in the self or the alter. Negatively expressed, there is no distinction between the feeling as individual experience and as projected, no distinction between the presuppositions in the two cases. In this organic sympathy we have the germ of a common meaning later to develop into feelings of participation, but as yet scarcely distinguishable from the "condition" feelings of simple appreciation.

(b) *The Rise of Assumption Feelings and Emergence of Distinction between Presuppositions—"Sembling."*

Nevertheless, such participation in the feeling of others, where there is lacking the sense of distinction in presuppositions, is undeniably limited to the most rudimentary form of organic sympathy, on the sensational and perceptual level. All that we can infer from these facts is that the distinction between real and imagined or presented feeling, which later becomes of importance, is, at least genetically, not ultimate. But as soon as the instinctive organic sympathy is in the least degree modified by arrest, there is readaptation in conative process, a change in presuppositions takes place, and with it, we shall find, a change in the content of projection. This change consists in the gradual substitution of explicit assumption for presumption, and with such substitution emerges a distinction between the feeling as merely felt and as projected.

The processes by which the subject comes to assume or imagine the existence of an inner life in the objects without him are in principle the same as those which condition, in its most general aspect, the passage from presumption to assumption.[1] All feelings of value presuppose at least the presumption of existence of the object. When such dispositions to desire or feel in a certain way have been created by relatively external

[1] Cf. chap. II, p. 51 f.

and objective conditions, the dispositions thus formed become a factor of *subjective* control, giving rise to assumptions of existence. In the case of organic sympathy, and its sympathetic projection, there are created certain dispositions to participate which go beyond the limits of organic sympathy, and thus give rise to Einfühlung of the playful semblant type, with its mere assumption of existence. This may remain mere æsthetic appreciation, or the assumption may develop into judgments of existence with their accompanying ethical feelings of a more serious character.

In this passage from simple presumption to assumption there is, therefore, a significant reconstruction of the situation. The subject now explicitly assumes the existence of the feeling in the alter. In the preceding stage no such explicit assumption is made, for the reason that there is no distinction between inner and outer control. But to assume explicitly the existence of the feeling is to assume its necessary presuppositions in the alter. These presuppositions, however, as well as the hedonic subjective aspect, cannot, as we have seen, be immediately or intuitively projected. They can only be *ejected* as conceptual constructions. In the attitude of assumption, therefore, we have the beginning of that ideal reconstruction of the experiences of immediate feeling which conditions their ejection into the alter and his characterisation as a person.

Certain important changes in the feeling of the subject accompany this change from presumption to assumption, and condition the further developments of ideal construction and characterisation. The feeling has become an assumption-feeling, and this, we have seen from our preceding studies, involves certain characteristic changes in the feeling. In the first place there appear those changes which we described as *abstraction* and *generalisation*. On the functional side the process was seen to be one of abstraction or detachment of the feeling from individual presuppositions.[1] The "feeling-in" of an attitude into another, with the assumption of presuppositions different from those of one's own feeling, gives to the feeling a quasi-general meaning, a schematic character, which raises it out of the sphere of simple subjective appreciation, and starts it upon a new path of objective meaning.

In the second place, in the assumption-feeling we found the beginning of a differentiation of certain aspects of the total feel-

---

[1] Chap. v, pp. 131-3.

ing-attitude—of the individual unpresentable aspect from the presentable form-qualities of the feeling. With this differentiation the feeling acquires recognitive and generic meaning. These characteristics of assumption-feelings which were developed in the abstract analysis of the earlier chapter, are now seen to get an additional significance in the processes of Einfühlung. On the one hand the rise of assumption-feelings, feelings of the imagination, with accompanying changes in content and function, is the condition of the extension of participation beyond the range of the simple appreciations of organic sympathy. On the other hand, the processes of Einfühlung continue the processes of generalisation and objectification of feeling-attitudes already begun. It is to this latter aspect, and its significance for the further processes of characterisation and ideal construction, that we must now turn.

These two characteristics of the assumption-feeling, or feeling of the imagination, its relative independence of individual presuppositions, and its differentiation of aspects of the total attitude, lead to important progressions or value movements in the characterisation of the self and the alter.

In the first place, such a feeling has acquired a dual character and function. It is at the same time both subjective feeling and objective presentation; it has both an individual and an over-individual reference. It is, so to speak, in a state of unstable equilibrium preliminary to new differentiations and determinations. This point must be emphasised if we are to make clear the nature of this transition stage in the total process of Einfühlung, for it is closely connected with a question to be raised presently—whether the projected content is a "real" feeling, or is merely imagined. To say that the sembled feeling is both subjective feeling and objective presentation seems at first sight paradoxical. But, according to the view already developed, feeling is the subjective meaning of a specific kind of content, a meaning which may be embodied in organic sensations, or may be transposed to more objective content of peripheral origin, when the feeling is said to be intuited. When, therefore, it is held that the sembled or presented feeling has a dual reference, both subjective and objective, it is meant that it stands in a representative capacity for the individual feeling, with its uniquely individual presuppositions, from which it has been abstracted and into which it may be re-converted on occasion, and that at the same time it has an objective over-individual reference.

This dual character develops further the "common meaning" already implicitly present in organic sympathy. In organic sympathy, presuppositions are not distinguished; but with the abstraction from individual presuppositions which comes with the assumption attitude, the feeling acquires a schematic character, which permits it to be read back and forth from the self to the alter. By its schematic character is understood precisely this abstraction from uniquely individual presuppositions and from organic sensation content, the characteristic which makes possible its dual reference, and makes it, to use Baldwin's terms, a "Person-Project," which may, in the further development of the process, be identified in explicit judgment with either the self or the alter.

Of chief importance in the rise of the objective and "common" meaning of feeling-attitude, is the fact that the schematic feeling of the imagination may acquire recognitive and generic meanings. With the intuitive projection of the feeling into the "other," appears the conscious recognition of the feeling as one's own. It has already been shown in another connection [1] that the condition of acquirement of recognitive meaning on the part of a feeling is that it shall become an assumption feeling. It is not the unique, individual aspect of the feeling which is recognised, but the schematic movement-form of the feeling of the imagination. In the semblant mode of Einfühlung we have precisely the condition necessary for the objectification and recognition of feeling-attitude, and for the reading back of the feeling, in terms of idea, into the self. Here also arise those further differences in the meaning of the feeling, between feeling as passive pleasantness-unpleasantness and as dynamic and expansive movement-forms, with their reference to conative dispositions,—those differences in feeling which lead on to ideal construction.

(c) *Feelings of Participation as Judgment-Feelings—Presuppositions as objects of Judgment—Conceptual Reconstruction of the Inner Life in Terms of Dispositions.*

The rise of assumption-feelings, and the semblant mode in participation, is the condition of the acquirement of certain

---

[1] Chap. v, p. 117 ff.

meanings and of further development in the characterisation of persons. It has already been shown that, while this stage of assuming or sembling of an inner life in other things and persons may remain a mere assumption, an intrinsic appreciation with the immanental values of the æsthetic, it may also lead on to a further stage in characterisation. The intuitive schematic feeling " project " may be merely instrumental to a stage where the vaguely assumed inner life is explicitly acknowledged in acts of judgment. This stage we may describe as the *ejection* of the presuppositions of the feeling in the form of conceptual construction of dispositions.

When this stage of the process is reached, the conditions of the *complete* inward value movement, toward the valuation of the disposition, are given. In the place of the mere presumption or assumption of the existence of a dispositional correlate for the projected feeling, judgment develops, and judgmental habit. It is these judgments of existence or non-existence of dispositions, in the self or the alter, which constitute the presuppositions of those feelings of value which we have described as personal and impersonal (social), and which find expression in those judgments of obligation and imputation described in earlier paragraphs of this chapter. Repetition of judgment, the formation of judgment-habit, gradually creates certain *implicit* assumptions or expectations, with which the subject making the worth judgment comes to the objects of judgment, the acts and dispositions of persons.

4. *Einfühlung as a Process of Valuation—The Nature of the " Feelings of Value" involved—Value Movements in Sympathetic Participation and Characterisation.*

(a) *The Projected Feelings are "Real" Feelings.*

We have now traced genetically the gradual change in cognitive presuppositions, together with the corresponding changes in feeling, which characterise the total process of participation as affective-conative process. The purely psychological study of changes in content and functional presuppositions which condition the acquirement of these personal and over individual meanings, requires to be supplemented at certain points by a more specific inquiry into the rôle of the feelings of participation in the processes of valuation.

This inquiry is obviously fundamental to the study of the

consciousness of personal and social, over-individual values, for these feelings of value depend upon Einfühlung, and one of the most important succeeding studies will be concerned with the application of the laws of valuation to these feelings. But as a preliminary to this study certain questions arise which belong properly to this psychological analysis. The projected feeling, with its individual and over-individual reference, is both subjective feeling and objective presentation. In addition to its individual presuppositions, as subjective feeling, it presupposes presumption, assumption, or judgment of existence beyond the subject, in another. Is the feeling when projected a *real* feeling of the individual, and, therefore, a feeling of value?

In the first place, the question has arisen whether feelings, when they lose their purely individual character, are still feelings, or whether, with the change in functional presuppositions and content described, they do not cease to be feelings and become presentations. This question, which is but a special aspect of the larger problem which has presented itself at different points, has received attention largely in connection with the study of Einfühlung in its æsthetic aspect. In this discussion it has been maintained, on the one hand, that only presented feelings could be projected, while on the other hand it has been insisted that the projected feelings are real feelings.

The question whether the projected feeling is an actual feeling or a presentation of a feeling, involves a further question. Is the immediate apprehension and appreciation of the feeling of another, with its presumption or assumption of existence, a feeling of value, or do feelings of value arise only when secondary *judgments* as to the existence or non-existence of real feelings or feeling-dispositions corresponding to the presented feeling are passed? We have already maintained that the projected feeling is a real feeling of value, with presumption or assumption of existence. It remains now merely to justify this position by a critical consideration of the psychological questions involved. The entire dispute may be referred, I think, to an inadequate conception of the nature of feeling, and to an ungenetic abstraction of the two terms,—function and content.

Witasek[1] maintains that only presented feelings can be

---

[1] Witasek, Zur psychologischen Analyse der æsthetischen Einfühlung, *Zeitschrift für Psychologie und Physiologie*, etc., XXV, 1901. Also *Allgemeine Æsthetik*, Leipzig, 1904, pp. 114 and 107.

projected. For, in the first place, actual feelings have certain presuppositions, sensational, organic, conative, and judgmental, which belong to the individual alone. Without these the real feeling cannot exist. But these presuppositions are different in the individual who projects and the other into whom the feeling is projected. The presuppositions cannot themselves be projected. While the projected feelings are imagined or presented, nevertheless, *actual feelings of sympathy, feelings of participation*, may arise when the subject affirms the existence of dispositions corresponding to these presented feelings. Groos,[1] on the other hand, maintains the real character of the projected feelings themselves, on the ground that organic sensations are present, thereby making them the criterion of real feeling, at the same time recognising that there may be projection of feeling in terms of pure presentation. Thus, I may be conscious of a man's anger or fear without experiencing the organic disturbance which is the basis of that actual emotion, and, again, I may have that presentation plus the organic disturbance, when I actually *feel* the experience *with* him. In both cases we have Einfühlung, but in one case the feeling is actual, while in the other it is presented.

It is apparent that in the case of both these views we are presented with but a partial aspect of the truth. Witasek finds "real" feelings of participation only on the higher level of ejection where dispositional presuppositions are *judged* to exist. They are, therefore, judgment-feelings. Groos sees in the primitive organic sympathy, with its presumption of reality, an experience of real feeling, but denies reality to the stage of imaginative projection, because of the absence of organic sensations. In neither of these views is the true criterion of real feeling given. With respect to the content aspect of feeling-attitude, which Groos has in mind when he makes the presence of organic sensations the criterion of real feeling, we have already seen in our analysis of feeling [2] that, while feeling is primarily the embodied meaning of certain forms of sensitivity, organic and motor, it is not dependent upon that content for its meaning, but may be transferred as *form-quality* to other content, relatively more objective, without losing its subjective reference and meaning. On the other hand, the same analysis of feeling has shown us that the assumption which underlies the view of Witasek—that the distinction between feeling and presentation is ultimate—will not

[1] Groos, *Der æsthetische Genuss*, p. 209.   [2] Chap. IV, pp. 100-3.

bear examination. If such a view is taken there is, of course, no question that the coëfficient of reality is lacking to the projected and intuitively presented feeling-attitude, but this view is without foundation.

The mistake at the root of both these misconceptions of the situation is, as has already been suggested, the neglect of the genetic point of view, the failure to recognise that the imaginative projection, with its quasi-presentational content, with recognitive and generic meaning, is but a transition stage between the simple appreciations of organic sympathy and the more developed feelings of participation which come with judgment and judgment-habit, or implicit assumption—an intermediate stage in which the " psychical " attitude is intuitively presented, recognised, and referred in acts of judgment to the self and the alter. As such, it has all the meaning of the primary feeling for which it stands, and into which it can be again converted by reinstatement of individual presuppositions. As such, it is also representative and anticipatory of the later feelings of participation, when presumption and assumption pass over into explicit judgment. What has been said, in more general terms, with reference to the *real* character of the affective abstract and affective sign [1] and its rôle as real feeling in the processes of valuation, may, therefore, now be repeated and again emphasised in connection with its function in the activities of sympathetic participation. The projected feeling is a feeling of value, whether that over-individual reference consist in a presumption, assumption, or judgment of its existence in another.

(b) *Value Movements in Participation and Characterisation.*

The conclusion of the preceding paragraphs—that the distinction between the feeling as individual and as projected and shared is merely genetic and relative, enables us finally to see the genetic relations between the different feelings of participation and the different cognitive attitudes in Einfühlung and characterisation of persons. As in simple appreciation of objects, so in characterisation of things and persons, there are value movements, in the latter case from organic sympathy to ethical and æsthetic participation and characterisation.

The difference between ethical and æsthetic participation is not a difference in affective content of projection, but in cognitive

---

[1] Chap. v, pp. 137-9.

presuppositions. In æsthetic Einfühlung, the presuppositions are assumptions, in ethical, judgments. In both cases the feeling as psychical content has been intuitively projected on the basis of the inducing conditions described, and with this has developed the conceptual construction of dispositions which are either judged or assumed to exist or not exist. It is the feelings following upon these judgments or assumptions which are different in the two cases. The ethical feelings are those of judgment, the æsthetic those of assumption.[1] In the case of a character of fiction or of the drama, as, for instance, Lear, we realise the despair and fury just as really as in real life, sometimes more clearly and vividly, and we have a certain kind of sympathy arising from a temporary assumption of the existence of actual presuppositions of the feelings. In ethical participation, on the other hand, we have the intuitive realisation of the feelings, but the presuppositions are *judged* to be real.

III. The Distinction between Personal and Impersonal Feelings of Participation

1. *Intensive and Extensive Projection.*

The preceding study of the processes of Einfühlung, of the origin of feelings of participation with their ideal objects, has failed to take account of one difference in acquired meaning which emerges very early in the process, namely, the distinction between *personal* and *impersonal* feelings of value. All feelings of participation have an over-individual reference, have a *common* meaning, but this common meaning may be specifically qualified as personal or impersonal. In the first chapter it was pointed out that the same object, the disposition to act or feel

---

[1] This analytical distinction, true as it is, may be pressed too far if in calling the assumption-feelings of æsthetic sympathetic participation, *Scheingefühle*, and the judgment feelings of the ethical, *real* feelings, the æsthetic are banished from the realm of worth feelings. We have already in our introductory definitions included the assumption-feelings among the worth phenomena, a procedure the importance of which will become especially apparent in the following study of the activities and values of characterisation. In the actual process of characterisation of the person and the imputed worths which arise in that process, we shall find the æsthetic participation worths entering as actual determinants in ethical valuation. Without going into greater detail in the present connection, it will be sufficient to point out that idealisation of character plays an important rôle in ethical judgments, and that these ideals are realised in æsthetic moments when assumptions take the place of judgments. The counsels of perfection whispered to our souls in these moments colour our ethical judgments in the real life that follows.

in a certain way, might be judged from two different standpoints, the personal and the impersonal. The feelings of value in these cases are qualified by different acquired meanings and references. The subject of the judgment represents two different selves, or, perhaps better, two different attitudes of the self. Our problem is to account for this differentiation of meaning and attitude.

This difference in attitude is fundamental,[1] and has its roots in the most elementary conditions and processes of sympathetic participation. Prior to all reflective judgment, to conscious judgment regarding the instrumental value of a quality or disposition for the purposes of the self or others, and, therefore, prior to the reflective distinction between egoism and altruism, there is a felt difference between the demand which is more intensive and personal, and that which is extensive and social, between the feeling of approval or disapproval which is more inward and personal in origin and reference and that which is more external and impersonal. These distinctions go back to a difference in presuppositions present in the most elementary forms of sympathy.

The fundamental difference we have in mind may be conveniently characterised as the distinction between intensive and extensive sympathy. By intensive sympathy and sympathetic participation, we understand, in the first place, that form of sympathy in which the processes of imitation, imaginative projection, and ideal construction, are confined to the ego and a single alter. Where the conditions of such relations are realised repeatedly, the common content with its common meaning becomes markedly individuated and personal. By extensive sympathy, on the other hand, we understand that form in which a larger number of individuals are included in the range of sympathetic projection, where the individual participates in the feeling and conation of social or racial groups. Between the extremes of intensive and extensive sympathy, there are, however, innumerable intermediate stages, and the terms obviously have merely a relative significance.

---

[1] It is a commonplace that the tribal morality of custom precedes personal morality, that the tribal conscience, with its more impersonal obligation, precedes the individual conscience with its personal obligations. And while, as we insisted in the preceding chapter, it is necessary to recognise a pre-ethical *impellent* mode, of quasi-obligation, prior to either personal or social construction, nevertheless we may admit that from the sociological point of view the more impersonal social demand is acknowledged in the form of obligation, prior to the more personal. At all events, the impersonal and social is equally fundamental with the personal.

Personal and Over-Individual Values

This relative significance is, nevertheless, important, for the reason that the more extensive the range of participation, the more unindividuated and impersonal the common meaning is. The grounds for this we shall seek to show in detail presently, but it is possible to see without further analysis that the more extensive the range of projection, the more generic and racial must be the feeling-attitude, and the less completely will it be identified with a single personality. If this is so, we should properly expect to find the implicit assumptions and the dispositions which they express, differing widely according to the intensive or extensive character of the processes of participation in which they are formed.

2. The Distinction due primarily to Differences in Inducing Conditions.

The inducing conditions of affective projection in general, considered without reference to the later distinction between intensive and extensive projection, have already been described. Organic imitation of movement-forms, perceptual or ideal, is the basis of sympathetic projection. When the objects of Einfühlung are persons, the perceptual movement-forms are bodily expression of various kinds, and those phases of motor expression which appear in the qualities of thought and speech. For the most elementary organic sympathy, similarity of motor attitude, of expression in general, is a necessary pre-requisite; and for imaginative projection, certain similarities of attitude or temperament, which, as we have seen, are reducible to similarities in the functional relations of affirmation and arrest of conative tendency, are equally necessary.

Taking attitude in the sense defined, it is clear that within any social group, whether large or small, there will be various differentiations of attitude. In the first place, to consider the most general and abstract difference first, individuals are found to differ in the degree to which they are predominantly affirmative or negative in type. Between the two limits—total absence of inhibition, and predominant arrest, such as we find in ascetics, there will be indefinite variation. At present we are not concerned with the causes of such variation—whether sub-social, biological, and economic, but merely with the fact of variation. This fact being recognised, it is further seen that within any organised society, or even group within a larger society, wherever there has been isolation enough to make such a group or society relatively homogeneous, there is a tendency for these variations to arrange themselves about a norm, the more individual variations, either in excess or defect of the normal, being eliminated or lost in the group attitude.

More specific variations in attitudes and emotional life are determined by the character of the fundamental conative tendency about which the other tendencies are systematised, and which in consequence has the greatest arresting and organising influence upon other tendencies. Thus, in every assemblage of individuals, sympathetic participation is determined by what we may describe as similarity or differentiation of *interests*, which colour in a noticeable way all emotional attitudes. Without pretending to an exhaustive treatment of the types and causes of this differentiation and its effect upon emotional attitude, the possibilities being really inexhaustible, we may content ourselves with reference to two lines of differentiation which have attracted special attention, namely, differences of function arising out of differences of sex and of employment. Recent studies in social psychology, especially those of Bücher [1] and Veblen,[2] have made much of the effect of differentiation of fundamental functions upon secondary or derived sentiments and emotions. The centre of affirmation and arrest varies so greatly, and becomes so fixed with generations of social heredity, that the sentiments and ideals of one class are with difficulty realisable by another.

When we turn to the fundamental differentiation of sex function, the effect of organic function in determining difference in derived sentiments and emotions is still more prominent. In addition to the generic difference which appears in the fact that to the man affirmation is more of a habit than in the case of the woman, there are the specific differences which arise from the different *locus* of the arrest in the two cases. Fundamental differences in feeling-attitude and in dispositional capacity for given sentiments and emotions, set certain definite limits to sympathetic participation, and ultimately, when ideal construction of dispositions has taken place, to differentiation in ideals of obligation and virtue.

---

[1] Bücher, *Die Entwickelung der Arbeit*, 3rd Ed., 1900.
[2] Veblen, *A Theory of the Leisure Class.* Also Simmel, *Ueber Sociale Differenzierung*, Leipzig, 1890.

From this brief sketch, it may be easily seen that there are causes at work differentiating and establishing, in larger and narrower groups, habitual attitudes and expressions which form the inducing conditions of sympathetic participation. These causes are doubtless both social and sub-social, the sub-social factors being biological and psychological in the narrower individual sense. But with the special character of these causes we are not immediately concerned. Our problem is rather this : granted the existence of such differentiations of attitude, how do they affect sympathetic participation and the feelings of value which emerge in these processes ?

3. *The Distinction Develops with Progress from Organic Sympathy to Ideal Construction.*

The most elementary differentiation of the personal and impersonal reference of " common feeling " occurs in organic sympathy, the first stage of sympathetic participation. It becomes more marked in the succeeding stages of imaginative projection, or sembling, and of ideal construction and judgment. In organic sympathy itself, prior to differentiation of presuppositions, the sympathy may have an individual or social reference. Group passions and emotions are as fully realisable sympathetically as are individual. We may well believe that what is called contagion of emotion is more completely realised on primitive than on the higher social levels. The individual subject to this contagion apprehends immediately, through inner imitation, the emotional attitude thus expressed, and projects it with presumption of its existence beyond the self. It is a common feeling, and for the participant has a common meaning, but it *is not*—and this is the important point—*localised in an individual* and then read back into the self. It remains external and impersonal in its reference, as an over-individual, impersonal demand.

The differentiation of personal and impersonal reference of the common meaning becomes still more marked when sympathetic participation is extended beyond organic sympathy, through sembling or feelings of the imagination. The inducing conditions of organic sympathy are similarities of motor attitude and expression, and the limits of such participation are definitely set by biological conditions which are sub-social and psychological. Beyond this point the projection becomes

s

imaginative, and the feeling of participation is an assumption-feeling. The condition of such imaginative projection, we have already seen, is abstraction of the feeling from its individual presuppositions and from its organic accompaniments. The significance of this fact for our study of the modification of the " common meaning " of feeling through extensive projection, is far-reaching. It follows that the more extensive the range of sympathetic projection, the more the individuals vary in expression and attitude, the more complete this process of abstraction must be, and the less personal will be the reference of the feeling.

This consequence may be shown in two ways. In the first place, only certain limited classes of feeling-attitudes are susceptible of extensive projection, and these are precisely those attitudes which are least individualised, most completely generic or racial. Within narrower groups, the derived and more highly differentiated emotional attitudes may be intuitively appreciated, but with the increase of extent of the projection, the assumption becomes more and more uncertain and the characterisation more and more fanciful; it is only the primitive condition worths which are susceptible of very extensive projection. I hear of some act of heroism on the part of a savage or an Oriental. Up to a certain point I can intuitively realise his attitude, especially if it is an act of heroism in connection with the fundamental motives of family or state, but even then, as a result of racial differentiations of habits of expression and thought, only incompletely, and in the case of more differentiated attitudes, not at all. This is especially true in the case of the *nuances* of his sense of honour. Into the background of presuppositions or implicit assumptions which determine his feelings and judgments, I can penetrate only with the greatest difficulty, for they have been created by activities of sympathetic participation and consequent imaginative and ideal construction differing in important respects from those which have determined my own. Social selection and differentiation have worked differently in the two cases. With the nature and laws of this selection we shall be concerned in another connection; here it is important merely to note the fact that beyond purely organic sympathy, sympathetic participation is distinctly limited.

In view of these facts, it can be easily seen that the judgments and implicit assumptions of existence or non-existence of more extensive social dispositions and demands, rest less and less upon immediate organic sympathy and intuitive projection, and more and more upon abstract inference and judgment, and that, consequently, the feelings of participation in this case become progressively more and more impersonal. It may be also readily seen that the implicit assumptions or expectations thus generated will vary widely, both in the character of the attitudes or dispositions demanded and in the amount expected, from the expectations or demands generated in more immediate personal intercourse. In these facts we shall find the explanation of those differences in personal and social obligation, personal and impersonal imputation, reference to which has been made at the beginning of this chapter. The further development of these differences and their explanation belong to succeeding chapters.

CHAPTER IX

I. PERSONAL WORTHS—THE VALUES OF CHARACTERISATION OF THE PERSON

1. *Definition: the Personal Attitude in Valuation.*

THE values described as personal constitute a well-marked sphere of meanings in our worth experience. Between the satisfaction of a simple sense-tendency, and its corresponding condition worth, and the satisfaction of a demand more deeply rooted in the personality, there is a difference which is immediately appreciated. No less clear is the distinction between the value of an act as a quality or expression of the personality, and as merely a means to other ends, either individual or social. If we had occasion to criticise the statement of Lipps that "every pleasure is conditioned by a personality worth," [1] it is, nevertheless, true that a certain class of worth feelings presuppose explicit reference to the ideal or concept of the person. These feelings are described as feelings of personal worth.

The objects of such feelings are primarily qualities or dispositions of the person. It is true that physical objects of condition worth may acquire a complementary personal value, but this is possible only when they are related to the primary objects through secondary associations or instrumental judgments. It is with the primary objects of intrinsic personal worth that we are here concerned. These objects, we have seen, are ideal constructions developed in the processes of sympathetic participation. Through the processes of Einfühlung, the feeling of the individual acquires a common over-individual meaning. The disposition corresponding to this feeling, now presumed, assumed, or judged to exist in another, has acquired a new meaning and value through the very fact of participation, of its being shared. But when the

[1] Chap. II, pp. 50 ff.

Personal Worths 261

disposition is thus cognised, and has this *subjective* "participation-value," it may be further intrinsically and independently valued as an expression of the person, the self, or the alter. This is its personal value or value for characterisation.

The attitude toward personal worths, of the self or the alter, is one which we describe in terms of respect or admiration, with their opposites, contempt and disdain. We clearly distinguish self-respect from self-complacency, and self-disdain from self-pity; and respect and disdain for others from mere liking or disliking and pity. The reason for this distinction is to be found in the fact that the first class of predicates represents personal worths, the second condition worths. Pity, like, and dislike are simple modifications of feelings of condition worth, adequately described in terms of pleasantness and unpleasantness. It is to these latter attitudes that the distinction between egoism and altruism alone applies, for it is only when we take the subjective feeling as end, to which the qualities of the person are related as means, only when we form the concept of our own or another's happiness, that the conflict between egoism and altruism arises. It is merely this subjective aspect of "condition worth" that has no common meaning, and that cannot be shared. Self-complacency and self-pity are, properly speaking, egoistic, self-respect and self-disdain are not. Pity for the unhappiness of another, or satisfaction in his pleasure, is altruistic; respect and disdain for another are neither egoistic nor altruistic. The intrinsic valuation of personality transcends the distinction.[1]

Equally clear is the distinction between the personal and the impersonal attitude in valuation. Within certain limits, which will be defined as our study proceeds, respect and disrespect, admiration and disdain, may be independent of the moral judgment of good and bad. Just as the personal attitude transcends the distinction between egoism and altruism, so, at points, it transcends the distinction of moral goodness and badness with which they are closely connected.

The preceding study of feelings of personal worth, their

---

[1] The feelings of hate and envy which are so often the accompaniments of the recognition of personal worths are but proofs of this position. We cannot hate or envy a man because of his personal worth. This is an acquired worth which is intrinsically recognised as good and desirable for us. It is only when we turn our eyes to the hedonic accompaniments, the condition worths which we infer to accompany the personal worth or with which we conceive the personal worth to be instrumentally connected, that we feel envy and hate. Thus, doubtless, the illiterate Athenian when he hated to hear Aristides *called* just, was always thinking of the rewards of the virtue. To envy a man because of his beauty, strength, or virtue is essentially a backward value movement.

objects and the qualities predicated of the objects, makes clear the more important characteristics of these feelings. Their meanings are acquired meanings, and their objects ideal constructs. Both the feelings and their objects presuppose the development of a certain sphere of meaning within which the judgments of characterisation are passed, a sphere or level of meaning which, while it develops by certain processes out of the lower level of feelings of condition worth, is now contrasted with that lower level.

Analysing these presuppositions in more detail, we find that they are certain implicit assumptions with which the subject of the feeling comes to the object. These assumptions, as we have already seen in the studies of the preceding chapter, are of the nature of expectations of the existence or non-existence of certain dispositions, certain tendencies to desire, feel, and act, on the part of the self and the alter. These assumptions, when made as a demand upon the self, give rise to feelings of personal obligation; when made as a demand upon the alter, they condition our judgments of praise and blame. In general, then, the presupposition of the sphere of meanings described as personal worths is the ideal construct of the *person*, individuated as the self or the alter, to which the objects of the feelings are referred.

2. *The Idea or Ideal of Personality: Its Meaning—How assumed in all Judgments of Personal Worth.*

In saying that the existence of the person is assumed implicitly in all feelings and judgments of personal worth, we have introduced the concept of personality, and in doing so we must proceed with caution if we are not to go beyond the limits of psychological method. Whatever may be said as to the ultimate metaphysical reality of the self, it is not, strictly speaking, an object of immediate experience, not an object of perception, nor, on the side of feeling, of simple appreciation, but is rather a construct of a higher order built up upon immediate perceptions and appreciations. The *self* is not first there as an object and then characterised, but is rather an object which is constructed and individuated in the very processes of characterisation. Constructed first for practical purposes, as a concept for the regulation of our expectations of sympathetic participation, it becomes individuated as an object with intrinsic value and meaning, to which obligations, responsibilities, merits, and demerits may be imputed, concepts which stand for certain acquired meanings of feeling. It is, first of all, a worth construction, and only secondarily an object of knowledge.

Such a self is always assumed in feelings and judgments of personal worth. And the self thus assumed is, in the first place, a generic and ideal self. To be more explicit, the ideal self is at the same time personal and over-individual. The specific disposition assumed has acquired an additional meaning through reference to the concept of the person, but the concept of the person is at first *schematic*, and not individuated into the ego and the alter as centres of unique interests and inner life. In order to understand this, it is necessary to recall the conception of the "person-project" developed in the preceding chapter.[1] There it was pointed out that the development of this ideal projection in the processes of sympathetic Einfühlung—the passage of simple organic sympathy with its presumption of existence, into feelings of the imagination in *sembling*, the abstraction of the feeling from individual presuppositions and its schematic character in general—makes it at once over-individual and personal, ready to be read either into the self or the alter, and acknowledged in judgment as identical with the self or the other.

II. THE CHARACTER OF THE IDEAL PERSON AS DETERMINED BY THE PROCESSES IN WHICH IT IS CONSTRUCTED

1. *Idealisation Involved in Sympathetic Einfühlung.*

The character of the presupposed personality is determined by certain factors inherent in sympathetic projection itself. The first of these may be described as the tendency to *idealise*. By idealisation is here understood the tendency, inherent in projection in its imaginative, *semblant* mode, to *enlarge*, so to speak, the feeling and feeling disposition as projected and assumed to exist in the "other." The projected feeling, abstracted from its individual presuppositions, is assumed to be deeper and broader, more completely identified with the person.

Illustrations of this fact are numerous. Most apparent in undeveloped persons, and differing in degree with differences in temperament, it is, nevertheless, present to some extent in all personal relations. The savage or barbarian, lost in

[1] Chap. VIII, p. 248.

admiration of the strength and pride of his chief, ignores the shadows, the negative factors of which he is conscious in himself, and it may be added, the negative condition worths, the pains which come to himself through this superiority. The child worships the "good and beautiful lady." The simple man believes the scholar's knowledge boundless. More developed persons are subject to the same illusion. The illusions of love will suffice for our purpose, since they are well adapted to show the psychological source of the illusion. The lover feels sympathetically the love of his adored, but as the result of the very conditions of sympathetic Einfühlung, i.e., abstraction from individual presuppositions, it is a purified and enlarged love that he beholds. In himself he is conscious of its dependence upon organic and other presuppositions—he is conscious of its admixture with condition worths, in this case lust—and though he may believe the disposition constant, he is conscious of the variations in feeling. Although intellectually he might infer similar conditions in the other, intuitively he is unable to project them, and, therefore, ignores them. The enlarged purified love he beholds is assumed to have a corresponding disposition—a correlate in the object of his devotion, and that disposition is assumed to have depth and breadth in the personality not realisable in himself.[1]

This imaginative projection, with its accompanying abstraction of the feeling from individual and limiting presuppositions, and its consequent enlargement, is, however, but the first stage of idealisation. The projected feeling has both an individual and an over-individual reference, and when that feeling is sympathetically realised as an attitude of the alter, it is again read back into the self. Idealised in the sense we have described, by imaginative projection, it is again referred to the self in its idealised form. Lipps has described the process in terms which I can do no better than quote in full. " As I look about me *the* man appears, now in this point, now in that, increased beyond the measure found in myself. That means, as we know, that expressions in others awake in me the idea of an increase of an element in my own nature. So arises in me a new idea of personality which, just in so

---

[1] Lipps, *Die ethischen Grundfragen*, p. 44. It is an empirical fact—upon which Lipps rightly lays considerable weight in his argument for the recognition of intrinsic personal worth in the alter, as opposed to its derivation from egoism—that the normal accompaniment of sympathetic projection is the contrasting of the assumed attitude or disposition in the "alter" with our own, in the direction of idealisation of the "alter."

far as it represents an extension of my real personality, is in comparison with the latter an ideal personality. There arises in me, finally, in the course of this process a representation of the ideal personality."[1]

2. *Division of the Personality—Extrusion of the Negative Moment Further Stages in Idealisation.*

In the process, as thus far sketched, we have but the beginning of the ideal construction of the personality. The primary contrast between worths of condition and of the person is the germ of the idealisation described, but the contrast, and the idealisation which it conditions, do not stop here. The contrast is thus far between the imagined and the actual feeling, between the feeling as projected into the alter or read back into the self, and as individual feeling with its individual presuppositions. The identification of this ideal project with the other, or in a return movement with the self, involves a further step in the process of characterisation, which may be described as contrast of the personal worth, now *identified* with the self or the alter, with the condition worths now conceived as sub-personal. This leads to a division of the personality.

The division of the personality, whether of the self or the alter, is a well-known phase of ideal construction. The distinction between the higher and the lower self is presupposed in all ethical judgments. The analysis of the situation shows that it arises out of an explicit acknowledgment, as an *opposition*, of what was at first merely a *felt* contrast. The identification of the disposition, as a positive quality, with the person, requires some corresponding acknowledgment of the opposing negative tendencies, and this gives rise to the intensification of the primary contrast in a conceptual division of the self. The contrast between the flesh and the spirit, between desire and will, are well-known characterisations of the situation. In such cases the objects, the " spirit " and the " will," acquire a new meaning, and are, through this contrast, more completely identified with the ideal personality.

We should fail, however, to understand the real significance of this stage if we did not realise that it may be but germinal to a later stage, in which division of the personality develops into complete extrusion of the lower tendencies, of the *negative*

[1] Lipps, *Die ethischen Grundfragen*, p. 37.

moment. Such a stage is reached, for instance, in the notion of temptation and in the personification of the tempting tendencies in the form of a hostile personality. The extreme of this externalisation we have in certain religious personifications where the highest personal worths are identified with the good God, while the evil is projected into opposing personalities and forces. The individual who identifies his will with the will of God frequently acquires, through the completeness of the contrast, the absolute value of complete sanctification, and to him is imputed by other persons the ideal values of sainthood. Similar heightening of the sense of value follows when the negative factor is externalised in an opposing social group, as when the personal worth of the martyr is increased through contrast with the surrounding evil. As a child of his age, some of its evil is probably in him, but the individuation of his personality about some supreme personal worth as a centre, brings with it extrusion of the negative elements. Such complete contrasts are commonly fully realised only in the isolation of the personality, in æsthetic construction where the negative moments are for the moment ignored, but there are quasi-æsthetic moments present in all ideal construction, and they are accompanied by belief in the ideal. Even purely æsthetic idealisations may, as we shall see later, under certain circumstances, pass over into belief, and affect our actual ethical feelings and judgments.

3. *Intuitive (Æsthetic) Individuation of the Personality—Acquirement of Complementary Value.*

Thus far in our study of the ideal construction of the personality, its schematic character and over-individual aspects have been emphasised. With the ideal imaginative projection of an individual feeling-attitude and its contrast with condition worths, it acquires a personal reference and meaning. But when the ideal construct of the person is thus formed, when a quality of that person is valued intrinsically as an expression of the person, further processes of individuation appear, and the quality or qualities in question acquire complementary value through their relations to each other as parts of a harmonious totality. The contrast or division of the personality, and ultimately the æsthetic or quasi-æsthetic isolation of the person, afford the necessary conditions for that individuating reconstruction and rearrangement of the elements of the personality which makes repose in the object possible, and gives rise to complementary immanental value. This individuation of the personality is of the intuitive type of construction discussed in a preceding chapter,[1] where certain forms of this individuating construction, both perceptual and ideational, were described, and their fundamental laws determined. In particular, we considered the emergence of new objects of appreciation, such as sensuous beauty, manners, cleanliness, through the rearrangement of sensational and perceptual activities; also the individuation of abstract ideal constructions, such as a sum of money, where the sum as a unity or totality, acquires an intrinsic value not constituted by the instrumental values of its separate elements. The individuating construction of the personality does not differ in principle from these types, but merely in the material elements.

The function of the *law of contrast* in building up the ideal personality is primary. In fact, the other two laws are, as we have seen, in a sense expressions of it. The contrast of a quality of a personality, with other qualities, by which it acquires complementary value, may be seen at two points. Such a quality may be contrasted either with the opposite qualities of surrounding persons, or with opposing qualities in the same personality which have been or are being overcome. Thus the holiness of a martyr stands out as completely identified with his personality, in contrast to the universal corruption about him. Augustine is all the more a saint for the opposition of his complete devotion to ideal ends in later life to the lower feelings and desires of his earlier career. Whether the contrast is between an inner and a more external self, or between the self and society—in either case the contrast enhances the sense of reality, and therefore of the value of the personality. The fondness of those who have undergone experiences of conversion for contrasting their present with their past, arises from the increase in the sense of personal worth, resulting from complete identification of present ideals with the personality, the sense of elevation, which results from the contrast.

The principle of the " total series," which was seen to be so important in æsthetic construction, has an important rôle to play in the real activities and judgments of personal worth experience. It may almost be described, perhaps, as the dramatic tendency in the characterisation of the self and the alter.

[1] Chap. VI, pp. 173 ff.

Unity and continuity form the goal, consciously or unconsciously, of all characterisations of personality. The ordering of the acts, of the expressions of a life, as they appear in temporal relations of succession, in such a manner that they have a qualitative order or meaning, as determined by relations of teleological dependence, is one of the chief sources of the complementary values imputed to personalities. This quasi-æsthetic characterisation of the personality is inseparable from any reconstruction of our own past or construction of our future, for the reason that the self is primarily a worth construction. It is equally inseparable from the biographical and historical reconstruction of other personalities.

Finally we may note the important rôle of the principle of "end feeling" in this characterisation of the personality. In general the tendency, already noted, to reconstruct the temporal relation teleologically through processes of selection and exclusion, leads to the selection of the end term of the series as the keynote of the whole, and as the chief determinant of the character of the whole. Even in the characterisations of the self and the alter of ordinary life, this ordering of the elements of the total character under the end-moments is much in evidence. The expression, in various forms, of the thought that no one is to be reckoned happy until he dies, shows the emphasis put upon the last moments. In like manner the importance of the last moments before death in determining the judgment upon a person as a whole is shown in the emphasis which religion puts upon the "making of a good end." But it is in the æsthetic characterisations of literature, where illusion-disturbing judgments are inhibited, and, to a degree also, in the quasi-æsthetic characterisations of biography and history, that the working of this law of ideal construction is most apparent, and the importance of the principle in the determination of the worth imputed to the personality as a whole is best shown. A moment of supreme manifestation of strength or self-sacrifice, at the end of a relatively meaningless life, may give it a supreme meaning and hallow all the other moments; may, indeed, through very contrast with the weakness or evil of the former acts, heighten the value imputed to the personality. Finality as purpose, is logically independent of temporal finality, but not for intuitive construction. In one sense it does not matter *when* the chief note of a man's life, as, for instance, his heroic moment, occurs, but in another sense it does. It is a timeless value, but for our unification of his character it makes all the difference in the world whether the heroic act came early and was followed by mediocrity or weakness, or whether a meaningless life receives meaning from a final beautiful act. As in the unities of the "temporal arts," music and the drama, so in the æsthetic characterisation of the person we seek to make the two kinds of " ends " coincide.

In the preceding principles of characterisation of persons are disclosed the laws according to which the process of idealisation, begun in sympathetic Einfühlung and consequent contrast of person and condition worths, is carried on in the intuitive individuation of the person. In both cases, there is acquirement of value. In the first stages of the process of idealisation the acquired value is transgredient, i.e., the projection of the attitude, its acquirement of common meaning, and its contrast with condition worths, issue in a new demand which is felt in the self as personal obligation, and with reference to the alter as a demand for intrinsic personal values. The acquired value of the individuating construction, on the other hand, is immanental, and arises from repose in the object, the unitary personality. Here the values are partially or wholly æsthetic, and the feelings of value find expression in the æsthetic predicates of perfection, nobility, beauty of character, etc. In the acquirement of this complementary immanental value, many qualities of the person are significant largely because of their rôle as necessary elements in the unique totality, and have only personal value, being without instrumental value for social ends.

4. *Conclusions.*

The general conclusions to be drawn from this study of the processes of idealisation of the person may be thus stated. In this process a new meaning is acquired, a new level of valuation formed. Through reference to the ideal of the person, and through contrast with condition worths, the disposition becomes the object of feelings *qualitatively* different from the feelings of simple appreciation. But not only is this qualitatively new meaning acquired. The feelings of value, with these acquired presuppositions, have greater transgredient and immanental reference, greater depth and breadth in the personality. They represent, therefore, an absolute increase in the *degree* of value or affective-volitional meaning. In general, personal worths have preference over condition worths. The demand to realise personal worths, as represented in feelings of "personal" obligation, is more intense than in the case of the quasi-ethical obligations attached to objects of condition worth. Personal qualities have in them a greater capacity for continuous valuation than objects of condition worth. These conclusions we shall see further substantiated in our studies of personal obligation and imputation of personal worth in the following chapter.

III. THE LAWS OF VALUATION AS APPLIED TO OBJECTS OF PERSONAL WORTH

1. *The Problem.*

The ideal schematic person, the existence of which is implicitly assumed or presumed in all feelings and judgments of personal worth, has now been sketched in its broad outlines. It is seen to be the conceptual term for a system of dispositions or affective-volitional tendencies which is assumed to exist, now in the self, now in the alter. As such it is the necessary background or presupposition of the entire group of values which we call personal. It was further shown how this schematic ideal may be individuated by the individuating principles inherent in ideal construction, and how the elements may acquire complementary value as part of a unique totality. It is, therefore, with such expectations, assumptions, demands, that the individual who judges comes to the objects of judgment, and his imputation of merit or demerit is the expression of the feelings of satisfaction or dissatisfaction following upon judgments of existence or non-existence of the expected dispositions.

These assumptions or demands are, on their part, expressions of dispositions generated in the processes of sympathetic participation, and have been determined by the selective processes of idealisation inherent in such participation. When this fact is duly recognised, it becomes apparent that our description has thus far abstracted wholly from one important aspect of the feelings of personal worth, and of their corresponding judgments, namely, the aspect of *quantity or degree*. Since the assumptions underlying judgments of personal worth represent the funded meaning acquired in processes of sympathetic participation and idealisation, the individual comes to the object of judgment, not only with a pre-disposition to assume the existence of certain qualities, but also to expect these qualities in certain amounts. Consequently the feelings and judgments of personal worth will be determined by the degree to which these expectations are realised. The relative value of any quantity, we have seen, is a function of the relation of that quantity to the amount of the presupposed demand. That demand, again, is determined by the dispositions to feel or desire created by previous acts of valuation. In this case the demand is the reflex of the ideal personality, that is, the funded meaning of the dispositions, acquired through reference to the construct of the person. Our task is now to define this demand in quantitative terms, to determine the laws of valuation of these ideal objects of personal worth.

2. The Problem in the Light of our General Study of the Laws of Valuation.

The solution of this problem is, in a sense, merely the application to a special question, to a specific class of worth objects, of the general principles developed in the chapter on the Laws of Valuation. It would seem that in defining the objects of personal worth as ideal and intrinsic, we have already determined the laws of their valuation, for it has been shown, at considerable length, that such objects have the capacity of continuous valuation, that degree of value increases with increase in the amount of the object. Objects of condition worth and of instrumental value we found to be subject to the law of Limiting Value, and the concrete judgments of value in these spheres were seen to reflect the working of this law, i.e., the thresholds and limits are determined by it. On the other hand, ideal intrinsic objects, with the capacity for individuation and acquirement of complementary value, are not subject to this law. From this conclusion it was further inferred that the presupposition or postulate of judgment in this sphere is the possibility of continuous valuation and of the existence of absolute values.

With regard to the special class of personal worths, it would follow, if these general principles are true, that the demand for such objects is unlimited, that the assumption underlying our judgments of personal worth, our judgments both of obligation and of imputation of merit and demerit, would be that indefinite increase of dispositions with personal worth means continued increase in degree of value. It would be "rational," to use the illustration of the earlier chapter,[1] to desire the increase of such dispositions indefinitely; and our judgments of obligation and imputation, in reflecting that desire or demand, would likewise be rational, would be but the reflection of actual facts and laws of worth experience.

This conclusion, based upon considerations of a general character, we shall find justified in the sequel, and an analysis of our actual judgments in this sphere will confirm the hypothesis. It will be seen that our judgments of personal obligation and imputation presuppose this postulate. Nevertheless, a special analysis of sympathetic participation and idealisation from this point of view will not only give a more concrete basis for this general conclusion, but will develop certain facts necessary for the adequate interpretation of judgments of personal worth.

3. *Feelings of Personal Worth as Modified by the Factor of Quantity of the Object.*

Analysis of the Factor of Quantity.

The feelings of personal worth have their origin in immediate sympathy and sympathetic participation, which is in the first place organic. Out of this develop imaginative projection and ideal construction of dispositions, with their assumptions and judgments of existence. It is clear that in our investigation of the effect of quantity on the degree of feeling we must keep before us this difference in objects and presuppositions of the feelings. In the case of simple organic sympathy the factor of quantity appears in two forms: as *repetition* of sympathetic participation, and as *intensity* of the feeling in which the subject sympathetically participates. When the level of ideal construction, i.e., assumption and judgment, is reached, the object is not the immediate emotional expression, but the disposition presupposed, and the factor of quantity is different. The quantity of the disposition may be displayed in two ways: either by *repetition* of the expression in acts, or by strength of disposition displayed in a single act. In the first case, the quantity of the disposition is measured in its extent, the degree to which it is habitual in the personality; in the second case, it is measured in its depth, the degree to which the disposition is fundamental in the personality.

---

[1] Chap. VI, pp. 186 ff.

(a) Organic Sympathy.

Organic sympathy we found to be genetically the lowest level of sympathetic participation. The effect of *repetition* upon these participation feelings is the ordinary one of dulling of sensitivity, leading ultimately to the arrest of participation. Analysis of experience leaves no doubt of this fact. It is apparent alike in æsthetic Einfühlung where the objects are impersonal and in ethical participation in the feeling of persons. In the case of " inner imitation," where the inducing conditions are perceptual movement-forms of nature, repetition is followed by the dulling of the organic resonance, as was clearly illustrated in the studies of the preceding chapter.[1] Still more is this true in the case where the inducing conditions are the expressions of persons. In organic sympathy with the joys and sorrows of others, such sympathy is distinctly limited to short periods and to favourable conditions, and loses its intensity with repetition.[2] In both cases, however, there is the possibility of substituting for organic sympathy an intuitive realisation of the feeling—more technically expressed, of feeling of imagination or emotional abstract—in the attitude of *sembling*.

The dulling of sensitivity with repetition has as its parallel a corresponding effect of *satiety*—i.e., when the intensity of the emotional expression, to be sympatheticaly realised, is above a certain normal amount. The emotional demand made upon the sympathetic person by an extreme of joy or sorrow, by unlimited enthusiasm, devotion, or sacrifice, as exhibited in the alter, may, as far as the organic resonance is concerned, have an effect entirely analogous to satiety in the sphere of other sensation-feelings, and especially so when the subject's temperamental equipment sets a limit to these emotional experiences. Here again, however, the limits of organic sympathy do not necessarily mark the limits of all forms of sympathetic participation. The substitutes for the full emotional resonance, the feelings of the imagination in sembling, may notably extend the range of our participation. In æsthetic participation, as in the drama, we find that, if certain conditions are met, an indefinite increase of feeling, as expressed by the actor, may be participated in sympathetically by the spectator in a manner and degree impossible in the case of those feelings described as " real." The æsthetic isolation and illusion bring

[1] Chap. VIII, p. 240.   [2] Chap. VI, p. 182.

about an unusual extension of our capacities of sympathetic participation, making possible a complete, though temporary, identification of the feeling of the self with that of the other and the identification of the sympathetic participant with the personality as dramatically presented.

(b) *Judgment and Assumption Feelings.*

Organic sympathy is, then, subject to the law of Limiting Value as determined by dulling of sensitivity and satiety. But organic sympathy does not mark the limit of sympathetic participation. There are forms of participation in which the feelings have as their presuppositions assumptions and judgments. Our further problem is clearly to determine the effect upon these dispositions, and upon their corresponding implicit assumptions, of actualisation of feeling through these cognitive acts. What is the effect of the factor of quantity in this sphere?

Here the problem is at first sight more complicated, but it is immediately simplified when we recognise that, whatever this effect may be, it is not one of dulling of sensitivity and satiety. These laws do not apply to judgment and assumption feelings as such, for they are not sensation-feelings.[1] With this negative conclusion, it becomes at once clear that we are not concerned with the mere mechanical effects of repetition and over-stimulation, but rather with the question of the limits of what we have called judgment capacity.[2] When the quantity of an object is apprehended in acts of cognition, the value of the quantity is either instrumental or intrinsic. When the feeling of value is mediated by instrumental judgments, it is subject to the law of Limiting Value for reasons developed in the chapter referred to, and which need not be repeated here. This law would apply to the value of a disposition, in so far as that value is instrumental. On the other hand, when the value is intrinsic, and presupposes the assumption of the existence of an individuated whole of which it is a part, the law of Complementary Values becomes operative, and the capacity of the object for continuous valuation depends entirely upon the degree to which individuation and isolation are possible. Whether, then, there is increase in degree of value, depends upon the degree to which, with increase in quantity of an object of personal worth, the object can be isolated and intrinsically valued. Whether these complementary values determine the *demand* for personal

---

[1] Chap. VI, p. 159.　　　　[2] Chap. VI, p. 171.

Personal Worths 275

worths presupposed in our actual judgments of imputation and obligation, depends upon the degree to which such intrinsic valuations modify the dispositions presupposed by these judgments.

4. The Effect of Idealisation on our Actual Judgments and Judgmental Dispositions.

(a) *Idealisation as Imaginative Construction.*

This intrinsic valuation is possible, however, only on the condition of æsthetic or quasi-æsthetic isolation of the personality, described in the study of the processes of idealisation. The preponderating rôle of imaginative projection, with its contrast and individuation, in the process of idealisation has been emphasised. Do these feelings of the imagination or assumption feelings enter into the formation of our permanent beliefs, or implicit assumptions of reality? Evidently the vital question in the present discussion concerns the effect of these feelings of imagination upon our dispositions to *actual* feeling, and therefore upon our worth judgments. This is, of course, but another aspect of the general question fully discussed in an earlier chapter.[1] There we insisted that feelings of the imagination, as well as judgment feelings, modify our feeling dispositions, our implicit assumptions, and are, therefore, of functional importance in the processes of valuation. Here we might apply that conclusion without further analysis of the facts, but our development of the present study will be more satisfactory if we make an independent analysis of æsthetic participation.

(b) *The Effect of the Semblant Mode in Simple Appreciation.*

The effect of the semblant, æsthetic mode in simple appreciation has already been shown, but a reconsideration of the facts at this point will enable us to understand better its rôle in the characterisation of persons. Cognitively considered, the attitude was found to be one of conscious self-illusion in that in most experiences of the æsthetic type, more particularly *artistic* creation and appreciation, the elimination of illusion-disturbing moments is a conscious process, and the judgments which would destroy the illusion are never completely inhibited. Nevertheless, even here the distinction between reality and illusion

[1] Chap. v, pp. 137-9.

cannot be pressed too far. The æsthetic mode of appreciation is genetically related to other worth attitudes, in that it is a value movement toward activity, in which assumption takes the place of judgment, and in which desire becomes dispositional. But precisely because of this genetic relation, the immanental value acquired in the movement modifies our actual feelings of value, as is seen in the phenomena of imputed value.[1] Even in art the assumption feelings are not without effect upon our actual desires and feelings. In such a work of art as Tennyson's *Lotos-Eaters*—a well-nigh perfect illusion of mood where, by the elimination of all illusion-disturbing factors, the dominant mood of peace and forgetfulness is completely realised—it is quite possible that its effect may persist in non-æsthetic attitudes. It is impossible, it is true, that the momentary assumption of the existence of such a land of dreams should pass over into actual belief in its existence, but since it was a real, though dispositional desire that was temporarily satisfied, the illusion may have its effect as an undertone in determining actual feelings and judgments. Such dreams not only create a belief which leads to its own realisation, as when Columbus said, " It was not astronomy or geometry, but his reading Isaiah's prophecy of a new heaven and a new earth, that set him on his discovery," but they may also form the basis of a critical judgment of actual conduct and life, which may lead to the realisation of the new heavens and the new earth of the reformer.

(c) The Effect of the Æsthetic in the Characterisation of Persons.

When we pass to the rôle of imagination in the characterisation of persons, and its effect upon the implicit assumptions underlying our personal judgments, the distinction between imagination and belief is still more vague. In our study of ethical and æsthetic projection, it was found that the difference lies, not in the projected feeling, but in the secondary participation-feeling following upon the judgment or assumption of the existence or non-existence of a dispositional correlate. In the case of *Lear* there cited, the projected feeling, as feeling, may be more fully realised than in actual life. It is the impulse or disposition to participate that is at a minimum, and therefore the corresponding feelings of participation may be said to lack reality. They are assumption-feelings. Neverthe-

---

[1] Chap. VII, pp. 229 ff.

less these assumption-feelings may pass over into judgment-feelings in several significant ways. The vulgar tendency to take the passions of the stage as real, and sometimes to act accordingly, shows this relation of assumption to judgment in a crude form. The ideal limiting case of the æsthetic attitude, desireless intuition, is but imperfectly realised. Will is present dispositionally, ready to flare up upon the crudest semblance to reality. Much more significant, however, for the larger life of worth experiences is what may be described as the "after-feeling of reality," the conviction or judgment, that such situations, such passions, etc., are actually real. We have here, then, the curious situation, the meaning of which has not been fully appreciated, that a feeling, the character of the presuppositions of which, as assumptions, was fully realised at the time, may gradually pass over into a real feeling with judgment as its presupposition. Phenomena of this sort are not far to seek. An æsthetic realisation of idealised passions and emotions may generate expectations which colour the actual judgments of real life. Similarly, a man may come to *believe* in his own dreams, which at first were recognised as dreams.[1]

(5) *Absolute Personal Values: They exist as Practical Absolutes.*

The self is an ideal construction of an individuating character involving contrast, serial order, and totalisation through the idea of finality. The working out of this construction involves an isolation and extrusion of the "negative moments," possible only in æsthetic idealisation. In such idealisation absolute values are realised, that is, situations appear where the object of personal worth is completely identified with the personality; the elimination of opposing elements is absolute and the ideal of perfection is realised.

---

[1] The nature of this transition from æsthetic, imaginative construction of a personality, with its mere assumption of reality and its conscious "self-illusion," to *actual belief* is well illustrated, in an extreme form, in some cases of illusions of mediumship. In that interesting and instructive study of mediumship, M. Flournoy's *A Journey to Mars*, it would seem to be established that the creation of secondary personalities was preceded by periods of incubation, in which an ideal fictitious personality was being constructed from materials got from reading, conversation, etc. Gradually there was a systematisation of tendencies and attitudes about a fundamental, and an accompanying arrest of illusion-disturbing tendencies. Finally the segregation became so complete that the system received a new name and became a new personality. The transition from assumption to judgment with its accompanying belief was gradual. What the trance contributed to the situation was simply that it afforded the conditions for complete auto-suggestion, arresting all tendencies which would be illusion-disturbing, which would again transform belief into assumption.

In actual ethical characterisation this ideal is only imperfectly realised. The ever-recurrent division of the self into the lower and the higher (the Kantian contrast between the empirical and the rational, intelligible will), is a necessary condition of ideal construction and of ethical judgment, but is normally incomplete. The complete identification of the ideal object of personal worth with the personality is merely an ideal to be attained, because of the difficulty of complete extrusion of the negative moment. There are, however, unique experiences, both in the processes of self-realisation and in the characterisation of the alter, where the illusion of complete identification, of perfection, which is ordinarily possible only in purely æsthetic experiences, becomes part of the real ethical process, where the æsthetic assumption acquires the conviction of judgment. These we may describe as practical absolutes.

The situations where these unique experiences, these supreme moments, appear are those in which the contrast between the individual and the surrounding social values, or between the ideal personal worths and the lower condition worths, is so complete that the negative moments are wholly externalised, and the personality is completely unified through identification with the ideal object; the æsthetic isolation and illusion is complete. This means that psychologically, for immediate experience, there are absolute personal worths—however these may be judged from a more objective impersonal and overindividual point of view. The ideal constructions of religious experience and the identification of the individual with these constructions are cases in point. The supreme sacrifice of Christ becomes an object of belief, and the identification of the individual will with his will has, at least in exceptional cases, produced the experience or illusion of complete holiness. Now the interesting feature of these religious experiences is that, while like the æsthetic they depend upon isolation (Christ is one with the Father and the believer is "*hid* with Christ in God"), in the religious experiences there is such complete arrest of all "illusion-disturbing" factors and all opposing elements, that assumption passes over into belief. They afford momentary realisations of supreme values which negate all questions of possibility and probability, and all such reference beyond the moment as characterises ethical and moral judgments. But the point should be emphasised that, while these experiences are conditioned by æsthetic and quasi-æsthetic detachment or *isola-*

tion, they continue to have effect beyond these momentary realisations. The æsthetic and religious assumptions generate expectations which function as ideal norms in the ethical judgments of obligation and imputation. The question at this point, it will be observed, is not whether the subject of these experiences has or has not the capacity for actual worth feeling of this character, or whether, indeed, individuals in actual life have the capacity for displaying such ideal dispositions, but merely whether psychologically the assumption generated in the æsthetic experience modifies actual belief and judgment.

It now remains to study the points at which these psychological absolutes are found, and to show the psychological conditions in which they are realised. They are what may be called *Tragical* or *Heroic Elevation*, and *Inner Peace and Harmony*. The first appears as the limiting case of transgredient worth, the latter as the limit of immanental worth. Tragical elevation may appear at two points : either where for an attitude which the person has completely identified with the self, and which is therefore a personal worth, all condition worths—including life, which is the presupposition of condition worths—are sacrificed ; or, secondly, where the individual sets himself in complete opposition to external worth judgments of society and goes to destruction for the worth which he identifies with himself. The point here made may be illustrated by saying that absolute personal worth has been realised even if the object for which the sacrifice has been made is, from the impersonal point of view of instrumental judgment, not considered worth the sacrifice. Psychologically viewed, the complete unity of the personality thus attained is a product of complete contrast or opposition in which the central quality of the personality is so emphasised that the minor elements are lost sight of, have become irrelevant, as have also the secondary judgments as to the effects of the act. The leader who champions to the death a lost cause is the object of absolute imputed worth, irrespective of the effect of the sacrifice—even if the cause was evil and should have been lost. In a similar manner the imperfections and weaknesses of the man are ignored or felt to be wiped out by the final act. It is the " end feeling " that gives the tone to the whole life. As long as the sacrifice and opposition is not complete, our judgments upon the man as a personality are complicated by secondary judgments as to the existence of negative elements and their social effects.

But let the sacrifice or opposition become complete, and these secondary judgments lapse. The person is, in very truth, elevated above them; they become externalised and irrelevant.

In a similar fashion, and corresponding to the ideal of the "heroic," the ideal of the "beautiful soul," or inner harmony, represents an ideal construction of the personality in which all disturbing moments are eliminated, and in which there is the repose of satisfied conation. Here, again, we have what may be described as an absolute moment in valuation, but in this case the passing of the relative into absolute value arises, not from a complete identification of the disposition with the personality through *one* supreme moment of effort and sacrifice transcending all relative estimation, but rather from the complete identification which comes with repetition and habit.

The realisation of either of these moments is possible obviously only through the quasi-æsthetic isolation of the personality, the conditions of which have already been described. Whether realised as a feeling of absolute personal value in the sublime moments of obligation, or as a sense of perfection of another revealed in glimpses of absolute sacrifice or perfect harmony of character, such experiences rest upon assumptions which are made possible only by abstracting from the causal and instrumental point of view. Such assumptions or postulates, with regard to the possibility or actuality of absolute personal worths, may, accordingly, fail of justification from other points of view, which include more general theoretical considerations. But the importance of these moments from the point of view of the present discussion is to be found in the fact that they are practical absolutes,[1] so to speak, points where conation, and with it all relative valuation, comes to rest. Though realised only when the isolation of the individual is assumed in æsthetic experiences, they create expectations which determine the norms and standards of actual ethical judgments of personal worth,

---

[1] For a similar use of the term "absolute" compare Simmel's *Philosophie des Geldes*, p. 213, where he distinguishes between absolute and relative ends: "Absolut—in dem hier fraglichen, practischen Sinne—ist der Wert der Dinge an denen ein Willensprozess definitiv Halt macht." The use of the term "practical absolutes" to describe these moments of tragical elevation and inner peace should be emphasised. They are practical in the sense that the objects, the belief in the existence of which gives rise to a satisfaction of conation beyond which relative increase is impossible, exist *for* the processes of valuation, the practical activities of feeling and will for which they are ends, but not *necessarily* apart from these processes. They are moments in which individual processes of feeling and conation come to complete fruition, but from a more objective, impersonal point of view, this belief in absolute objects might appear illusory.

as the succeeding studies of these judgments will show We may, then, conclude this discussion by affirming that objects of personal worth may acquire absolute value, in so far as they are intrinsically valued as qualities of an individual, and that, moreover, the implicit assumption which underlies all judgments of personal worth is precisely this belief.

CHAPTER X

Personal Worths (*Continued*)

I. Interpretation of the Concrete Judgments of Personal Worth in Terms of the Preceding Theory of their Origin and Nature

1. *The Problem.*

It has been maintained that the feelings and objects of personal worth constitute a well-defined region of worth experience, and the studies of the preceding chapter have gone far to justify this view. The valuation of persons as persons constitutes a relatively independent type, one which presupposes a differentiation of object and attitude, and which is characterised by specific presuppositions and postulates. If this view is justified, we should expect to find these conclusions substantiated by a detailed analysis of the actual judgments in this sphere—the judgments of personal obligation, and of imputation of personal merit and demerit, already distinguished. We should expect these judgments to disclose certain empirical uniformities, both in the *qualitative* predicates employed and in the *quantitative* aspects of the judgment, i.e., in the way in which the degree of value varies with the amount of the object of value. Such uniformities a careful analysis of the phenomena discloses, and, when properly interpreted, they are seen to reflect the laws of valuation of personal worths already developed. To such analysis and interpretation we must now turn, seeking in the facts of judgment a proof or disproof of our theory. The problem of this chapter is, accordingly, the formulation and interpretation of the empirical laws of characterisation of persons and of estimation of personal worth.

The first condition of such a study is obviously the isolation of the phenomena in question, the judgments of personal worth, of personal obligation and merit or demerit, from other types of judgment. In order to interpret adequately these judgments it will be necessary to differentiate: (1) the objects of judgment, and (2) the terms and predicates in which the characterisation and estimation take place, from the objects and predicates in other types of worth judgment. It is further necessary to differentiate the norms or standards, the expectations or implicit assumptions with which the judging subject comes to the characterisation of the person, and to the estimation of personal worth, from similar norms in other types of estimation. If such differentiation of attitude, such isolation of phenomena is possible, we may hope to account for the worth judgments in question by tracing them back to the processes of sympathetic participation and ideal construction in which the objects, predicates, and presuppositions arose.

2. *The Objects of Personal Worth.*

The distinction between objects of "condition" and "personal" worth is implicit in our experience prior to any reflective distinction between egoism and altruism. It has already been shown that there is a well-defined sphere of *intrinsic* appreciation of dispositions and qualities of the person, quite apart from the estimation of the *utility* values of those dispositions or qualities, as instrumental to condition worths of the subject. The objects of personal worth are ideal objects which have acquired a common over-individual meaning through the processes of sympathetic Einfühlung and ideal construction; and therefore have acquired a further complementary value through reference to the individuated whole, the person. It is as a quality or expression of this whole that it has its meaning and value. We have already traced the processes in which the objects of personal worth are constructed and contrasted with condition worths, and need not repeat this here. It is sufficient to emphasise the fact that this contrast of objects of personal with objects of condition worth is present in all concrete worth judgments, and will presently appear in our study of the predicates employed in the characterisation of persons and in the quantitative estimation of personal worth.

The objects of personal worth judgments are, then, qualities or dispositions of the person; and value, in the form of merit or demerit, is imputed to the person on the basis of possession or non-possession of these qualities. But there is a further differentiation in concrete worth experience which must be taken into account in our isolation of personal worth judgments, one to which more detailed study must be given. These ideal objects, qualities, and dispositions may be judged from two distinct points of view, the personal and the *over*-personal or, in its extreme form, impersonal. As an object of *personal* value the quality or disposition is judged intrinsically, as part of the ideal whole, the person. In personal judgment, the judging subject abstracts from all reference of the disposition to social, over-individual ends, from the instrumental value which the disposition in question has for the ends of social participation. The personal judgment, as such, presupposes the isolation or detachment of the person from social references, and the characterisation of him, and estimation of his value, in the light of expectations generated in immediate sympathetic participation and ideal characterisation. In the over-personal attitude, on the other hand, the subject abstracts from just these personal references and meanings of the quality or disposition, and ultimately, by processes to be described later, reaches a relatively impartial or impersonal point of view in which his judgments are determined by the demands or expectations of a wider social consciousness.

This difference comes out strikingly in certain characteristic facts which will be immediately recognised. We may describe them in general terms as the shifting of the centre of interest or attention, the affirmation of one system of assumptions, and the negation or inhibition of another. In all those cases where the specifically personal attitude is uppermost, and where the intrinsic ethical or æsthetic predicates of respect and admiration are called out, our characterisation of persons almost constantly puts the qualities which we may describe as "lovable," the purely personal quasi-ethical qualities, before the more moral attributes with their larger social reference. So also the more æsthetic qualities, such as harmony or strength of character—often irrespective of the acts in which they are shown—may take precedence of the more moral, directly social virtues. Limiting cases appear where personal devotion and admiration, not to say worship, exists with almost total suppression of moral judgment. The fact seems to be that there are some personal qualities the reference of which to wider social values is the most remote and indirect, others which have a significance both for personal and social judgment, and still others, perhaps, almost wholly impersonal and social in their reference. The important point is that the demands or assumptions, in personal participation, differ in significant ways from those which represent the subject in his capacity of participant in the larger demands of society. Such isolation of the person is, nevertheless, always *relative;* it approaches to completeness only in the activities of æsthetic characterisation, where the conditions of detachment and isolation are most favourable, but it is present as a determinant in all concrete judgments of personal worth.

For this distinction between the personal and impersonal attitudes in judgment the terms *ethical* and *moral* have been used. This distinction corresponds fairly well with popular usage, the terms moral and immoral being employed with reference to those standards which are universal and impersonal—what Kant described as the region of *perfect* obligation; while ethical and unethical are employed to designate that larger and more indeterminate region of differentiated personal ideals, but of *imperfect* social demand. We shall presently see in detail how the personal and impersonal judgment of the same disposition differ both qualitatively and quantitatively as a result of this differentiation of attitude, but before considering this question we must make a preliminary study of the terms or predicates employed in judgments of personal worth.

3. *The Terms of Estimation of Personal Worth.*

The terms in which a person is characterised are, as we have already seen, ethical and æsthetic. The ethical predicates, good and bad, are imputed to a character on the ground of the possession or non-possession of qualities demanded of him as a person in personal relations. The æsthetic predicates, nobility, vulgarity, beauty, ugliness of character, represent complementary values arising from the harmonious or inharmonious relations of qualities within the personality.

An analysis of the ethical predicates good and bad, as used in the characterisation of persons, and in estimation of their personal worth, shows clearly the differentiation of object and attitude, the relative isolation of the personality already described. In the first place, when once the qualities and dispositions which are instrumental to, and the condition of, personal participation or intercourse have been differentiated and fixed by the selective processes of Einfühlung, and are intrinsically valued, their value is estimated wholly in terms of their depth and breadth in the personality, the degree of their identification with the person. The various virtues are all estimated in these terms. They extend all the way from those quasi-ethical qualities which are significant merely in the characterisation and appreciation of the individual, the lovable and admirable qualities, to the more fundamental virtues, such as courage, integrity, persistence, etc., having wider social instrumental value. In so far as the attitude is personal, characterisation of the person as *good* means simply supremacy of personal over condition worths, and as *bad* the supremacy of condition over personal values. The distinction between the two levels, and between forward and backward value movements, having once been made, the choice of ease and comfort, of bodily good of any sort, instead of such qualities as have a more personal reference, is always the object of negative judgment. With the exception of certain limiting cases to be considered later, this law is practically universal.

The terms of estimation of personal worth are, therefore, *intra-personal*. They reflect the relative isolation of the personality from social judgments, and abstraction from the instrumental social value of the quality. This comes out more clearly when we contrast the terms in which the personal worth of a quality is measured with those employed in the measurement of its social impersonal value. In order to measure the degree of personal worth, the extent to which the valued quality is identified with the personality, its depth and breadth in the person, it is necessary to have some means of comparison, and this is found in the contrast between personal and condition worths. All estimation of relative value involves two factors, a positive and a negative; the degree of value of an object is measured indirectly by the extent to which other objects are sacrificed for it. In the case of imputation of personal worth, the worth of a person is determined by his readiness to sacrifice condition to personal worth. The terms of estimation are, therefore, wholly intra-personal, within the ego, and reflect the division of the self involved in the ideal construction of the person.

This is, however, in striking contrast to the terms of estimation employed when the disposition or quality is measured from the more specifically moral point of view. Here the moral value of a disposition is measured in terms of sacrifice of the *individual* for the *over-individual*, of egoism for altruism.

In this attitude of judgment, both condition and personal worths are lumped together as individual, and set in opposition to over-individual social values. From this point of view, estimation of the value of a disposition abstracts entirely from the intrinsic value of the disposition as a quality of a person, and considers it wholly in the light of the disposition to participate in over-individual ends displayed by the quality in question, the degree of which disposition is measured by willingness to sacrifice both condition and personal worths. It is true that in the main personal worths may *on reflection* be seen, in the light both of their genesis and meaning, to retain a potential reference to social ends. It is also true that in general social values have complementary personal values which can be reflectively worked out. But this is not *absolutely* true, as will be shown in the sequel. Personal and social values are at some points indifferent in the sense that the concepts individual-ethical and socially valuable are only partially and occasionally identical. There are certain qualities and actions which come under the concept of the individual-ethical which from the standpoint of social morality are indifferent, as well as certain social demands which may be in abeyance in personal relations. The full extent and bearing of this fact will be discussed in another connection.[1] The point of importance here is that these remote relations, if they exist at all, are irrelevant for the specific judgment, in the specific situation.

An illustration will bring the situation into clearer relief, and emphasise still more strongly the relative isolation of the personality involved in imputation of personal worth. Any individual of more than ordinary character, displaying to an unusual degree the most fundamental personal worths of strength, daring, and persistence in the pursuit of his ends, forms his own standard, and to a certain extent finds it accepted by others. We may estimate the acts of some unscrupulous master of men, or, in fact, of an ordinary robber, low indeed when we view them in the light of our normal expectation of what his attitude should be toward social ends. But when, suppressing these judgments temporarily, we consider merely his courage and perseverance, his readiness to sacrifice condition worths for what are to him personal worths, our estimate is largely modified. For the time being, at least, these qualities dominate us, and we seem to get a glimpse into ultimate realities of will deeper than the superficial

[1] Chapter XIV.

distinctions of egoism and altruism. This employment of a double standard, as involuntary as it is disconcerting at times, is indicative of a real duality in our conception of the good which must be worked out completely before it can be overcome.

In this connection a final question appears. There are two ways in which the supremacy of personal worths, their identification with the personality, may be realised. The same relative supremacy might be attained, either by actual increase of the disposition which has personal worth, or, indirectly, by the decrease or weakening of the disposition which has merely condition worth. Is the imputed value the same in both cases? Experience has, I think, an entirely unequivocal answer to this question. In so far as our judgment is one of purely *personal* worth, increase of personal worth may be acquired only in the first way. The mere weakening of the condition worths decreases the personal worth in that, however idealised and spiritualised these personal qualities may become, they have their roots in those more elemental qualities of strength and spontaneity of instinct and will to which, as we have seen, a quasi-ethical, sub-personal, and sub-social obligation attaches. The weakening of these impulsions involves the weakening of the personal values with which they are set in contrast. If, on the other hand, our judgment is purely social and impersonal, the way in which the desired relation of personal to condition worths is attained is irrelevant, for we are concerned only with its extrinsic effects, i.e., with the instrumental value of the disposition in question for social ends. The point to be emphasised is that our specific judgments are always relative and partial. It is immaterial for practical purposes, for our " snap " social judgments, whether correct personal habits and qualities arise from mere weakness of passions or from strength of will. The effect is, in either case, the same. But for our judgment upon the person it makes all the difference in the world.

4. *The Difference in Relative Value of the Same Objects (Dispositions or Qualities) according as the Value is Personal or Over-personal.*

The difference in objects and in terms of estimation of the two spheres of personal and impersonal judgment has shown clearly the tendency to isolation of the person in judgments of personal worth. The difference becomes still more marked when the *quantitative* aspect of these judgments is considered. There are, as has been shown, some qualities or dispositions which have both a personal and impersonal reference, and toward which our attitude is mixed. Even here, however, it is not difficult to separate the personal from the impersonal attitude, for the reason that the *quantity* of the disposition displayed brings out strikingly different judgments, according as the attitude of judgment is personal or impersonal.

This is, first of all, evident in what may be described as the difference in *sensitiveness* of the personal and impersonal or social thresholds, the difference in the standard of personal and moral imputation. The same absolute amount of disposition displayed by an act may have a very different relative significance in the two cases. Such a disposition as truthfulness, which has both a personal and a social reference, affords a good illustration. A painful scruple or a slight divergence from strict truthfulness may have a value for personal participation, and, therefore, for personal imputation, while it is negligible for impersonal social participation. On the other hand, it is equally true that in the case of some dispositions the threshold of *moral* worth judgment may be passed without any variation in the personal worth judgment. This is most apparent in those cases where we recognise that the moral norm has something of the conventional in it, where its reference to important ends is, though real, somewhat remote and indirect. My friend may have slightly transgressed, and as representing the social attitude, I call him to account; but the very expression of my face and the tone of my voice shows that my personal attitude has not altered. This is also true in more important situations. Candour compels one to recognise that even variations from more fundamental norms, as, for instance, those which regulate the relations of the sexes, may, when they are the expression of a frank, generous, and spontaneous passion, leave the personal attitude *essentially* unchanged.

In the second place there are numerous *nuances* of personal appreciation which, while significant for personal participation and for personal judgments, do not call out strictly moral approval or disapproval. This fact we have already observed in its qualitative aspect. There are extensive regions of personal qualities which are only remotely significant from the abstract moral point of view; those qualities, for instance, which were described as "lovable." But this fact becomes

U

still more apparent when we view the situation from its quantitative side. In the case of those qualities which call out both the personal and impersonal reaction, there are wide variations in quantity of disposition which *fail to influence the moral judgment*. In imputing worth on the basis of a disposition displayed, if the imputation is personal, the *total* disposition out of which the action springs is taken into account, as an expression of the personality, and the degree of value imputed tends to vary directly with the amount of disposition displayed. In specifically moral judgment, on the other hand, we judge rather in the light of the minimum of disposition without which the act could not take place, i.e., its instrumental value for society. All else, excess of disposition beyond the constant of social expectation, whatever of uniquely individual emotion and sentiment is displayed by the act, tends to be irrelevant, and, if included in the judgment at all, receives an imputed value slight in proportion to the amount of disposition displayed.

A consideration of the preceding phenomena confirms the view that the judgment of personal worth is a relatively distinct type of judgment, involving distinct attitudes and presuppositions, and one which may be isolated from other types for more detailed study.[1] This well-defined difference in the significance of qualities or dispositions, in respect both to quality and quantity, according as the point of view from which they are judged is the personal or impersonal, indicates that what we have described as imputation of personal worth follows its own laws, as determined by its own distinctive presuppositions. If we can define these presuppositions we shall have the basis for the explanation of this type of judgment and its laws.

---

[1] Meinong, *Psychologisch-ethische Untersuchungen zur Werththeorie*, p. 295, has, to an extent, developed the same distinction without, however, recognising the full significance of the personal attitude in worth judgment. He describes the difference as one between emotional and intellectual imputation. In intellectual imputation the subject of the worth judgment is not the person in immediate personal relations with the object of the judgment, but the impersonal subject representing the total social consciousness. In emotional imputation the subject is an individual in immediate sympathetic relations with another person. In like manner in intellectual imputation the act, upon the basis of which value is imputed, is judged wholly in the light of its instrumental value for social ends. The emotional aspect of the act and the place in the total personality of the disposition which it presupposes, are irrelevant, while in emotional imputation these determine judgment, and the instrumental values tend to become irrelevant.

II. THE PRESUPPOSITIONS OF RELATIVE ESTIMATION OR MEASUREMENT OF PERSONAL WORTH

1. *The Thresholds and Norms of Personal Obligation and Imputation: their Origin in the Processes of Sympathetic Participation.*

The presuppositions which underlie judgments of personal worth are clearly different from those which determine the so-called moral and impersonal judgments. The preceding attempt to isolate the phenomena of personal imputation justifies this conclusion. The question now arises whether it is possible to define these presuppositions more explicitly, and thus to derive the concrete phenomena of personal imputation from them.

The presupposition of feelings and judgments of personal worth is, expressed in the most general terms, what we have described as the *ideal personality*.[1] More closely examined, this ideal was seen to consist in certain implicit assumptions as to the existence or non-existence of qualities or dispositions in the person, certain expectations generated in sympathetic participation and ideal construction. When these expectations are met, when the object is judged to exist, the feeling is one of satisfaction and the judgment is positive; when the object does not exist, the feeling is one of dissatisfaction and the judgment negative.

The demand for the existence of certain qualities or dispositions, their possession by the self or the alter, is the presupposition of the feelings of personal worth described. The qualities in question are the necessary condition of personal participation, and of those feelings of respect and admiration for the person as such. But, as we have also seen, these assumptions or expectations have a quantitative aspect, as determined by the laws of valuation applied to feelings of participation. The degree of feeling, and therefore the degree of worth imputed to the person, is, consequently, a function of the relation of the quantity of disposition displayed, of the supply, to the demand presupposed As in the sphere of condition worths, the intrinsic and instrumental values of economics, the degree of value of the object is a function of the

[1] Chap. IX, p. 262.

two factors, demand and supply; so also here the value imputed to the person is a function of the relation of existential judgments as to the amount of disposition displayed by the person to the implicit assumption or expectation presupposed.[1]

In our more general study of the Laws of Valuation,[2] it was pointed out that all judgments of value, on whatever level, presuppose certain norms and limits which define in conceptual terms the capacity of the demand or feeling-disposition presupposed. These we defined as the Thresholds of Value, and, while they were described in detail only in the case of " condition " worths, it was shown that the same conception might be applied to the higher levels of valuation. As in the case of economic worth judgment, in order to measure the relative value of different quantities of a good, it is necessary to define the demand quantitatively, that is, to determine the conceptual points within which the demand moves, its norms and its limits, and the law of increase and decrease of the demand with change in quantity of the good, so also here, in the sphere of personal worth, the same requirements must be met.

We have already applied these concepts in our preliminary demarcation of the region of quasi-ethical and ethical personal worths from the impersonal moral worths. These points of difference, expressed in the most general terms, consisted in the two facts: (1) that an act expressive of a certain quantity of disposition might call out a personal worth feeling in emotional imputation when it would not rise above the threshold of impersonal moral judgment; and (2) that increase of quantity of disposition, displayed in such act or acts, continues to call out personal reaction long after, from the impersonal moral point of view, the increment has become worthless or has passed over into negative worth. The limits of personal

---

[1] Doubt may naturally arise as to the applicability of the concepts of demand and supply in this connection in that, while the judgment of value seems to be determined by the demand or expectation presupposed, the ethical demand seems to be unaffected by the supply. This very general and uncriticised assumption is just the point at issue. The ethical demand, as an abstract norm and as theoretically formulated, does have the appearance of such independence. The ideal of personality as expressed in the demand to " be a person and respect others as persons" can be said to be thus unconditional for the very good reason that it is practically meaningless. It is only when the ideal becomes specific, when the demand is for a specific quality or disposition of the personality, that it becomes the basis of actual concrete judgments of value. But such demands in the individual are, as we have already seen in our study of the ideal construction of the personality, determined, both as to what specific qualities are demanded and as to the amounts expected, by the empirical conditions of personal participation.
[2] Chap. VI, p. 146.

worth are, therefore, much wider than in the case of moral or impersonal worth judgment; the lower threshold is lower, the upper threshold is higher. These facts indicate that the region of ethical and quasi-ethical personal worths, which presuppose relative isolation of the personality, is a wider region than the moral. We must now seek to determine the thresholds of personal worth feeling more definitely, since they constitute the critical points in all imputation of personal worth.

(a) *The Normal Threshold—The Norm of Characterisation.*

All imputation of personal worth, whether positive or negative, whether of merit or demerit, takes its start from, presupposes, what may be described as the *normal threshold*. The normal threshold represents that amount of disposition which corresponds to the normal expectation, the habit or implicit assumption, generated in personal intercourse, in sympathetic participation and its accompanying ideal constructions. As a result of repeated processes of "reading back and forth" of feeling and feeling-dispositions, the subject comes to expect, of himself and the "other" alike, acts expressive of a certain constancy of disposition. Expressed in the more definite terms of estimation of personal worth, he expects a certain degree of supremacy of personal over condition worths, he expects certain personal worths to have acquired a certain depth and breadth in the personality. Since this expectation constitutes the normal presupposition of the characterisation of persons which underlies personal intercourse, we may describe it as the *characterisation norm*.[1]

It is clear that this constant, this norm of characterisation, corresponds to habit, and that, when the amount of disposition displayed by a person merely fulfils the demands of the "correct," meets the implicit assumption with which we approach him, it does not call out any explicit judgment, positive or negative. To the person who displays a disposition corresponding to our normal expectation we impute neither merit nor

[1] The significance of this concept becomes clearer if we contrast it with another conception of which we shall make use later, namely, the *participation-norm*. When we come to the study of the impersonal, specifically moral, judgment upon acts (as distinguished from the ethical and quasi-ethical personal), we shall find that there also a certain normal expectation can be clearly distinguished and defined. But it is different from the normal expectation in judgments of personal worth, and is determined by different laws. It represents that amount of a socially desirable disposition which is normally expected of an individual, and is determined by its instrumental value for social ends.

demerit. It is only when the disposition in question varies appreciably in the way either of excess or defect, that any explicit reaction and judgment takes place. But from this point on there is imputation of degrees of merit or demerit proportional to the amount of variation of the disposition above or below the normal. We must now seek to determine the limits within which this variation moves.

(b) *The Upper and Lower Limits of Personal Worth—The Characterisation-Minimum.*

In the case of any given quality or disposition which has become inseparable from the ideal of the *person*, indispensable for personal relations and the values of characterisation, there grows up, as we have seen, a normal expectation or norm of characterisation. From this norm there may be considerable variation. With excess of disposition there is imputation of positive worth or merit; with defect, imputation of negative worth or demerit. But the character of this series of judgments is determined by certain limiting presuppositions or assumptions, beyond which the attitude and type of judgment undergoes a change. These limits or thresholds depend upon what we may describe as the *characterisation-minimum*.

By this minimum of characterisation is meant the smallest amount of a disposition or quality necessary for personal sympathy and personal relations, and for the feelings of respect and admiration which are characteristic of personal attitudes. This term, constructed on the analogy of the *existence-minimum* in the sphere of condition worths, denotes a conceptual point marking the division between condition worths and acquired personal worth. The minimum of existence marks the limit of relative condition worth where it passes over into absolute worth, and is the term used to describe the smallest quantity of an object necessary for existence, and for which no substitute can be found. The minimum of characterisation is the smallest quantity of the disposition of a person necessary for personal participation, and therefore for valuation as a person, and without capacity of substitution. When the amount of the disposition sinks below this limit, the person becomes worthless from the personal point of view, and this minimum constitutes the *lower* threshold of personal imputation. But, on the other hand, since it represents the minimum of an indispensable personal good, it may acquire *absolute* worth, and complete sacrifice of condition worths for this indispensable minimum may call out imputation of absolute value. This point represents the *upper* limit of relative estimation of personal worth. The minimum of characterisation appears, therefore, in two concrete situations. In the first place, as the amount of the disposition falls below the normal expectation, the imputation of demerit becomes more and more emphatic, until a point is reached where the worth judgment experiences a qualitative transformation. The personal attitude passes over into impersonal judgment or into mere altruism, which, as we have seen, is a feeling arising upon the recognition of the condition worths or *un*-worths, the pleasures or pains, of the person judged. The minimum necessary for personal participation has been reached. Such a situation we sometimes describe by such phrases, as an act or person is "beneath criticism" or "perfectly worthless." In the second place, such a minimum appears as a functional moment in another concrete situation. When an individual, for the sake of a minimum of personal worth (say honour), sacrifices all his condition worths, even life itself, our judgment passes over from the negative to the positive side, and indeed from relative into absolute valuation; the moment of the heroic or tragical elevation is reached. This situation is entirely in harmony with what we have found to be the character of personal worths. In thus completely identifying himself with the minimum of personal worth necessary for his own and others' ideal construction of his self, through sacrifice of condition worths, the subject has displayed another personal worth, courage or devotion, on the basis of the recognition of which positive worth is imputed. There has been what may be described as a certain substitution of personal worths.

2. *The Substitution of one Personal Worth for Another—Its Limits.*

This leads us to a consideration of the entire question of substitution of personal worths. The minimum of characterisation exists only in the case of qualities or dispositions for which there are no substitutes. We have also seen that such a minimum of characterisation is presupposed, or is present as an implicit assumption, in all imputation of personal worth. Are all personal worths without this capacity of substitution? To answer this question properly, we must make a distinction between dispositions which are without substitutes in *particular situations* of personal participation and dispositions which are without capacity of substitution *absolutely*. In economic thinking, the crust of bread is the minimum of existence only under certain conditions of time and place which make substitution impossible. So also in personal or ethical imputation—a given minimum of a disposition may be without substitute in certain relations of sympathetic participation, and therefore in the valuation of the self or the alter. Thus if we take the more superficial personal worths, beauty, fame, intellectual power, tact, we find that, while the more intimate personal relations are impossible without them—and those who do not exhibit the necessary minimum are judged impersonally rather than personally, nevertheless, they are really goods with the capacity of substitution, for a display of the deeper personal worths, such as honour, devotion, courage, strength, etc., may restore the relation of personal imputation.

Even more fundamental values than these, such as chastity and honour, usually without capacity of substitution, may, under exceptional circumstances, be sacrificed for still more ultimate personal worths, still more primitive qualities. Thus we find that, while the personal worth of chastity is, in women, normally without capacity of substitution, that of honour normally without substitute in men, at the same time there are cases where the loss of both may be compensated for by the display of still more ultimate personal worths. To the woman who sacrifices her chastity for her starving child, or for the love of a man, or for love of country, if the love be great enough, and the lost chastity a real sacrifice, we impute a personal worth which may reach the absolute moment. The same is true of the sacrifice of honour for love. What has taken place here is that a still more ultimate personal worth has been substituted for a lower. And the failure thus to sacrifice, as in the *Statue and the Bust*, calls out negative worth judgments. It would appear, then, that the only qualities which are absolutely without substitutes are the most fundamental personal worths, strength and harmony of character. In so far as there is isolation of the personality, our sense of personal worths is emphatic on these points.

Nevertheless, it must be recognised that the situations here described are limiting cases. The isolation of personality, with the consequent detachment from social demand, is, for most of us, perhaps fortunately for society, confined to the purely æsthetic moments. In most of our judgments upon actual personalities, these personal judgments are so complicated with social moral judgments that the laws of personal imputation do not stand out clearly. The isolation of personality which is presupposed in all personal judgments is only imperfectly realised. But the fact that it can be realised æsthetically, and that, when thus realised, the judgments of imputation follow the laws here described, is significant for the whole theory of value.

3. The Rôle of the Characterisation-Minimum in Personal Obligation.

To this study of the significance of the minimum of characterisation in imputation of personal worth to the alter, should be added a word as to its reflex meaning for the self, in his feelings of personal worth as reflected in the sense of personal obligation. Here, too, the minimum of characterisation is presupposed in all sense of relative obligation—not as the limit of personal participation, but of ideal characterisation of the self.

Two illustrations will be sufficient to show how it functions. We are told most enlightening accounts of transformations in the sense of personal obligation, which take place in the case of those who by circumstances are compelled to live for long periods in uncivilised regions, apart from personal participation in the life of those among whom their sense of obligation has been acquired. Personal worths are socially derived, and frequently we find them dropping off for lack of continuation of the processes of sympathetic participation in which they were acquired. We find a regressive substitution of more elemental for more developed attitudes. Among others, cleanliness and manners are often lost. But we are also told of pathetic cases where, for the sake of cleanliness, or other habits which distinguish a gentleman, most important condition worths will be sacrificed, and in extreme cases cleanliness may become an indispensable minimum, for which life itself is risked, if not actually sacrificed. The situation obviously is this. Through contrast this personal worth, normally, perhaps not absolutely without substitutes, is, nevertheless, now so completely identified with the personality, that it becomes a symbol of all other personal worths, and for it even life is sacrificed. Here the most emphatic obligation is found at the minimum of characterisation.[1]

There seems to be no question of the existence of some personal worths—in the region of personal obligation as well as of imputation, for which there are no substitutes. They constitute the irreducible minimum of certain dispositions necessary for personal participation in the experience of the alter and of personal attitude toward him, as well as the irreducible minimum necessary to that ideal characterisation of the self which is the condition of the continuation of valuation on the higher level of personal worths. As such they have absolute value. It does not follow, however, that these same dispositions, in their aspect of instrumental value for social over-individual ends, are equally without capacity for substitution. The over-individual, instrumental value of dispositions is determined by other laws.

III. Analysis of the Laws Governing Feelings of Personal Worth as Illustrated in Imputation of Merit and Demerit and in Personal Obligation

1. *Imputation of Personal Worth to the Alter.*

With these norms and limits as conceptual instruments of analysis, we may now turn to a quantitative study of feelings of personal worth as expressed in the judgments of imputation and obligation. The worth of the disposition is measured directly by the changes in the emphasis of the judgments of imputation, indirectly by the strength of the feeling of obligation as expressed in the judgment " I ought." The imputed worth expresses the degree to which the expectations generated in sympathetic projection are satisfied; negative worth judgments reflect the degree of variance from the expectation. Similarly,

[1] In Conrad's novel, *Lord Jim*, Lord Jim, the chief character of the book—having, by processes of imaginative construction, identified most completely his personal worth with the attitude of bravery, and failing, through weakness of the flesh, to perform a brave act which he demands of himself, i.e., the rescue of shipwrecked people—feels his sense of personal worth completely lost, and devotes his entire life to its recovery, a recovery which is finally realised only in the tragical elevation of self-sacrifice. One of the interesting features of this study is that this sense of personal obligation is represented as persisting independently of any social demand, in a savage environment where his past is wholly unknown. Here we have the significance of the characterisation-minimum at its clearest, an illusion perhaps from the point of view of social obligation and imputation, but for our empirical study of the worth consciousness a very significant illusion.

the degree of obligation measures the extent to which the ideal object, the disposition, has been identified with the personality, and therefore has worth. In tracing out the modifications in these feelings, and their corresponding judgments—between the limits of the normal threshold, at which the imputed value is null, and the characterisation minimum where the imputed value is absolute, we shall have the means of determining the validity of our analysis of the origin and nature of personal worths.

We may begin this discussion by taking as our object of study feelings or dispositions irrelevant for moral judgment, that is, for impersonal participation, but decidedly significant for personal participation; thence proceeding to the consideration of dispositions significant for both personal and impersonal participation, but which, after a certain minimum of the disposition is reached, become irrelevant, if not superfluous, for the demands of impersonal participation.

As illustrative of the first we may take some *nuance* of conjugal or filial sentiment too fine to rise above the threshold of the moral sense, one which is essentially the product of sympathetic Einfühlung between two persons. Such are the finer and more spiritual faiths and loyalties which may be demanded as the basis or unspoken presupposition of intimate personal relations, but which can scarcely be demanded in the more impersonal but still moral relations which are the concern of the impartial spectator. The somewhat romantic demand for absolute trust, for the faith which believeth all things despite appearances, is the necessary condition of the higher forms of love and friendship, of conjugal and filial relations, but lies beyond the sphere of the strictly moral. A certain minimum of the crasser conjugal and filial attitudes our moral sense does indeed demand, but with others, it is strictly speaking, not concerned. The individual not concerned with them is aware of them indeed only through æsthetic presentation. When once such an attitude of trust or loyalty has been identified with a personality and a certain expectation formed, personal worth feeling may run through a whole gamut of positive and negative changes without the threshold of impersonal moral judgment having once been crossed, just as there may be considerable modifications in our moral judgment, as, for instance, judgments of disapproval upon disposition and act which are not significant for the law.

Given such a disposition as a personal worth, the judgments of imputed value, between the two critical points of expectation, the norm and the minimum of characterisation, arrange themselves as follows. Decrease in disposition below the normal expectation is followed by corresponding increase in the demerit imputed, until the minimum of characterisation is reached, a point which, of course, varies with individuals and circumstances. But when this point has been passed, the indispensable minimum of personal participation having been reached, the distinctly personal relation has been severed, and either mere condition worths become significant or an impersonal moral attitude appears.

The phenomena at this point are very interesting. When the minimum of characterisation has been reached, one of two fundamental changes in attitude on the part of the subject of judgment takes place. Either he may substitute an attitude of pity on the basis of his appreciation of the "condition" worths or *un*-worths of the alter, or he may substitute the intellectual, impersonal attitude of moral judgment for the personal, and emotional. We have already, in our discussion of the minimum of characterisation, considered the former possibility. It is a value movement of the backward type in which organic sympathy takes the place of the intuitive projection upon which personal worths are founded, or in which the conceptual construct of the pleasure or pain of the other is made the end of altruistic acts, instrumental to increase of pleasure or decrease of pain. The other possibility is the substitution of the impersonal attitude, in which the isolation of the personality ceases and the impartial moral judgment takes its place. In connection with the personal worths considered, conjugal and filial attitudes, both types of substitution are in evidence. Love passes over into pity or into scrupulous justice. When the minimum of personal participation has been reached, valuation does not cease, but object and attitude change. It is significant that the minimum may be passed and the personal relation severed when, from the standpoint of the impartial spectator, the distinctively moral predicate "bad" cannot be applied. Similarly, as we shall see later, the personal worth relation may be maintained long after, from the moral point of view, the person is the object of judgments of disapproval. There is a sense in which feelings of personal worth are beyond the moral region of good and bad, above and below.

If we turn now to those dispositions which are **significant** for both personal and impersonal imputation, but which in certain *quantitative* aspects are no longer relevant for moral judgment, we find the same laws, with slight modifications, at work. The sense of honour, as a disposition calling out both personal and moral judgment, is a good illustration, for it is the class name for a group of dispositions significant from different standpoints of judgment, varying all the way from the purely personal, through social groups of varying extension, to the impersonal impartial standpoint. It needs no discussion to point out that the expectation in these different cases varies greatly. As in the similar case discussed above, an individual may lose all personal honour for his friend or social group long before he has done anything which will call out strictly moral judgment. It is also equally true that an excess of sacrifice for the ideal of honour may, from the personal standpoint, call out an absolute personal value, while from the social moral point of view it is irrelevant or indeed quixotic, if not the object of distinct disapproval. In fact, the indispensable *minimum* which is demanded of an individual in a purely personal relation, or even in a limited group, may exceed the *normal* demand in impartial moral judgment. Thus we find that the sacrifice for honour is susceptible of indefinite increase, and that with this increase there is a corresponding increase of personal worth, *in so far as we have the condition of isolation of the personality fulfilled.* On the other hand, in so far as the social moral point of view, with its intellectual instrumental judgments, intervenes, excess of disposition beyond a certain point tends to call out negative worth judgments.

It will be worth while to consider one more disposition which may be judged both as a personal and social worth, namely, altruism, especially since it is at this point that the most interesting problems of the relation of personal to social values appear. By altruism is understood the disposition to sympathetic participation in the worth feeling of others. This disposition may obviously be valued both intrinsically as a personal worth and instrumentally with reference to its value for social ends. Now for certain reasons, which will be developed in the following chapter, the instrumental value of the altruistic disposition, the disposition to sacrifice condition and personal worths for over-individual values, is not susceptible of indefinite increase. We shall find that a certain *normal* display of altruism is demanded, but that increase in excess of that norm is governed by a law analogous to the law of Diminishing Utility in the sphere of economic goods. A point is finally reached where sacrifice is no longer approved, and may indeed call out negative judgments of disapproval. But it is significant that if the altruistic individual be isolated from social moral judgment, he may acquire personal worth indefinitely through such sacrifice of condition and personal worths. In so far as the disposition is valued intrinsically, as an attribute of the personality, it is not subject to this law, but with the increase of the disposition there is a corresponding increase of imputed worth. The limiting case is the tragical elevation which comes with the sacrifice of all condition and personal worths for over-individual good, the sacrifice of life itself. Such sacrifice, if its value were determined by impersonal intellectual judgment, would not be found to have the absolute value which we attribute to it intrinsically as a personal worth. And when we thus value it intrinsically, we do so, it should be observed, as expressive of the capacity of the individual to identify himself with the over-individual object, abstracting from the instrumental value of the act. As a personal worth, altruism may acquire absolute value, as a social worth it is not susceptible of indefinite valuation.

This difference in the standards of value applied to the same disposition, according as it is referred to the personality or to over-individual objects, will come out more clearly in the succeeding chapters, where the norms of over-individual values are developed, and the laws of preference between personal and over-individual worths are studied. Here it is sufficient merely to note that in this intrinsic valuation the question of the effect of increase of disposition is ignored as irrelevant. Secondary instrumental judgments are suppressed in the immediacy of the personal relation, or at most are represented by a vague assumption of indefinite reapplicability, or instrumental value, of the disposition in question. In the terminology of ethical discussion, the motive alone is considered, and not the effect. Whether this attitude, this assumption, does not involve an illusion is, of course, a question. The whole problem of worth illusions will present itself for consideration at the conclusion of the chapter.

2. Personal Obligation as Reflecting the Laws of Personal Worth.

The individual's feelings of the worth of his own qualities, as distinguished from his sense of the worth of the qualities of the alter, are more obscure than the latter. In general, however, it may be said that his sense of the importance of his personal qualities is reflected in his feelings of personal obligation. The degree of the feeling of obligation represents the extent to which the quality has been identified with the personality, and, therefore, the degree of its transgredient reference. The depth of the feeling of satisfaction and inner peace, when the obligation is met, reflects in a similar manner this acquired personal meaning.

The feeling of obligation, as analysed in a preceding chapter,[1] was found to have three forms, to show three shades of meaning which are appreciatively distinguishable. Condition worths may acquire an instinctive sub-personal and sub-social obligation, through arrest of conative tendency, as illustrated in the obligations which appear as the objects of condition worth approach the existence minimum.[2] Psychical objects, qualities or dispositions of the personality which emerge in the processes of sympathetic participation and ideal construction, arouse feelings of obligation which may be personal or social and over-individual, according as the object is referred to the self, as intrinsic quality of the person, or to some over-individual social demand. The feeling of obligation toward these psychical objects may be personal or over-individual, according as the demand is felt as personal or social. There are some attitudes or dispositions to which merely personal obligation attaches, while there are others which have both personal and over-individual or social obligation. It is with the feeling of personal obligation that we are now concerned.

These purely personal obligations are not difficult to distinguish either from the sub-personal, instinctive, or from the impersonal moral. If, as was indicated in a previous chapter, it may be said that strength, sex, etc., have certain obligations which are not the reflex of ideal projections, either personal or social, it is also true that there are some qualities of the personality which have obligations which are irrelevant for social participation, more specifically for social demand. Their ful-

---

[1] Chap. VII, pp. 209-11. [2] Chap. VII, pp. 213-16.

filment is not significant for social demand; they do not rise above the threshold of impersonal moral judgment. Nor does failure to meet these obligations call forth any self-condemnation in so far as our attitude is impersonal and moral. The distinction sometimes made between perfect and imperfect obligation describes the situation. Perfect obligation applies to those fundamental dispositions demanded as a condition of social participation, demanded universally, and in a certain amount which constitutes the minimum for participation. Those more individual and personal obligations, on the other hand, which attach to dispositions not demanded generally, and to dispositions in excess of the minimum demanded, are described as imperfect.

The phrase "Noblesse oblige" includes many of these personal, and from the impersonal point of view imperfect, obligations. Thus, to take the obligations of nobility in its original class sense, such obligations, as the result of intimate sympathetic participation, will be more intimately personal than the more extensive social obligation. Deeper still are the more personal obligations of the thinker to truth, of the artist to beauty, and of the saint to holiness. They frequently transcend completely any cognisable social reference; and the obligation remains, even when the attitude, the disposition to which it is attached is, either by reason of its uniqueness or its excess, not only irrelevant, but even inimical to wider social participation.

The chief characteristic of personal obligation is, then, that its objects do not necessarily correspond to the objects of impersonal social obligation. Much more noticeable is this discrepancy when we consider personal obligation in its quantitative aspect. The intensest personal obligation is always about the minimum of characterisation, but this minimum may represent an amount of the disposition in question far in excess of the normal or correct as demanded by social judgment. And, whereas the impersonal obligation falls off in intensity as the amount of disposition demanded by a given act exceeds the normal, the personal obligation still remains.

This divergence arises from differences in the processes of sympathetic participation in which these two worth attitudes have their origin, and thus in differences in the demands felt as obligations. In the case of all those attitudes or dispositions which have *both* over-individual and personal obligation, there is a certain normal disposition which we may describe as the "correct," how determined we need not in the present connection consider, about which the intensest over-individual obligation is found. Any variation from the correct, in the way of lack, is felt as obligation to make good the deficiency, and this feeling of obligation finds its expression in the obligation to sacrifice personal and condition worths. But when the sacrifice reaches a certain point normally demanded, or when the over-individual good to be attained by the sacrifice is so minute as not to be significant for social participation, the over-individual demand or impersonal obligation lapses. Not so, however, if the attitude or disposition is identified with the personality, as a personal worth. The personal demand or obligation continues beyond this point, and if the disposition is a personal worth for which there is no substitute, it may reach the absolute point at the minimum of characterisation. The illustration of cleanliness, already considered in connection with the discussion of this minimum, is a case in point. To this, as an ideal object of desire, attaches both social and personal worth; it is the object of both over-individual and personal demand. The intensest over-individual obligation is found at the minimum demanded for social participation, and the sacrifice demanded will be greatest at this point. But when the sacrifice exceeds the maximum demanded, over-individual obligation begins to fall off. It does not follow, however, that personal obligation has ceased. On the contrary, when, as in the case cited,[1] cleanliness has been identified with the personality as a good for which there is no substitute, it constitutes an indispensable minimum, and the demand for sacrifice may be absolute. It is noteworthy that quantitatively this minimum for characterisation may exceed that which constitutes the minimum for participation. In the case before us the degree of cleanliness which constituted the characterisation-minimum was far in excess of the social demand. The obligations to honour and altruism are of the same general character. Personal obligation to an ideal of honour may continue long after all feeling of impersonal over-individual obligation has lapsed; and in this particular case, the personal obligation may be in contradiction to the social, as when the obligation to avenge one's honour conflicts with the moral obligation to abstain from personal vengeance.

In the case of altruism we have the most striking illustration of the relation under discussion. A certain degree of altruism

---

[1] See above, pp. 297 ff.

constitutes the maximum of social demand, the maximum required for social participation. Beyond that point impersonal obligation falls off, but not necessarily personal obligation. The intensest personal obligation is felt at the characterisation-minimum, and the amount of the disposition which constitutes this minimum for a given individual may be far in excess of the maximum of social demand. The characterisation minimum constitutes the indispensable minimum for the ideal construction of the self, and a disposition which ceases to have value for over-individual ends may acquire intrinsic complementary value through reference to the total personality.

3. *The Rôle of Æsthetic Complementary Value in Judgments of Personal Worth.*

The preceding paragraphs seem to indicate that objects of personal worth, as measured by the feelings of merit and obligation, may acquire absolute value. Through the processes of sympathetic participation and isolation of the personality, dispositions may be so identified with the personality as to be without capacity of substitution, and to demand indefinite sacrifice of condition worths. With the increase of this demand for sacrifice, there is a corresponding increase of the individual's sense of worth, increase of the transgredient reference of the feeling; and with increase of the disposition to sacrifice, there is a corresponding increase of the merit imputed to the personality. This law appears to hold, however, only when the individual is isolated, and when judgments as to the participation or instrumental value of the dispositions in question for social good are suppressed. The limiting case, both of personal imputation and personal obligation, is reached in the feeling of tragical elevation which comes with complete identification of the attitude with the personality through complete sacrifice of other worths, even of life itself.

But an analysis of actual worth judgments seems to indicate that personal worths are thus "steigerungsfähig," susceptible of indefinite valuation, and may even acquire absolute worth, when the identification with the personality is not measured in terms of sacrifice, i.e., is without the elements of opposition and contrast. If the personality may be isolated and tragically elevated by the extreme of sacrifice, it seems equally possible for it to be æsthetically isolated by the display of an inner unity and harmony of character which shows no traces of effort and struggle. For it is, in the first place, a fact long observed that many of the finer attitudes of personal worth are of such a character that they lose their unique quality when their display involves sacrifice and effort. Love, devotion, gratitude, honour, are feelings which cannot be forced without losing something of worth. We care neither to *demand* them of others nor *to have others demand* them of us. The moment of spontaneity and harmonious expression which constitutes what has been called the " beautiful soul " seems to be a fundamental factor in determining personal worth.

Now, while there can be no doubt that worth is imputed to this element in personality, and that the degree of worth increases with the increase of the disposition above the normal, it would be a mistake to interpret such imputed worth as merit. The condition of the imputation of merit is the sacrifice of condition to personal worths, the contrast and opposition which arises from the ideal construction of personal worths. In the case before us, however, it is precisely because this distinction has lapsed, and the objects of personal worth are desired with the same spontaneity as the objects of condition worth, that the new quality enters into our feeling of the worth of the personality. It has been held that these values presuppose the consciousness of effort and sacrifice in the same way that the feeling of the worth of a work of art, a picture, or a piece of music, may include in it a realisation of the effort involved in mastering the difficulties of execution.[1] That such an element does enter into many æsthetic valuations of personality is beyond doubt, but it has then ceased to be, as in the case of imputation of merit, a *measure* of value. The situation is rather this. The feeling in question is of the æsthetic immanental worth which comes from the assumption that the disposition desired is fully realised in the personality. This is the positive source of the worth feeling. But such repose in the personality presupposes its isolation, and this isolation involves the extrusion of all negative moments; otherwise the assumption of such complete realisation cannot be maintained. The cognition of past efforts and sacrifices adds nothing to the intrinsic worth of the object, but merely *strengthens* the assumption and isolates the object. This, I am inclined to think, is the hidden emotional logic of the religious consciousness in its worship of

[1] Simmel, *Einleitung in die Moralwissenschaft*, Vol. I, p. 227.

such ideal persons as Buddha and Jesus, a factor in the ideal construction of which there is always the story of supreme temptations. The temptations add nothing to the intrinsic value, but they serve to isolate the person and to strengthen the assumption upon which the worth feeling rests.

It should be noted that the isolation of the personality, and these corresponding æsthetic valuations of persons in art and in life, are unique and fleeting moments in experience, for the reason that the assumptions upon which they rest can be sustained for but short periods and under special conditions. But, as has already been pointed out, there are some moments of worth experience the value of which does not lie in repetition, but which, when once experienced, create expectations which determine succeeding worth judgments.

Of equal importance for a comprehensive view of the values of characterisation is the more subjective correlate of these judgments of personal worth, namely, the individual's sense of inner peace, or absolute worth, which comes with the exclusion of all negative elements, and with them of effort and conflict. This is undoubtedly a real factor in experiences of personal worth, although, like the experiences of the preceding paragraph, it is of the unique and non-habitual type. Unlike the feeling of tragical elevation, which comes with the isolation of complete sacrifice, and which supervenes upon effort, these experiences, of which the mystical religious is the extreme expression, isolate the self by identifying it with a Supreme Being. The complete identification of the individual will with the will of God, in which the self is "lost in wonder, love, and praise," is the characteristic feature. The disposition which has personal worth is increased to the absolute point by identification of the individual with a being in which the absolute is assumed to be already realised. The essentially æsthetic character of this experience, as distinguished from the ethical character of the feelings of obligation, appears in the fact that that which, ethically, is always a goal, is, in the religious experience, assumed as already realised.

There can be no manner of doubt that such "practical" absolutes exist, and that they are believed to correspond to actual reality. There is also no doubt that this belief finds expression in our actual judgments. Whether repeated or not, they stand as representative, as the measure of the capacity of the individual for worth experience. As such they determine his obligations and judgments.

4. *The Question of the Validity of these Judgments of Personal Worth and of the Implicit Assumptions or Postulates upon which they rest.*

Our analysis of the actual judgments of personal worth has justified the main contentions of this chapter—that personal worth may be acquired indefinitely; that there are absolute personal worths; and that this assumption is presupposed as the postulate of all characterisation of persons and all estimation of personal worth. Psychologically, this belief, this implicit assumption, is explicable. The preceding chapter was devoted entirely to the study of the genesis of the assumptions presupposed in feelings of personal worth, and their effect in determining our actual judgments—both qualitatively and quantitatively. The recognition of this postulate as underlying all judgments of personal worth was the culminating point of the discussion.

But when we turn from the purely phenomenological aspect of the problem to the question of the validity of these judgments, and therefore of the assumptions which they presuppose, a somewhat different problem arises. May not these assumptions, these ideals be unfounded in fact, and, therefore, the judgments of personal worth be illusions? When absolute worth is imputed to a personality in the moments of tragical elevation and inner harmony, it is on the basis of the assumption of complete identification of the person with the ideal object. When the subject feels absolute obligation toward a personal worth, or the feeling of complete inner peace which comes with the satisfaction of that obligation, it is upon the assumption of the possibility of realising the object or the belief that the object is already realised. If these assumptions should be unfounded from the point of view of an external system of " matter of fact," would not the feelings in this case be feelings of the imagination, real enough as psychological phenomena, but unreal in the sense that their cognitive presuppositions are unfounded? These assumptions themselves have their origin psychologically in imaginative constructions which presuppose the æsthetic isolation of the personality. May not reflection upon the " causes of things " show this isolation to be unreal, and the assumptions created in such experiences without any foundation in fact? If such should turn out to be the case, we might very properly describe them as "pathetic fallacies," on the analogy of the use of the term in literature and art, where we read into inanimate objects of nature sentiments and ideas which are not there in reality. In this case our fallacy would be that we read into persons, and into the system of things in general, imaginative constructions which do not exist, and assume them to be *real* instead of the æsthetic illusions that they perhaps are.

This problem, it will be readily seen, involves the whole question of the "rationality" of these assumptions and beliefs, a question already discussed in a preliminary way in a preceding chapter, where the conditions of the solution of the problem were stated. The question as to what constitutes reality and as to what is illusion in our worth experience, now appears in a more concrete and pressing form. The attempt at a solution we shall reserve for the *axiological* discussions of the concluding chapter, where the general problem of the relation of judgments of value to judgments of fact and truth will be considered. Meanwhile, we must turn to the investigation of another class of values, the social and over-individual, and of their relations to the personal and individual. It is frequently the facts and laws of these more objective valuations which seem to throw doubt upon the assumptions of the personal sphere.

CHAPTER XI

I. Objects of Impersonal, Over-individual Value—Their Nature and Origin

1. *Definition.*

A THIRD class of objects of value, and with it a third type of valuation, was distinguished in our introductory chapter, a class of objects described as over-individual and a type of valuation characterised as impersonal. Objects of over-individual value are those, the value of which is founded on processes of desire and feeling which are *social* and *over-individual;* and their valuation by the individual is impersonal, in so far as his feelings and judgments presuppose participation in the impersonal over-individual desire and feeling. Through process of participation in the worth consciousness of others, the feelings and desires of the individual acquire a new meaning, an over-individual reference to ends beyond the self.

Two classes of over-individual objects were distinguished, the moral and the economic. That which they have in common is the fact that both are founded in a certain over-individual demand, a demand which may be variable in extent and intensity, but which is, nevertheless, always felt as more than personal. Their *difference* lies in the character of the objects. The economic object is primarily a physical object of condition worth which has, through processes of ideal reconstruction consequent upon the individual's participation in the worth judgments of others, acquired the over-individual reference that makes it an object of exchange value. The moral object is an act, or disposition represented by the act, which is no longer valued merely for the condition worths which result, or for its intrinsic worth for the personality, but for its participation value, its reference to this over-individual demand. An economic object is an object of condition worth with the acquired capacity of exchange; a moral object is a disposition of a person which has, in addition to its immediate subjective and personal meaning, the acquired capacity of being instrumental to certain over-individual ends, participation in which is socially desirable. Its value is, therefore, a social *participation value*. Both values are objective and social, objective *exchange* and objective *participation* value. It is evident that the similarities of these two types of value extend so far that in both cases the individual who passes such judgments of value, economic or moral, becomes, for the time being, an " impartial spectator," represents an attitude in valuation attained by abstraction from the individual and personal references and meanings of the object, and which therefore, to the extent that this detachment is realised, is impersonal.

In our discussion of the equivocations in judgments of value,[1] we found that it was possible to attribute to the same object positive and negative worth, according to differences in attitude or in the presuppositions of the feeling. Thus I may attribute objective value to objects, e.g., diamonds, although subjectively, as objects of condition worth, they are distasteful. To reach this objective impersonal attitude, a certain abstraction from subjective appreciations is necessary. Through participation in the worth processes of others, the object is removed from immediate appreciation and becomes mediately, as an exchange value, instrumental to more remote appreciations. A certain ideal reconstruction of the object, described in a previous chapter,[2] has taken place. I now conceive the value of the object to lie in its capacity of exchange, and this acquired meaning is founded on a series of judgments, which in constructing the over-individual demand, have at the same time abstracted from immediate appreciation.

An entirely similar situation exists in the case of the morally qualified judgment upon acts and dispositions, the psychical objects of moral judgment. Here also my impersonal, objective judgment upon an act may differ widely from my personal judgment. In the moral judgment that which determines the value of the act is not, as in the case of personal worth, its significance as indicative of a feeling-attitude or disposition intuitively realised by the subject, but its meaning as an instrument for furthering the over-individual ends of society. The moral participation value of a relation of the sexes " without benefit of clergy " is low for the reason that, not conforming

[1] Chap. II, pp. 22 f.   [2] Chap. VI, pp. 169 f.

to over-individual demand, it set limits to further participation in other ends. But the personal worths and worths of appreciation which grow up in this relation may possibly be of the highest order, perhaps even *because* of the social isolation and the contrast which comes with it. No one who has studied human experience closely, from an unbiased point of view, will feel disposed to deny the possibility of such a situation, or to deny that circumstances are conceivable in which the personal obligation to such relation might be very emphatic, and in which the disposition displayed, in so far as we ignore the impersonal point of view, might lead us, not only to condone, but actually to impute worth to, the personality involved. But from the standpoint of the distinctively moral or social judgment such emotional accompaniments are irrelevant.

2. *The Impersonal Standpoint in Moral Judgment—The Morally Qualified Act and the Morally Qualified Judgment.*

Economic and moral values are alike objective and social, and the judgment of the individual in such cases is impersonal. It is the impersonal moral judgment upon dispositions which concerns us here, since a detailed study of economic values is not within the province of this investigation. The origin and nature of economic values has been treated in a general way in the chapter on the Laws of Valuation.[1] With this present comparison of the two classes we may, therefore, turn directly to the study of the moral values of dispositions.

Returning, then, to the illustration already given of the distinction between ethical and quasi-ethical or personal judgments and moral or impersonal, it is quite evident in such a case —and this is merely an extreme instance of very frequent contradictions between personal or private, public or moral judgment—that while the object of the judgment, the *act*, is superficially the same in both cases, the meaning of the act is radically different in the two situations. The presuppositions of the act itself, as well as of the attitude of judgment upon the act, represent different acquired meanings. One meaning of the act is irrelevant from one point of view, the other equally so from another point of view. For the personal attitude and judgment, the act has meaning as a spontaneous expression of a personality, and is measured wholly in terms of sacrifice of lower

[1] Chap. IV, pp. 142 ff. and 167 ff.

condition worths. For the moral point of view, it has meaning as readiness or failure to participate in an over-individual demand, and is measured in terms of readiness to sacrifice individual and personal desires and demands.

This appears in both the morally qualified act and the morally qualified judgment. The morally qualified act is determined by the motive presupposed. An act is thus qualified when it expresses a disposition to impersonal participation, the response to an impersonal, over-individual demand. The act is moral precisely in the degree to which subjective and personal motives are abstracted from; and, whereas in personal imputation the degree of imputed personal value is measured in terms of sacrifice of condition to personal worths, in impersonal imputation—as we shall see later, in more detail—the *moral* value of the disposition is estimated in terms of sacrifice of egoism for altruism, egoism including from this point of view both condition and personal worths, and altruism being a term used to designate all dispositions to participate in over-individual ends. Similarly, the *morally* qualified judgment is the judgment determined exclusively by the consciousness of the over-individual demand, and presupposes abstraction from individual and personal demands. It is the judgment of the "impartial spectator," who abstracts from the subjective participation value of an act, and from its acquired complementary personal values, and reflects in his judgment merely the objective participation value of the disposition.[1]

3. *Relativity of the Distinction between the Personal and the Impersonal Attitude.*

But while the morally qualified act and judgment upon that act represent *ideally* the impersonal attitude upon the part of the actor and spectator alike, nevertheless, neither particular

[1] That the foregoing distinction between ethical and moral values—and the consequent definitions of the *morally qualified* act and judgment—will commend themselves immediately to the reader is perhaps too much to expect. The confusion underlying the identification of the two has been too prevalent, and of too long standing in ethical writings, to be easily cleared away. For this very reason, the limitation of the term moral in our way is perhaps to be deprecated: a term entirely unequivocal in meaning would have been preferable, if indeed such were to be found. But, on the other hand, there are in favour of this restricted usage two reasons which to the writer seem decisive. In the first place, it is but making more rigorous for accurate analysis a real distinction which, as we have already seen, is present in all valuation of acts, and is even recognised by the distinction between the personal and the moral. In the second place, it is justified by its fruitfulness in analysing and interpreting concrete moral judgments, as they are presented to us in the following chapter. The results of that analysis must decide whether the distinction is valid or not.

Objects of Impersonal Over-Individual Value 315

acts nor judgments upon these acts ever show the moral attitude in its purity. Actual situations are always more complex. In the sphere of concrete judgments the distinction between the personal and impersonal is only relative. In our study of personal worths, we have already seen that, while there were some aspects of the person, some dispositions, which are wholly irrelevant for impersonal, moral judgment, many of them have significance for both types of judgment, and become irrelevant for moral judgment *only in certain quantities*. Our moral judgment takes cognisance of them only when they reach a certain minimum, and ceases to find them relevant when they reach a certain maximum. Thus it was found that, in the valuation of the same object, at certain points the personal passes over into the impersonal and the impersonal into the personal attitude.[1] Again, the impersonal attitude itself, as the specifically moral, is merely the limiting case of a series of degrees between the purely personal and the impersonal. Between the complete isolation of the personality, which is the limiting case of personal imputation, and the complete abstraction from the personal moment, which is the ideal of moral judgment, there are those judgments in which the over-individual worth, which gives the disposition its participation value, is a group, class, or perhaps national worth. The ideal object " honour," already considered in our study of personal worths, is a case in point. Between the standard of honour which holds between friends and that which is abstractly " human," many specifications of the standard appear, as determined by class and racial consciousness. The objects of quasi-ethical, ethical, and moral worth judgment tend to overlap, and the subjects of these judgments are, therefore, but relative differentiations of attitude acquired through differences in the psychical processes presupposed. Moreover, the impersonal attitude of the " impartial spectator " is but an ideal limit at which the personal reference is still more or less present.

The difference between personal and impersonal judgment is further characterised by the distinction between *emotional* and *intellectual* imputation.[2] Here, again, the relativity of the distinction is apparent. Every worth judgment, as worth judgment, is the expression of some feeling. Accordingly, when the impersonal, moral judgment is said to be intellectual, the expression of practical *reason* as opposed to emotion, it is

[1] Chap. x, pp. 283 f., 300 f.   [2] Chap. x, p. 290 note.

meant merely that certain emotional aspects of the personal relation which are determinants in personal imputation have become irrelevant—not that the attitude itself has become purely cognitive and has ceased to be emotional. More specifically, the apprehension of the over-individual meaning of the individual's act and disposition, and the entrance of that cognitive act as a presupposition of the feeling of value of the object, inhibits those emotions which are significant merely for immediate and personal participation.

Two facts stand out clearly—first, that the objects of moral judgment are but a narrower, differentiated class within the larger group of ethical and quasi-ethical worths, and partially identical with them; and, secondly, that the impersonal moral attitude of the subject of the judgment is attained by abstraction from personal and emotional elements, whether as determinants of the act or of the judgment upon the act. From these facts we may draw certain important conclusions in regard to the origin and nature of the moral standpoint and object. In the first place, it is clear that the presuppositions of both types of judgment, the implicit assumptions and demands, of the personal and impersonal attitude alike, are acquired in processes of sympathetic participation, and that the objects are products of ideal constructions founded on these processes. As has been shown in our sketch of sympathetic participation, the feeling-attitude of the alter has first an immediate appreciative value for the subject, what we may in this connection describe as the *subjective* participation value of the attitude. Out of this, on the one hand, develops the characterisation of the person, and the independent, intrinsic valuation of the attitude as an expression of the person. This is the personal value of the disposition. On the other hand, from this "subjective" participation value, develops the *objective* participation value, the over-individual value reflected in the impersonal moral judgment, the instrumental value which the disposition has as contributory to social over-individual ends. But in the second place, it is equally apparent that the objective over-individual values, consciousness of which is presupposed in moral judgment, are determined by social demands in which the individual merely participates; they are the product of social interaction, or sympathetic participation in its social aspect.

Our task is now to define these objective social values more fully, to determine their origin, nature, and laws, and to show

Objects of Impersonal Over-Individual Value

how they are presupposed in moral judgment. The present chapter will be devoted to this study of objective participation value, while the following will attempt to show that the moral judgment, in its two aspects of obligation and imputation of praise and blame, reflects these values and their laws.

II. SUBJECTIVE AND OBJECTIVE PARTICIPATION VALUE OF DISPOSITIONS

1. *Their Relations.*

The over-individual " participation value " of a disposition or quality is, it has been said, a function of the relation of that object to social over-individual demand, and the *moral* judgment of the " impartial spectator " has as its presupposition a consciousness of this relation. With this statement of the situation, it becomes evident that the problem of the ensuing study is twofold. In the first place, we have to consider the nature and origin of this over-individual demand and of the ideal, over-individual objects of the demand; and, secondly, the manner in which the individual participates in this demand, and how the meaning acquired in this process determines his feelings and judgments of impersonal value—how the consciousness of over-individual ends and demands becomes a presupposition of his feelings. The problem is, accordingly, one involving both individual and social psychology.

By this statement it is meant that the over-individual demand, in which the objective participation value of a disposition is founded, must be studied in two aspects: as a social fact, the product of social interaction; and as a cognised presupposition of the individual's feelings and judgments. As an objective social fact, it is the product of social interaction, of sympathetic participation in its objective social aspect. But *as a product of social interaction* it is the resultant of modifications of the subjective feelings of value of individuals, as determined by these processes of sympathetic participation. There is, therefore, a definite relation between the subjective and objective participation values of dispositions. This relation we must now seek to determine.

2. Collective Desire and Feeling—Social Synergies Demand and Supply.

External to the individual, and often apart from any consciousness in him of their existence, there are certain collective or aggregate desires or demands which may be described as the social will, and which may be localised in larger or smaller social groups. These collective desires or trends owe their existence to the simple fact that, in consequence of uniformity in the organic and biological conditions of psychical life, men have similar instincts and desires, and, consequently, similar passions and emotions. It is possible that such desires and feelings may be shared without any accompanying consciousness of their "common meaning." A demand to which I am myself a contributing factor might conceivably exist, indeed often does exist, without my being conscious of its existence. As such, my desire is but a part of a collective or aggregate demand. But it is possible that I may also be conscious of the demand of which my desire is a part. Not only has the object of desire then acquired a common meaning, but I have become conscious of that common meaning, and in so far as this consciousness enters as presupposition of my feeling, my desire is itself modified, and with it my feelings and judgments of value.[1]

Collective desire and feeling, when it has acquired this "common meaning," when the object of desire and feeling is consciously held in common, we may describe as Social Synergy;[2] and the objective, over-individual values may be described as the resultants of social synergies. The introduction of this term has for its purpose the clearest possible distinction between social forces as conscious and as sub-conscious. It is with the former that we are here concerned, and our problem is to analyse these social processes of conscious inter-action by which the objective over-individual values are determined. These processes are

---

[1] Cf. in this connection Baldwin's study of aggregate, con-aggregate, and public meaning, *Thought and Things*, Vol. I, Chap. VII, sects. 5–10, and of their higher stage, syndoxic and synnomic meaning. Ibid., Vol. II, chap. III.

[2] The term *Synergy* is here used on the analogy of its use in Psychology (cf. the definition of the term in Baldwin's *Dictionary of Philosophy and Psychology*), where by motor synergy is understood the working together of motor tendencies to form a totality. The term *Co-operation*, while more in use, has this disadvantage, that it covers only a limited field of the phenomena with which we are concerned. Co-operation implies participation in the intellectual processes of devising means to ends, while many phases of participation are purely sympathetic and emotional.

Objects of Impersonal Over-Individual Value 319

the activities of sympathetic participation and ideal construction already studied from the point of view of abstract psychological analysis of the individual. Our task is now to study them as factors in the creation of those social synergies, those factors of " demand and supply " which determine the over-individual participation value of dispositions.

The two factors of social synergy, *demand and supply*, the demand for socially desirable acts, and the readiness of individuals to supply them, are, in so far as they presuppose this common meaning, the products of social thought and sympathy, that is, of the sympathetic participation of the individuals in common ends. Through sympathetic participation in collective desire and feeling, the individual becomes aware of the over-individual demand, and this awareness modifies his disposition to act or to expect actions from others. The social supply is similarly conditioned. It is the product of the acts of individuals contributing to the social end, and the dispositions of the individuals to participate and to contribute to the social supply is determined by consciousness of the demand acquired through sympathetic participation. This consciousness, although beginning with emotional contagion and simple appreciation of common organic function, passes through common judgment and belief, to common sentiments and ideals.

The objective participation value of a disposition is, then, a function of the two factors of social synergy, supply and demand; and these factors are determined by the consciousness of common meaning on the part of the individuals participating. In order, therefore, to determine the nature of these factors and their laws, it is clearly necessary to discover how this consciousness of common over-individual meaning modifies the individual's disposition to participate and to demand participation on the part of others. From these facts and laws of *subjective* participation value it may, then, be possible to deduce the laws of social synergy and of the objective participation value of dispositions.

In the chapter on the Laws of Valuation we found, it will be remembered, that economic method consists in the analysis of the laws of subjective value, on the assumption that the objective or exchange value can be developed from the laws of subjective value, a procedure which justifies itself. The situation here is analogous, for, as in the case of an economic good, its exchange value is a function of the laws of desire and feeling, of subjective worth in the individuals desiring the good, so the participation value of a given disposition is a function of the laws governing the tendency or disposition to participate of the individuals involved. Consequently, having studied the phenomena of sympathetic projection and the consequent modifications of feelings of value and dispositions in the individual, we may pass to the objective, social point of view.

III. THE LAWS OF SUBJECTIVE PARTICIPATION VALUE

1. *The Individual's Feelings of Participation Value as Determined by Social Sympathy—Extensive Sympathetic Projection.*

The individual becomes aware of collective desire and feeling through extensive sympathetic projection. In this process his feelings of value acquire an over-individual reference and meaning. Analysis of extensive projection, and its inducing conditions,[1] leads, moreover, to the following general conclusion: with the extension of the range of sympathetic participation, the feeling of participation becomes more and more impersonal, and the object of participation value becomes more and more abstract. Let us recall briefly the grounds for this conclusion.

In the first place, the feeling becomes *over-personal* in character. Its transgredient, over-individual reference is beyond the personality. Even on the level of simple organic sympathy, immediate participation in group emotion or passion "takes the individual out of himself." The forces of group suggestion inhibit the more individual and personal feelings and reactions, until finally the abstraction of the feeling from its purely individual presuppositions reaches such a point that it is no longer referred back to the self and identified with the self in an act of judgment. The presupposition of the feelings of value in such organic sympathy is the vague presumption of an over-individual trend or demand not definitely localised in a personality, either in the self or the alter. While still implying the self remotely, it is now free from explicit reference to private and personal meanings. In the second place, the conditions of extensive projection, the character of the inducing conditions, lead to a certain *selection* among the feeling-attitudes of the individual. Only the most fundamental and general attitudes are susceptible

[1] Chap. VIII, pp. 253 ff.

Objects of Impersonal Over-Individual Value

of extensive projection, and of acquiring this impersonal, over-individual reference. The condition of projection of an attitude of an individual into social groups is abstraction from the individual and personal presuppositions and references of the feeling.[1] From the consideration of these facts it is apparent that the over-individual demand, as immediate or merely *felt*, is already over-personal in character. The demand for a given attitude or disposition, though vaguely felt, is not localised in any person, either the self or the alter, and may thus ultimately become the presupposition of a relatively impersonal and impartial attitude.

With the emergence of this impersonal qualification of the transgredient reference of feeling, begins the ideal construction of over-individual ends to which the feeling is referred. As in the case of feelings of personal worth, the acquired meaning of the feeling is referred to the ideal construct of the personality, so here the acquired impersonal reference leads to conceptions of an over-individual will and of impersonal ends. But it is at this point that the chief difference between the two types of feelings and of their presuppositions appears. The ideal construction of the " person " is, as we have already seen, individuating and intuitive in character, while the over-individual objects are abstract and conceptual. Beginning with the initial contrast between condition and personal worths, and the idealisation of the person described, the detachment of the individual from social relations further advances until he is intrinsically valued as an end in himself. The disposition of the person in question is intrinsically valued as an expression of the person, and acquires complementary value through its relation to the person conceived as an individuated whole. In the case of the ideal construction based upon extensive sympathetic participation, the situation is otherwise. With the growing impersonality of the feeling, the ideal construct to which it is referred becomes more and more abstract. With every increase in the extension of the concept of the over-individual end to which the feeling refers, it is progressively more and more difficult to refer it back to the person as an intrinsic personal end, in other words, to visualise it concretely. Thus the individual is felt to be merely the *locus* or the bearer of these social over-individual ends or ideals, and his dispositions are conceived as merely instrumental or contributory to their realisation. The consequences of this are significant. As soon as immediate

[1] Chap. VIII, p. 257.

sympathetic participation develops into ideal construction and judgment, the feelings of value have as their presuppositions instrumental judgments, and the demand represents not intrinsic but instrumental values.

2. *Feelings of Participation Value as Modified (Quantitatively) by Extensive Projection—The Laws of Social Sympathy.*

The modification through extensive projection, of the presuppositions of the individual's feelings, and their consequent change in reference have now been shown. A certain relation between the extension of the common meaning, the impersonality of the individual's feeling, and the degree of abstractness of the object of the feeling has appeared. Is it possible to establish any relation between this extension of the common meaning and its intension, between the degree of expansion of sympathy and its intensity? If such a relation appears, it may afford the basis for the formulation of the laws of subjective participation value, and ultimately of objective social values.

The primary condition of the sense of over-individual value is, as we have seen, sympathetic participation in its aspect of extensive projection. Beginning with its simplest form, where the conditions are similarities of organic conditions, and developing through the stages of imaginative and ideal construction, the extension of the range of sympathetic projection involves abstraction from personal presuppositions and references, and therefore a qualitative modification in the direction of impersonal reference. This qualitative change is also accompanied by characteristic changes in the quantitative aspect of the feeling. In order to understand these changes we must make a careful analysis of the quantitative factors involved.

The factors here under consideration are, on the one hand, the degree of sympathy felt, or its *intensity*,[1] and, on the other hand, the *extension* of the range of the sympathetic feeling, through the inclusion of more and more individuals in the group in which the individual participates. What is the effect of extension of sympathy upon its intensity? And further—since the desire to participate in over-individual ends is a function of the intensity with which the over-individual demand is felt,

---

[1] The term intensity is here used in the general sense of *degree*, not "sensational intensity" (Cf. chap. III, pp. 73 f.).

how is this desire affected through the satisfaction of the demand by the acts and dispositions of others?

If we begin with that form of extensive sympathy described as participation in group desire or emotion, immediate participation in collective attitudes, we find that the effect of such participation upon the feelings of the individuals participating is clearly marked. We have already seen that in such cases of "contagious emotion," expansion of the feeling is possible only in the case of relatively primitive and undifferentiated emotional attitudes, and is limited to relatively short periods. Within relatively small groups, and for short periods, the emotion or passion may attain a high intensity *and* complete expansion, so that the group feels intensely and as one man. We may almost speak of a mob soul. As reflected in the individual thus participating, the effect is seen in an intensification of his feeling of over-individual reference. Within limits, the degree of sympathy, and with it the intensity of the over-individual demand, increases with the extension of the range of sympathy. This temporary increase in the feeling of value is manifested in increase of disposition to participate, to respond to the social demand, and in increase of demand for similar response on the part of others. But it is a well-known fact that such participation, based upon organic sympathy, is followed by phenomena analogous to the experiences of dulling of sensitivity and satiety, which we have seen to accompany all excess of organic sympathy. Extensive sympathy of this fortuitous kind, based upon external and often superficial similarities of attitude, and made possible only through the arrest of more individual and personal attitudes and habits, is followed by reaction. The temporary presumption of existence of objects and ends, corresponding to the group emotion or passion, fails to develop into judgment and judgmental habit, or implicit assumption.[1]

It is obvious that while the experiences of immediate participation in group emotions and passions may afford the basis of consciousness of over-individual ends and demands, this is, in the very nature of the case, limited to rare occasions and to relatively small groups. Any extension of social sympathy beyond these limits must rest upon imaginative and

[1] The well-known effect of emotional revivals in producing dulling of sensitivity and satiety is a case in point. In certain regions of the West the people have a significant word for these effects. They speak of the region visited by such mob emotions as "burnt out!"

conceptual constructions. Our ability to realise sympathetically over-individual trends and demands depends upon conditions of a more intellectual character. Imaginative projection, with its assumption of the existence of corresponding dispositions, depends upon similarity of attitude. How does extension of the range of sympathetic projection modify the conditions of such sympathetic participation, and, therefore, the degree of sympathy?

It has already been shown that the condition of imaginative projection is abstraction of the feeling from its purely individual reference, that it is only in this way that the " person project " acquires its common over-individual meaning. It has also been shown, however, that if the processes of abstraction from private and personal meanings continue, the reference of feeling becomes impersonal; the feeling-abstract is no longer referred back to the person, but is projected and localised beyond the person. Now the important point in this connection is that, owing to the nature of the inducing conditions of imaginative projection, we find with increase in the range of sympathy, decrease in similarity of inducing conditions, and, consequently, growing abstraction and impersonality of the feeling. It may be shown, I think, that, with this decrease in resemblance and consequent growth in abstractness and impersonality of the feeling, the feeling of sympathy, and with it the feeling of value of the attitude in question, will decrease in intensity.

Several significant facts indicate the truth of this inference. In the first place, as has already appeared, extensive projection exercises a selective influence among our feeling attitudes. Owing to the variations in individuals, the nature and conditions of which have already been considered, there is a weeding out of all feeling-attitudes which are unique and personal, these being retained for intimate and personal relations alone. Certain others will be stamped as class and group attitudes, and only the most fundamental attitudes will survive in more extended sympathetic projection. But a similar selection is made with reference to the quantitative aspect of feeling-attitudes. Even in the case of those attitudes which, so to speak, survive extensive as distinguished from intensive projection, there is a characteristic modification of the intensity of the projected feeling. Gradually the extremes of feeling, the unique and individual variations, are inhibited in favour of a certain normal intensity which in actual experience has been ound to meet with response. Accordingly, we may go a step further and say that, with increase in the range of sympathy there is not only decrease in similarity of inducing conditions, and consequently growth in abstractness and impersonality of the feeling, but also, as the result of these, decrease in intensity.[1] Immediate sympathetic participation, whether it be conditioned by similarity of organic conditions or by similarities of ideal presuppositions of the feelings, is thus limited by the psychological nature and conditions of sympathy. This fact evidently has a meaning both for individual and social psychology. It states both the law according to which the feeling of the demand to participate is modified in the individual's consciousness, and also the law of this demand in its more social aspect.

Viewing sympathetic participation in this objective, sociological way, we find the truth of this law manifest in illustratrations which are numerous and instructive. Among primitive men, social sympathy, and the concomitant sense of collective values, is intense and immediate. The limitations of the group, the relative homogeneity of their affective experience, and of its corresponding expressions, are conditions which favour rapid expansion of feeling and its dominance over the consciousness of the entire group. Within more highly organised societies, where the organisation consists in differentiation of smaller groups within the larger whole, we find the most intense emotional participation in connection with those affective attitudes which correspond to limited groups. And as a further consequence, we find the actual feelings of obligation and judgments of praise and blame more emphatic with reference to *group* attitudes. We need call attention only to those specialised obligations and virtues of the politician and the labourer within our own civilisation, and to the equally specialised obligations of military classes in societies of the aristocratic type.

[1] It is facts of this character which Giddings (*Inductive Sociology*, p. 217) has sought to gather together in his formulation of the so-called "Law of Sympathy." "Using the word sympathy," he says, "for all the feelings which are included in the consciousness of kind, the law of sympathy is, the degree of sympathy decreases as the generality of resemblance increases." Further, "it loses intensity as it expands to the more remote resemblances, and becomes intense as it contracts to the narrower degrees."

3. *The General Law of Subjective Participation Value—The Law of Limiting Value.*

The conclusion thus far reached is that, while, up to a point, with extension of sympathy its intensity increases, with *continued* extension the degree of sympathy decreases. With the growing impersonality of the reference the intensity is lowered. This general law finds its explanation, apparently, in the limits set to social sympathy by the nature of its psychological conditions. Immediate sympathy, with its intuitive projection of the feeling attitude, becomes more and more impossible with extension of the social group. Our feelings and judgments of value, in so far as they presuppose this immediate sympathetic participation, with its underlying assumptions, manifest the working of this law. Nevertheless, all our feelings and judgments of participation value are not *necessarily* conditioned by this *immediate* intuitive sympathy. On the basis of immediate sympathetic participation, conceptual constructions of dispositions and over-individual ends, to which these dispositions are instrumentally referred, are built up, and when once these concepts are formed, the dispositions are valued instrumentally. What is the effect of increase of quantity of such dispositions upon the individual's feeling of their value?

The quantity of the supply of such dispositions may be increased or decreased either by the addition or subtraction of new individuals to the number of participants, or by increase or decrease in the amount of the given disposition in members of the social group. The question is: What is the effect of these quantitative factors upon the individual's feelings of value —and consequently upon the affective-volitional disposition to participate which these feelings presuppose? How does the increase of the quantity of the over-individual good affect the individual's desire to add to it by participation, and his feeling of value when others add to it by acts of participation? I think there can be no question that these feelings of participation value, and consequently the dispositions to participate, are subject to the general law of Limiting Value developed in the chapter on Laws of Valuation. In general, with each additional judgment of the extension of the area of participation, or of increase in the area of the common good through these increments, there is a relative falling off in the increment to the degree of worth, until finally a point is reached where

Objects of Impersonal Over-Individual Value 327

additions to the total good are without appreciable effect upon worth feeling.

There are several facts which indicate in a significant manner the existence of this law. In the first place, the individual's desire to participate—and ultimately, we shall see, his feeling of obligation to participate—reflects this situation. When once the demand for the over-individual object has been created, the individual's desire to add to the sum of social good seems to depend upon the degree to which the good is already realised. The greatest energy of participation appears normally where the lack of the social good is most apparent, and falls off as the disposition to participate becomes more and more general. Where voting is a general duty and opportunity, and where the act of voting constitutes a contribution to over-individual impersonal good, we feel both the desire and obligation to vote when the participation is least; and as it becomes more general our feeling of its worth and our desire to participate diminishes. In like manner, any contributions to social worths, such as acts of politeness, are felt as of most worth when in contrast to a more or less general lack of civility. They do not rise above the threshold of worth judgment when such participation is universal. On the other hand, up to the point at which these deficiencies are emphatically felt, and we identify ourselves with the rising minority demand, there is a tendency to fall in with those who abstain from the acts in question, for the reason that it is of no use to do otherwise. The actual *participation* value of our act is insignificant.

In general, then, the subjective participation value of a disposition, whether it be intrinsic or instrumental, whether it be immediate or mediate, seems to be subject to the law of Limiting Value. Of course such an abstract, general statement of the facts must be modified in important particulars, as we shall see in more detail presently, when to the impersonal participation value of the act personal and group worths are added as complementary values. When the object with over-individual reference has also a personal or class reference, acquired in immediate emotional participation, this law will be modified in the same manner as the law of Marginal Utility for objects of consumption is modified by the principle of complementary values. Just as the details of a feast or of dress, or an insignificant fraction of our total wealth, themselves without appreciable instrumental value, may acquire value as part of a unique and harmonious totality, so acts such as those described above, in themselves also without appreciable value for social participation, may acquire complementary value as a part or a sign of a harmonious personality, or as a mark of a coherent social class or group.

IV. THE OBJECTIVE PARTICIPATION VALUE OF DISPOSITIONS AS DEDUCED FROM THE LAWS OF SOCIAL SYMPATHY—THE LAWS OF SOCIAL SYNERGY

1. Objective Participation Value.

The preceding studies have had as their object the determination of the laws governing the changes in the individual's feelings of over-individual value, immediate and mediate or instrumental, as conditioned by the extension of the range of sympathetic participation. The question now arises whether from these facts it is possible to deduce the laws of objective, over-individual value, conceived as objective laws abstracted from the individual subjects of the feelings of value. We have maintained that the individual's feeling of value, in so far as it is impersonal, reflects the actual social value of the dispositions he thus impersonally judges. If this is true, the quantitative laws governing his feelings of over-individual value must correspond to similar laws of social value. Only on this condition would the norms and standards of impersonal judgment, presently to be considered, correspond to actual social values.

The objective participation value of a disposition is a function of two factors, the quantity of the demand and the quantity of the supply. Both of these factors are determined by the feelings and feeling-dispositions of the individuals participating in the collective will which creates the demand or supply. These feelings of the individuals are, however, as we have seen, modified in certain specific ways by extension of the range of the sympathetic feeling; and with this modification there is a corresponding change in the individual's desire or disposition to participate. From this it may be easily seen that there is a direct relation between the laws governing the individual's feelings and feeling-dispositions and the objective value of those dispositions as determined by the interaction of the individuals. More explicitly stated, the social demand and supply, and the objective values of which they are the determining factors, are in some sense the product of the individual's disposition, considered as modifying the demand or supply, as the case may be. As the intensity of the individual's feeling of over-individual value, expressed either in the degree to which he participates in the social demand or in acts supplying the desired dispositions, is determined by the degree to which the dispositions are universalised, so the intensity of the over-individual demand, when conceived as abstracted from the individuals participating, must be determined by the degree to which the disposition is universalised, i.e., by its quantity. Our problem is now to state the law of this dependence more definitely, and to formulate, on the basis of the principles governing this interaction, the law of the participation value of over-individual objects.

2. *The Law of Marginal Participation Value.*

A disposition or quality of an individual may, as we have seen, have a twofold value—the participation value which it has as the condition of wider social intercourse, i.e., as contributing to common over-individual ends, and the personal value which it has as expressive of a total personality. The latter is complementary to the participation value. From the point of view of the present study, we are interested in the individual's disposition merely as it affects the quantum of the social good. Participation through acts expressive of dispositions may then be conceived as additions to or subtractions from this good. The supply may be increased in two ways. Either there may be increase in the amount of the disposition of the individuals involved, as displayed in increase of the energy of participation, or there may be increase through the addition of individuals to the group. There may be increase in the intensity or extension of the supply. Corresponding to this objective social supply there is a social over-individual demand. What, then, is the effect of changes in the supply brought about by these two factors upon the quantity of the collective demand? This collective, over-individual demand is, like the supply, a variable quantity, and a quantity which is determined by the desire of the individuals concerned for acts with participation worth, that is, for expressions which may be the inducing grounds of sympathetic projection. This demand in the individuals may be satisfied by increase either in the intensity of sympathetic participation or in its extension. We must, then, consider the effect of each factor in the supply upon the demand of the individuals.

It is clear, in the first place, that, according to our law of sympathetic projection, the effect of expansion of the group as a factor in the increase of supply is to lower the intensity of emotional participation in the individuals, and, therefore, the intensity of the demand. The effect of increase of intensity of the supply is of the same nature, but, the situation being somewhat more complex, it requires closer analysis. Let us suppose that in some manner, how it does not matter— whether through imitation or more conscious choice—a disposition which has participation value increases in an individual or a number of individuals considerably beyond the average intensity. Will not such an increase in the supply bring with it, through suggestion and imitation, a corresponding increase in demand? In other words, cannot such a disposition increase in intensity and extension simultaneously?

At first sight it would appear so, but upon reflection doubts arise. For, according to our analysis of sympathetic projection, a variation from the average intensity of the disposition presupposes a variation from the normal in attitude, and the greater this variation from the normal, the smaller the group in which sympathetic participation is possible. Clearly, then, additions to the supply, through increase above the normal of the amount of disposition in individuals, involves new group segregations. The demand would be increased in individuals and groups, but such increase in intensity above the normal would be secured only by the limitation of the extensity of the demand.

From these facts it would appear that we are justified in inferring that the over-individual value of these objects is governed by a law analogous to the law of Marginal Utility in the sphere of economic values. Ehrenfels has formulated the same law, and developed it in a somewhat similar fashion.[1] He characterises it as the law of Grenz-frommen, to distinguish

---

[1] Ehrenfels, *System der Werttheorie*, Book II, chap. III, especially p. 86.

When we examine more closely the nature of these over-individual objects or goods, the participation value of which determines their morality, we see that all the conditions necessary for the application of such a law exist. For the application of the economic law of Marginal Utility to any object of condition worth it is necessary: (1) that the object be limited in amount; (2) that it have capacity of substitution; and (3) that the desire corresponding to the object have the tendency to highest possible activity. An examination of the processes of sympathetic projection which create

it from the law of Grenz-nutzen in the sphere of economic goods. But since we have defined social good, of which the moral sense is the reflection, wholly in functional terms of participation, we may preferably speak of the law of *Marginal Participation Value*. This law, it is further apparent, is but the resultant, in the sphere of objective social values, of the law of Diminishing or Limiting Value operative in the sympathetic participation of individuals.

3. *The Laws of Social Synergy.*

If the line of reasoning which has led to the formulation of this law is sound, we are justified in concluding—thus far upon merely theoretical grounds—that the individual's feeling of over-individual value, and his judgments of value, precisely in so far as they are impersonal and reflect this feeling, correspond directly to the objective social participation value of the dispositions judged. Our thesis has been that moral worth judgments, in their aspect both of obligation and imputation, are impersonal judgments upon acts, and reflect the participation value of these acts for over-individual ends. An analysis of these judgments, to which we shall presently turn, will show this correspondence. It will become evident that the consciousness of over-individual value presupposed by these judgments, reflects the working of this law, i.e., that the norms and limits presupposed by these judgments reflect this law of participation value. In the meantime, and as a preliminary to this analysis, we may here develop certain important consequences of the law significant for our later studies. These consequences are twofold, and may be properly described as corollaries from the law of Marginal Participation Value. This law, together with its corollaries, may, then, be described as the laws of Social Synergy, for they are the laws governing those social processes of sympathetic interaction and valuation which have been characterised as social synergy.

these over-individual objects shows that all these conditions are in force. The desire for the object springs out of the tendency to participation, and this tendency, in its primitive organic form, seeks the highest possible activity both in intensity and extension. The amount of the disposition is always limited, both in extension and intensity, by the conditions of sympathetic projection; and, finally, as we have seen, while dispositions in their personal or limited group reference are, under certain special circumstances, without capacity of substitution, no specific disposition is as such ultimately indispensable for social participation.

(a) *Corollaries from the Law of Marginal Participation Value.*

In the first place the working of this law results in the establishment of certain norms and limits of participation value for these different social dispositions. The normal demand for participation on the part of an individual, i.e., for acts which will add to the social good or satisfy any given social demand, as well as the minimum and maximum demanded of him, will be determined by the extent to which the disposition is already universalised. Judgments of imputation and obligation, in so far as they correspond to actual social values, in so far as their reference is impersonal and over-individual, will constitute a reflection in the individual consciousness of these objective norms and limits.

In the second place, we shall find that the inevitable consequence of this law of social synergy is social differentiation and group segregation. The tendency to complete universalisation or expansion, which is inherent in every social disposition or tendency, is followed by loss of participation value. This arrest of social demand is followed by value movement to new objects, as in the case of discontinuous value movements in the individual (Chapter VII). But as in individual, so in social valuation, there is another type of value movement, the continuous, in which the same object acquires complementary values, ethical or æsthetic. In the former it is through detachment or isolation and individuation of the object or person that the new value is acquired; in the latter it is through the isolation of a group, its organisation and unification about an ideal or value, and its contrast with other groups. Through these contrasts arise new complementary group values, which are imputed over and above the actual value which the object would have in virtue merely of the functioning of the primary law of social synergy, and which therefore modify the norms and limits of moral over-individual judgment. Only by the consideration of these two phenomena in their inter-relations shall we be able to interpret the concrete social judgments of obligation and imputation.

(b) Norms and Limits of Participation Value—Social Value Movements.

The first consequence of the application of this law to social values is that it enables us to distribute conceptually these social worths about three critical points. The working of this law, the principle of Grenz-frommen, as Ehrenfels calls it when applied to social worth dispositions, results in a mutation of value in which three phenomenal phases may be distinguished, as aspiring, normal, and outlived values (Ehrenfels's [1] *aufstrebende, normale, und überlebte Werthe*). These we may describe in the following way. An aspiring social value is one the intensity of demand for which in a given social group is great, corresponding to a limited expansion or diffusion in the social consciousness. A normal value may be described as one in the case of which the intensity of the demand and the extent of its diffusion are more nearly equal. In the outlived value the diffusion has become so great that decrease in intensity, and finally loss of value as it approaches universality, follow. We have here the stages of a social value movement, from social passion and emotion to habit and indifference, analogous to the similar stages in the instrumental valuation of objects by individuals.

This law of the mutation of social values is most apparent in the superficial changes in fashions. In the case of fashions in clothes and manners, the value is chiefly found in the functional significance of the object for social participation and contrast, and the value movements are correspondingly rapid and superficial. The period of intensification of personal and group values through novelty and contrast is quickly followed by imitation and universalisation until, when the objects become " common," their value, which has been conditioned largely by temporary demand, expires and is finally *outlived*—and new forms of distinction and contrast become necessary. The working of the law is seen here at its purest because the greater part of the demand for the object or act is an expression of their value for immediate social participation, the more indirect value they may have for specific individual and social ends being relatively little. This is seen in the fact that when the *mode* is past the greater part of their social esteem and economic value or *price* has gone. It is the paradox of fashion that when it is most prevalent, when the demand is at its height, its decay has

---
[1] Ibid., Book II, chap. III, par. 17.

already set in. Up to that point it is the extension that stimulates imitation and creates its value; when that point is reached it is this same extension which destroys its value and leads to its wholesale abandonment. It is just because of this emptiness of all meanings except the commonness of superficial contagion that the pursuit of fashion is so essentially self-defeating.

When we turn to the more important region of the socially desirable dispositions and common ideals of men, we find that, while they are more permanent conditions of social participation—the ends which they serve being more ultimate and permanent—nevertheless, they are subject to the same law. The value movement, it is true, is extended over a longer time, and is, therefore, more difficult to detect. Moreover, the social participation value is much more complicated with fundamental personal worths, and the dependence of its intensity upon its social expansion is not so clearly marked. Nevertheless, analysis enables us to distinguish the two elements.

The most patent illustrations of these value movements are to be found in the sphere of social and political ideals and shibboleths, although similar laws govern the more ultimate moral ideals which underlie them. The ideals of "liberty, fraternity, equality" of the French Revolution may be said to have gone through these phases. In contrast to the opposing ideals of the old régime they were first *aspiring*, and participation in them was accompanied by intense personal and group worths. The *normal* stage was reached when they became the presupposition of judgments of morals and legislation. They had then become diffused enough to find institutional expression, and were still felt intensely enough to make them a moral force. At this point, the specific dispositions for which these ideals with their suffused emotion stood (the disposition to acknowledge manhood suffrage, etc.) having secured practically universal assent, they are *taken for granted*. Social habit appears, and the usefulness of the ideals for social participation decreases. They begin to be outlived, and their demands are not strongly felt. The old symbols become empty words, lacking the social emotion of the aspiring value or the social sentiment which accompanies habit. They do not correspond to actual values, and therefore lack real obligatory force. It may, of course, be said that the spirit of these ideals is far from realised, and that they will constantly take on new forms. This is true, but each new form means the differentiation of a new specific disposition and a new concrete ideal, and the intensity with which that ideal is felt will again depend upon the same empirical conditions, the degree of expansion which the ideal has attained.

All this may be easily misunderstood—may be taken to mean that the ideals which have undergone this transmutation into "things taken for granted," or social habits, have lost all relation to actual social values. This is far from the truth. They have become the platform of implicit assumptions upon which new values may be built up. Emerson's epigram "that culture is the measure of things taken for granted" may well be applied here; we may say that civilisation is the measure of socially desirable dispositions or habits taken for granted. But when all this is admitted, it is still true that *on the platform of things taken for granted* new ideals suffused with emotion must arise if conscious social values are to continue. A potential value can become actual and dynamic only by becoming a *felt* value. In order to continue, value must forever be taking on new forms.

This brings us finally to the question of the possible existence of certain social ideals and dispositions, underlying the more superficial values, which are said to have absolute value and to escape the social value movement here described. In the preceding case it was said "the spirit remains, even if the form changes," and it is not only a popular assumption, but also in many quarters a philosophical postulate, that there are certain fundamental acts and innermost dispositions to participate which have absolute and unconditioned value. But when we examine the acts or dispositions in question, we discover that in every case they have acquired this unique sanctity only by abstraction from concrete reality. The assumption of absoluteness has had its ground either in a narrowness of historical and social perspective—in which case the feeling of absoluteness has attached itself to a concrete act or disposition which is in reality neither universal nor eternal, or else, perhaps, in a process of logical abstraction—in which case the object is so abstract that no actual felt value whatever is attached to it, and the postulate of universality and eternity cannot be challenged. This illusion is furthered by the fact that different dispositions pass through these phases of value movement in widely varying periods of time, and that some dispositions remain in the normal phase through long periods, so that it is difficult to determine whether there has been any appreciable movement toward the loss of intensity which characterises the outlived value. Moreover, actual changes in worth dispositions may be perfectly consonant with long-continued retention of the old name.

Such a conclusion evidently has an important bearing upon our conception of moral values. Underlying the normative law of "universalisation," whatever its form, whether utilitarian or idealistic, whether in the Kantian form or in Fichte's modification ("act so that the maxim of thy conduct may become for thee an *eternal* law"), is the assumption that moral values escape the laws inherent in the temporal character of values. But the difficulties in such a conception are not to be hidden. Universalisation of a given disposition, or even indefinite increase of the supply, must involve such a modification of the demand as in turn to change the actual objective social value of the disposition. To act as though the maxim of one's act were an eternal law is to act as though frequency of repetition would have no effect upon its value, an assumption which experience does not allow us to make with respect to the objective values of any object. Whatever validity such an assumption may have for the worth experience of the individual, it cannot be taken as a norm or measure of actual social values.

With the postulate of absolute value in its logical or axiological aspect we are not here concerned. That "value is eternal," in the sense that continuity of valuation is presupposed in every value judgment, is the necessary postulate of every judgment of value; that it is universal in the sense that my value judgment is in some way continuous with the judgments of all other subjects of valuation is an equally necessary postulate. But to infer from this that the participation value of any concrete disposition or act is either eternal or universal is unwarranted. Such an inference would be justified only in case we could show that for the instrumental participation value of certain dispositions there are no substitutes. But beyond the idea that whatever possesses actual social value must persist in one form or another, we cannot pass; and of these future forms we cannot form any definite ideas, for experience shows us a continual readjustment according to the laws already described. That many of these social values may, as ideals, and therefore as centres of organisation for individuals and groups, acquire the meaning of practical absolutes is a possibility we have already suggested, and will consider more fully presently, but *as social values* they are always relative.

Objects of Impersonal Over-Individual Value

(c) Social Values as Reflected in the Individual.

Assuming the truth of this schematic picture of the mutation of social values, of the value movement that every social value undergoes, and therefore also of the distribution of values in any given cross-section of the social consciousness, how does this situation reflect itself in the individual's consciousness of over-individual values? It is clear that values in all three stages will be represented. Those dispositions which belong to the class, normal values, will constitute a central region which we may describe as "moral" worth dispositions. They represent a degree of constancy of habit in worth judgment which other dispositions cannot attain. This constancy has two aspects. On the one hand, these moral worths represent the most completely universalised dispositions, and consequently the expectation, or demand for participation in them is relatively universal. On the other hand, the intensity of participation expected is relatively constant, and represents the norm of expectation in judgments of obligation and imputation. As a result of this element of constancy in the normal moral disposition, the judgments which spring out of this norm approach most closely to the impartial impersonal ideal which constitutes the standpoint of morality.

About this region of "moral" values as a centre, gather the aspiring and outlived values which, in contrast, may be described as ethical or *quasi*-moral worths. They are so named because, while social and over-individual in their reference, they lack the impersonal reference of the impartial spectator. They are limited group values which shade over into personal worths.

The *aspiring* values are supra-normal worths in that they represent great intensity with limited expansion. To take as an illustration the new values taught by Christianity in its early days, within the Christian fellowship itself the demand for manifestation of its virtues exceeded the normal, while it was clearly felt that a different standard must be recognised for those outside. In the case of such ideals the expectation is not "standardised"; individual variation is more marked. But for this very reason the intensity with which the individual participates is also greater than in the case of normal values—in direct proportion to the absence of the virtues in others. Moreover, the value imputed to the individual thus participating is proportionally greater.

z

The *outlived* social value, on the other hand, is below the normal, in that expansion so outruns intensity that participation is no longer emotional but purely intellectual and formal, in so far as the mass of individuals is concerned. The social demand, as reflected in the individual, is, therefore, normally much less intense than in the case of the other classes of worth dispositions, the aspiring and the normal. Thus there are certain conventional acts and standards, such, for instance, as church-going in some communities and certain forms of charity, which were at one time motived by a vital and immediately felt disposition to participate in common worship or in the common good, but which are now kept going merely by an intellectual recognition of their formal instrumental value for social solidarity. A good test of an outlived value is just this conscious effort to keep it up when the real disposition for which it stood has passed away or has been transferred to some other act. The loss of belief in these forms of piety and charity does not necessarily mean weakening of the energy or will to participate which underlies them. They simply draw in, and contract to more ideal and personal forms, awaiting perhaps the time of a new embodiment in a social ideal which shall again call forth feelings of reality.

An outlived value makes itself felt, therefore, in this way. As a positive ideal it is still upheld, and is often the more eloquently preached the more its vitality wanes, but its non-observance is less and less noted and disapproved until finally it is entirely detached from the direct relation to feeling and will which formerly gave it life. In the consciousness of every individual there will, therefore, be certain faint social obligations which reflect outlived values.

In general, then, as has already been stated, the individual's consciousness of over-individual values will reflect the actual social values of these objects, and his disposition to participate and to demand participation on the part of others will be modified in the ways described. But we should not overlook the fact that, as in the case of the aspiring values, so in the outlived, the working of this general law of value movement may be modified. The outlived value may become the ideal or the centre of intrinsic values for individuals and groups, and may acquire a new participation value through contrast and opposition, as in the case of reactionary and radical groups. An outlived social value, such as class ideals of honour and bravery belonging to a military type of civilisation, may survive in an industrial régime, the monastic ideals of humility and contemplation may survive in a time when they correspond to no widespread social demand, and through this very contrast and opposition they may become the objects of intense loyalty and of emotional participation. For such reactionary individuals and groups they again become aspiring values. The worth thus acquired is, however, an ethical, personal, or group worth, and the demand is no longer impersonal and over-individual. To the radical, on the other hand, these same socially outlived values become the stimulus for the development of new ideals and values, and in seeking *freedom* from the old conventional sentiments and ideals he thereby develops the new. This leads us to the phenomenon of social differentiation and its bearing upon the development of values.

(d) *Social Differentiation—Group Segregation.*

The second consequence of the law of Marginal Participation Value, social differentiation, is closely connected with the phenomena of social value movements which we have been considering. The tendency to complete universalisation and expansion which is inherent in social dispositions is followed by loss of participation value and by value movements to new objects. In these movements appear new group formations and contrasts, with acquirement of complementary value through these contrasts. In the sphere of objective social values also we find, within certain limits, a modification of the law of Marginal Participation Value similar to the modification of instrumental values in other spheres,—through acquirement of intrinsic complementary value.[1]

Social differentiation, group segregation, consists in the unification and organisation of a group about some ideal end. It is the product of two factors, the tendency to complete expansion and homogeneity inherent in imitation and sympathetic participation, and the tendency to individuation and intensification of sympathetic feeling through contrast. The first factor produces social habit. Aspiring values become normal and normal values become outlived. But this process is held in check by individuation of the group through idealisation and contrast. The processes here involved are in principle the

[1] Chap. VI, pp. 171 ff.

same as those employed in the idealisation of the person. The disposition in question is *assumed* to be universalised within a group, a class, a race, a party, etc., and this homogeneity is deepened through contrast with opposing groups. Such ideal construction may go so far as to individuate the opposing groups about the negative, evil dispositions and ends, in which case, by a well-known contrast-effect, the negative elements are extruded, and the unity of the group idealised. We have already seen how this individuation and isolation of the group is to a degree possible in organic sympathy. For short periods, and in connection with fundamental desires and passions, the solidarity of the group may be complete, and the sympathy may be intensified by group contrast. But such isolation is only temporary, and the presumption of homogeneity is likely soon to lose its force and to prove illusory. More important in creating permanent assumptions of group solidarity are the idealisations of the group through æsthetic and religious constructions, which we shall presently study in detail. Through these ideal constructions groups are organised about the aspiring and outlived values, and these objects acquire an intrinsic meaning for the individual group which is quite apart from their objective instrumental value.

This is but a special application of the general law according to which instrumental values, on becoming intrinsic, acquire complementary value. As the law of Marginal Utility for objects of instrumental value, more especially for wealth in general, was seen to be modified in certain significant ways, i.e., a quantity of wealth acquires a complementary intrinsic value, not found in the instrumental value of the parts, so we find a similar modification of the law of Marginal Participation Value. The valuation of a sum of money as a whole, where the separate instrumental judgments are suppressed, where its indefinite applicability to condition and personal worths is assumed, and where it is referred immediately to the personality, gives to the sum of money, as a unity, an intrinsic value which may greatly exceed its actual instrumental value. In a similar way, when an over-individual good, a social disposition with participation value, is identified with a group, and assumed to be universalised in that group, it acquires an intrinsic worth which goes beyond the limits of instrumental valuation. Emotional participation is extended beyond the limits set by the working of the law of instrumental judgments. Doubtless the specialised dispositions and ideals of special groups and classes all have had, or still have, certain instrumental values for society at large. The specialised dispositions of military classes, the ideals of free expression of the artist class, the ideals of contemplation and renunciation of religious orders, all have instrumental values for society. But in every case their value is conditional upon their not being universalised.

There can be no doubt that the condition of the highest realisation of participation value is group segregation. How far this individuation or isolation of a group may go in the direction of creating absolute permanent worths, and what are the limits of the process, we shall have occasion to consider, but that it is a factor to be reckoned with in accounting for the phenomena of actual social values, and the individual's participation in them, is clear. For, not only does it come in to modify, at least temporarily, the inevitable tendency of all social values to pass into social habit where emotional participation ceases, and thus to maintain in the form of group worths the class described as *outlived* longer than would otherwise be possible, but it also, by its intensification of *aspiring* worths, enhances their value. Moreover, it affords the conditions for the intensification of personal worths, or, from a more objective point of view, for the development of great personalities.

If we may make use of a biological analogy, with a distinct consciousness of its purely suggestive value, this group isolation may be compared to isolation in the sphere of natural selection. There it is generally recognised that, in order that a new variation may be fixed in the species, isolation of the species, either through environmental conditions or the impossibility of breeding with other species, must be assumed. Otherwise the variation would soon be lost again through panmixia. In a somewhat similar manner, in order that there may be continuance of intrinsic valuation of definite and fixed attitudes, isolation of groups is necessary, or at least contributory. Here we have the springs of class jealousy, once group segregation has taken place. Social pan-mixia, the breaking down of class barriers, makes impossible that fixity and contrast of ideals which constitute the condition of many personal and group values. Such class jealousy often connects itself with the preservation and isolation of ideals and standards which, from the point of view of wider, more impersonal judgment, seem fictitious, as, for instance, in the case of the seemingly fine spun and arbitrary notions of honour which characterise certain classes. They are indeed fictitious, but only in the sense that *many* personal values are, in that they are ideal constructions made in the interest of continuity of valuation. As the primitive tribesman finds himself in the arbitrary and conventional tribal marks which adorn his brother's person, so individuals of a later civilisation find in intrinsic and conventional attitudes those contrasts and oppositions which deepen, if they do not broaden, the feeling of participation.

It is not necessary to insist at any length upon the fact that we are not here concerned in the least with any evaluation of these phenomena, with the determination of the teleology or dys-teleology of social differentiation. Whether salvation consists, as with Tolstoi, in wiping out these fictitious values and getting back to those which are most universal and primitive, however that may be conceived to be possible, or as with Nietzsche, in affirming still more distinctly these same segregating attitudes, or as with Guyau, and in a more scientific way with Simmel, in bringing about an ordered continuum of social values in which the individual can easily pass from one to the other, is a problem of social philosophy and practice. Our interest is merely in the psychological processes involved in social differentiation.[1]

4. *The Limits of Participation Value of Dispositions—The Question of Absolute Social Values.*

The consideration of these laws of social synergy—the law of Marginal Participation Value, and its two corollaries with reference to value movement and group formation and differentiation—would seem to lead to the conclusion that the social over-individual value of qualities and dispositions of persons, no less than of economic goods, is always relative, the degree of value being relative to the quantity of the dis-

---

[1] The phenomena of social differentiation have ordinarily been studied from the objective point of view, as an extra-psychic, social fact, part of the order of nature. Viewed in this way, apart from the value consciousness of the individuals involved, it has been studied in two aspects: (*a*) causally and genetically, as the product of sub-conscious forces of selection, defined now as economic, now as biological, now as a combination of the two,—as a product, in other words, of a specification of functions; or (*b*) logically, or, perhaps better, teleologically, in that the thinker seeks to rationalise, and sanction, social segregation by showing that such differentiation is instrumental to the realisation of some abstractly defined good— according to one or other of the hypotheses most in vogue, the idealistic or the hedonistic, either the fullest ideal life or a maximum of pleasure or utility. With neither of these aspects of the problem are we primarily concerned. Both types of explanation are, strictly speaking, extra-psychological.

Objects of Impersonal Over-Individual Value 343

position or the degree of its universalisation. This, if true, would exclude the possibility that any disposition, no matter how fundamental, should acquire absolute social value. The very fact that, as *social*, the value is instrumental and not intrinsic would necessitate this consequence. From this it would follow that judgments of value of the individual, in so far as they are impersonal and moral and reflect actual over-individual value, would be always relative and never absolute, as in the case of personal worths.

Nevertheless, while this conclusion seems to be inevitable—and we shall find it substantiated by an analysis of the concrete phenomena of impersonal moral judgments of obligation and imputation, we cannot accept the conclusion without further analysis. It is at least conceivable that, as in the case of personal worths, so here, a disposition having social value may become intrinsically valued, and thus acquire absolute complementary value. If it is impossible that a social good should attain absolute participation value, and that the moral obligation to that good should be unconditional, it is still conceivable that the abstract moral point of view might be so modified by other activities of valuation, as, for instance, æsthetic and religious, that the instrumental value might become intrinsic and acquire absolute complementary value. In the sphere of personal values the ethical reaches an absolute moment through æsthetic characterisation. There, we found, in the very processes of characterisation are contained the necessary presuppositions of absolute personal worths, the æsthetic isolation of the individual, the suppression of instrumental judgments and repose in the object. The hypothesis of absolute personal worths was then found substantiated in the actual judgments of personal obligation and merit. May it not be that in the processes of social participation and ideal construction there are similar activities creating absolute values?

In the foregoing study of social sympathy and its consequent ideal constructions, we have already had occasion to call attention to the fact that, while the normal law of social sympathy, as determined by its conditions, is that with the increase of the range of sympathy the degree of sympathy decreases, nevertheless, this law is modified by group isolation and contrast. Similarly, it appeared that through this group isolation and contrast the conditions are realised which make possible, within limits at least, the individuating reconstruction of the group and the acquirement of complementary value. The question for consideration now is, how far this individuating construction may go in this direction.

There are two types of social ideal construction or idealisation which create complementary values and extend the range of social participation and valuation, the æsthetic and the religious. In the beginning strictly limited in their scope, confined to the function of enhancement of group and racial values, the range of their constructions has expanded until some æsthetic and religious idealisations lay claim to absolute and universal validity, on the one hand as expressing the purely and simply "human," on the other as having reached the divine. How far these constructions are able to create absolute social values we must now decide.

Taking up the problem from the side of æsthetic idealisation, there can be do doubt, it would seem, that æsthetic feeling does extend immensely the capacity for social participation—both in intensity and expansion. In the chapter on Value Movement [1] we had occasion to criticise one view of the origin and nature of æsthetic attitudes and constructions which, because of their great significance for the expansion of social sentiment and its maintenance on a high level of intensity, sought the conditions of æsthetic expression wholly within the social. While we were compelled to look for the presuppositions of the movement toward the æsthetic in the individual, and thus to criticise the merely social theory of its origin, we did not ignore its significance as a vehicle for the extension of social sympathy. In smaller groups, and on the level of emotional contagion—where the inducing conditions of sympathetic participation are largely perceptual, as in the dance of primitive peoples—this function of art is very much in evidence. On the higher ideational level also, and in much larger social groups, national and racial, where the sentiment shared is a funded meaning of some great over-individual ideal, there may arise something which may quite properly be described as a *racial assumption* of the reality of that ideal and of its complete expansion. In that racial assumption the individual may feel an absolute over-individual worth, and may realise the moments of inner peace and sublimity. All this may be admitted, and yet, when we examine more closely the forms in which this great group faith or illusion incorporates itself, the inherent incapacity of the æsthetic to make social worths absolute shows itself.

[1] Chap. VII, pp. 221 f.

Objects of Impersonal Over-Individual Value 345

The very condition of æsthetic repose is individuation and isolation. Only thus can an object acquire immanental worth, only thus are the instrumental judgments which otherwise determine the worth of the object, and which give us only relative value, suppressed. But this individuation and isolation is possible only when the racial ideal, the virtue or capacity, is incorporated in some great individual, the "hero," or in some relatively small group. The meaning of the ideal in all its fullness can be expressed only by limiting its expansion. Thus all great racial art which approximates to the expression of absolute worths is essentially monarchical or aristocratic. A democratic art, in the sense that it may be shared, is possible—it may be actually prevalent and generally appreciated,—but in the sense that it represents only that which is common and undifferentiated in human nature, it is a contradiction in terms.

An interesting proof of this position from the negative side is to be found in the incapacity of æsthetic social ideal constructions to create illusion. Utopian pictures of a society in which the social worths or worth dispositions, which now have value merely instrumentally with reference to social need and demand, are universalised—where communism not only of goods but of ideals abounds, where altruism reigns, although no longer needed, and justice without injustice to be righted—leave us strangely cold. The reasons for this incapacity of impersonal social ideals for the acquirement of intrinsic immanental worth are to be found, not only in the fact that such constructions must remain abstract and conceptual, but also because it is impossible for us to *assume* their existence, or at least rest in the assumption, with any degree of *belief*. The emotional conditions of belief are wanting, and intellectually, the assumption of the indefinite applicability of these dispositions to social ends, when subjected to scrutiny, will not maintain itself. It is only when, as in the case of the religious ideal of the Kingdom of Heaven, the ideal is made supernatural—when, i.e., the assumption underlying the æsthetic contemplation is frankly detached from empirical conditions and is grounded in a supernatural personality, contrasted with the entire system of nature, that belief is possible.

This incapacity of purely impersonal over-individual worths for æsthetic idealisation does not, however, prevent them from being the object of absolute immanental worth for individuals and groups. The relatively complete expansion of an aspiring worth, or even an outlived social worth, within homogeneous groups, may create the illusion of complete universalisation. The conditions here are favourable to the isolation and individuation of the group which would make possible such an assumption. The very contrast and opposition of such groups, as utopian societies and saintly orders, afford the conditions for such a degree of intensification and expansion of these worths within the group as to arrest critical existential and instrumental judgments, and to favour the assumption of actual realisation. These conditions are indeed favourable to the realisation of personal worths of elevation and inner peace, but they are then no longer impersonal.

Religious construction is closely connected with æsthetic in that it projects its social worths into ideal personalities, but it shows this important difference that, whereas the æsthetic construction is all directed toward repose in a worth already realised, toward an hypostatisation of the immanental tendency in worth experience, the religious construction is, in its purest form, directed toward making absolute the transgredient moment. As such, it projects the over-individual worth into a person or persons with whom the individual or society is in volitional relations. This difference appears in the different rôle which the negative moment plays in the two constructions. In the æsthetic constructions the tendency is simply to eliminate or ignore opposing tendencies as illusion-disturbing moments. In the religious consciousness, before it is affected by philosophical reflection, the tendency is to intensify the consciousness of the reality of the ideal by opposing it to certain negative forces to which equal reality is ascribed. In both cases value is intensified by contrast and detachment, but the result is attained in different ways.

Now, in so far as religious construction is a social phenomenon, it is clear that it is simply an extension of sympathetic projection. If it is true, as comparative religion seems to indicate, that "fear first made the gods," if the first projection beyond the social group, in over-social persons or forces, is that of the negative or opposing moment, such a fact is easily understood on the basis of our analysis. The dispositions with participation value remain longest instinctive and intra-social because they constitute the attitudes and dispositions which through sub-social forces were selected and fixed as the instinctive basis of participation. But once the negative

Objects of Impersonal Over-Individual Value 347

dispositions have been projected, the positive or good dispositions with participation value soon follow. From this point on the process is fairly clear. The persons of the gods in whom the worth dispositions are projected correspond at first directly with group distinctions. Tribal or national gods are the *good* gods, the bad deities being the gods of the enemy. The highest form of religious construction, on the social side, is attained when the racial limits are transcended and the god becomes *one* god and the god of all men. It would seem, then, that in the religious construction we have the possibility of the universalisation of over-individual values, and at the same time of emotional participation of the individuals in these values, which is the real condition of absolute worth. If in the religious consciousness group limits may really be transcended, and if in the ideal constructions of religion we have an object for universal emotional participation, we have a situation of the greatest possible significance, for we have here the possibility of an *absolute* over-individual demand for participation, and such participation would have absolute not relative value. Does the religious consciousness really transcend these limits?

In order that there may be emotional social participation in these over-individual constructions, two conditions seem to be requisite: (1) the personalisation of the deity, and (2) the opposition of the deity to negative tendencies, preferably personalities. The religious consciousness, if it is to be both emotional and social, cannot transcend these limits. I mean by this to say that there may be a certain type of emotional participation of the individual in a being conceived to transcend these limits, but the moral and social sphere has been left behind. Attempts have been, and are constantly being made, in the interests both of purely intellectual and of worth continuity, to transcend these limits; and these efforts take the form of a pantheistic monism in which the fundamental notes are universalisation of some worth attribute and abstraction from anthropomorphic personal and group limits. It is with these constructions only in so far as they are worth constructions, and with their capacity for becoming objects of absolute worth, that we are here concerned. When viewed in this aspect, as a worth construction which shall at the same time be completely over-personal and the object of worth feeling, the process is seen to be self-defeating.

The facts which show this may, for the sake of emphasis, be put in the form of a dilemma, which may be described as the dilemma of all pantheistic worth constructions. When the worth attribute, whether it be pure reason—and reason in these constructions is always a worth attribute—or some ineffable form of experience which transcends reason, is thus universalised and made absolute, one of two things happens. Either it ceases to be a worth construction with any intrinsic meaning whatever, and becomes a purely instrumental intellectual construction, or else it passes from the sphere of impersonal worth objects into the region of the subjective and personal. In either case it has transcended the region of the moral. In the great historic pantheistic constructions this emotional logic is everywhere apparent. Hinduism can attain the purely impersonal worth object only through atheism, and the object thus created can remain an object of feeling only by becoming identified with the self, as in the famous phrase, " That art thou ! " The attempt to make absolute the over-individual worth construction reduces the social moral world to illusion, and in the moment of attainment it is no longer an impersonal but a personal worth of inner peace that is achieved.[1]

We are justified, then, in concluding this study with the statement that religious construction in its social aspect may, like the purely æsthetic construction, enhance the consciousness of over-individual value, but it cannot transcend the laws inherent in social construction. Religion may give complementary values to social ends, and intensify the feeling of social obligation, but to do so it must remain dualistic and anthropomorphic. This dualism is overcome in moments of contemplation and faith, but the condition of these experiences is *Einfühlung* in its æsthetic individuating form, not impersonal participation. The personal and impersonal values fuse in an absolute intrinsic value. As immediate, it is over-personal and over-social in its meaning. But it still remains a personal value in the sense that it is only as a *practical* absolute, as the limit of a series of personal experiences, that it has axiological meaning and validity.

Whether this implies that personality in its æsthetic and

---

[1] The intellectual love of Spinoza and the cosmic emotion of Clifford are also doubtless real, or at least possible, experiences, in which absolute immanental worth is attained, but it is a personal worth with which we are concerned in both cases. Such emotion does not attach to the purely impersonal world order when abstracted from the subject which constructs and individuates it. The mechanical world order, the immensities of space and time are, as such, worthless. It is only when the soul whispers to itself, in varied dialects to be sure, the magical and mystical words, " *That art thou*," that the " that " acquires worth.

religious form is the highest category of worth experience we need not here inquire—since our interest is confined to the dynamics of valuation. If it is, it must take up into it all the meanings of the social consciousness. What we must insist upon is that religious and æsthetic experiences have axiological validity, and are not merely empty mysticism, only in so far as they retain as their content and indispensable presuppositions, the meanings acquired in personal participation. It is as means of enlargement, not loss, of personality that they have significance.

CHAPTER XII

OVER-INDIVIDUAL VALUES (*Continued*).

I. INTERPRETATION OF CONCRETE MORAL JUDGMENTS IN THE LIGHT OF THE PRECEDING ANALYSIS AND THEORY

The Problem.

WE come now to the study of the concrete phenomena of moral judgment which must test the truth of the preceding theory—the analysis of judgments of moral obligation and imputation.[1] If moral values are actual values, determined by processes of social participation and by the laws of social synergy, then these judgments should reflect, in their qualitative and quantitative aspects alike, the expectations and demands created by these processes. The situation here is entirely similar to that which presented itself in the sphere of personal worths. As a result of our study of their genesis, certain laws were developed, and these were shown to be reflected in the phenomena of personal obligation and imputation. A theory of the nature and laws of *moral* values has likewise been developed, and the phenomena of moral judgment, if we succeed in isolating them, should reflect these laws. More specifically, since moral values are the objective participation values of dispositions, and since these values are by their very nature subject to the law of Marginal Participation Value, we should expect the moral judgment to reflect in its quantitative aspects the operations of this law. An analysis of the empirical laws of moral judgment will show this hypothesis to be justified.

1. *The Object of Moral Judgments—The Morally Qualified Act.*

The prerequisites of such an empirical study are, as we have seen in a similar analysis of personal worths, the isolation of

---

[1] For similar studies of these phenomena, and also for some of the terminology used in this discussion, the reader may be referred to Meinong, *Psych.-Ethisch. Untersuchungen zur Werttheorie*, chap. III of Part II (Vom moralischen Sollen); also Ehrenfels, *System der Werttheorie*, Part II, pp. 195-205 ; also Simmel, *Einleitung in die Moralwissenschaft*, Vol. II, p. 323.

the object of judgment, the fixation of the terms in which estimation of moral value takes place, and the definition of the presupposed demand in terms of its norms and limits—that is, the limits within which the estimation moves. The definition of the morally qualified object, as already given, isolates the phenomena in a preliminary way. The morally qualified act we found to be an act which expresses a disposition to impersonal participation, the response to an impersonal demand. The morally qualified judgment upon such an act is one in which abstraction is made from all subjective and personal elements, and which reflects a disposition to judgment as determined solely by the over-individual demand. It is the judgment of the " impartial spectator." Further studies have, however, caused us to modify this definition somewhat. If, as has appeared, over-individual demands, to be felt at all, must be related to the concrete interests of a group and can never be wholly abstract and universal, then, strictly speaking, there is no purely impersonal participation and no wholly impartial spectator. The morally qualified act and the morally qualified judgment, as at first defined, would alike be ideal limits never actually realised. This conclusion we may admit. The moral value of an act is always an *actual* social value, and the demand presupposed by moral obligation toward such an act, and by moral judgment upon it, always represents a concrete, relative value determined by the laws of social synergy. Moral values are actual, not ideal, as in the case of personal values. To this statement the " ideal society " for which the reformer works seems to present a contradiction. The values there are ideal, and at the same time apparently moral and social. Nevertheless, the contradiction is only apparent. In so far as they are ideal they are personal and intrinsic. The reformer's utopia may be intrinsically desirable, but it cannot yet be determined whether the ideal can be actualised. Only those ideals which have already been at least partially actualised, and have taken form in an over-individual demand, institutional, legal, or social, can form a standard for an impartial judgment of the actual moral value of an act. Thus even the reformer who works for ideal conditions would hesitate to judge the men of his time by any other than the best actualised standards.[1]

---

[1] Even when the "radical" promulgates ideals and standards in opposition to the social valuations of his time, and seeks to organise groups about these ideals, he does

2. The Terms of Estimation of Moral Value—Egoism and Altruism.

All estimation of relative value, we have repeatedly seen, takes place in terms of two variables: affirmation of conative tendency and its arrest, which stand for the positive and negative moments. In the case of impersonal judgment upon impersonal participation, the positive factor is the tendency to participate in over-individual trends, to contribute to over-individual goods, while the negative moments are the " condition " and " personal " worths which may arrest this tendency to participate. In estimating the participation value of the act we measure its positive altruistic quality in terms of the strength of the egoistic tendencies sacrificed for the altruistic.

It will be observed that in this social or moral reckoning the distinction between condition and personal worths, fundamental in personal imputation, becomes irrelevant, and both are subsumed under the general term of egoistic tendencies and dispositions, a clear indication of the process of abstraction by which the impersonal point of view is reached. The dispositions described as altruistic may include attitudes or tendencies to participate which display different degrees of impersonality. Thus one may sacrifice individual ends for the good of another individual, for the good of a limited group, or for relatively abstract social ends. But the essential of such participation is that there be some contrast between individual and over-individual good—otherwise we have purely personal relations and personal worths. The extreme of altruism, as understood in this reckoning, is the case where the object or person for which the sacrifice is made is so remote from our personal sympathies that the participation is wholly unemotional.

Moral imputation, as distinct from personal and ethical, is therefore, strictly speaking, judgment upon the act as thus qualified. An act is said to be " correct," deserving or blameworthy, according to the relation between the egoistic and altruistic tendencies expressed by the act. These qualifications of the act, and the degrees of emphasis with which they are

---

not seriously, in ordinary social relations at least, judge his fellows by these standards. Except for purposes of pedagogical effect (as in the case of Bernard Shaw, perhaps), he does not in actual situations go beyond the normal demand. His sense of humour, if not of justice, and his intellectual apprehension of the principle of " economy of the truth " (especially when the truth is so *very* inner and ideal) is usually sufficient to guard him against such fallacies of worth judgment. Nietzsche's personal and social relations are excellent illustrations of this fact.

Over-Individual Values 353

predicated, are, moreover, reducible to a function of these positive and negative moments. But while moral judgment is primarily upon the act, and upon the act as instrumental, that is, as contributing to over-individual worths, the moral judgment may easily pass over into the ethical and personal. Altruism, as we have seen, may be judged both as a personal and a social worth; and, while in the concrete worth experience the two are not kept distinct, yet it is necessary for our scientific purposes that they should be.

(a) *The Amount of Altruistic Disposition as Measured by the Character of the Individual Good Sacrificed.*

If now we turn to a more specific examination of this reckoning in terms of egoism and altruism, we find that the dispositions thus described may vary in several significant aspects, each type of variation affecting the moral judgment, which is a function of the two variables. In the first place, there is the amount of the disposition to participate, as measured by the *character of the condition and personal worths sacrificed*. Condition worths may vary along the whole scale from the existence-minimum to the wholly worthless, personal worths from the characterisation-minimum, which is without capacity of substitution, to the most superficial personal quality. As an illustration we may take the case of the rescue of a human life (an act of high participation value): (*a*) by the sacrifice of a few hours of ease and pleasure; (*b*) by the risk of one's good name; (*c*) by the loss of all one values of condition and person, or even loss of life itself. If we bring no other elements into the reckoning, it is obvious that the degree of altruism is a steadily increasing one in these three cases, and that, other things being equal, the moral value of the act increases accordingly.

(b) *As Measured by the Character of the Over-Individual Good for which Sacrifice is Demanded.*

A second factor enters into our estimation when we take into account the character of the over-individual demand to which the given act constitutes a response. This demand differs: (*a*) according to the nearness or remoteness of the object from personal or group sympathies; and (*b*) according to the degree to which the demand for the object has become universalised. The latter factor we may call the "coëfficient of projection or participation," by which is meant the character of the demand as representing a *normal, aspiring,* or *outlived* value.

In the first case, the nearness or remoteness of the object determines the emphasis of our judgment, of our positive judgment when the act takes place, of negative when the act is omitted. Thus sacrifice of condition or personal worths for one's child will receive less praise than sacrifice for a friend, for an unknown man, or for an abstract principle. And, in the same order, the failure to sacrifice will call out disapproval or negative judgment—strong disapproval in the case of failure to sacrifice for one's child, less and less disapproval as the objects become more and more remote from the emotional participation of the individual. Again it may be observed that our judgments take into account the projection co-efficient of the sentiments, participation in which is demanded. Sacrifice for a value which has already attained a high "expansion-coefficient," large social recognition, let us say duty to the family, integrity in business, freedom in the State, is rated less highly than sacrifices for worths which have attained less expansion, which are not normal, but rather aspiring values, as, for instance, new ideals of truth or social justice just beginning to be strongly felt. It would appear, then, that when we take the attitude of the impartial spectator we cannot abstract from a consideration of the instrumental value of the sacrifice itself, i.e., from the relative importance of the object sacrificed and of the over-individual demand to which the sacrifice is a response. Altruism as a social value is not possessed of the capacity of indefinite increase; its felt importance has a limit determined by the laws of social participation already developed.

It cannot be denied, of course, that absolute sacrifice is actually demanded of ourselves and others, that an act which is so insignificant as to be below the threshold of instrumental value may not only become so important as to demand such sacrifices, but the sacrifice may actually acquire absolute value, as was seen in our study of personal worths. It is important to recognise, however, that this value is no longer merely impersonal and over-individual, that which it has for the impartial spectator, but is a complementary value which is acquired through reference to the concept of the personality or to quasi-personal constructions.

II. THE THRESHOLDS AND NORMS OF MORAL JUDGMENT

These general facts with regard to the conditions which determine the changes of emphasis in our moral judgments being established, we may now turn to a quantitative study of these changes. And if the preceding analysis, largely qualitative, made our hypothesis probable, the facts now to be considered make this probability a practical certainty. In a general way we have seen that, if no changes in the character of the overindividual object be introduced, the moral value imputed to the act, within certain limits which will presently be determined, varies directly with the amount of sacrifice of condition and personal worths. The question now arises whether this variation, its laws and its limits, can be more accurately determined—in order that we may connect them with the psychical processes which condition these judgments, and compare the region of impersonal with that of personal worth judgment.

The first requisite of such a study is the determination of conceptual points or thresholds from which the increase and decrease of judgmental emphasis rise and fall. Two such critical points may be distinguished. They may be described as the *Norm of Participation* or the "correct," and the *Participation-Minimum*. In general the correct represents the normal expectation, fulfilment of which is accompanied by neither praise nor blame. The minimum of participation represents the smallest quantity of a social good for which sacrifice of individual good is demanded. These conceptual points are in principle not difficult to determine, although, owing to changes in social values, they are not always easy to define in a given concrete situation.

1. *The Norm of Participation or the "Correct"—The Normal Expectation of Social Participation.*

In defining the region of the "correct" the first thing to be noted is that, in comparison with the normal threshold of personal worth, it is much cruder, much less sensitive. The sphere of the correct includes wider variations than the corresponding sphere in personal worth feeling. Praise and blame come less quickly in impersonal than in personal valuation. The "correct" in wider business circles allows of considerable of the group or the nation, as an indispensable part of a total complex. The merit imputed in such a case is not the reflex of an over-individual demand, but of a personal demand which arises through identification of the attitude with the personality. The importance of this will be especially apparent when we come to study the laws of preference between personal and over-individual worths.[1]

(c) The Significance of these Terms of Estimation.

When the results of this analysis are properly weighed, they are seen to constitute strong grounds for the hypothesis that moral judgments reflect the working of the laws of social sympathy, and more specifically the law of Marginal Participation Value. Estimation of the degree of moral value in terms of the character of the individual good sacrificed and of the over-individual end for which it is sacrificed, turns upon the degree of concreteness and immediacy or abstractness and remoteness of the goods and ends.

For, in the first place, this imputation of value in degrees varying with the remoteness of the object from emotional sympathetic participation, is precisely what we should expect in the light of the law that intensity of sympathy decreases with increase of the generality of resemblance. It means simply that our sense of over-individual value is relative to our capacity to represent in sympathetic projection the affective-volitional meaning of others. Again, the variations in degree of emphasis of the judgment, corresponding to the differences in social sentiment described as normal, aspiring, and outlived values, indicate the working of the same law, according to which the intensity of an over-individual trend decreases with its expansion. Where, as in the aspiring value, the intensity is in excess of the expansion, there the emphasis is greater than in the case where the relation of intensity to expansion is more nearly normal. These are all aspects of the law of Marginal Participation Value.[2]

[1] Chap. XIII.
[2] It should also be noted that the emphasis of judgment varies with the degree of probability of realisation of the over-individual end. For the law of Limiting Value is a law of instrumental values where the feelings presuppose existential and instrumental judgments. Our judgment capacity is strictly limited, and when the object becomes more and more remote in probability and possibility, or approaches to absolute certainty of realisation, participation becomes less and less significant. Compare in this connection chap. XI, pp. 337 f.

variation from the standard demanded in personal intercourse. The sacrifices of his personal interests for the larger interests of his profession demanded of the physician as correct, may seem quixotic, or be wholly unintelligible, to wider business groups. The reason is not far to seek. Social and impersonal participation is instrumental, and a display, either of egoism or altruism, does not become significant, does not rise above the threshold of the correct into the regions of praise and blame, until its importance can be felt by the cruder sense of the multitude. But the fact must not be overlooked that the region of the correct expands and contracts with differentiation or fusion of sentiment, with group segregation or combination.

The region of the correct in impersonal moral judgment represents, then, the normal disposition to participate, the normal sacrifice of egoistic to altruistic interests, whether for individuals or for social ideals. In any particular case of moral judgment, this norm of sacrifice is strictly relative to the significance of the over-individual object or ideal, as we have defined that significance above,[1] for which the sacrifice is made. The disposition normally expected is, therefore, a direct product of the laws of social synergy as we have defined them.

2. *The Participation-Minimum—The Lower Threshold.*

At the point of the *correct* there is no imputation of praise or blame. To remain in the social niveau is not meritorious, and, by reason of the crudeness of the social sense at this point, slight variations in excess or defect of the normal are not readily marked. But as the variations increase the judgments of praise and blame appear. As the altruistic disposition to sacrifice increases, so within certain limits the judgments of praise also increase. This increase of altruism may, as we have seen, be measured in two ways: either in terms of the character of the over-individual object for which sacrifice is made, or in terms of the character of the individual good sacrificed. Now, measured in either way, there is a limit to the praise imputed for the performance of an act or of blame for its omission. This limit is the participation-minimum already described, the minimum of the over-individual good for which sacrifice is demanded, or, what amounts to the same thing, the maximum of sacrifice of individual good demanded. When this minimum for participation

[1] Cf. above, pp. 353 f.

is reached, in so far as the praise or blame is purely moral or impersonal, the performance of the act is not praised and its omission not blamed.

The existence and function of this participation-minimum appears clearly in certain concrete cases. The demand for truthfulness, respect for property, and benevolence, are more or less completely universalised sentiments. But, from an impersonal, impartial point of view, we do not expect a man to sacrifice important personal interests, or ultimately life itself, for a merely formal adherence to an insignificant truth. Neither do we expect him to make such sacrifice for the comfort of a total stranger, nor to suffer pain or death rather than appropriate an insignificant object to which his name is not attached.

III. Judgments of Imputation and Obligation— as Related to these Norms and Limits

1. *Imputation of Praise and Blame.*

The minimum for participation represents that minimum of the over-individual good beyond which sacrifice is not demanded by the impartial spectator, and the demand for sacrifice falls off as the good approaches this minimum. Any exhibition of altruistic disposition in excess of this demand will then be supra-normal. Let us see how the judgments of praise and blame are constituted at this point.

A disposition in excess of the normal may, for reasons which we have seen, not be noticeable at first, but when it becomes apparent it calls out judgments of praise, for the very good reason that in general altruism is in demand. But the increase of the disposition is not accompanied by a corresponding increase in the degree of praise. Altruism, as a social good, is not susceptible of indefinite increase. As the excess of the disposition in proportion to the object becomes more and more marked, the judgmental emphasis begins to fall off, and finally a point is reached where praise passes over into blame. A good illustration is that of the mother who persists in sacrificing important personal and condition worths, health, strength, and her own interests of various kinds, for minor worths of the child. In such a case the moral value of the act decreases relatively to the excess of the sacrifice over the normal, and threatens to pass over into the region of the blameworthy. In the same manner failure to sacrifice is accompanied by judgments of blame, but with less and less emphasis until, as the minimum is reached, the failure becomes negligible.

How different all this is from personal imputation is patent. There it was precisely at these points, at the minima of characterisation (and of participation also when the over-individual good is identified with the person), that absolute worths appeared. Thus in the case of the preceding illustration of the mother, if we participate in her act emotionally, that is, isolate her æsthetically from the social value-process, an absolute sacrifice for a trivial end may acquire absolute value. In such a case we have intrinsic valuation of the mother as such, repose in the idea, and the principles of intellectual imputation are transcended. The ethical theorist might say—*upon reflection*— that the reason the moral judgment takes this form is that, as a result of her excessive sacrifice for the child, other services to society at large, and even to the child itself, are made impossible —more important values of *the same kind* are sacrificed to lower. Such a logical relation, such an ultimate harmony of ends and norms, may conceivably be worked out by a philosophy of ethical values, but the presuppositions of concrete judgments are not derived reflectively, but result from the working of the empirical laws of valuation.

In this connection another fact, already noted in the preceding chapter, is significant. In personal characterisation the emotional accompaniments of the act are relevant. In immediate personal participation we infer the disposition presupposed from the emotional expressions which constitute the inducing grounds of our sympathetic participation. Whether the act of participation is accompanied by passive participation, lively sympathy, apparent readiness to offer oneself, or enthusiastic sacrifice, is a question of decided moment. A person with sensitive feeling for personal worths would prefer—and rate higher— an insignificant act with evidence of gracious insight and feeling, to a much more important act done with a sullen, or even cool, sense of duty. There is ample room for the " pathetic fallacy " here, yet most of us prefer our illusions because of their fruitfulness for life and faith. But these very accompaniments, so significant in emotional imputation, are irrelevant for the impersonal imputation of moral judgment. A minimum of disposition requisite for the bringing forth of the normal act is demanded, but all beyond that is more or less irrelevant. I say "more or less," for while it is, in a measure, taken into account, because the impersonal judgment is never pure, nevertheless, the value imputed to these manifestations is far from being in proportion to the excess of disposition displayed. When a man is righteous overmuch, the excess is but grudgingly acknowledged and approved by social judgment.

2. *Moral Obligation.*

When we turn to the more internal aspect of the over-individual demand, as it finds expression in the individual's sense of impersonal demand or obligation to participate, we find the same general laws at work, determining the conditions of the demand's being felt at all and the intensity with which it is felt. Oligation being but the reverse side of imputation of praise and blame, this is what we should expect; and, while it is perhaps more difficult to isolate impersonal from instinctive and personal obligations than to distinguish between personal and impersonal imputation, nevertheless, the phenomena are sufficiently distinguishable to enable us to show the working of these laws, the laws of actual over-individual values.

a) *It Reflects Actual Objective Participation Values.*

In conformity with the nature of moral values as *actual*, we find that, in order that impersonal obligation may be felt at all, there must be as a necessary presupposition the judgment of the existence of an actual over-individual demand. Moreover, and this is still more significant, there must be presupposed the certainty, probability, or at least possibility, of the act in question being instrumental to the realisation of the over-individual social end. The degree of obligation decreases according as the judgment is one of certainty, probability, or mere possibility, and lapses entirely with the judgment of impossibility. This condition of impersonal obligation, which a further analysis of the facts will clearly show to exist, is in striking contrast to the conditions of personal obligation, where, as we have seen, the feeling of obligation to personal ideals is not so conditioned.

A vivid characterisation of the critical point at which over-individual obligation lapses is given in Robert Louis Stevenson's fable of the two men on the sinking ship. The captain of the sinking ship, it must be premised, has just found one of the hands smoking in the powder magazine. "'For my own poor part,' says the captain, 'I should despise a man who, even on board a sinking ship, should omit to take a pill or to wind his watch. That, my friend, would not be the human attitude!' 'I beg pardon, sir,' said Mr. Spoker, ' but what is precisely the difference between shaving in a sinking ship and smoking in the powder magazine?' 'Or doing anything at all in any conceivable circumstances?' cried the captain. 'Perfectly conclusive. Give me a cigar!' Two minutes after the ship blew up with a glorious detonation." With the lapsing of all possibility of there being social significance to the act, lapsed all obligation toward the ordinary duties of life. Personal obligations, the captain would probably admit, still remain. Just as one may not be nasty in the dark, so when courage is of no more avail, we do not expect a man to lose his personal worth of manliness. Obligations of the instinctive, appreciative order, of strength, etc., also still remain. But with the lapsing of the possibility of realisation of over-individual good, all social obligation lapses.

The situation is brought out still more clearly in the obligation to vote at an election. The feeling of obligation is undoubtedly strongest, other moments being neglected, when the vote is thought to have almost certainly an effect upon the election. As that certainty decreases, the feeling of obligation, in so far as it is impersonal, also decreases until a point is reached where it may lapse entirely. This situation may arise in two ways. Either there may be so many voting the same way as to make the individual's vote negligible; or else, through corrupt practices, the effect of the vote may be nullified. If the individual is absolutely certain that his vote will be of no effect, ordinarily his feeling of social obligation lapses. It is quite possible, of course, that personal and narrower group obligations may still persist. He may owe it to himself to fulfil his duty. Loyalty to a class ideal, or even to an abstract principle, as an object of personal worth, may still influence him, but his feeling of obligation loses that over-individual reference which characterises impersonal obligation. This accounts, it would seem, for that peculiar sense of futility which the principle of " performance for performance's sake " arouses in us when it is justified

[1] Quoted from Taylor, *The Problem of Conduct*, p. 265.

merely by reference to future and indirect instrumental values. The fear that failure to do one's abstract duty completely, even when there is no point in doing it, may lead to undermining of a good habit, seems to be a form of unworthy timidity. The robust conscience, to use Ibsen's phrase, lets the good habit take care of itself. But the intrinsic value of the act at the moment—its purely personal value—is another matter.

(b) *It Reflects the Norms and Limits of Objective Participation Value.*

Moral obligation is intimately related to moral praise and blame. It is the more subjective aspect of the demand presupposed in moral judgments. There must, accordingly, be a definite relation between the degree of strength or intensity of the feeling of obligation and the degree of emphasis of moral judgments of praise and blame. We have already seen that the degree of praise and blame is determined by certain norms and limits, the norm and minimum of participation. How is the intensity of obligation related to these?

In studying the phenomena of imputation it was found that the norm of participation represents the zero-point. To remain in the social niveau is not meritorious. Those who perform the normal duties of life, who fulfil the normal expectations, both as to the quality and amount of disposition displayed, acquire no merit except through contrast with exceptional demoralisation. But when we turn to the more subjective aspect of the situation, impersonal obligation, we find that it is *precisely at this region of the " correct " that the feeling of impersonal obligation is most intense and emphatic*. Moreover, the intensity of the obligation falls off as the quantity of the object, the social good, approaches the participation minimum, or as the object passes out of the region of the normal into that of the supra-normal, where the values are ideal and aspiring, and the disposition to sacrifice is beyond the normal. In these cases the obligation to participate is less and less intense; while, as the distance from the region of the correct increases, the neglect or refusal to participate appears more and more admissible.

The facts of the moral life bear out this analysis, and the reasons for the facts are not far to seek. Even a limited observation convinces one that in those cases where the objective social demand appears in its purest form, in those cases, namely, where men of action and affairs live the unreflecting life of their day and class, uncomplicated by more general and ideal reflections—it is the acts which represent the "sacred average," in some cases of the race, in others of a class, which mark the limits of social obligation and effort. It is what "one does," and even more emphatically, what "one does not," in other words the correct, which constitutes the whole duty of man. To the achievement of this necessary minimum all *conscious* moral effort is devoted, the rest being left to the control of obligations of an instinctive kind. Strongly confirmatory of this view is the fact that in more developed, as well as in more primitive communities, the conventional demands of ceremonial morality and of etiquette are easily confused with the more strictly moral. It has been said that one's conscience often pricks him more severely for a *faux pas* than for a sin, and, while this is perhaps not quite true, it is still true enough to indicate that it is at the correct, the habitual, that the stress of the over-individual demand is chiefly felt, often irrespective of the question of the ends which the social demand subserves.

The reason for these characteristics of impersonal obligation is to be found in the fact that, in the main, the correct or the participation norm represents the indispensable minimum of social participation and cohesion. Its value is instrumental and not intrinsic, and consequently increase of the disposition above the amount demanded, while it has value, becomes progressively less and less significant. It is for this reason also that law, with its legal norms, is almost wholly concerned with giving additional sanctions to the average normal duties, with the preservation of the indispensable minimum of moral or altruistic dispositions. The objective value of *this minimum*, experience has shown; but it would be impossible to predict what changes in value would follow the enforcement by law of more personal and individual obligations. We may conclude then that moral obligation, as well as the moral judgments of praise and blame, reflects actual participation values as determined by the laws of social synergy.

(c) *Moral Obligation is Relative—not Absolute.*

But with this conclusion we find ourselves, it cannot be denied, in apparent conflict with the supposed "moral sense," and with much of ethical theory. Moral obligation often seems to reflect in terms of feeling an absolutely impersonal, over-individual law, universal and necessary. Such is Kant's categorical imperative, which he thinks he finds attached to attitudes and dispositions demanding complete universalisation, not realising, apparently, that the condition of this demand being felt at all is precisely the lack of universalisation. Clearly in such a situation one of two things must be true. Either our entire theory of moral values, and the analysis of facts upon which it rests, must be at fault, or else this supposed deliverance of the moral sense, and with it the theory based thereon, must represent some distortion of the worth consciousness, some misinterpretation of the facts which a closer analysis will discover.

We shall scarcely be open to criticism if, after that which has gone before, we choose the second alternative. Nor is it difficult to show that we *are* here concerned with a misinterpretation, and to point out wherein it consists. The moral values, as distinguished from the ethical and quasi-ethical, belong to that innermost group of dispositions described as normal, representing social habit, i.e., the maximum of expansion consistent with the minimum of intensity necessary to *felt impulsion*. As social habit, the feeling of obligation is not the reflection of an absolute impersonal law, but of a concrete social synergy, and of actual objective values. As such the demand is limited in intensity and extension. How, then, does the concept of absolute, or perfect and unconditional, obligation arise—that is, the idea of a demand for every individual and for an individual under every circumstance?

The idea of perfect, in the sense of universal, obligation rests upon an abstract ideal construction. A certain minimum of a given disposition is demanded of all the participants in a given social group, for which it has normal participation value. An individual who feels this demand idealises it; he assumes that, were it universalised, it would still have the same or greater value. In this assumption he is further influenced by the fact that for these fundamental normal attitudes there are certain class names, such as the cardinal virtues, which, although they include under them in the course of time greatly varying attitudes, nevertheless, create the illusion of permanence and universality. Through the working of the laws of social value movement there may be, as in the case of the change in meaning of the virtues of courage and chastity from Greek to Christian times, actual change in attitude with relative permanence of name.[1]

The illusion of perfect, in the sense of unconditional, obligation arises in a somewhat similar way. The act which has value with reference to a certain specific end, and in certain circumstances, is assumed to be applicable under all circumstances, and the disposition expressed by the act to be of value in any amount. Such an assumption with regard to personal values which are intrinsic is, we have seen, in a sense justifiable, but with reference to instrumental values it is illusory.

[1] See above, p. 335.

CHAPTER XIII

SYNTHETIC PREFERENCE

I. The Relative Value of Different Classes of Worth Objects

THERE still remains a chapter in our investigation of these judgments without which the preceding studies would be flagrantly incomplete, a chapter which is in a sense both the completion and the test of our preceding analyses. We have sought to isolate the various objects and standpoints in valuation, to study their laws, their norms, and their limits, in the light of their psychological genesis and of the character of their psychological presuppositions. But we have continually recognised that there is an artificial and abstract element in this procedure, that any given concrete act of valuation may represent the resultant of various motives, and that, moreover, many of these concrete acts of valuation consist of preferences, not only between objects of the same class, on the same level of valuation, but between objects on different levels. We have analysed the conditions which determine the relative values of objects within the same general group, but it is not yet clear that we can infer without further study the laws which determine the relative values of the different groups. To this question we must now turn.

Some steps in this direction we have already taken. We have analysed the fundamental appreciative distinctions between condition, personal, and over-individual impersonal values, and have sought to account for these distinctions in terms of the acquired presuppositions of the feelings. Each of these classes represents a meaning acquired in some process and determined by certain characteristic presuppositions. As instruments of analysis we made use of the concepts of the *threshold* and of *capacity for continuous valuation*, as determined by the laws of valuation, seeking to determine these laws for the different levels. As a result we found that, in general, personal values represent a higher level of meaning than condition worths, and over-individual values a higher level than either. The question now arises whether the acts of valuation which consist of *preferences among these different worth objects* can be explained as resultants of the facts and laws already developed, or whether new principles must be called in to account for them. This may be described as the problem of Synthetic Preference, in contrast to the laws of analytic preference developed for the several levels of valuation.

The characteristic of all such acts of preference is sacrifice. What Böhm Bauwerk has said of economic goods is, *mutatis mutandis*, and, with certain limitations, true of all worth objects. " We find occasion," he says, " to pass judgments of value only under two conditions : first, when it is a matter of letting a good pass out of our possession by gift, exchange, or use ; and, secondly, when it is a question of adding a good to our possessions." This is true in all those cases where the judgment of value takes place after conflict of motives, although, as we have seen, there are certain types of judgments which merely register feelings of value having as their presuppositions the habits or implicit assumptions which follow upon adjustment. But in all cases of conflict, estimation of value takes place in terms of two variables, a positive and a negative factor. The question of preference and sacrifice is simple enough, at least in principle, within the separate spheres of values. It is simply a matter of more or less, and the judgment is analytical. By this is meant that the judgment or preference is the result merely of the distinction, according to their degree, between objects or qualities within the same general class of values. Thus in the sphere of condition worths, the relative value of different objects, and quantities of objects, is a function of the specific laws of valuation in this sphere, of the capacity of the object immediately to satisfy desire, or to acquire complementary values through rearrangement and association with other objects. Similarly in the other spheres of personal and social values, definite and specific empirical laws determine the relative value of different objects, of acts and dispositions. When, however, it becomes a question of sacrifice of an object of one type for an object of another qualitatively different type, the problem is more complicated.

II. RATIONALISTIC AND MONISTIC THEORIES OF PREFERENCE AND SACRIFICE—CRITICISM—VOLUNTARISM AND SCEPTICISM

The history of ethical theory is full of attempts to explain these facts of preference and sacrifice by reference to some monistic principle, some single conception of end or good out of which all relative values spring, and to which they may be referred. Now with these conceptions as metaphysical theories of the ideal end we have in this connection no concern. It is conceivable that a philosophy of values might be able to formulate a concept of a single ultimate ideal, the mere thinking of which would include its obligatory character, its normative objectivity, in the sense that the conception of " the most perfect Being" was said to include its existence. But it does not necessarily follow that from this logical obligation, if we may so call it, the actual felt demands can be deduced. We must avoid carefully the confusion between obligation as a logical category and as an actual experience. It is with the latter phenomenon, with the empirical facts of obligation and imputation in the more complicated form of conflicts between different spheres of values, that we are here concerned, and our interest in the different theories of a single end is in this connection confined to the one question : to what extent do the single ideals actually maintain themselves in practical situations, to what extent can our actual feelings of obligation be shown to refer to a single conscious end ? Should they turn out to do so, the idea of a science of ethics would so far find confirmation. But, on the other hand, even if a single conscious end should be shown to be empirically untenable, it does not follow that a science of ethics is impossible, nor indeed that it is impossible to show a *functional* unity in the processes of valuation. To this more ultimate question we shall return, but for the present we must examine these theories of preference in detail.

Viewed from the empirical standpoint, as hypotheses for interpreting the concrete facts of preference, the monistic theories present difficulties, for in every case they are the products of abstraction in which one conceptual construct, developed in the course of the concrete processes of valuation, is abstracted from these concrete processes, and taken as an equivalent for all types of values. Thus Hedonism, in all its forms, takes the abstract equivalent for condition worths, quantities of pleasure, and seeks to reduce all affective-volitional meanings to these terms. All preferences are reduced to choices between quantities of pleasure. The self-realisation hypothesis does the same thing with the fundamental concept of the personal level, striving in vain to show a reference to the "self" as the presupposition of all acts of preference. Still another theory finds the solution in the reduction of all condition and personal worths to abstract impersonal ends.

But all these hypotheses have shown themselves more and more incapable of *explaining* the manifold and complicated phenomena of synthetic preference—i.e., it seems impossible to reduce all preferences, all resolutions of conflicts, to the *conscious* introduction of any one of these ideals as norms; and the problem has accordingly been brought to a head by the absolute denial, in recent discussions, of any monistic and rational principle in terms of which these preferences may be explained. This denial has found expression in two forms: in the revival of intuitionism, of which Schwartz's voluntaristic type is a good example; and, on the other hand, in a thorough-going scepticism, of which Simmel's is the most conspicuous illustration.

The essential point in Schwartz's position [1] is that, while the preference which takes place in the different spheres of condition, personal and over-individual worth objects is analytical, and may be seen to be determined by the empirical laws of valuation, preference *between* these different groups can be understood only as *synthetic*, as due to an immediate unanalysable judgment that personal worths shall be preferred to condition worths, and over-individual to personal and condition worths. This law is absolute and is not reducible to any empirical laws growing out of the genesis and character of worth objects. Leaving out of account the failure of this law as a description of fact, a point which we shall consider in its proper place, it is sufficient to note in this connection that such a method of solving the problem, by magnifying relative appreciative distinctions into eternal principles, implies a failure to recognise the essential nature of these distinctions as genetic and relative.

Scepticism is always a near neighbour to intuitionism, and the scepticism in this case takes the form of denying the ex-

---

[1] Schwartz, *Psychologie des Willens, zur Grundlegung der Ethik*, Part II, chaps. I and II.

istence of any single law to which these preferences may be referred. The two monistic conceptions which have especially called out this sceptical attitude are the concept of an extra-experiential or metaphysical *Self*, of which these different worth objects represent different stages of realisation, and that of hedonistic utilitarianism which conceives these different worth objects, with their differences for appreciation, as reducible to a common equivalent, quantity of pleasure.

The inadequacy both of the Self-realisation and of the Hedonistic hypothesis is shown by Simmel's criticism of the two concepts.[1] The keynote of his criticism of the unity of the personality as the supreme norm of worth experience is to be found in the fact that he sees in it a transference of the supreme *logical* category of epistemology to the sphere of worth experiences where it does not necessarily apply. To infer the actual unity of the ends of volition from the logical unity of the subject of knowledge is to go beyond the worth experience itself. We do indeed find the empirical unity of the subject, or self, an object of desire and of worth judgment, and, within limits, a standard of values, just as we find individuation a motive in the construction of worth objects, but the individual, and the processes of individuation, are empirical and not logical.[2] In like manner the concept of pleasure is an abstraction from our experiences of feeling of value, an abstraction which ignores the appreciative distinctions in feeling to such a degree that it no longer includes the appreciative differences of depth and breadth, and the personal and impersonal meanings of the feelings. It is a workable equivalent only for what have been described as condition worths.

It is undoubtedly true that neither of these conceptions will establish continuity between the different spheres of values. And the reason is that in both cases the standards of a particular type of worth judgment are abstracted from the processes in which they are constructed, and applied as norms to a different type of activity. Within a certain class of relative judgments, concerned with condition worths, pleasure is a well-founded object of desire and quantity of pleasure a well-founded

---

[1] Simmel, *Einleitung in die Moralwissenschaft*, Book I, chap. IV, Book II, chap. VI.

[2] An instructive criticism of the first of these monistic principles is to be found in Taylor's *Problem of Conduct*, where it is shown at what points actual worth experiences prove refractory to such reduction. The great single moments of experience, both of supreme assertion and supreme negation, do not lend themselves easily to this conception of Self-realisation.

standard of judgment. The ideal of unity of the personality is also undoubtedly the presupposition of an entire group of worth judgments—of personal obligation and of imputation of personal worth—and as such constitutes, within those limits, a well-founded object of desire and a standard of judgment. The ideal of the sacrifice of the subjective and personal, it is equally obvious, is a well-founded ideal within the limits of strictly moral judgment. But no single one of these conceptions has been able to supply a satisfactory standard for synthetic preference, and scepticism as to the existence of such a standard has resulted. The only way open to us, then, is to take these pre-scientific distinctions between condition, personal, and over-individual values as heuristic conceptions, and, by empirical analysis of actual preferences—the conflicts between obligations on these different levels and between personal and impersonal imputation, to determine to what extent these preferences show uniformities, to what extent higher unities and continuities of preference may be established. If any such higher laws of preference emerge, it may be expected that they will be more general expressions of the empirical laws already found operative in the different spheres.

III. ANALYSIS OF THE FACTS OF SYNTHETIC PREFERENCE AS EXHIBITED IN JUDGMENTS OF OBLIGATION AND IMPUTATION

The point at which Simmel's scepticism becomes most incisive is in his discussion, in the last chapter of his work, of the conflicts of duty. It is just the impossibility of accounting for the *actual* resolutions of the conflicts between our different obligations in terms of any single highest end, any monistic principle of valuation, that leads to the denial of such a principle. In particular he insists that we have no standard in terms of which we may estimate the relative importance of the *extensive* and *intensive* aspects of obligation, i.e., judge between the duty which is more *intensive* because more personal and emotional, and that which is less intensive but more extensive, because more general and over-individual in its reference. Preference between an extensive duty with weak intensity and a narrower duty with marked intensity is, he maintains, determined by forces in the darker life of feeling which cannot be adequately expressed in terms of our knowing consciousness. In this statement of the difficulty we have the problem of our own study presented in our own terms, that is, what determines our choice between ideal objects of condition, personal, and over-individual worth, where degrees of obligation can be reduced neither to differences in degree of intensity of feeling nor to the explicitness of reference of the object to the self. And the same difficulty inheres in our attempts to rationalise our judgments of imputed worth.

Let us, then, begin our study by returning to that other form of denial of a monistic principle of continuity, the voluntaristic intuitionism of Schwartz, according to which our consciousness of value, as expressed in feelings of obligation, always demands the sacrifice of condition to personal and over-individual values, and the sacrifice of both condition and personal to over-individual values. Some facts of experience must have motived this formulation, otherwise it would not have the element of truth that it certainly has. For it contains at least this much truth—that it constitutes a broad generalisation of the facts. It is one of those pre-scientific formulations which precede more detailed analysis. More than this, it corresponds to what we have found to be the genetic levels of meaning. In general, normal over-individual values have greater transgredient reference than normal personal values, and personal values greater than condition worths. In general, also, we find this fact reflected in our feelings of obligation.

But when we seek to carry out this generalisation in detail, we find that it is by no means an accurate picture of the facts. If it were so it would mean, as Schwartz admits, that our sense of obligation would demand the sacrifice of the most important personal to the least important over-individual good, and the greatest condition worth to the smallest personal worth, a consequence which the analysis of actual judgments by no means bears out. It is, therefore, precisely at this point of the limits that the critical question arises. An analysis of how our sense of value reacts at these limits or points of conflict of obligations, will not only have the negative result of showing the points where this intuitional formula breaks down, but will also have the positive result of disclosing the empirical principles which determine the actual resolutions of such conflicts.

1. Conflicts between Personal and Impersonal Obligations.

Especially enlightening for our study is a striking illustration of this intuitionist point of view from the pen of Tolstoi.[1] With his customary fondness for intense and clear-cut assertions, he raises the question of the limits of self-sacrifice, and answers it by affirming that our conscience recognises no limit. He presents us with a picture of beggars coming one after the other to the house of the moralist, and receiving all his money, food, and shelter. At last there appears a disreputable tramp, who asks for the moralist's last bundle of straw, the final barrier between him and the certainty of death. Should the moralist give it? Yes, not only share it, but give it completely. To all questions of limits or compromise Tolstoi answers with a determined "No!" Even the minimum of existence, and all the personal worths which it involves, must be sacrificed, be the consequences what they may. There can be no doubt that there are many who would honestly feel no such obligation, and yet this is not the extremest form in which the demand might be stated. Conceivably the last bundle of straw might be asked merely for some minor purpose of the beggar—not for the protection of his life and health. Or it might be asked as a charity for one who is not only far removed from the immediate sympathies of the giver, but one with whom he would never come in contact, and yet the demand would be the same in principle.

Assuming that for some, as, for instance, Tolstoi himself, this *would* be a real obligation, for many others it certainly would not. And if this be granted, it would appear that, not only does the a priori principle itself fail of universality, but that this fundamental difference in worth feeling, at such a point, affords some basis for that scepticism which denies the possibility of our finding any explanation for preferences of this sort. The first inference we may admit, but the second only in case the laws which we have already developed fail to give us any clues to the explanation.

In attempting to find these clues we must first recall the fact, frequently insisted upon, that any concrete practical attitude of obligation or imputation is a complex, the total force of which is analysable into several motives. The sense

---

Tolstoi, *Acte der Selbst-Opferung*, Wiener Rundschau, October 1, 1899. Quoted from Kreibig, *Psychologische Grundlegung eines Systems der Wert-theorie*, p. 152.

of worth which Tolstoi expresses in this extreme judgment of obligation may very well represent, not only his sense of the moral or participation value of his act, the over-individual value, and therefore obligation, but also a sense of its personal worth, and therefore personal obligation for him. We should in such a case have, not a pure over-individual demand as the determinant of the judgment, but such a demand as modified by complementary personal worths. Such a preference would then be at least partially explicable upon our principles.

We may best approach this question by taking the other side of the apparent antinomy, that of the man who *would not* feel such obligation. This we should have less difficulty in understanding psychologically. In the extreme case, as the situation was presented—where the beggar is far away and the object which means life or death to the giver is of only secondary importance to the recipient, the participation value of the act is so remote and indirect that it is practically below the threshold of worth feeling. It is below the participation-minimum, as we have defined it.[1] On the other hand, the value of the object for the individual sacrificing—since it is the minimum of existence and constitutes the indispensable presupposition of other acquired values, is practically absolute. If, then, the laws of "condition" and of over-individual, social values were alone operative, there can be no question which way the preference would go. In that case, too, where the bundle of straw is also the minimum of existence for the beggar, the obligation would still not be felt by many, and with perfect honesty, because of the remoteness of the beggar from their sympathy, and because of the absolute value of the object sacrificed. In this case, as well as in the first, the value of the over-individual object is far below the minimum of participation, the amount of the over-individual good for which the sacrifice is normally demanded, while the sacrifice here demanded is far above the maximum of altruism expected in the normal working of over-individual demand. The judgment of the man who honestly does not feel the obligation to such extreme sacrifice seems to be in accord with the normal laws of valuation.

Does it not then seem that such a preference as Tolstoi's, such a feeling of obligation, must be irrational, or at least suprarational, in the sense that it transcends all the empirical laws of worth feeling? Some extreme voluntarists have so held,

---

[1] Chap. XI, pp. 357 f.

Synthetic Preference

finding in self-denial a mystery which transcends all empirical explanation. But this seems as hasty an inference as is the claim of the extreme rationalist to explain these experiences in terms of a conscious rational ideal. It is just cases like these which give us the clue to our empirical analysis. We have already seen in an earlier chapter[1] how altruism, as measured in terms of sacrifice of condition and personal for over-individual worths, may itself become a personal worth, and, as such, is indefinitely *Steigerungsfähig*, susceptible of indefinite increase, when as an impersonal worth it is not. It is quite possible that the supreme worth of tragical elevation enters as a determining moment in such an act of preference. In fact it would seem that Tolstoi is himself a case very much in point. James, in his study of Tolstoi's conversion to his extreme altruism with its accompanying religious feeling, lays stress upon the preceding moment of satiety and loss of value upon the part of other objects. "A well-marked case of anhedonia," he calls it, "a passive loss of appetite for all life's values."[2] We have, then, in the absolute intrinsic value ascribed to altruism, apparently, merely the substitution of one personal worth for another, and not really the sacrifice of all condition and personal worths to the smallest over-individual worth. If Tolstoi realised the *relative* participation value of such acts, i.e., felt their demand merely in the degree which would follow upon the normal working of the ordinary laws of sympathetic participation, there would be a limit to the over-individual obligation to sacrifice.

(c) *Confirmation of this Explanation by the Judgments of the "Impartial Spectator."*

When we turn to the judgments of the impartial spectator upon such acts of sacrifice, we find this view substantiated. There is a fundamental difference between what we may *demand* and what we may *admire* in these matters. The ordinary man would say, I suppose,—if he could become articulate and if he would consent to use the terminology of the present discussion, "I cannot help imputing emotionally absolute worth to such a personality when he thus, by an act of extreme self-sacrifice for an insignificant over-individual worth, displays such strength and singleness of disposition, but I am at the same time unable,

---

[1] Chap. x, p. 301.   [2] James, *Varieties of Religious Experience*, p. 149.

when I take the impersonal point of view of moral judgment upon the act, on the basis of its participation value, to demand it of every person. Nor is the moral value which I impute to it in any sense proportional to the strength of the disposition displayed. For when I take the impersonal standpoint in judgment, I become aware of the fact that such absolute self-sacrifice means the sacrifice, not only of condition and personal worths, but of other over-individual values of which the existence and self-realisation of the individual in question are presuppositions. The individual is the meeting-point of various over-individual demands; in him inhere various group worths, of family, state, knowledge, art, etc." It would seem, then, that in his judgment of the participation value of an act, the impartial spectator cannot avoid taking into account what may be described as the "personality-coëfficient" of the individual sacrificing and of the individual for whom the sacrifice is made, that is, the relative significance of the system of values for which each stands. But when this is once admitted, it is clear that the a priori principle of preference enunciated by Tolstoi is not reflected in our judgments of imputation.

2. *Conflicts of Condition and Personal Worths.*

The actual resolutions of the conflicts between personal and condition worths seem equally refractory to subsumption under one general principle. The proposition that *all condition worths should be sacrificed to personal worths* also falls short of being an accurate picture of our real feelings of obligation. That it describes in a general way our feeling of the relative value of the two classes of objects is beyond doubt, but here again, when we examine the limiting cases, difficulties arise.

In order to understand the situation properly, we must recall the fact that there are instinctive obligations on the level of simple appreciation or simple condition worths, prior to activities of characterisation, and that it is in the region of the existence minimum that these obligations arise. It is a question, therefore, of preference between two kinds of obligation, not between mere desire unqualified by obligation and the feeling of obligation, and here again we may be disposed to say with Simmel that the determining forces lie beyond the ken of our knowing consciousness.

But to consider first the facts themselves, it seems fairly

clear that objects of condition worth, in so far as they are of relative and instrumental value, are normally felt to be of less value than personal worths; they should always be sacrificed to the least important personal worth. They have more capacity for substitution and have less capacity for continuous valuation than personal worths. Such obligation as may attach to merely instrumental and condition worths is only indirect, and is dependent upon their relation to the necessaries of existence or to personal worths. But when it comes to a choice between the *minimum of existence* and *minor* personal worths with capacity of substitution (more or less external personal worths, such as pride in one's position, name, beauty, etc.), our judgment is not wholly unequivocal. When this type of personal obligations comes into conflict with fundamental condition worths, with obligations which arise in the struggle for existence, we are disposed to think that such personal values are more or less fictitious, or at least have capacity of substitution, and should therefore be sacrificed. While we may admire absolute sacrifice of condition worths for such personal worths, in that thereby a new personal worth is revealed, we cannot demand it for the reason that such personal worths are relative and not absolute. They are not without capacity of substitution. If they are lost more fundamental personal worths may take their place.[1] The minimum of existence, on the other hand, is without capacity of substitution.

The real test of the formula appears when the conflict lies between absolute personal and absolute condition worths, between the minimum of existence and the minimum of characterisation. Illustrations in point would be conflicts between starvation, or extreme bodily pain, and honour. Extreme bodily pain, for example, approaches the psychological absolute of supreme evil in the sphere of condition worths. Otherwise expressed, in the moment of extreme bodily pain, or in imagination of it with belief in its imminence, cessation or removal of the evil has absolute worth, constitutes the existence-minimum. Let us suppose that a person, subjected to cruel torture, has sacrificed, one after the other, minor personal worths which are not without capacity of substitution, until finally nothing but the sacrifice of his honour, it may be by the betrayal of a comrade or by obedience to a demand to recant, will purchase the relief which now has for him absolute value. We expect him

[1] Chap. X, pp. 295 f.

to hold out, for we believe, however the belief may have been created, that such persistence is possible and has taken place. If the personal worth triumphs we hail such triumph as heroic, and the worth imputed to the personality is absolute. But suppose it does not? Our reaction in that case is not instinctive and unequivocal. We have already seen in our study of personal worths [1] that at this point two reactions are empirically possible. When the minimum of characterisation is sacrificed, either all personal relation is abrogated, the person is beneath contempt, and our attitude passes into one of purely impersonal moral or judicial judgment, or else the attitude of personal respect and admiration passes into one of profound organic sympathy and pity which may amount to a sanctioning of his act. We may admire such extremes of sacrifice, but we do not demand them universally. Our feeling of obligation seems to be similarly equivocal in such situations. There are some individuals for whom this extreme of sacrifice would be obligatory, others for whom it honestly would not be. The significance of these facts seems to be that in the limiting cases of conflict between condition and personal worths the general norm of preference may break down. Our judgments are not unequivocal and a priori.

IV. CONCLUSIONS FROM THE ANALYSIS OF SYNTHETIC PREFERENCE

1. *Summary of Results.*

The preceding examination of the facts of synthetic preference leads to certain conclusions, in the light of which it is possible to formulate a theory of more general philosophical significance. Returning to the question with which the analysis started, the grounds are now apparent for the negative conclusion that, whatever continuity there may be in the processes of valuation, it cannot be shown to spring from the consciousness of any single rational end or principle. There is no single ideal which shows itself to be ultimate in the sense that it always constitutes the controlling factor in the solution of these conflicts. In the second place, it seems equally certain that there is no universal a priori law governing these preferences. While the norms and ideals of the different genetic levels constitute

---

[1] Chap. X, pp. 300 f.

Synthetic Preference 379

a continuous series of values, the appreciative distinctions are not ultimate in the sense that they maintain themselves *absolutely* in the limiting cases of conflict.

Nevertheless, our study has not been wholly barren of positive results. Modest as our insight is in comparison with what is claimed by those theories of the standard which we have been considering, still we have, up to a point at least, learned something of the principles operative in synthetic preference. In so far as these concrete and individual experiences can be rationalised at all, they seem to be resultants of the laws of valuation already developed. They reflect, in a general way at least, the relative capacities of the different objects for continuous valuation and for substitution, and therefore the acquired meaning of the objects. By the method of ethical experimentation we have employed, in which it was sought to test the relative capacity of the different ideals to persist in the face of arrest, and to discover the range and limits of our judgments of obligation and imputation, we have secured results which agree in the main with the laws of acquirement of value.

But that these values *are acquired*, that the distinctions between the different groups of worth objects are acquired and not ultimate, is apparent in the breakdown—at the limits—of the so-called a priori law of preference. At these points the distinctions tend to lapse. In the case where the distinctions are wholly within the Ego (between worths of condition and person), there seem to be supreme moments of assertion of the will where the distinction disappears, where the ideal objects and their acquired meanings and obligations fall away, giving place to simple immediacy. Personal ideals may acquire absolute value, that is, may become practical absolutes in the moment of tragical elevation. But so may a supreme necessity of organic life. In the one case it is the minimum of characterisation, in the other that of existence, which has absolute value. Whichever alternative triumphs in a conflict, we cannot properly speak of a victory either of condition or personal worth, for the conceptual distinction between the idea of pleasure and of the self simply does not exist. Similarly, the man who, in the supreme moments of preference between personal and over-individual worths, chooses the absolute personal worth, is no longer, strictly speaking, an egoist. Nor is he who chooses the over-individual worth, with its moment of tragical elevation, an altruist. The relative distinction between egoism and altruism lapses. Again we are face to face with an absolute moment of simple immediacy in which relative distinctions vanish.

On every hand, then, we are forced to the conclusion that the supreme moments of affirmation or abnegation transcend the relative distinctions which the intellect makes in the service of the will, and consequently in part elude our conceptual descriptions. The acquired distinctions and meanings of these ideal objects are appreciative descriptions, volitional norms, formulated in the interest of continuity of appreciation and valuation. This is the important point. The monistic theories we have been considering fail to take sufficiently into account the elements of discontinuity which the analysis of value judgments discloses. They invariably seek to deduce the concrete norms, or psychologically determined presuppositions of value judgments, from logical conceptions of the relation of the individual to the universal, i.e., from ultimate logical presuppositions. The philosophy of supreme moments, to which we have been led by our analysis, seems to negative such conclusions. Rather does it appear that the moments of absolute worth experience may be equally those of self-affirmation and self-abnegation, and ultimately moments in which even these intellectualistic conceptions lapse. Viewed phenomenally, the activity of the will seems to be an oscillation between supreme moments within the different spheres of values, and a principle which should explain them would have to give us the laws of these oscillations, the larger concept which would comprehend them in a higher unity.

2. *The Bearing of these Results upon Larger Conceptions.*

The attempt to formulate such a larger philosophical conception does not lie within the province of this study, but we may offer in conclusion certain suggestions, as much by way of avoiding misunderstanding as for the sake of completeness.

Throughout this entire study, including the present chapter, the standpoint and methods of empirical analysis of valuation have been consistently maintained. In so far as the monistic theories of the ideal are considered, it is with the object of determining their function as *conscious* ideals, as *actual* presuppositions or norms of judgment and feeling—not as attempts to characterise the ultimate logical presupposition of valuation required by a philosophy of values. That such a philosophy of values is possible, or that the single ultimate presupposition upon which valuation, when thus logically viewed must rest, can be characterised, we need not deny. In order that valuation shall be not only describable in terms of its empirical conditions, but also intelligible in the light of its ultimate meaning, such an axiological re-reading of our judgments of value in the light of their ultimate logical presuppositions is probably necessary. All that we have here been concerned to show is that no unity and continuity of *conscious* ideals and norms is discoverable, no *single* content has *for feeling* unconditional value.

That the logical presupposition of all valuation must be a *single incontestable or unconditional value,* follows from the logical unity of the subject of the value judgment, and from the claim of the value judgment to objectivity. But from this logical unity of the subject we cannot pass to the empirical unity of *conscious* ends and of *felt* values; from the logical postulate of an unconditioned value we cannot pass to the unconditioned value of any concrete content. Such a transition is made impossible, we have seen, by the equivocal character of the actual feelings of obligation and of intrinsic appreciation or approval and disapproval in the limiting cases, and by the oscillation between the ideals of self-realisation and self-abnegation. But, despite this discontinuity of conscious ideals and of empirically derived norms, there can be no question of the *functional* unity and continuity of valuation itself. Even in those cases in which the outcome of the conflict is equivocal, and in which the acquired distinctions break down, the choice is always of the nature of a falling back upon a value which is without capacity of substitution, and which represents the necessary presupposition of continuity of volition and valuation—in other words, is a practical absolute in our sense of the term. It is conceivable, therefore, that, while no single ideal can be taken to represent absolutely the whole end and meaning of this continuity—for the reason that no conceptual construction can, because of its empirical origin, be universalised and applied continuously, and while, consequently, no single norm embedded in such ideal can be applied in every empirical situation, it may still be possible to formulate a metaphysical conception of this functional unity and continuity which shall be compatible with the actual plurality of *conscious* ends and of empirical norms or presuppositions.

Accordingly—thus it is argued by the monistic philosophies

of value—we cannot dispense with the concept of a metaphysical or met-empirical will, whether personal or impersonal and over-individual, if the functional unity and continuity of valuation is to be intelligible, the realisation of such a will being presupposed in every realisation of finite ends and in every particular judgment of value. The facts here examined do not prove the impossibility of such logical unity and continuity, but merely that the attempt to formulate that implicit presupposition in terms of conscious ideals must remain incomplete. The breakdown of the distinctions between personal and condition worths, between egoism and altruism, simply means that the content of the ideal has been conceived too narrowly, and that out of these conflicts and oppositions a larger ideal arises which includes these distinctions. The question must, therefore, assume this form—not *is there a single conscious purpose to which all other ends are subordinate*, but rather *is there not, for reflective evaluation at least, some absolute intrinsic value logically presupposed in these empirical ends*, to which, as an ultimate presupposition, the implicit assumptions, the empirically derived norms, in the various judgment situations, may be logically reduced?

When the problem is thus stated the situation is materially changed. For a monistic philosophy as thus contemplated, there is support in our actual experiences of value. The presence in our experience of what we have described as *practical absolutes* indicates clearly that such an absolute unconditioned value is presupposed, and that, while this value is not realised in any empirical content conceived as end, it *is* realised in moments of intrinsic appreciation where the empirical will comes to rest in the assumption of complete realisation through identification with the met-empirical will.

It is not our purpose to pursue these suggestions as to the possibility of a philosophy of values further in this connection. How the ultimate postulate of valuation is to be defined—whether as self-realisation or as realisation of an impersonal over-individual will, whether as " will to power " or as will to " Selbsterhaltung der Welt "—or whether indeed the functional unity and continuity of values presupposed in the empirical experiences of feeling and will can be defined in *any* such abstract terms, is a question which for our present purposes may be left unanswered. In the following chapter we shall undertake a consideration of the entire axiological question of the evaluation of values, of the meaning of the distinction between subjective and objective values, of the meaning of the presupposition of reality implicit in every feeling and judgment of value, and of the ways in which that presupposition is actualised and acknowledged. From this larger view of the problem we may again return to this point. The object of these paragraphs has been merely to show the bearing of the results of our empirical analysis upon this question, and here the conclusion of importance is this. While a monistic philosophy of values is possible, it must be such as to allow us to take the facts of actual value judgment at their face value. We must not distort them by subsuming them all under one empirically derived ideal and norm, for they are *practically* discontinuous. There are situations where condition worths have supreme value without the consciousness that they are the necessary condition of personal and overindividual values. Personal values may have supreme worth without the consciousness that they are the means to the realisation of social ends. There are cases where altruistic acts are chosen without the idea that thereby the self is realised. In general the principle must be recognised that the feelings of value—of obligation and of intrinsic appreciation, approval, and disapproval—are not to be conceived as determined by the logical relations of subordination to ultimate ends, but as feelings attaching directly to specific content, and as conditioned by empirically derived demands. In the light of an ultimate postulate these demands may be interpreted and made intelligible, but they cannot logically be deduced from a single end.

CHAPTER XIV—(*Conclusion*)

VALUATION AND EVALUATION

I. The Problem—Restatement of the Axiological Point of View

WHATEVER else the course of this investigation may or may not have succeeded in bringing to light, it has at least led us to a point where we may see the justification of the concept and method of a general theory of value as outlined in the introductory chapter. Through the genetic treatment of the different types of value judgments and their laws, a more intensive analysis of the facts of worth experience and a more comprehensive view of their inter-relations have been made possible. Every advance in intensive analysis and in comprehensive correlation should bring with it greater power of interpretation; and this test of fruitfulness has been applied at various points, with the result that many types of value judgment, hitherto not sufficiently understood, have been explained in terms of the general laws of valuation.

But such increase of insight as we may have gained cannot have failed to bring more fully to consciousness the other aspect of a general theory of value described as axiological, to have emphasised its importance, and to have made clearer the nature of the problem. In our introductory chapter we sought to state this problem, and in doing so we examined critically a certain view according to which the two problems of description and evaluation are wholly unrelated. Between the feeling of value as an experience of the individual, conditioned by psychically derived and determined presuppositions, and the judgment of value with its claim to objectivity, and therefore its logical presupposition of a world of unconditioned values, there is, it is held, no common ground. According to this view our task was properly concluded in the preceding chapter, and our inability to discover any absolutely unconditioned values constitutes a condemnation of our entire method. At this point a *philosophy* of values must begin with an entirely different purpose and method, its task being to discover and to formulate the single absolute value logically presupposed in all specific forms of value, and from this to develop deductively " a closed system of pure values," uncontaminated by any admixture of empirical feeling and will. Without raising any question as to the abstract possibility or impossibility of any such ideal—although after our study of actual valuation it cannot fail to appear to rest upon a false reading of the meaning of the claim to reality and objectivity in value judgments, we may easily see that this is not the nature of the problem as it presents itself to us. At numerous points we have seen specifically—what was stated in general terms at the beginning —that the question of validity or evaluation is in some way closely bound up with the facts and conditions of valuation, and that the axiological problem rises directly out of the psychological. The problem of evaluation being the adjustment of the implicit claims to reality which our feelings of value with their presumptions, judgments, and assumptions make, it is necessary to interpret those claims in terms of their empirical origin and conditions.

It is, therefore, with a much more concrete body of questions that axiology, as we have conceived it, has to deal,—with those questions, namely, which arise when in practical situations we seek to distinguish between the subjective and objective value, between the founded and unfounded judgment of value. Such problems are everywhere present, not only in practical reasoning but in the sciences of value. It was in fact with a view to their solution that the distinctions between actual and imputed, real and ideal, subjective and objective, values have arisen in practical judgments, and have been developed in scientific usage. But their significance is still more clearly seen in all those discussions, as for instance between individualism and socialism, about ethical and social ideals, where the dispute rests upon certain assumptions as to the possibility of economic or moral motives, the truth or falsity of certain ideals —whether they are founded or unfounded. More specifically, then, we have the problem of illusions and fallacies of value judgment, a problem which came to the surface at various points in our special studies. Æsthetic and quasi-æsthetic appreciations, personal and social ideals, religious hypostatisations—

all these give rise to certain ideal and imputed values. In what sense are these values real? Or are they indeed real at all? Now from the standpoint of psychological process, all these intrinsic ideal and imputed values arise in the processes of actual valuation, and, as such, are in a sense real. They all rest upon assumptions which have the feeling of reality. The question is whether from some other point of view they may not be wholly subjective and ideal, fictitious and illusory, as opposed to real. What is the standpoint of ultimate judgment in such cases—how shall the ultimate criterion of reality be defined in a way which shall include predicates of worth as well as of truth, attributions of value as well as of fact?

II. Reflective Evaluation—Normative and Factual Objectivity

1. *Analysis of Axiological Distinctions.*

These are questions of reflective evaluation, and any solution of them must involve the development of the meanings and implications of the various axiological distinctions which reflective evaluation introduces. The origin and nature of these distinctions we have already seen. Analysis of the value judgment (Chapter II) has shown us that, while the judgment is assertorial, there is always some implication of relation of values to reality. But while judgments of value presuppose reality, while they presume, assume, or judge their objects to be, or to exist, it is not always clear *in what sense* that existence is claimed. Unreflective value judgments are not unequivocal, and it is for the purpose of removing the various equivocations which arise that the distinctions between subjective and objective, intrinsic and instrumental, actual and potential, actual and imputed, real and ideal or imagined values, are introduced. These distinctions we have already found of use as guides to the analysis of presuppositions of feelings of value, and with their help we were able to determine the subject and object and the dispositional and actual presuppositions of different types of value judgment. But their implications are ultimately normative, and it is with the development of these implications that we are here concerned.

The whole problem is bound up, therefore, with the question

Valuation and Evaluation

of the ultimate meaning, in all its extension and intension, of the presupposition of reality implicit in all feelings and judgments of value. What are the possible meanings of reality as employed in reflective evaluation, and what is the common logical core of all these meanings? The answer to these questions will enable us to see the relation of values to fact and truth, of normative to factual and truth objectivity, as they appear in actual judgment. From a study of these relations we shall then be enabled to understand the ultimate meaning of the postulate of realisation, and to develop specific criteria for determining the extent to which it is fulfilled.

2. *Meanings of Existence and Truth.*

As to the first aspect of the problem we may get our starting-point by retracing the processes of reflective evaluation, and developing the implications of the axiological distinctions there employed. Reflective evaluation consists in the clarification of the meaning of reality implicit in judgments of value by the development of explicit existential and truth meanings. Through the development of these distinctions, subjective valuation is controlled, this element of control being, as we have seen in the Introduction, the practical significance of normative objectivity.

In their first and more limited meaning, the terms actual and real, when applied to values, signify that the presupposition of reality—presumption or assumption, as the case may be, is directly or indirectly convertible into already completed factual or truth judgments, independent of the value judgment. The terms potential, ideal, and imputed, on the other hand, mean that the values thus described have presuppositions not thus convertible, or at least not *wholly* convertible, into such judgments. What are the meanings of existence and truth employed in such evaluations?

(a) *Existence: Outer and Inner.*

The first and most obvious meaning of the presupposition of reality is that of *physical* as distinguished from psychical existence. If this is what the presupposition means, then in order that the value may continue it is necessary that *this specific* meaning of the presupposition of reality shall be fulfilled. If this meaning cannot be realised, if conversion into the object cannot take place, then the value is subjective and imaginary. In the case of the so-called "condition" worths, both immediate and mediate or instrumental, this is what the distinction between subjective and objective values means. In order to satisfy directly, or to be instrumental to more ultimate satisfactions, the object must have physical existence. A feeling of the imagination has in this case merely representative, not actual, value.

Again, for some purposes of normative control a value is said to be actual and objective when its object *exists*—not in the physical sense, as an object of sense perception, but still in the outer sense of being the object of a demand external to and independent of the will of the subject. When a desire, expectation, or demand of the individual subject finds fulfilment in, or is continuous with, the demand of others, individuals or social groups, the value is said to be actual. Sympathetic participation in the feelings and wills of others gives rise to the construction of dispositions; and the assumption of existence in this case means outer existence in wills other than our own. Such is the meaning of existence implied in all judgments in which a quality is said to belong to, or to be possessed by, an individual, and it has its psychological correlate in the concept of disposition. Such also are the economic and moral social values determined by processes of demand and supply. The value exists, and in a sense only in will or mind, but in the collective will or mind as distinguished from the individual. A subjective value is said to be actual, to have objective grounds, when it is in some sense continuous with, or convertible into, the social value. From this point of view, as we have already seen in our analysis of impersonal judgments, whatever of the individual and personal feeling and feeling dispositions is convertible directly or mediately into a supply for that demand, has actual value, in that it is founded in an existential judgment. All else is irrelevant, and is described as ideal and imputed value.

These are the chief meanings of the predicate of existence, but there is still a third which is equally important in distinguishing the subjective from the objective, the real from the unreal in valuation. In this case the distinction is *within* the individual subject. The demand which is acknowledged as objective and as a norm for the control of the fleeting subjective experi-

Valuation and Evaluation

ences, is not "outer" in either of the preceding senses. It is an inner demand which represents organised and permanent dispositions as over against temporary desires and feelings. Any form of will which has become ineradicable, any expectation, demand, or assumption which is incontestable, acquires a normative objectivity which, in contrast to the desires and feelings which it controls, makes it an existent which must be taken into account. It is, accordingly, merely this persistence, continuity, or control which is acknowledged when the predicate of existence has this meaning of *inner* reality.[1]

(b) Truth: Outer and Inner.

The preceding meanings of reality include all those cases where the claim to objectivity is acknowledged in predicates of *existence*—where continuance of value requires the possibility of direct conversion of presumption or assumption into existential judgment. There are, however, other cases where satisfaction of this claim to objectivity does not require this direct and immediate conversion, but only acknowledgment of *truth* as objective. What is the meaning of the objectivity of truth? Here, as in the case of the predicate of existence, there are several meanings which we may conveniently classify as "outer" and "inner" truth.

By "outer" truth is understood in ordinary speech "correspondence of idea with reality," reality being taken in the special sense of existence. Propositions said to be true or false in this sense are general propositions about existents of the physical, social, or individual worlds, or connections, causal and other, among these existents. The concept of correspondence includes the further assumption that, while the ideas themselves are not existents, they are founded upon existents, and are hypothetical in the sense that their truth is conditioned upon the assumption of the existence of the objects about which the propositions are made. The external control, though remote, is assumed to be real. While to ground the objectivity of a value, it is sufficient to say that the idea or concept to which the feeling of value attaches is thus true, still there is always implied in the conception of *outer* truth

---

[1] For a similar discussion of the meanings of existence, from the standpoint of Epistemology, see Baldwin, *Thought and Things*, vol. I, chapter x, §§ 9, 10, 11. Also his discussion of "primary, secondary and tertiary conversion," in vol. II, chapter III.

the belief that the judgment of truth will lead to, or may be converted into, the judgment of existence. Outer truths of this sort are in general the causal laws of the physical, social economic, and individual-psychical spheres. They are organised and retrospective propositions about existents, and many ideals and anticipations of value must, in order to make good their claim to objectivity, conform to these laws.

But there are certain meanings of truth not exhausted in this description, cases in which truth is *not* " outer " in the sense that it claims correspondence with external existents. Here truth is said to be merely an internal relation among ideas, correspondence of idea with idea, identity and lack of contradiction. The claim to objectivity in this case is interpreted as logical consistency, necessity, and universality. It is sometimes held that this meaning of the objectivity of truth is also the ultimate meaning of the claim to objectivity in values. Whether this is true or not we have still to consider, but we may at least admit that there are certain values, e.g., of knowledge, where, in order that the presupposition of reality may be fulfilled, they must conform to this demand.

3. *The Relation of Normative to Factual and Truth Objectivity.*

Evidently, after this analysis, the next question is—to what extent normative objectivity is identical with factual and truth objectivity, to what extent, in other words, the terms real and objective, when applied to the *values* of objects, have the same meaning as when applied to objects apart from valuation. There can be no question that at some points they are identical. At others they are closely related, and at still others they may, perhaps, be independent. The answer to this question involves the whole problem of the relation of judgments of value to judgments of truth and fact.

(*a*) *Normative and Factual Objectivity.*

There are some cases where normative and factual objectivity are clearly identical. Here continuance of subjective value and feeling of reality requires that the presumption or assumption of existence created by subjective dispositions shall be convertible into an existential judgment. When the

Valuation and Evaluation 391

home-sick mariner imagines his desired haven near, this feeling of the imagination has representative value, but it will not continue unless the assumption develops into existential judgment, either through perception or by inference from observations by means of his nautical instruments. Similarly, in the case of Gaunilo's Island, the mere formation of the image and assumption of its existence is not sufficient; there must be conversion into existential judgment of the first type, in order that it may have real value.

In the second place, it is clear that normative objectivity is frequently identical with factual objectivity of the second type. Wherever the reality of a value is conditioned by the belief that the object desired is also the object of desire and will on the part of others, individuals or social groups, there factual objectivity is implied in the normative. Thus in all cases where the value judgment of the individual lays claim to objectivity in the sense of the impersonal economic or "moral" judgment, this judgment can receive its validity only from an existential judgment of the second type, which predicates of the value an existence in social demand and supply independent of the individual. "Normal" exchange values or prices, "normal" moral or participation values, are both facts and norms—facts in that they have a kind of outer existence independent of the subject, and norms because the subject must take this outer reality and control into account. They have normative objectivity precisely because they have factual objectivity. In so far as actualisation of subjective feelings of value is conditioned by exchange or participation in social activities, economic or moral, the individual's judgment of the value of the object or disposition must conform to, and be fulfilled in, the objective social value. Such norms we may describe as *instrumental;* and they must have factual existence in the sense that they are founded upon social demand.

(b) *Normative and Truth Objectivity*.

In general it may also be said that, when the value is instrumental, normative objectivity is identical with truth objectivity of the outer type, or with propositions about relations among physical, social, and individual-psychical existents. Whenever the actualisation of any ideal or anticipation requires the application of physical objects or participation in economic and social processes, this ideal must conform to the general laws or truths of these spheres. All instrumental values presuppose first direct conversion, and if that is not possible, indirect conversion into existential judgments.

But, as we have said, there are other values, ideals, and anticipations which transcend the claims of this kind of outer truth, and which, in order to be valid, do not require this direct or indirect conversion into existences. Such are the ideal values of ethical, æsthetic, and religious experience. The assumptions of ultimately desirable ethical dispositions, and of objective beauty as distinguished from the subjectively effective, are ideals of this sort. Developed though they may have been in social interaction, and retaining, as they undoubtedly do, a secondary instrumental value for social participation, they are, nevertheless, now primarily significant as the conditions or presuppositions of the continuity of individual and personal values. Inner truth and reality such ideals have; they are ideal constructions which are realised or fulfilled in the individual experience which they control. They are not empty imagery, *mere* objects, for they have a funded meaning or value which can be converted into actual feelings of value. But their presupposition of reality cannot be wholly converted into existential and truth judgments. There are æsthetic values which do not claim the physical existence of their object. There are personal ethical ideals the objectivity of which is claimed in every feeling of obligation, in every judgment of imputation of which they are the grounds, and yet this normative objectivity does not imply that they are actually realised, or even capable of complete realisation, in specific individuals or societies.

We are thus led to the conception of " inner truth," as the last of the pre-formed and organised definitions of the meaning of the presupposition of reality. Surely here value and truth are ultimately and completely identical; all values presuppose at least inner truth or validity. It all depends upon whether truth, when thus defined abstractly and retrospectively, can also be defined comprehensively enough. The most comprehensive definition of abstract intrinsic truth attainable is, as we have seen, that of logical consistency, with its assumption of universality and necessity. Can the postulate of valuation be identified with this logical postulate? Or is there a last meaning of inner truth not definable apart from the judgment of value

Valuation and Evaluation 393

in which it is implied? We have already suggested doubts of this identity of truth and value, and a fuller examination of the question establishes these doubts more firmly.

This lack of identity may be seen at two points. On the one hand, such ethical, æsthetic, and religious ideals, though still claiming inner truth, often appear in an indeterminate form, which makes them not comparable with abstract conceptions, a fact especially apparent in æsthetic and religious symbolic truth. It may be said that this fact means merely that the implicit claim is *never pushed*. But this is hardly true, for the reason that the presupposition of reality is satisfied *without* pushing the claim; and in case the attempt is made, for extrinsic reasons, to turn the reality into abstract truth, and the attempt to do so is unsuccessful, the feeling of inner truth still persists. On the other hand, this same lack of identity is apparent from the fact that logical necessity does not always include realisation of inner truth. It by no means follows, as we have seen in the preceding chapter, and shall see more clearly still in the sequel, that such logical necessity includes reality for the will and for appreciation generally. Nor does logical contradiction necessarily mean incompatibility for volition. Intellectual conviction does not always include realisation.

We are therefore forced to conclude, either that certain forms of value judgment are independent of truth judgments, or else that such truth as they presuppose is not definable in retrospective or logical terms. In the former case, appreciation includes reality unconditionally, and there is no criterion other than this immediate appreciation. In the latter case, there is still an implicit hypothetical reference to judgments of existence and truth not reducible to any of the retrospective formulations or organisations of experience thus far described. The latter is probably the true interpretation of the situation. While these ideal values, in order to make good their claim to normative objectivity, do not demand conversion into existential and truth judgments of the types defined, they still have a reference to matter of fact and truth. Just what this hypothetical reference may be, can be determined only after the postulate of valuation itself is developed in all its meaning. In either case however, this much is certain—there is only partial identity between normative and factual objectivity, between the axiological and epistemological predicates. The distinction between subjective and objective values is one which arises within the function of valuation itself with a view to the control of this function. The axiological predicates of existence or truth get their meaning from their place in this function, and this meaning is always relative to the special intent of the subjective experience to be controlled. Every value is in a sense real. An unreal value is a contradiction in terms. The only question is as to how this reality shall be explicitly acknowledged and characterised in terms of reflective definition.

4. *Proof of this Conclusion in the Value Judgments of Religion.*

Religious values furnish an admirable illustration of the truth of this analysis of the relation of judgments of value to judgments of truth and fact—of their relative independence at certain points. They are, as Höffding has well said, value judgments of the second degree, in that they express the feelings which arise from the consideration of the fate of primary personal and social values in reality; they express the demand for conservation of values already acquired. As a consequence of this character, the judgment of value is bound up originally with existential judgments, the real meaning of which is not always at first apprehended.

The object of religious belief and devotion is psychologically an appreciative construction externalised and given "outer" existence in the manner already described (Chapter XI). The presupposition of reality is acknowledged in existential judgments of the most elementary type. As a consequence, for the unsophisticated religious consciousness, appreciative and existential meanings are often inextricably mixed. Literal paradises and hells arise out of this state of primitive undifferentiation; the heights and deeps of our experiences of value are so confused with temporal and spatial magnitudes that belief in the reality of the values is made to rest upon the belief in the physical existence of the symbols. But when this first fusion —and confusion—is broken up, as it ultimately is when the interpretation of the presupposition of reality in this way is no longer possible, i.e., when the object is neither perceptually verifiable nor continuous with other truth judgments, a readjustment of reality-meanings takes place. A restoration of the value in the form of a conception of symbolic or inner truth appears, and, if the value involved is vital, the presupposition of reality outlasts the cruder factual and truth judgments. The history of religions, of Christianity no less than the others, shows this progressive clarification of reality-meanings, the historical culmination in the case of Christianity being the attempt to identify the presupposition of reality implicit in the ideal of perfection with logical or truth objectivity in its most abstract form. The failure of this attempt, as in the Ontological Proof, marks the full realisation of the primacy of values. Experience has shown the remarkable power of religious beliefs to recuperate and readjust themselves, and from this vitality we may probably infer that, until the values of men themselves change, the value judgments of religion need fear nothing from the appearance of new judgments of fact and truth.

III. THE SUFFICIENT REASON OF VALUATION—THE GROUND OR SANCTION OF VALUE

1. *The General Problem of Sufficient Reason or Sanction.*

The situation which our preceding analysis has disclosed is one which has, in many quarters, compelled the abandonment of that form of intellectualism which makes objective value derivative from preformed and already organised judgments of fact and truth. The several meanings of reality and realisation show clearly that normative objectivity, and, therefore, the predicate of reality when applied in the only sense proper in the sphere of values, cannot be *completely* identified with factual and truth objectivity in the narrower sense, either of physical and psychical existence and connections among those existents, or of logical validity. With the realisation of these facts has come the various forms of *a logism*, seeking for concepts and criteria of validity which shall embrace and legitimatise the various reality-meanings not thus reducible, and finding expression, therefore, in a reaching out, either after an independent principle of sufficiency for value judgments, or toward an expansion of the concepts of reason and truth to include grounds not recognised in the older logical and epistemological theories. This general problem—of which our search for the meaning and grounds of normative objectivity is but a special form, may then be properly described as the formulation of a theory of the *Sufficient Reason of Valuation*—or, if the term "reason" seem too intellectualistic in its connotation, *Sufficient Sanction*. It includes the discovery of the ultimate core of meaning in the various demands for reality, and the determination, in the light of this conception, of the various types of experience which constitute sufficient fulfilment of the specific demands. We are thus led to the second aspect of our general problem.

The proposal to develop an independent Sufficient Reason of valuation seems, at first sight, to give away the whole case. Because of the intellectualistic connotation of the word *reason* the task appears predestined to failure, the use of the term reason or ground seeming to refer wholly to grounding in preceding judgments of fact or truth. But the history of the term, as well as its present usage, shows that it has a much wider connotation, and is used interchangeably for truth and value. Leibnitz constantly interchanges the two, and in applying his principle of *sufficient* reason, not only grounds judgments of value in more ultimate judgments of value, but judgments of truth and fact in judgments of value. As synonymous with his principle he sometimes uses the phrase "principle of fitness" (*convenance*) or harmony. We give the sufficient reason of a thing, he says, when, in addition to its abstract possibility, we show its compossibility with other things; and in developing that compossibility he often introduces a concept of *inclining or moral* compossibility—evidently pure worth conceptions. Rationality is ultimately identical with continuity of experience in all its forms. It is true, as I have elsewhere shown,[1] that in the succeeding developments of the principle the tendency has been again to restrict it to judgments of factual and truth objectivity of the types defined, but this has merely had the effect of developing a counter-tendency to the various forms of alogism which characterise the thought of the present.

2. *The Pragmatic Criterion—Criticism.*

This general tendency to alogism appears especially in connection with the problem of illusions and disillusionment which has become so prominent with the development of the causal or scientific point of view. Some of its most interesting

[1] *The History of the Principle of Sufficient Reason: Its Metaphysical and Logical Formulations.* Princeton Contributions to Philosophy, No. 1, The Princeton Press, 1897.

expressions have arisen in connection with just those problems which have emerged in our study of the phenomenology of valuation—whether, namely, the ideal objects with their imputed values are merely illusions, or whether they have some relation to reality. It is present, for instance, in all the works of Guyau, but is especially emphasised in his *Esquise d'une moral*, where in developing a purely positive morality *sans sanction*, either theological or metaphysical, he finds certain value judgments and obligations resting upon assumptions which, from the external point of view of the existential and truth judgments of science, are wholly unfounded, and therefore, illusions. But they are "fruitful" illusions—fruitful for life, and must therefore have some ultimate reality and meaning. Again, it appears to Ehrenfels that, while from the point of view of actual social values the assumptions upon which many subjective worth experiences rest seem fallacious, nevertheless, though illusions, they still have some instrumental value. Finally, we may note the pragmatic point of view of James in his estimate of the subjective and personal worths of religious experience. He deduces their truth from their fruitfulness, and from their value for life is disposed to argue some objective existent. Moreover, and this is an important point, he distinctly denies the jurisdiction of the existential and truth judgments of science, more particularly of physiology and pathology, in the sphere of worth judgment.

In all these cases we have, broadly speaking, an application of the pragmatic criterion. And when closely examined, this latter further seems to be but a special application, with greater intensity of purpose, and to a wider range of phenomena than formerly, of a philosophical formula by no means new, and one which has deserved a more whole-hearted application than it has hitherto received. The formula, wherever there is appearance there is reality, or, in Herbart's terms, " wie viel Schein, so viel Hindeutung auf Sein," has been accepted in some form or other by all except the most extreme intellectualists, but in most cases—and notably in the case of Herbart himself— inveterate rationalistic prejudices have prevented the full development of its implications. The turn which the pragmatist has given to the formula seems to be but an over-emphasis upon one type of indirect conversion of the implicit presupposition of reality, namely the instrumental, and to be due historically to the peculiar emphasis of the present time upon the utility conceptions of biological evolution, with which in fact the pragmatic conception of truth is closely connected.

With that phase of the pragmatist's contention which insists upon a broader conception of reality and truth, one which will include and legitimatise certain incontestable presuppositions of reality implicit in values, we may confess ourselves in sympathy. We have seen that, while values presuppose reality and truth, they do not always presuppose such conceptions of truth as can be abstractly defined in terms of " correspondence of image with object " or of " logical consistency." These, to be sure, constitute grounds of fulfilment or realisation in particular cases, as analysis of the meanings of reality shows. When the presupposition of reality *means* physical or psychical existence or ideal consistency, these constitute the test of reality. But the presupposition of reality means more than this, and the application of such specific criteria as though they were absolute negates the more general conception already formulated, and gives us a generous crop of illusions. With the criticisms of the formulations of " truth in general " and their direct application as criteria of realities, we are therefore in accord, but it is doubtful whether the criterion which is proposed in their place, that of utility or of indirect conversion through instrumental judgments, is adequate either as a definition of the meaning of truth, or as a test of the validity of the various implications of reality. All values have a reference to reality, but the meaning of that reference cannot be exhausted in the concept of utility.

It must, nevertheless, be admitted that the test of utility does from the ground of many judgments of value which have an inner presumption of reality, but are not directly convertible into judgments of existence. The concept of utility has, moreover, been so broadly interpreted as to include all types of instrumental relations, biological, social, and individual. But it is not difficult to see that this concept of pragmatic sanction owes its value primarily to its generality and that it suffers from the same difficulties as the other criteria. As soon as the abstract concepts of " utility," or " fruitfulness for life," are defined and applied to particular situations, certain equivocations arise, and with them certain difficulties.

Thus, if our pragmatism is of the crude type, if we conceive " life " in an external way, then our criterion still fails to include many internal meanings, many intrinsic and individual values which cannot be thus related to the external biological and social existences. Taken in this sense, the criterion is still external, in that it really does not transcend the crude distinction of physical and psychical reality. For the concept of instrumentality, the relation of means to ends, can be applied only to pre-established existents. An idea or ideal can be instrumental to the production only of existences, physical goods, or psychical experiences, and to be thus instrumental it must itself be an existent.

But even if utility is taken in a broader sense, if our pragmatism is of the more refined type, i.e., if we include in our world of pragmatic truth ideal meanings which are individual and intrinsic, such as the ethical and religious "practical absolutes," we can do so only by resorting to a shifting use of the terms utility and instrumental value. Thus, when Augustine says, "I seek thee *in order that* my soul may live," he attributes in this utterance only mediate value to the object of his faith, but when in other utterances he speaks of God as the highest or only good, as goodness and truth itself, the object of his faith appears invested with immediate value. Between the two the pragmatist seems to find no difference, when, as a matter of fact, even pragmatically viewed, there is all the difference in the world—a difference not only in the meaning of the presupposition of reality, but also in the type of experience in which it is realised. This fallacy of equivocation is one to which the pragmatist is constantly prone. He uses his concept of utility primarily to apply to truths in the case of which the value is in the strict sense instrumental, but when he finds truths and values of a purely intrinsic kind, of the higher type of immediacy where the value is immanental and not transgredient, he covers the situation by the use of the general phrase "fruitful for life." This appears in the relative truth which James has been recently according to the concept of the absolute.[1] He admits its function as *practical*, as the means to "moral holidays," and again as the presupposition of the immanental values of æsthetics and religion, but does not realise, although other pragmatists apparently do, that the whole instrumental concept is here in danger. For to realise these experiences, these "holidays," at all, the very condition is that you do not make them conscious ends, and still less means to ends. The condition of their functioning at all is that they

---

[1] James, *Pragmatism*, Longmans, Green & Co., 1907, Lecture II, pp. 73–79.

remain implicit assumptions—otherwise the process is self-defeating. This is what is meant at bottom by the criticism that, as a theory, pragmatism itself lacks pragmatic value. We may conclude, then, that the pragmatist's attempts to characterise in retrospective terms the presupposition of reality in all its meanings is no more ultimate than those which it criticises, and that any conception of the primacy of values which shall be satisfactory must not confine itself to the instrumental conception.

3. *The Ultimate Meaning of the Presupposition of Reality and of its Fulfilment—The Demand for Continuity.*

What, then, is the ultimate ground or sanction of value judgments? The answer to this question evidently involves a deeper analysis of the ultimate presupposition of reality and its satisfaction, one that goes beyond the pragmatic interpretation, valuable as it is as a protest against the logical deduction of values, and as an attempt to widen the concept of sufficient reason. It is equally apparent that the problem centres about those intrinsic values the objects of which are ideals not reducible either directly or indirectly to judgments of fact or truth, and not related instrumentally to values the objects of which have been already acknowledged as true or existent. There are, as our study has abundantly shown, forms of realisation or satisfaction which do not depend for their validity upon either of these kinds of acknowledgment, where, indeed, realisation is possible only on condition that the assumption of reality merges directly into realisation, and that we do not seek to reduce it to retrospective judgments of fact, truth, or utility. The objectivity claimed for the ideal values of ethical, æsthetic, and religious experience cannot be defined in terms of any of these conceptions of direct or indirect conversion into existential and truth judgments. *To determine just what constitutes their sufficient reason we must know what the demand for reality ultimately means.*

A definition of this demand, as a postulate of reflective evaluation, requires a comprehensive analysis of the common element in all the various forms of presumption and assumption as they appear on the different levels of unreflective experience. Here it is no longer a question of the genesis of specific forms of the common presupposition, but of the intelligibility of the

Valuation and Evaluation 401

common element or the logical core which gives it meaning, and which survives its transformation into various forms. If, then, we review our analysis of the axiological predicates—this time, however, with a view to their intension rather than to their extension,—we find but one element which is clearly common to them all, namely, the postulate that our experiences of feeling and will, as subjective and individual, are in some way identical or continuous with a reality that transcends our momentary experience. They have a reference, either transgredient or immanental, beyond themselves. Sometimes this postulate means, as our analysis has shown, that the object, as desired and enjoyed by us, exists in the physical sense; and the value is said to be objective and valid when the feeling of value continues after presumption has passed into existential judgment. Valid also is that subjective feeling of participation when the object of *our* subjective feeling is also the object of other wills than our own, when our feeling and will is continuous with an over-individual experience. Again a subjective feeling of value is valid when it is identical or continuous with dispositions or forms of will in ourselves which have already attained an objective and over-individual reference. These direct, together with the corresponding indirect, forms of conversion through judgments of truth, constitute the usual meanings of realisation. But finally—and this is the most significant point—in the case of intrinsic ideal values the postulate means only *inner identity and continuity of the will with its objects or with itself*, through successive empirical moments of realisation. This internal identity and continuity, as over against the discontinuity of momentary and isolated desires and objects, creates an objectivity within the subject's experience, and constitutes the last meaning of objectivity as reality.

The character of this ultimate form of the postulate gives the key to the meaning of the postulate of identity in all its forms. Here the transcendental reality presupposed is clearly *will*, and the axiological predicate of inner truth means identity of will with will. The other expressions of the postulate are but more indirect and disguised forms of the same claim of identity of subjective with more objectified forms of will. They are specialised demands which have developed as secondary meanings; and, while the desire for existence as such, and for abstract truth, *may* appear apart from other desires, normally factual and truth objectivity are demanded only as instrumental to that inner reality and truth which arises from identity of one act of will with another, and all secondary distinctions are made with a view to the maintenance of that continuity.

The presupposition of reality in all valuation is, then, the identity or continuity of subjective volition with forms of will which transcend the individual and momentary experience— not merely identity of subjective "image" with objective "thing," of subjective will with over-individual in the sense of social will, nor yet of subjective will with itself as objectified as a disposition of a person—but, ultimately *identity of subjective will with a met-empirical will not completely expressed in any of these forms*. Whether that identity is acknowledged, that continuity maintained, by explicit existential judgment after arrest, i.e., after distinction between outer and inner, or by explicit postulation or acknowledgment of persistent assumptions or ideals, or, finally, by the mere continuance of an implicit assumption,—in every case some form of reality or being is acknowledged because of identity of subjective with objective will.

The realisation of this postulate of identity in any of the specific forms of empirical continuity gives objective value. Complete identity would mean absolute value; and, could we formulate this met-empirical will in such a way as to deduce from it its actual content or objects, a system of absolute values or of unconditioned satisfactions could be developed. For objects which could afford the basis of such complete identity would be universal and eternal values, unmodifiable by any empirical conditions, objects of an over-individual will or longing unaffected by the desires and feelings of the individual.

The attempts to define the met-empirical will in terms of realisation of self, or realisation of an impersonal over-individual will interpreted socially, have been criticised in the preceding chapter. The wholly acquired and intra-experiential character of these distinctions and meanings makes it inconceivable that either should be completely identical with the total meaning of the over-individual will; and the analysis of actual value judgments in these spheres showed their relative nature. It is still conceivable, however, that, if the meaning and content of volition should be abstractly enough defined, it might be found ultimate enough to form an absolutely necessary presupposition of all actual volition, and at the same time broad enough to include these, as well as all other, forms of realisation—

and thus to be an incontestable value. The many attempts thus to characterise the unconditioned act of will presupposed in all relative and subjective volitions—as "the will to love," "the will to power," etc., can logically lead only to an abstraction in which all elements of individual desire and emotion are eliminated, and finally to the emptiest of logical abstractions —the will to *pure being*. Such is the recent attempt to ground all values in an over-individual longing, an over-individual will to the self-maintenance of the world, or, more briefly, " Wille zur Welt." [1] Suggestive as this characterisation of the ultimate presupposition of reality undeniably is—as a logical characterisation, it is too thin an abstraction upon which to build a world of actual values. For, either it includes in it the concrete content of an already defined and realised world, or else it means nothing more than mere persistence or continuity of will. In the first case, the relativity of all ideal construction makes it impossible to show the absolute identity of actual ideals and their realisations with such a will; the postulate of eternity of value does not include the eternity of specific objects of value. In the second case, the very abstractness of the meaning of will as thus defined makes it so empty a concept that it is useless as a criterion of evaluation until it is reduced to the specific forms of the demand for continuity. Viewed in either way, it is useless as a point of departure for developing a system of absolute values.

From such reflections it seems necessary to conclude that the presupposition of reality, realised in various forms of actual worth experience, cannot be defined in such a way as to deduce from it absolute values. It can be characterised merely as a postulate of the continuity of value, the persistence of will and its satisfaction beyond *any empirical forms* which it may assume. The logical, or better axiological, postulate of identity of the empirical with the met-empirical will becomes for practical purposes the demand for continuity of empirical desire and feeling, for continuity of subjective with already objectified forms of will. The real problem is, then, to find the empirical forms in which the demand for continuity appears, and to determine the extent to which the empirically derived objects fulfil these demands.

[1] Hugo Münsterberg, *Philosophie der Werte: Grundzüge einer Weltanschauung*. Leipzig: Verlag Johann Ambrosius Barth, 1908.

4. The Postulate of Continuity: Acquirement and Conservation of Value—Practical Absolutes.

The two forms in which this demand appears in immediate experience are the transgredient and immanental references of feelings of value. When, however, these references become the explicit demands of reflective evaluation, they appear as the postulates of *acquirement* and *conservation* of meaning or value. In order that the function of valuation may continue, that volition may persist, new values must be acquired, and those already acquired must persist or be conserved in new objects on new levels. Every specific form of the demand for continuity may, therefore, be comprehended in these two aspects of the general postulate of valuation.

It is, perhaps, idle to raise the question as to which of the two aspects is ultimate. In his admirable discussion of religious values, Höffding [1] makes the concept of conservation the more ultimate, deducing the demand for acquirement from conservation on the ground that the condition of the persistence of value is the creation of new values. But further reflection seems to require a reversal of this relation. The inmost principle of sufficient reason of volition, and the ultimate criterion of normative objectivity alike, are to be found in the fact that an act of will affords the basis for ever new forms of will, and that a value is but the starting-point for new values. But in this principle is included the further postulate that any volition already fulfilled, any value experienced, is conserved in some form as the platform for new volitions and values, that any essential value persists in new forms of reality. The postulate of conservation is a retrospective formula having reference to those implicit assumptions which constitute the indispensable conditions of continuity of valuation.

In the recognition of this fact—that the postulate of conservation is included in the ultimate presupposition of reality, we have finally the basis for an understanding of the function of the axiological predicates of existence and truth. The judgment of value, while an appreciation, is one which includes reality; while assertorial in form, it has a hypothetical reference to reality. The predicates of existence and truth are, when

---

[1] Höffding, *The Philosophy of Religion*, translation from the German edition. Macmillan & Co., 1906. pp. 215 ff.

used axiologically, the explicit meanings developed in the interest of conservation of the implicit presupposition. As prospective ideals, values require merely that *inner* truth which is identical with value. As norms conserving the values already acquired, and forming the basis of new values, they must have that *outer* existence and truth which makes them objective and over-individual. The demand for outer existence and truth in its various forms is but an expression of the demand for persistence and conservation, and the predicates in which this demand is acknowledged are the signs of such conservation.

It is also clear that any form of existence or truth may, under certain circumstances, have absolute value. Any of the objects of actual desire, any of the ideal constructions developed in the empirical processes of valuation, may become practical absolutes in that their persistence is demanded unconditionally. The will to live, the will to be a person, and the will to participate may, as we have seen, under certain circumstances, be unconditional, and the realisation of certain objects of will, as for instance, the minimum of existence, of characterisation, or of participation, may have absolute value. The feeling of absolute obligation in its several forms appears in connection with those objects which are without capacity of substitution, and which are therefore assumed to be the indispensable conditions of continuity of valuation. In general it may be said that the feeling of absolute value of the existence or truth of certain concrete objects thus arises because, under the empirical conditions of their origin, already described, they are the objects in which the met-empirical postulate of identity finds concrete expression in an individual demand. While there are no absolute values in the theoretical sense that the object of the individual empirical will can be shown to be absolutely identical with the object of the met-empirical will, the empirically derived presupposition identical with the logical presupposition, there are, nevertheless, as we have seen, practical absolutes, objects which in specific situations are the indispensable conditions of realisation of the postulate of continuity.

5. *Axiological Sufficiency—The Well-Founded Value.*

The presupposition of reality, the claim to objectivity, means then, ultimately, the fulfilment of the postulate of continuity of value in its two forms of acquirement and conservation.

The significance of this conclusion is far-reaching. If this is what the postulate of valuation ultimately means, the sufficient reason of any assumption of reality, any subjective experience of feeling or will, is to be found in just this continuity, in the fact that it maintains itself in succeeding experiences of feeling and will. Unhindered activity or continuity is the source of reality and value. Judgments of existence or of logical consistency are merely special forms of registering the fact that specific presuppositions have maintained themselves. They are but secondary modifications of the primary feeling of reality. An incontestable assumption, postulate, or belief registers the same fact.

This is the axiological meaning of certain facts brought out in our psychological analysis. We have seen (pp. 42–49) that it is not the entrance of a new element, the existential judgment, which makes the *mere idea,* until now unreal, objective and real; but it is rather the process of abstraction—by which an "objective," with primitive presupposition of reality, is turned into a *mere* object, that creates the feeling of unreality. When this abstraction has taken place, when the presumption of reality is disturbed, it must, to be sure, be restored in some explicit acknowledgment of the presupposition of reality, but unless disturbed it is valid. No less valid, it may be added, are any secondary and derived assumptions and postulates which form the basis of continuity of actual experience of value.

This being the meaning of the presupposition of reality and of its fulfilment, it is clear in what direction the criterion of its realisation must be found. It is apparent that we must look, not for *absolute grounds,* but for *sufficient sanctions* of value judgments, not for absolute norms, but for well-founded ideals of value. The postulate of identity of the empirical with the met-empirical will is realised, not in absolute, but in *sufficient* identities—i.e., sufficient for the continuity of value. Here, then, in this question of the nature of axiological sufficiency lies our real problem. For, if it is true that we cannot find points of absolute logical identity between the objects of the empirical and met-empirical will, it is no less true, as we have already seen, that the concept of mere continuity is useless until made more concrete and practical. A closer scrutiny of the concept of sufficiency is demanded, and here again the thinking of Leibnitz is suggestive.

For him, as we have seen, rationality and continuity are

identical. But complete continuity of finite objects with the ultimate reality, and therefore absolute grounding, would require, as he says, "infinite analysis." Nevertheless, in order that a phenomenon may be "well-founded," in order that practical distinctions may be made between the subjective and the objective, such infinite analysis is not necessary. It is required merely that the analysis shall be sufficient, that it shall satisfy a specific form of the demand for continuity, i.e., sufficient in the sense in which we say of a certain magnitude that it is sufficient when it satisfies a given equation.[1] In like manner, recalling the steps of our argument up to this point, we may say that a value is well-founded when it fulfils a *specific* presupposition of reality. In the case of a value judgment, the "equation" to be satisfied is formed by the analysis of the specific presupposition of reality or demand for objectivity implicit in a value judgment, and its solution consists in determining the specific meaning of the predicate of reality which satisfies that demand. The entire question is one of relevancy. With regard to the world of cognitive judgment, Leibnitz says: "Although this entire life were said to be nothing but a dream, and the visible world nothing but a phantasm, I should call this dream or phantasm real enough if we are never deceived by it, when we use our reason rightly."[2] In like manner, paraphrasing Leibnitz's thought for the sphere of practical value judgment, we may say: a value is real and objective enough if it maintains itself, if the ideal continues when we reason and will rightly, i.e., if we do not take the presumption or assumption of reality to mean that which, in the light of its place in the system of our experiences, it does not, and indeed cannot mean.

The applications of this principle to the practical reasonings, anticipations, and postulates of our individual and social, of our economic, ethical, religious, and æsthetic life, are comprehensive and varied, and to some of these applications we shall direct attention in the sequel. Here we may note, merely in the light of what has preceded, that it introduces into our application of the criterion of continuity that element of *control* which gives it practical axiological value. For it tells us this much negatively at least—that the objectivity or reality implicit in a value, although well-founded, need not necessarily

---

[1] R. Latta, *Leibnitz: The Monadology, etc.* Oxford: The Clarendon Press, 1898, p. 236, note.
[2] *De Modo distinguendi phenomena realia ab imaginariis.* Ed. J. E. Erdmann, Berlin, 1840, 444a.

mean identity with factual or truth objectivity of any of the types described. Reality of ideals does not necessarily mean their translation into terms of social objectivity or existence; nor can we infer that specific appreciative constructions or ideals will continue in precisely the same form. We have found that, except in the case of the most ultimate personal worths, these ideals have capacity of substitution. As long as new experiences arise, so long there will be new valuations. A highest value, other than the practical absolutes of the personal sphere, is not demonstrable. Value can be preserved only by transformations, and all that we can say is that, since value persists, the essential value in any ideal will be acknowledged in new constructions and new existential judgments.

IV. Application of the Principle of Sufficient Reason or Sanction of Valuation—Its Relation to Concrete Norms and Assumptions

1. *The General Problem.*

The criterion of normative objectivity, of reality in the only sense in which it is applicable to values when conceived comprehensively, has now been developed. Its implication with respect to an ultimate postulate of worth continuity, and its further implication that sufficiency is always relative to a specific presupposition of reality, includes, I think, all that is significant in the pragmatic criterion and furnishes the key to the ultimate grounds of valuation. In the concept of *sufficient* as distinguished from *absolute* ground of value, and in the definition of sufficiency as relative to specific continuities and specific presuppositions, we have, moreover, the point of connection between the axiological and phenomenological points of view—between the specific presuppositions, presumptions and assumptions as genetically derived, and the presupposition of reality as logically interpreted. Our task is, therefore, not to deduce logically a system of values from one absolute incontestable value, but rather to interpret the actual demands and presuppositions of valuations axiologically, i.e., to show the relation of the actual presuppositions of concrete values to the ultimate logical presupposition of valuation, the degree to which continuity of valuation is realised in specific ideals.

Of the possible meanings of the claim to reality or normative objectivity, only that of inner reality and truth requires special consideration. In the other cases normative objectivity is identical with factual and truth objectivity, and the realisation of the presupposition of reality requires acknowledgment in specific existential and truth judgments. Only by such conversion of presumption and assumption into judgment is continuity of valuation possible, is the value as a subjective experience well-founded. The test of the well-founded value in this case presents no special problem. The claim to reality is specific in its meaning, and the illusions which follow its misinterpretation are manifest to all who tamper unwittingly with the physical and economic worlds. But with the claim of intrinsic ideals to inner truth and reality the case is different. Here validity does not involve complete conversion of assumption into already determined fact and truth; the faiths embodied in such ideals need not be completely actualised in the specific spheres of physical and social reality. What, then, are the specific tests which such claims must fulfil in order to be accepted as well-founded?

(a) Inner Truth has a Reference to Inner Existence or Psychical Matter of Fact.—The Nature of this Reference.

The fact that ideals transcend experience in the sense that they do not demand complete conversion into factual and truth judgments, i.e., continuity at every point with the objective world of science, has been taken to mean, as we have seen, that here the presupposition of reality is to be interpreted as an assumption of universality and eternity of the values involved. If this is its meaning, then, of course, there are no empirical tests of sufficiency, any reference to actual empirically conditioned feeling and will being irrelevant. But this interpretation of the presupposition of reality we have found to be a logical distortion of its meaning. While the ultimate postulate of valuation is an assumption of the eternity of value, it does not include the eternity of specific objects and concepts of value; while it assumes identity with an over-individual will, it does not assume that identity without a difference comprehended in the concept of logical universality. Again, while ideals transcend experience in the sense defined, they nevertheless have their roots in certain regions of experience and fact.

Founded as they are upon psychical matter of fact, they contain an implicit reference to retrospectively defined reality which must be made explicit and subjected to test. Can the nature and measure of this reference be defined, and can this definition be applied reflectively to the evaluation of ideals and the judgments based upon them—in other words, to the differentiation of valid ideals from " pathetic fallacies " ?

The nature of this reference is not difficult to define in general terms. Whenever the claim to objectivity is made in the case of ideal values and their norms, this claim includes the belief that they are realisable in some fashion. We live by ideals, it is true, but only because they are at the same time realities. An ideal, as soon as it becomes practical, is an anticipation of reality. The claim to universality and eternity has no meaning until in that claim we admit the temporal anticipation that, with the actual empirical extension or persistence of the ideal, there will be a corresponding actual fulfilment in empirical realisations, that the postulate of continuity will be realised in its two aspects of acquirement and conservation. But anticipations are meaningless and groundless unless based upon some reference to fact, and in this case the " matter of fact " is what we call broadly "human nature," human feeling and volition in its various aspects and forms.

This very general characterisation of the reference to matter of fact implied in all ideals can, moreover, be made more definite for the purposes of axiology. Using the form of words employed in the Introduction, and now charged with a fuller meaning, we may say : every assertion of value involves *ipso facto* an assertion of its conformity with the laws of feeling and will. The abstract formulations of the normative sciences, their ideals and norms, cannot be anything else than the development, in other terms and for other purposes, of what, from another point of view, we call psychological laws. As now understood, the empirical laws of valuation have axiological significance ; it is through them that the specific empirical demands are to be interpreted. For the processes of feeling and will, in which ideals are constructed, permanent dispositions are formed, and the presuppositions of value judgments are established, are *real processes of the real will*. They determine the specific conditions of the realisation of the met-empirical will presupposed in all valuation ; they create spheres of actual and possible experiences which in turn condition the inner reality of ideals. The sufficient reason or sanction of ideals must therefore include the question whether they are axiologically possible, and in what sense and within what limits they are possible.

This conception of the relation of validity to psychical matter of fact is inevitable for any one who holds that every actual experience of value, while presupposing objective validity, is, nevertheless, in one aspect a subjectively conditioned feeling, that every judgment of value, however over-individual its reference, must express the *felt* realisations of some subject. Nor does such a view commit its holder to that form of *Psychologismus* which identifies continuity of feeling as a mere psychical fact with continuity of value as an axiological principle. It merely sets him in opposition to the view which holds that realisation and satisfaction are unrelated to empirical feeling. For us the disjunction between logical validity and psychical fact is not complete; the genetic conception, with its implication of the reality of the developing processes of feeling and will—an implication which we have seen underlies all appreciative description and the genetic method to which it gives rise—constitutes a middle ground. Upon this middle ground our solution of the problem must be based.

(b) *Axiological Sufficiency and Possibility*.

The sufficient reason of a judgment which contains any implication or presupposition of reality must, as Leibnitz long ago pointed out, include a reference to possibility. In addition to possibility every such judgment must have a further mark, which Leibnitz describes as the special characteristic of sufficiency—" compossibility," or compatibility of the given judgment with other established judgments. The region of the possible is negative, and is determined by the application of the principle of non-contradiction; that of compossibility is more positive, and is determined by the harmony of the given concept, judgment, or postulate with the entire system of experience and the ultimate postulate of continuity which underlies it.

That sufficiency must include possibility and compossibility is clear, but, in order that we may apply these conceptions to the region of worth experience, we must see just what meaning they have in connection with valuation. That there may be contradiction between facts and values which make values, at least in the form originally conceived or presented, impossible, that there may be disharmonies or incompatibilities between values and values, between ideals and ideals, which require the elimination or reconstruction of ideals, are facts which are patent to all. But these contradictions and disharmonies cannot be reduced to logical terms. As it is impossible to say that a logically necessary conception is *ipso facto* a felt value, so it is impossible to say that a contradiction in feeling and will is necessarily reducible to abstract logic. What, then, is the meaning of the possible and compossible in the sphere of valuation, and what is its axiological interpretation?

The whole question is evidently one of relevancy. What realms of fact and what laws are relevant in the determination of axiological possibility? This question we have already considered in a general way in the concluding paragraphs of Chapter VI. It is a pertinent question, we found, to ask whether an ideal is possible—whether, for instance, to consider again the illustration there used, it is rational for a man to desire indefinite increase of a valued disposition on the assumption that with this increase there would be increase of value. It is not pertinent, however, to answer the question by showing that the assumption is in contradiction with inferences from the principle of the conservation of energy. The only question that is relevant is whether such an assumption conforms to inner psychical matter of fact, to the laws of feeling and will. Again, it is pertinent to ask whether certain ideals of social good are possible, whether, for instance, the will to universalise altruistic dispositions, or to make the maxim of one's conduct an eternal law, presupposes assumptions which are or are not in harmony with the fundamental facts and laws of social value. The assumption in this case is that amount, i.e., frequency of repetition, is accompanied by corresponding increase of instrumental value, an assumption which is not in harmony with the laws of participation value. But here also there is *only* one type of existential judgment which is relevant —namely judgment concerning the psychical dispositions determined by the working of the laws of sympathetic participation. In general it may be said that, while there are specific regions of inner psychical fact which must enter into the retrospective evaluation of any such ideal or assumption, there are entire regions of outer fact and truth which are totally irrelevant, namely the causal and mechanical generalisations of physical science. They are without competency in this connection, because they are formed for an entirely different purpose, and by abstracting wholly from the experience with which we are here concerned.

The question of compossibility or compatibility of value judgments involves something more than possibility. Here the question is one of compatibility of the presuppositions of one value judgment with those of another; and it arises in all those cases of judgment and volition which involve transition from one norm or ideal to another—either continuity between different types or levels of valuation, or the reduction of norms and standards to a single ideal. The working of the fundamental laws of valuation and worth construction, the value movements from lower to higher levels, create those appreciative distinctions or qualitative differences in the meanings of our feelings, which, while not absolute and a priori, nevertheless are *practically* absolute in the sense that they fix the limits to the activity of specified ideals. It is chiefly in the attempts to universalise specific ideals, as, for instance, the ideals of pleasure, perfection, and self-sacrifice, that incompatibilities appear.

The general relation of possibility to compossibility is now clear. In the former, the creation of psychical disposition determines the possibility or impossibility of certain feelings and volitions. In the latter, the development of dispositions, ideals, and levels creates certain conscious meanings and distinctions, certain universes of appreciative discourse which mutually limit and determine each other. In the main it may be said that the special studies of the different types of value feelings and judgments—their conditions, laws, and limits— were studies in axiological possibility, while those concerned more specifically with the problems of synthetic preference and valuation dealt with problems of compossibility.

Having thus distinguished the two concepts of possibility and compossibility, it is possible to unite them again in a more comprehensive concept. As the well-founded ideal value is that which makes possible continuity of valuation, so the ideal which is not well founded is that which develops discontinuity. Where impossibility and incompatibility appear the process is "self-defeating." In this concept of the self-defeating process we have a negative test of validity.

The full significance of this concept is apparent only when it is recognised that it is volitional in meaning and transcends the sphere of merely logical contradiction. That it is capable of almost purely logical statement is evidenced by the extensive use of the principle of "endless regress" and of self-defeating activities of thought, as seen especially in the antinomies. But even here, as Bosanquet [1] has pointed out, the real meaning is ultimately affective-volitional. The wearisome vanity of these empty repetitions without hope of unity or finality, without repose of realisation and satisfaction of the will, is what really leads to value movement to new types of activity and ideal construction. That this is Kant's ultimate meaning appears, I think, from the close connection of his doctrine of antinomies with his practical philosophy. The transition from the agnosticism of the theoretical to the faith of the practical reason is a value movement on a large scale. Be this as it may, that the principle is essentially one of volition and valuation rather than of thought and logic, appears from the fact that, while, as we shall see later, all logical applications of the principle are referable to volitional categories, not all applications to valuation are logical. This is especially apparent in the so-called hedonistic paradox, where the pursuit of pleasure is said to be self-defeating—not because of a logical contradiction, but of an inherent character of the practical will. The self-defeating process is accordingly one which arises when we will an idea in connections in which the ideal is untenable, wherever there is demand for a type of realisation which is inherently impossible. Correspondingly, all fallacies of valuation arise in the acknowledgment of the primary presupposition of reality in spheres of existence and truth not comprehended or implied in this presupposition.

2. *Application of these Principles to Specific Problems.*

In this conception of axiological possibility and compossibility, we have the sufficient sanction of ideal values, the sufficient reason or criterion of their inner truth. The application of this criterion in connection with the specific problems which have emerged in the course of our investigation, and which have been emphasised at the beginning of this chapter, would involve practically the rehearsal of the entire content of the preceding discussion. Though tedious, it would not be difficult to show that the entire question of what are realisable and

[1] *Logic*, Vol. I, p. 173.

well-founded ideals, in the various forms in which it presents itself in the economic and moral, individual and social life, must ultimately find its solution by reference to this sort of truth and rationality. The disputes between the individualist and the socialist, for instance, as to what are possible and impossible motives, practicable or impracticable ideals, imply certain assumptions, on the part of both, which can be tested only by the application of such axiological criteria. Thus the question of the desirability of certain forms of distribution of economic goods, of the extension of certain moral dispositions—their effect upon values—raises the further question of the relation of individual to social values, whether, more specifically, certain values are not conditioned by their being exceptional and isolated by personal and group contrasts, and whether, even if their extension were economically and psychologically possible, such a process would not be axiologically self-defeating in that they would then be incompatible with other values.

With equal truth it may probably be said that whatever fallacies appear in such reasonings about and anticipations of values, are in the main a specific axiological form of the material fallacies of composition and accident, fallacies which arise from what may, perhaps, be called false quantities in volition. Thus the assumption that a motive which has its origin in a limited participation in class consciousness, and which has attained its intensity and extension within that class by the fact of contrast and opposition, would, if universalised, exist in the same clearness and intensity, is one which requires examination, and may possibly contain a fallacy which vitiates the entire argument in which it appears. When the socialist argues that the motives which have been characteristic of special classes, such as the military, artistic, or philanthropic, could be extended to all industrial activity, he may be right—there may be certain universal elements unmodifiable by specific function, but any prediction of the form they would assume, or of the results of such universalisation, is liable to errors of this type. Equally doubtful is any argument which proceeds upon the assumption that the ideals which actuate men in exceptional situations, and which are perfectly legitimate expectations in the sphere of personal obligation and imputation, are susceptible of repeated application in normal circumstances or of universal extension. On the other hand, we have the converse fallacy when we apply the laws of social value judgment of men *en masse* to individual situations and persons—when we seek to argue from economic and sociological generalities, made for certain purposes, to the nature and capacities of individual originators of values.

(a) *Again the Monistic Theories of Ultimate Value.*

But with such special problems we are not here concerned. Our object is rather to show in a general way the principles which underlie all reflective evaluation of ideals and values. Nevertheless, while we cannot take up this criticism in detail, we may in conclusion profitably return to a reconsideration, from our present point of view, of the question of ultimate ideals and norms as presented in the preceding chapter. To such assumptions of ultimate ends, and their corresponding norms, all the special assumptions which we have just been considering in turn go back, and the question of their validity or workableness is closely connected with the more ultimate question of the validity of the ideals on which they rest.

In all reasonings and anticipations of the type described, some single ideal, such as happiness, self-realisation, or realisation of over-individual social good, is usually presupposed, either explicitly or implicitly. These ideals are implicitly assumed as norms of certain types of judgments of obligation and imputation, but, in the several monistic theories discussed, each has also been taken separately as the absolute ideal of valuation, as the single explicit end of all volition. Examination of our actual feelings and judgments has shown us that they do not afford ground for such monistic theories. The method of testing these ideals and norms employed in the preceding chapter showed that they break down at the limits. Now, with our present conceptions of possibility and compossibility, we may see why these single ideals, *as single ideals*, are not well-founded.

In general it may be said that, with reference to certain situations, in connection with certain processes and levels of valuation, each of these ideals is well-founded, in that the funded meaning finds realisation, in that the postulate of continuity, as we have defined it, finds fulfilment. These ideals or assumptions prove illusory and fallacious, however, when, abstracted from the specific processes in which they are developed and which they in turn control, they are universalised and conceived to hold absolutely and unconditionally. It is then that impossibilities and incompatibilities appear; and they appear just because the very act of taking them unconditionally involves a misinterpretation of the presupposition of reality. These general principles have been applied, either consciously or unconsciously, in the many criticisms of Hedonism which have sought to show its self-defeating character and to display its practical fallacies, but they have significance for us only in their general logical bearings, and these can be shown in a few words. The ideas of pleasure or happiness are, as we have seen, ideal constructions. As objects, as passive states, they are abstractions, the product of a process of abstraction exercised upon our "condition" worths, including the primary condition worths together with the complementary values, ethical and æsthetic, which arise on that level. Now, within certain limits, this abstraction has a basis in reality, i.e., the desire for pleasure is well-founded. When we believe pleasure to exist, and assume that it may be attained, our belief and assumption are justified by the fact that up to a certain point the assumptions are realised, not indeed in "pleasures," but in actual worth feelings. This "point" is determined by the nature of the processes and laws in which the ideal is implicit or embedded. As a convenient representation of objects of condition worth, and within the limits of the laws governing such values, it is a well-founded object of conation. But when applied beyond that sphere—to represent personal worths, for instance, its capacity as an object of continuous valuation disappears, as may be seen in the fact that it is not a substitute for personal worth. No less fallacious is the attempt to substitute a sum of pleasures for over-individual, social good; for the fulfilment of the demand for this good does not include necessarily, i.e., in so far as the test of experience can show, the realisation of the demand for pleasure.

The self-defeating or paradoxical character of Hedonism as a monistic ideal appears, therefore, at two specific points. If I assume pleasure to be an object of absolute value, in the sense of a perpetually tenable end, my experiences will probably prove such an assumption unfounded and illusory, for the reason that it is in contradiction with the laws of *condition* worths in connection with which the idea alone has meaning. The assumption is axiologically impossible, for it is contrary to the laws of valuation. On the other hand, if I proceed upon the assumption that pleasure may be taken to represent indiscriminately all values on whatever level, I am equally subjected to practical illusions; my assumption turns out to be incompatible with those fundamental appreciative distinctions which have been genetically developed, and is, therefore, axiologically incompossible. In both cases the presupposition of reality in the ideal of pleasure has been misinterpreted, reality has been claimed where the claim cannot be realised.

No less paradoxical and self-defeating is the universalising of the ideal of over-individual and impersonal good with its corresponding norm, for here, again, such a process involves a misinterpretation of the presupposition of reality. The classical criticisms of this ideal, as for instance Schiller's criticism of the Kantian conception of obedience to an absolute law uncontaminated by individual feeling, and Spencer's criticism of absolute altruism, emphasise the unreality of the ideal, its incompatibility with other fundamental values. Wherein does this unreality consist?

Our study of the nature and origin of the ideal of over-individual and impersonal good has shown it to be also an abstraction standing for certain concrete social ideals which emerge in the processes of social participation. As such it has a certain reality. But in this case the presupposition of reality, the demand for realisation implicit in the ideal, can mean only one thing—namely, that type of outer existence described as social, which consists in the fact that the ideal as subjective experience finds its fulfilment or realisation in a corresponding over-individual and social demand. If it cannot be thus fulfilled, the ideal is empty and lacks reality, and the judgments of obligation and imputation founded upon it are fallacious. Normative objectivity implies factual objectivity, i.e., an ideal in order to have reality must have actual participation value. Such ideals are well-founded, therefore, just in so far as they are in conformity with the laws of participation value which determine both the nature and the extent of the demand which gives them their reality.

When, however, the subject acts and judges as though the presupposition of reality or claim to objectivity means, not this factual objectivity, but that purely logical objectivity characterised as universality and eternity, fallacies both of obligation and imputation arise. Ideals and their norms are abstracted from the empirical processes of emotional participation of persons and groups, and instead of being treated as founded upon actual desire and its satisfaction, they are held to be determined by a wholly over-individual and impersonal will. The self-defeating character of such an assumption appears in the fact, as shown in detail in preceding chapters,[1] that the ideal either becomes an unreal abstraction or passes over into a wholly individual and personal value.

We are finally brought, then, to the question of the reality of the personal ideal and of personal values. Here the claim to absoluteness takes the form of the ideal of perfection; "perfection is eternal." A certain paradoxical and self-defeating character has been charged to this ideal also, and without doubt it may give rise to fallacies both of judgment and action, which must engage our attention. Our first task, however, is to determine to what extent it is well-founded, what is the true interpretation of the presupposition of reality.

Like the ideals already considered, it is an ideal construction developed in certain empirical processes. In these processes funded meaning is acquired, and within certain limits this funded meaning is realised in certain actual feelings, ethical, æsthetic, and religious. The forms in which the ideal of personal value appears are, as our study has shown, the ideal of absolute sacrifice at the characterisation minimum and of complete inner harmony. That these ideals have a certain basis in reality is indicated by the fact that they form the presupposition of the very real experiences of personal obligation and of æsthetic realisations of intrinsic values. But the condition of the realisation of these values is the isolation of the personality. The ideal of perfection is the organising principle of the personal series, but it is realised only in so far as it remains implicit in that process. The presupposition of reality or the claim to objectivity in this case means just that inner continuity and reality of the ideal which we have found to be the ultimate meaning of normative objectivity. In so far as the ideal remains thus an implicit organising principle of experience, it is an assumption which includes its own reality, fulfilling the demands of possibility and compossibility alike, as our study of the laws of valuation in this sphere has shown. The personal obligations felt, and the æsthetic and religious values imputed on the basis of the belief in perfection, are not pathetic fallacies, but the highest realities. But let this meaning of reality be misinterpreted, let us seek to convert this inner reality into outer reality through

[1] Chapters XII and XIII.

existential and instrumental judgments, and illusions and unrealities appear.

Of these false applications of the ideal of personal perfection, the one most commonly emphasised is that which appears when we make the implicit presupposition or norm of personal obligations and imputations an explicit end, single and conscious, to which other ends and values are sacrificed. In this case the process is self-defeating, and pathetic sentimentalities and unrealities appear. Self-forgetfulness is no less the condition of perfection than of happiness, and those single experiences which come by the grace of the gods are not to be repeated at will. The quasi-æsthetic moment of isolation, deeply as it is rooted in reality, is not to be petrified into a permanent attitude without loss of value and reality. The fallacy of the situation is again misinterpretation of the presupposition of reality. In this case the subject of the illusion assumes that realisation of the ideal means its actualisation in certain psychical states. Assuming that reality means psychical existence, an intrinsic ideal is turned into a means to ends; it becomes instrumental to certain psychical experiences, and the inevitable consequence is the "backward value movement" to the hedonic accompaniments of the ideal. No less fallacious is that other application of the ideal in which the assumption of its reality is interpreted as demand for existence in the social sense. As social ideals and norms become empty and unreal when abstracted from the empirical processes of participation in which they are constructed and which they control, so here expectations generated in the ideal construction of the personality do not necessarily find fulfilment in social demand.

(b) *Inferences from the Application of Axiological Principles to Special Problems.*

From this axiological criticism of ultimate assumptions two conclusions may be drawn. In the first place the working out of our principle—that the sufficient sanction of an ideal with its assumption of reality is always relative to the specific meaning of reality implied, has shown us that, while it is the nature of ideals to transcend experience, in that they are not completely convertible into factual and truth judgments, nevertheless they are real, and control experience only in so far as they are well-founded anticipations of experience. Some reference to experience already organised is necessary.

But a second conclusion of even greater importance may be drawn—namely, that the general principle of indifference of judgments of value to judgments of truth and fact *at certain points* is substantiated by an examination of the grounds of different judgments. This relative independence is seen first of all in the indifference of judgments of value, where the presupposition of reality means one kind of fact or truth, to other judgments of value implying another kind of fact or truth, where, to be more explicit, distinctions of inner and outer truth are drawn. Thus a certain indifference of personal and social values has shown itself at various points, and has become so constant as to be almost of the nature of a fundamental principle, into the meaning of which we may well inquire more fully.

If we view social values and their mutations from the external point of view of mere matter of fact, we must, as we have seen,[1] judge certain values to be normal, others to be aspiring, and still others to be outlived. But to the individual who casts in his lot with any of these values, who realises himself in identifying himself with them, our judgments of fact are relatively indifferent. The reactionary judges or assumes what you, as an impartial spectator, have inferred to be an outlived value, to be of absolute worth, and if he realises, in sacrifice of self for it, the highest personal worth, *that is his test*, and *your* existential judgments are irrelevant. The same may be said of a reformer who throws himself into an aspiring worth, and even of the normal man who finds harmony and peace in living the life of his day.

On the other hand, it is equally true that much that is of significance from the personal point of view is irrelevant for objective social values as a system of forces. The fate of the personal worths is a matter of indifference. They seem to play the rôle of epiphenomena. The working of the laws of personal worth construction may produce the values of inner peace and tragical elevation in connection with narrow group worths and outlived values which, from the point of view of the factual judgments of the objective system, are merely individual in their meaning, and luxuries which have no appreciable instrumental value, or which, if they have any value

[1] Chap. XI, pp. 333 ff.

at all through social imitation, are practically negligible. Often they appear as pathetic fallacies, resting upon judgments and assumptions which do not conform to the system of values judged as a system of fact. Our valuation of extremes of altruism is often possible only by an abstraction of the person from his relations to society.[1]

But the relative indifference discoverable at this point becomes still more marked when we leave the sphere of ethical and social judgments and consider judgments of value in their relation to the more neutral or "*wertfrei*" judgments of science. If there is indifference at those points where judgments of value and fact seem most closely related, it is needless to say that the indifference will become much more pronounced where the scientific constructions and formulas are still more remote from value judgments, and abstract still more from appreciation in their descriptions. The indifference of judgments of value to the constructions of science becomes progressively more marked as we pass from the centre to the periphery, from social and economic to physiological, biological, and physical constructions. It is only when the abstract conceptions of science are really not abstract, when they still contain an appreciative connotation, that conflicts arise. Only when science uses symbols which have a worth connotation, when she talks of the abysses of space, of fate, of the reign of law, of the struggle for existence, of survival of the fittest, etc., does she come into contradiction with values. And these contradictions arise precisely because when she thus talks another language she becomes progressively more and more symbolic and equivocal. But this indifference is always, it must be remembered, relative and genetic, not absolute.

V. Conclusion
1. *Existence—Truth—Value.*

The development of a point of view in evaluation distinctive enough to merit the special term axiological, or, in other words,

---

[1] For a fuller discussion of the point, see the writer's two papers, *The Individual and the Social Value Series*, Philosophical Review, Vol. XI, Nos. 2 and 3. Also *Ehrenfels: System der Werttheorie*, Vol. II, p. 153. An impartial observation of the empirical data, Ehrenfels confesses, shows us that the concepts "socially valuable," and "individual-ethical" are only partially and occasionally identical, that, as a matter of fact, "there are certain dispositions and actions which come under the concept of the individual-ethical which from the standpoint of social morality must be designated indifferent."

of a special principle of Sufficient Reason or Sanction of valuation and value judgments, seems to have found its justification in the concrete problems which it both reveals and solves. The fact that judgments of value have as their " objective " a reality not fully exhausted by factual and logical objectivity is made clear by the merely partial and relative identities of normative with factual and truth objectivity, and by the principles of practical estimation of values which the recognition of this fact brings about.

But while we have in these axiological principles the grounds for the practical distinction between subjectively and objectively conditioned values, between practical reality and illusion, there is still unquestionably something to be desired from the more theoretical point of view. The concepts of existence and reality, of truth and value, are left sufficiently unrelated to give some ground for the criticism that the full implication of our discussion of the relations of these concepts is still to be developed. Somewhere, it will be said, there must be a point of ultimate anchorage, a point of complete identity between reality—the " objective " of judgments of value and fact alike, and one or the other of these subordinate concepts, an identity so complete and definite—of reality with value or reality with truth—that in the one case all facts and truths may be seen to be forms of value, or, in the other, all values aspects of truth. Ultimately we must face this last question: Does all truth and fact rest upon an incontestable value, an absolutely tenable attitude of will, or do values rest ultimately upon an undeniable truth the opposite of which is unthinkable? Is the ultimate statement of the situation to be in intellectualistic or voluntaristic terms?

That some answer to this question is implied in, and, in a sense perhaps demanded by, our preceding discussions, can scarcely be denied. And there can be no doubt that the whole drift of our discussion has been in the direction of a concept of the primacy of value and of the value judgment, in the sense that the " objective " or intent of the predicates of reality is always value, and that the existential and truth judgments are but special forms of valuation. Let us, then, in conclusion, seek to find the logical ground of this inference, to take this last logical step.

2. The Meaning of the Concepts of Indifference and Relevancy.

Evidently the point in our discussion where the logical implications were not completely drawn is to be found in our conceptions of relative indifference of value and truth, and of merely partial identity of normative with factual and truth objectivity. To some such position we were driven by our analysis, and with the admission of the fact we apparently accepted the old dualism between appreciation and description in a new though none the less serious form. Nor would such an inference be entirely without foundation, although there is, it should be observed, a significant difference between such a principle of indifference formulated at the close of our investigations, and the antithesis between appreciation and description which from the beginning makes impossible such description of worth experience. But as a matter of fact this is not an adequate view of the situation, for the principle, as we have formulated it, has two aspects, a positive as well as a negative. Not only does it warn us against deducing the reality of values from the outer truth or existence of the objects valued, but it also tells us that value itself involves an inner truth and reality not describable in these terms.

The negative significance of this principle has been fully developed. It tells us explicitly that the complete intent or meaning of the presupposition of reality cannot be exhausted in any abstract definitions of existence and truth, and that, therefore, the predicates of reality as used in valuation cannot be wholly tested by such norms. Its value is methodological and as fundamental for axiological method, I believe, as the principle of psycho-physical parallelism for psychology. As the latter tells us that the psychical can never be reduced to the physical, nor the physical to the psychical—so long, at least, as we remain on the plane of scientific description, so the axiological principle of indifference warns us not to seek to reduce all values to factual and truth objectivity, all worth experiences to mere effects of social processes or means to social ends, i.e., again, so long as we remain on the axiological plane.

But the positive implications are even more significant. The very reason for this injunction not to identify reality with existence and truth is that the intent or meaning of the presupposition of reality transcends any retrospective definitions of existence and truth. Analysis of the predicates of reality in their extension and intension, has shown us, not only that the meaning of these predicates is varied, but also that acknowledgment of the presupposition of reality in existential and truth judgments is always relative to the specific intent of the presupposition. To put this into more general form for our present purposes, we may say—the criterion of knowledge as such is always relative, and arises, not out of the relation of a special intent to an absolute intent, but from relations of special contents to special intents. Error and fallacy consist in discrepancy between special content and intent. Attempts to generalise these proximate intents, to formulate concepts of " truth in general " in such a way as to make it all inclusive and to give it intrinsic meaning, serve only to emphasise their relativity. When truth is defined as " correspondence of idea with reality," as " contradictionless experience," or even pragmatically, as " instrumentality of ideas for life," such formulas prove, as we have seen, to be either too narrow to fulfil the intent of truth, or, when they are sufficiently broadened to satisfy our sense of rationality, so little self-sufficient as to force us beyond concepts of existence and truth to modes of immediate experience or of intrinsic appreciation which they presuppose.

We are thus led to the conclusion that judgments of existence and truth, far from being exhaustive of the intent of reality, themselves have axiological meaning only in so far as they serve, by acknowledgment of fulfilment of a special intent, to lead to that identity of the empirical with the met-empirical will which constitutes the essence of value. In other words, they are not predicates of total systems of experience. Judgments of existence and truth apply only to relations among our impressions and ideas. It has been well said that the totality of experience is as little describable as existent or true as the totality of matter is describable as heavy.

But if we admit that existence and truth cannot be exhaustively interpreted except with reference to concepts or postulates of valuation, and therefore, that value may logically be prior to existence and truth, it still remains an open question whether the identity of value with reality can be so characterised as to make the relations of value to existence and truth intelligible. It may be that totalities of experience can be only appreciated, that only values can be the predicates of such total experiences. As we found it impossible to characterise a total experience as absolutely true, it may be equally difficult to say what would make a total experience absolutely valuable. Now, for value and reality to be identical means that an experience, in order to be real, must be satisfying. Could we say what the object of absolute satisfaction is, there would be no longer any points of indifference ; we could deduce the nature of truth and existence from it. Such definition is, as we have seen, impossible, but it is not inconceivable that we may be able so to describe appreciatively our ultimate values as to show that they transcend truth and existence and include them. It may be possible for " the inspirations of reason, appreciative of values," to use Lotze's fine phrase, so to apprehend the ultimate nature of the will and its satisfaction as to enable us to adumbrate that incontestable value in the light of which we can pass from the object of thought to its reality.

Lotze's own well-known attempt so to apprehend ultimate value leads him to find this final satisfaction in the feeling or consciousness of harmony, including all those forms of activity in repose, of unity and continuity, describable as love, beauty, perfection. In these experiences—the highest inspirations of reason—reason finds its own inmost essence ; in them is realised—in practically absolute moments, the assumption of identity of the empirical with the met-empirical will. It would be " *intolerable* " that these ideals, formed in the activities of ideal construction, should have no existence, power, or validity in the world of reality. They *are* true he holds : we can feel them when we cannot think them. From these ultimate appreciations he then deduces the relative validity and value of those special forms of continuity, between inner and outer existence, inner and outer truth, which are the indispensable conditions of this realisation.

Now it may well be granted that these inspirations of reason far outrun its reasoned convictions, and that this insight into the identity of value and reality cannot make itself wholly intelligible. Our handling of the speech of valuation is still inept, with its crude distinctions of feeling and knowledge, and its unworthy slavery to the prejudicial connotations of the term feeling. It may, indeed, be further granted that precisely at this point, in his use of the concepts of feeling and thought, Lotze's presentation of the concept requires decided modification. But with all these admissions, it remains true that his fundamental insight into the identity of value with reality and the priority of value to truth and existence remains incontestable.

Valuation and Evaluation 427

This doctrine of priority means, when properly interpreted, that worth experience in its entirety corresponds to a larger world of reality than the limited regions of existence and truth. There are forms of harmony of intent with content of experience which are not comprehended under the specific meanings of these terms. The standards of knowledge are but special formulations of the ideals of unity and continuity; and of the total realm of ideal objects judged or assumed to be real, only a limited number will conform to these standards, these specialised demands. Many do not thus conform, and yet contribute to the unity and continuity of affective-volitional meaning. The ideal makes itself felt, and finds satisfaction in many ways which fail to conform to these definitions. It is no less true that the standards of value are special and relative formulations of this demand. There are forms of harmony not exhaustively interpreted in terms of the realisation of any of the ends to which these standards refer, forms of harmony in which the experience transcends ideal construction of ends no less than of truths. This we have fully recognised in the preceding chapter in our conception of *supreme moments* in which distinctions of ends and norms lapse. But this merely serves to emphasise the priority of value. Practical absolutes may indeed come at the limits of volition, relative values may be sublimated into absolute; but, so far as I know, a relative truth may become absolute only by becoming the presupposition of an absolute value.

To the final question, therefore—how are judgments of existence and truth related to ultimate appreciations with their intrinsic values?—our answer is simple and evident. They establish relations between experience and experience, between idea and idea, which lead to new appreciations or conserve those already acquired. The specific predicates of existence of truth, already considered, have meaning only when they add to the intrinsic value or reality of an impression or idea. There are cases where the acknowledgment of the presupposition of reality in these predicates does add value and reality to the idea, e.g., where the presupposition of reality already includes a retrospective explicit definition of existence or truth. But such addition is not a necessary consequence of such acknowledgment, nor is such acknowledgment a necessary condition of appreciation. As the critics of the Ontological Proof have clearly seen, the proof of the truth or existence of the idea of the perfect being adds nothing to its reality. In the intrinsic appreciation of the meaning of the demand or postulate of such a Being, whatever reality it has is already included. Its central place in the spiritual life, its value, must guarantee its reality, and the attempt to translate such ultimate reality into the subordinate concepts of outer existence and truth can certainly add nothing to that reality, and may even, by falsely interpreting the presupposition of reality, lead to error and unreality.

This is the final point to which our axiological study brings us. The implications of valuation when fully worked out lead to the claim of priority. Yet, since there is always the further implication of an inner truth which, while not exhausted in the predicates of existence and truth already considered, is still not in ultimate contradiction with them, since, in other words, life and experience show themselves progressively more and more capable of statement as a system of truth, there remains always the assumption of the ultimate intelligibility of every value. A still higher form of experience in which the two claims are equally satisfied, a form of contemplation which transcends will and thought alike, must ever be the goal, acknowledged or unacknowledged, of all metaphysics. Such a state of equilibrium would indeed be the Beatific Vision. Whether it is attainable or not, and if attainable capable of being held, it is not for us to say.

THE END

INDEX

A

Absolute values, 19, 335, 342 ff., 363 f., 370, 380, 384 f., 396 ff., 402, 406, 425 ff.
Absolutes, practical, 150, 277, 295, 374, 376 ff., 382, 399, 404, 427
Act, cognitive, as related to dispositions, 51, 53, 64, 95
Æsthetic feeling, 31, 45, 53, 251
Æsthetic mode, presupposition of, 45, 70, 122, 220, 235 n., 240, 275
Æsthetic values, of simple appreciation, 205, 217, 221, 224, 229; of characterisation of the person, 266, 277, 296, 306; in social participation, 334; validity of, 309, 399, 422 ff.
Affective continuity (substitution, subsumption, transition), 121, 130
Affective generalisation, 77, 120, 131, 133 f., 244
Affective abstract (See Affective generalisation.)
Affective memory, 113 f., 116, 131
Affective sign, 105 f., 112, 129, 241
Alogism, 395
Alter, the ego and the, 211; as ideal construction, 234, 248, 261
Altruism, egoism and, nature of distinction, 261, 264 n.; as personal worth, 301; as social value, 314, 352 f.; limits of, 359, 374 f.
Appreciation and description, 6 ff., 17, 19, 57, 424
Appreciation, intensity-less, 128 ff., 274; and hedonic redundancies, 76, 162, 166, 185. (See also, Intensity-less feelings.)
Appreciation, simple, 30, 32, 192; objects of, 30; meanings of, 59, 67; value movements of, 199, 234
Appreciative description, nature of, 8, 14, 55; of feeling and will, 83 f.; terms of, 59 ff.; and scientific, 57, 62
Apprehension, imageless, 125
Apprehension, of inner life in others, 237

Art, and æsthetic experience, 166; origins of, 222; the element of order in, 225 ff.
Aspiring values, 333 f., 337. (See also Value Movements.)
Assumption, as cognitive act, 38, 42, 47, 52; as presupposition of worth attitudes, 70, 137 f.; implicit and explicit, 48, 70, 115, 132; in affective memory and generalisation, 115, 131 f.; in value movement, 199 f.; in *Einfühlung* and sympathetic participation, 233, 245, 259
Assumption, implicit, rôle of in characterisation, 280, 290 ff., 309; in social participation, 313 f., 316, 334 f., 356 f., 362
Assumption-feelings, 48, 115, 118, 138, 150, 162, 166, 181 ff., 245. (See also Feelings of imagination and Intensity-less appreciation.)
Augustine, 399
Axiology and Axiological method, 16 f., 24, 188, 309 f., 384
Axiological sufficiency, 405, 411. (See Valuation and Evaluation.)

B

Baldwin, J. M., on genetic method, 15; on cognitive and existence meanings, 28 n., 47 n., 389 n.; on semblant mode, 70, 127; on *Einfühlung*, 234, 235, 248
Bentham, 157
Bernoulli, 157
Böhm Bauwerk, 367
Bosanquet, B., 414
Brentano, F., on judgment, 44; on hedonic redundancies and intensity-less feeling, 57, 76, 159; on feeling and will, 90

C

Characterisation, values of, 30, 71, 234, 260 f., 284. (See Personal worths.)

Complementary Values, law of, 145, 173 ff., 178 ff.; in relation to other laws, 151, 229, 173; in economic valuation, 174; in extra-economic valuation, 175; in simple appreciation, 193, 214, 229; in characterisation, 266 f., 306; in social participation, 340, 348

Condition, worths of, definition, 30, 147 f., 190, 197, 294; and value movement, 205, 213, 229; and of person, 261, 264, 269, 286, 300 f., 367, 372, 376

Consumption, economic, 143, 160, 170; as modified by other values, 177, 213, 229

Continuity of value, postulate of, 15, 404 ff.

Correct, the. (See Norm of Participation)

D

Degree of worth or value, 72, 74, 76, 108, 152; measurement of, 79, 156 f., 171, 282 ff., 288 ff., 291, 322

Demand and Supply, in economics, 142 f.; in personal worths, 292; in social values, 318, 327, 329

Depth and Breadth, of feeling, 50, 72 ff., 155; as determined by disposition, 50, 76, 183, 206, 209, 217; in the personality, 264, 269 f., 286, 296, 304, 371. (See Degree of worth.)

Desire and value, 35 ff., 70, 82, 85, 94, 148 ff.

Diminishing Utility. (See Diminishing Value.)

Diminishing Value, law of, 145, 156, 158; extent of application of, 167, 171 ff., 181; as related to value movement, 145, 193, 203; in personal worths, 272 ff.; in social values, 326 ff.

Disposition, concept of in definition of value, 33 f., 37, 50, 53, 77; in genetic method, 14 f., 82, 95, 104; and implicit assumption, 121, 127, 133, 138, 248, 258 f.

Disposition, ethical and moral, 233, 248 f., 258 f., 260 ff., 283 ff., 291, 294, 298, 311 ff., 342, 351 f., 375 f. (See Norm of Characterisation and Participation.)

E

Economics, and theory of value, 3, 311, 367; laws of, 142 f., 169, 174, 177

Economic values, definition of, 143, 311; thresholds of, 146 ff.; laws of, 169, 174; as related to other values, 213 ff., 229, 311

Ehrenfels, Ch. von, on definition of value, 35 ff.; on feeling and will, 86; on laws of valuation, 156, 186 ff., 330 f.; on value movements, 195, 333; on moral obligation, 350 n., 397, 422 n.

Einfühlung, and valuation, 72, 102, 234 ff.; psychology of, 236, 238, 241, 255; ethical and æsthetic, 245, 252; and real feelings, 240, 249 ff., 273. (See Participation, sympathetic.)

Elsenhans, T. R., 129

Emerson, 335

Emotion, as feeling of value, 64; analysis of, 88, 97, 100 ff., 119

Emotional Logic, 76 f., 112 f., 121, 139, 203 f.

Ethical and Moral values, 285, 314. (See also Personal and Impersonal values.)

Ethical scepticism, 5, 370

Ethics and theory of value, 4, 368, 380 ff., 416

Existence, judgment of, 42; as presupposition of feeling of value, 38 ff., 66, 80, 95, 118, 133, 162, 199, 248; as related to other presuppositions, 47, 51, 66, 69 ff., 77 f., 94. (See Judgment-feelings.)

Existence, meanings of, 22, 387 ff. (See Presupposition of reality.)

F

Fechner, 159, 180

Feeling, analysis of, 62, 93 f., 103 f.; dimensions of, 59 ff., 62, 83, 100 ff.; presuppositions of, 41 ff., 47, 64, 66; genetic relations of, 51 ff., 104; theories of, 57, 82, 94, 96 ff.

Feeling and value, 35, 39 ff., 53, 64 f., 95

Feeling and will, theories of, 57, 83, 85, 89 ff., 93 ff.

Feelings of value, presuppositions of, 35 ff., 47, 62, 66

Feelings of the imagination, in valuation, 115, 133 ff., 138; in *Einfühlung*, 245 ff., 250 ff.; in ethical judgment, 263, 276. (See Assumption-feelings.)

Flournoy, Th., 277

G

Genesis and Validity, 6, 16, 384, 424 f.

Genetic method, in worth analysis, 44 ff., 68, 81, 137, 191, 234, 252

Index 431

Genetic levels of valuation, 51, 190, 230, 282 ff., 314, 366, 379, 384
Genetic Theory of feeling and will, 89, 104
Gestalt-qualität ("form of combination" of elements), of emotional complexes, 100, 110, 119, 132, 238 ff.; and complementary values, 179 ff.; in æsthetic characterisation of persons, 225 ff., 266 f.
Giddings, F., 325
Gossen, 157, 166
Group Segregation. (See Social Differentiation.)
Gross, K., 217, 240, 251
Guyau, J. M., 210, 342, 397

H

Habit, and disposition, 50 f., 83; and feeling of value, 50 f., 83, 103 ff., 120, 133, 161, 183 f.; and affective abstract, 133, 158; and implicit assumption, 48, 67, 107, 121, 133, 249, 259; dulling of sensitivity with, 158, 161, 183, 203, 323; and normal expectation, 293, 333 ff., 356, 361
Hedonic redundancies, of feelings of value, 77, 108, 129 f.; as affected by repetition, 163, 166, 273; rôle of in valuation, 155, 185, 197, 261. (See Intensity-less appreciation.)
Hedonism, ethical, 84, 370, 417
Hegel, 203
Herbart, 397
Hirn, Yrjo, 74, 222
Höffding, H., 20, 65, 394, 404
Höffler, A., 152

I

Idealisation, of the person, 263, 265 f., 275 ff.; of social wholes, 342 ff., 363 f.
Impartial Spectator. (See Impersonal attitude.)
Impellent mode. (See Obligation.)
Impersonal attitude in valuation, 27 f., 232 f., 313 f., 350 f., 375 f., 378
Impersonal values. (See Over-individual values.)
Imputation, of merit and demerit, 233; emotional and intellectual, 290, 315; personal and ethical, 260 ff., 291, 298 ff., 307, 309; social and moral, 290, 293, 302, 314, 356, 358 ff., 375 f.
Imputed value, 22 f., 174, 177, 214

Inner Peace, 279, 307 f., 344, 380. (See Tragical Elevation.)
Intensity-less feelings, 34, 77, 106, 128
Intuitionism, ethical, 369 ff.
Isolation (or detachment), æsthetic, 266, 278 ff.; as presupposition of personal values, 285 ff., 296 f., 299, 301, 307, 312; of social groups, 339, 344 f., 359

J

James, William, 12, 137 n., 126, 182, 375, 397, 399
Jevons, S., 149
Judgment-feelings, 38 ff., 47, 53, 64, 93 ff., 138, 248. (See Existence, judgment of.)

K

Kant, 205, 278, 285, 336, 414
Kraus, Oskar, 157, 172
Kreibig, J. C., 27, 86, 156
Krüger, F., 39, 50 ff., 153

L

Leibnitz, 396, 407, 411
Limiting Value, law of. (See Diminishing Value.)
Lipps, Th., 49 ff., 264
Lotze, 130, 426

M

Marginal Participation Value, law of, 329 f., 332; and social value movements, 333; and moral judgment, 350
Marginal Utility, law of, 149, 156, 169 ff., 174, 327, 330. (See Valuation, Laws of.)
Marshall, H. R., 217
Meaning, worth as affective-volitional, 15, 26, 30 ff., 93 f.; acquired and funded, 8, 82, 111 ff.; "common," 232, 253; recognitive, 113, 117, 248; generic, 121, 125, 139, 248; of existence, 22, 24, 55, 387
Meinong, A., on definition of value, 35 ff., 41 ff.; on judgment and assumption, 138; on ethical and moral judgment, 27, 290 n.; on moral obligation, 350 n.
Merit and Demerit. (See Imputation.)
Minimum of Characterisation, 294, 297, 304, 377
Minimum of Existence, 148 ff., 214, 294, 353, 373, 377
Minimum of Participation, 357, 361, 374

Modes of consciousness of value, 55, 67 ff.
Monistic theories of value, 368, 380, 416
Moral judgment, the, 313, 350 ff., 356. (See Impersonal attitude.)
Moral obligation. (See Obligation.)
Münsterberg, H., 11, 73, 94, 183, 403

N

Nietzsche, F., 2, 192, 342, 352 n.
Norm of Characterisation, 293, 299 f., 304
Norm of Participation, 293 n., 333 f., 356 f.
Normal values, 333 f., 391. (See Value Movements (social).)
Normative and Descriptive, 16 ff., 384 ff., 424 f.
Normative objectivity. (See Objectivity of values.)

O

Objectivity of values, 17, 22 f., 187 f., 309 f., 384 ff.; relation of, to fact and truth, 386, 390 ff. (See Sufficient Reason and Well-founded value.)
Objects of value, classification of, 29
Obligation, analysis of, 68, 207; quasi-ethical, 209; ethical and personal, 297, 303 ff.; social and moral, 360 ff; perfect and imperfect, 285, 304, 364; conflicts of, 373 f., 376, 379
Ontological Proof, and primacy of values, 395, 427
Organic sympathy, 244, 273, 322 f.
Outlived values, 333 f., 338, 341, 354. (See Value Movement (social).)
Over-individual values, 30, 311 f., 366; laws of, 328 ff., 342; estimation of, 350 ff.

P

Participation, sympathetic, nature and laws of, 234, 238, 244 ff.; extensive and intensive, 253 ff., 320 f. (See *Einfühlung* and Sympathy.)
Participation, values of, definition of, 30, 71, 254; personal and impersonal, 253 ff.; subjective and objective, 261, 316, 328 f.; laws of, 320, 326, 328 ff., 333, 342
Pathetic fallacies, 310, 359, 410
Patten, S. N., 197 f.
Paulhan, F. R., on genetic theory of affective attitudes, 105 ff.; on affective memory, 113; on "affective sign," 124, 129.
Personal worths, definition of, 270; origin and laws of, 263 ff., 270, 277; objects of, 283 ff.; norms and limits of, 291 ff., 348, 359, 361, 373, 376, 419
Personality, and value, 49, 262; ideal of, as assumed in judgments of personal worth, 262 ff., 291; construction of, 248 f., 263 ff.; idealisation of, 266, 275. (See Isolation, æsthetic.)
Person-project, 248, 263
Pleasantness-unpleasantness, and feeling of value, 39, 50, 57, 62 f., 96, 108, 114; and the laws of valuation, 142, 152, 158, 166, 176, 184; and æsthetic values, 217 ff.; and personal worth, 50, 261, 300, 368 f., 417
Poe, the Raven, 123, 140
Practical Absolutes. (See Absolutes, practical.)
Pragmatism and pragmatic criterion, 396, 398
Praise and blame. (See Imputation.)
Presumption of existence, as cognitive attitude, 43, 477 ff., as presupposition of feelings of value, 43, 66, 190, 245; and implicit assumption, 52, 118, 257
Presupposition of reality, in feelings of value, 24 ff., 38 f., 47, 53, 66; ultimate meaning of, 400 ff.
Presuppositional method, as form of the genetic, 14 ff., 81, 384.
Projection. (See *Einfühlung*.)
Psychology of valuation, the, 9 f., 14
Puffer, Miss E., 219

Q

Quasi-ethical and quasi-moral. (See Ethical and Moral and Obligation.)

R

Reality-meanings. (See Meaning and Presupposition of reality.)
Religious value, 346 ff., 394 f.
Ribot, Th., on affective memory, 113, 115; on affective generalisation, 124, 129
Royce, J., 62, 126, 234

S

Sanction, ethical, 122; Sufficient. (See Sufficient Reason of valuation.)

Index

Satiety, law of, 164 ff. ; and appreciation, 183, 203, 221, 237; and sympathetic participation, 273, 323
Saxinger, R., 119, 133 f.
Schiller, F., 418
Schwartz, H., 58, 77, 85, 192 f., 369
Self-realisation, theory of, 370, 419 f.
Semblant mode. (See Æsthetic mode.)
Sensitivity, dulling of, 159 ff., 161, 185 ; in appreciation, 203, 221, 231 ; in sympathetic participation, 240, 273, 323. (See Habit.)
Sensitivity, feeling as, 96 ff.
Shaw, B., 352 n.
Sigwart, 46
Simmel, G., on ethical theory, 12, 370 ; on feeling of value, 57, 69, 96 ; on laws of valuation, 171 ff. ; on definition of obligation, 69, 207 ; on practical absolutes, 280 n. ; on social differentation, 256 ; on moral obligation, 350 n.
Social Differentation, and valuation, 322, 339
Spencer, H., 418
Spinoza, 348 n.
Stevenson, R. L., 361
Störring, G., 62
Stout, G. F., 44, 100, 125, 128, 155
Stuart, H. W., 31, 112
Stumpff, C., 155
Sufficient Reason of valuation, 395, 400 f., 406 f.
Sympathy, social, 322 ff.
Synergy, social, 318, 331, 351, 357
Synthetic preference, 366, 368 ff., 371, 378 f.

T

Taylor, A. E., 361 n., 370
Tennyson, Lotos-Eaters, 123, 140, 276
Thresholds of value, economic and extra-economic, 146 ff. ; as modified by complementary values, ethical and æsthetic, 151, 215, 230; in personal worth, 293 ff. ; in over-individual value, 356 f.
Tolstoi, 342, 373
Tragical Elevation, 279, 295, 298, 302, 306, 375, 380. (See Inner Peace.)
Transgredient and immanental references of feelings, to dispositions presupposed, 9, 11, 60, 69 f., 71, 150; in simple appreciation, 201, 206, 210, 216; in personal values, 269, 277, 303, 307 ; in impersonal values, 320, 344, 346 ; axiological meaning of, 401, 404, 410

Truth, meanings of in evaluation, 389 ff., 394, 409, 422 ff.

U

Universality in morals. (See Absolute values.)
Utility, values of, 30, 143, 169, 311. (See Diminishing Value and Marginal Utility.)

V

Valuation, nature of, 21 ff., 142 ; levels of, 51, 147, 190, 230, 314, 366, 379, 384
Valuation, laws of, 79, 142 ff., 145, 156, 167 ff., 173 ff., 185 ff., 193, 202, 270 ff., 320 ff., 328, 371, 379, 384
Valuation and Evaluation, relations of, 24, 61, 185 ff. 309 f., 384 ff. (See Normative and Descriptive.)
Value, definition and analysis, 21 ff., 95 ; actual and imputed, 22 f., 174, 177, 214, 386 ; intrinsic and instrumental, 22, 148, 152, 169 f., 174, 195, 206, 261, 269 ff., 311, 327, 342 f., 386, 391, 396 ff., 400 ; primary and derived, 67, 71, 192 ; real and ideal, 22 f., 309, 342 ff., 386
Value, the judgment of, as assertory, 21 f. ; types of, 31 ; the subject of, 27 ; objects of, 28 ; relation of to judgments of fact and truth, 384 ff., 422 ff.
Value, theory of, 1 ff.
Value Movements, 15, 67, 191 ff. ; and laws of valuation, 145, 193, 202 f. ; of simple appreciation, 67, 199 ; of sympathetic participation and characterisation, 232, 252 ; social, 333 ff.
Veblen, T. B., 12, 256
Voluntarism, 368 f., 403, 422 ff.

W

Well-founded value, the criterion of, 19, 185, 309, 405 ff., 409, 413, 416 ff.
Wieser, F. von, 3
Witasek, St. von, 31, 53, 101, 235, 250
Worth. (See Value.)
Worth predicates, 22 ff., 55 ff., 78 f., 233, 282 f., 285, 352 ff.
Worth suggestions of feeling, 61, 64
Wundt, W., on three-dimensional theory of feeling, 63 ; on feeling and will, 90 ff., 97, 100 ; on law of "resultants," 180, 204

For Product Safety Concerns and Information please contact our EU representative GPSR@taylorandfrancis.com
Taylor & Francis Verlag GmbH, Kaufingerstraße 24, 80331 München, Germany

www.ingramcontent.com/pod-product-compliance
Lightning Source LLC
Chambersburg PA
CBHW070603230426
43670CB00010B/1390